The Films of
Larry Buchanan

The Films of Larry Buchanan

A Critical Examination

Rob Craig

McFarland & Company, Inc., Publishers
Jefferson, North Carolina, and London

LIBRARY OF CONGRESS CATALOGUING-IN-PUBLICATION DATA

Craig, Rob, 1954–
The films of Larry Buchanan : a critical examination / Rob Craig.

p. cm.

Includes bibliographical references and index.

ISBN-13: 978-0-7864-2982-0
softcover : 50# alkaline paper ∞

1. Buchanan, Larry — Criticism and interpretation.
I. Title.
PN1998.3.B8C73   2007   791.4302'3092 — dc22   2007007507

British Library cataloguing data are available

©2007 Rob Craig. All rights reserved

No part of this book may be reproduced or transmitted in any form or by any means, electronic or mechanical, including photocopying or recording, or by any information storage and retrieval system, without permission in writing from the publisher.

On the cover: (top to bottom) Poster art from *The Eye Creatures,* 1965, and *Mars Needs Women,* 1967; Libby Booth as *The Naked Witch,* 1961; and the Gill Monster in the 1967 film *Creature of Destruction*

Manufactured in the United States of America

*McFarland & Company, Inc., Publishers
Box 611, Jefferson, North Carolina 28640
www.mcfarlandpub.com*

for Elisa

Acknowledgments

The author would like to extend thanks to the following people, without whom this book would not exist: to the Buchanans (Jane, Jeff, Barry, Randy and Dee), for their enthusiastic support of the project; to Larry Buchanan's right-hand man, Lynn Shubert, and his wife, Betty Shubert, for their insight into the *real* Larry Buchanan; to Doyle Greene, for his astute editorial suggestions; to Greg Woods, for allowing me to forge a rudimentary study of Larry Buchanan's films in his visionary magazine, *The Eclectic Screening Room*; to Greg Luce and Mike Vraney, for their lifelong crusades to save forgotten film; to Mark Hill and Gregory Walker, for supplying vital research; to my father, R.L. Craig, for founding my love of writing; to my wife, Elisa Vegliante, for her endless inspiration. And finally, a nod of gratitude to all filmmakers and artists for whom the creative act is paramount; their tireless labor is our everlasting bounty.

Table of Contents

Acknowledgments vii
Preface 1
Introduction 3

1. Orphan in the Storm 5
2. Among the Missing 13
3. That's Exploitation 20
4. *The Naked Witch* 32
5. *Naughty Dallas* 42
6. *Free, White and 21* and *Under Age* 53
7. *The Trial of Lee Harvey Oswald* 67
8. The Azalea Pictures 76
9. *The Eye Creatures* 84
10. *Zontar, the Thing from Venus* 96
11. *Curse of the Swamp Creature* 110
12. *Mars Needs Women* 122
13. *In the Year 2889* 133
14. *Creature of Destruction* 144
15. *It's Alive!* 159
16. *A Bullet for Pretty Boy* 171
17. *Strawberries Need Rain* 177
18. *Goodbye, Norma Jean* 184

19.	*Hughes and Harlow: Angels in Hell*	193
20.	*Mistress of the Apes*	202
21.	*The Loch Ness Horror*	209
22.	*Beyond the Doors*	218
23.	*Goodnight, Sweet Marilyn*	226
24.	The Ghost of Larry B	233

Filmography	237
Chapter Notes	247
Bibliography	253
Index	255

Preface

I first encountered the films of Larry Buchanan on a sunny Sunday afternoon in 1967. Channel 7, the New York ABC affiliate, had announced the New York television premiere of something called *Zontar, the Thing from Venus*. As a monster-movie buff, I was intrigued by the lurid pulp-fiction title. When the film began, I was immediately struck by the garish color, familiar middle-class settings and low-budget sensibility. When it soon became apparent that *Zontar* was virtually a shot-for-shot remake of a B-movie classic, Roger Corman's *It Conquered the World* (1956), I was perplexed and fascinated. Not knowing at the time that *Zontar* was an authorized and commissioned remake, I considered it a strange occurrence of "outlaw cinema" ripping off a genre picture in a primitive style more akin to home movies than professional filmmaking.

Needless to say, Larry Buchanan become something of an obsession with me. The more of his films I encountered the greater the mystery became. His Azalea telefilms were excitingly crude productions, virtually experimental in many places, and were unlike any other feature films shown on television at the time. When I finally caught up with Buchanan's more mature works, including *Goodbye, Norma Jean* and *Free, White and 21*, I understood that Buchanan was a filmmaker with great talent and range, someone who could make thrilling melodramas under modest budgets. Additionally, he liked to play around with accepted history on topics as diverse as racial equality, celebrity, political conspiracy and the military-industrial complex.

I had the profound fortune of speaking with "Larry B" (as he liked to be called) in the late 1990s, after the publication of his autobiography, *It Came from Hunger: Tales of a Cinema Schlockmeister*. I had sent Larry some early reviews of his Azalea telefilms, and we eventually spoke on the phone several times. Buchanan proved to be what I had imagined him to be: an intelligent, soft-spoken gentleman, passionate about his films and full of theories about pretty much everything going on in the world. His enthusiasm for life and film was infectious.

The films of Larry Buchanan contain a special quality, a certain soul or spirit, an abiding intelligence which elevates them above the majority of independent product of the day. I am awestruck by the evocative melodramas which Buchanan was able to create with the absolute minimum of resources. Buchanan's expansive mise-en-scène successfully mimics much of Hollywood's output, often at a mere fraction of the cost. He was a master of utilizing available resources to their best advantage, and his lyrical screenplays ensured a bigger-than-life cinema experience.

This humble volume, written from the perspective of a fan, attempts to give the reader an overview of the unique body of work Buchanan created. More importantly, it will attempt to bring into focus some consistent themes and energies in the films. I do not pretend to be an expert in the field of critical studies; my postulations come more from intuition and personal observation than from formal academic study. There is more work to be done in studying the films of Larry Buchanan. I hope this volume will begin that assuredly revelatory project.

Introduction

Perhaps no other independent filmmaker of the latter twentieth century elicits such a disparity of response from general movie audiences and cult film buffs alike as Larry Buchanan. The general public have likely never heard of him, even though many of his films have entered the popular lexicon of film mythology. Even in the rarified air of cult film studies, Buchanan's name provokes either gasps of horror or hushed sighs of awe. To many, the creator of such grungy throwaway product as *The Naked Witch*, *Mars Needs Women*, and *The Other Side of Bonnie & Clyde* is a mere hack, a cultural anomaly unworthy of further consideration. To others, films such as *Zontar, the Thing from Venus* and *Mistress of the Apes* do deserve note, but only as amusing examples of "badfilm," of low-rent cinema gone haywire, good only for chuckles, not adoration or exploration. Yet, when one seeks serious study of the work of this prolific, innovative filmmaker, there is nary a whisper. Other B-movie auteurs, once neglected or dismissed, have now achieved legendary status, including Sam Fuller, Edgar G. Ulmer, Roger Corman and Oscar Micheaux. Larry Buchanan deserves a similar status.

Larry Buchanan was a unique filmmaker whose oeuvre ranged from low exploitation to high art, yet always he slaved within the budgetary constraints of the B-movie universe. Whereas many filmmakers of "B-product" often settled for thinly sketched, meandering collages of quasi-dramatic set pieces, pseudo-documentary montages, or even unabashedly plotless, nonlinear stock footage compilations disguised as feature films (Barry Mahon, Willis Kent and Edward D. Wood, Jr., among many others), Buchanan invariably crafted his films using the classical three-act narrative structure, even when it became apparent that neither the market nor his backers applauded or even noticed such a move.

This may have been due to Buchanan's lifelong love affair with the classic dramas of the golden age of Hollywood. Films like *History Is Made at Night* (1937, d: Frank Borzage), with their succinct story structure, always appealed to Buchanan, and it is surprising to find the same sophisticated narrative structure on many of Buchanan's "throwaway films," most notably the Azalea telefilms. Conversely, Buchanan was a devout fan and student of European art films, and his work bears the indelible influence of Ingmar Bergman (witness his homage to Bergman, *Strawberries Need Rain*, 1970), Michelangelo Antonioni (reflected in *Mars Needs Women*, 1967), and Jean Cocteau. Lured by the easy money and lax restric-

Larry Buchanan performs his duties as a singing cowboy in *Homer Goes Hygienic* (ca. 1951), one of several U.S. Army–sponsored films he graced as performer before turning his energies to filmmaking.

tions of the exploitation film market—where Buchanan could devise his own rules provided he gave the producer and audience an hour of film, a good title, and some sexy titillation—he used these modest pictures to refine his art.

Buchanan was also a political filmmaker, crafting his art in a most unique environment: Texas, the mythic hotbed of singing cowboys, fearless outlaws and murdered kings. Working in the convulsive upheaval of the 1960s assured that his films would bear an indelible stamp of his time. Above all, Buchanan was a subversive director, both in form and content. He took traditional Hollywood genres (monster movie, courtroom drama, biopic) and revamped them according to his artistic sensibilities, as well as the sociopolitical filters of the times. One can easily see the particular brushstrokes of Buchanan in the wild aesthetic revisionism of his monster movies or in the inflammatory historical revisionism of his biographical dramas. Buchanan presented the secret places of the military-industrial complex, the CIA and the U.S. government, the bared teeth behind the false smile of Hollywood, the decay behind the tacky pasteboard façade of suburbia, and ultimately shone a healing light to animate humanity's journey through the modern, despairing void.

1

Orphan in the Storm

Larry Buchanan was born Marcus Larry Seale on January 21, 1923, in a tiny hamlet called Lost Prairie, deep in the wind-parched dustbowl of Texas. An Aquarian, he would change his name twenty years later to the day, at the prompting of the casting office at 20th Century Fox. Buchanan's adoring mother died when he was only nine months old. According to her son, she was a simple, deeply religious person.[1] Buchanan's father was a cop, during the time of Bonnie and Clyde and an epidemic of daring bank robberies. He was once shot at by "Pretty Boy" Floyd Hamilton, an event which would have significant reverberations on young Buchanan. Fearing for his life and safety and wondering who would provide for his family should tragedy strike, Buchanan's father placed his kids in a Baptist-run orphanage in Dallas, the Buckner Orphans Home.

Young Larry, however, considered himself abandoned, and for many years called his father a coward and a deserter. A bright and creative adolescent, Buchanan questioned the historical Jesus taught to him at the strict Baptist orphanage. The matrons of the institution were "monstrous," according to Buchanan, and his queries were met with corporal punishment both "swift and terrifying."[2] If the nervous teenager wet his bed, he would be locked in the "wet closet," with all the soiled linen, for an entire day. He was fed Epsom salts and cod liver oil against his will. The only respite from the punitive home regimen were the weekly screenings of recent Hollywood movies in the orphanage recreation hall. Buchanan was able to endure his Jobian trials by reliving the previous week's movie fantasy over and over in his mind. Movies, it could be said, saved his life. The movie Buchanan claims changed his life forever was Frank Borzage's *History Is Made at Night* (1937). From the moment he saw this haunting romantic melodrama, Buchanan became obsessed with movies, and was determined to be a part of them.

Due to ongoing accusations of sex scandal at Buckner, there were eventually sweeping revisions to the corrupt institution, resulting in its takeover by a professional management team. The bright teenaged Buchanan was singled out for several functions in the "new" Buckner, including editor of the school newspaper. Most telling, however, was his being chosen as the "traveling ambassador" to the institution. Buchanan became a teenage preacher, speaking in church congregations across the South and Southwest, raising funds

In 1936, a young Marcus Larry Seale enjoys some of the perks of his evangelical work for the Buckner Orphan Home.

for the rapidly expanding group home. Soon the handsome young man was a "hit" junior preacher on the Lone Star Baptist evangelical circuit, "a post-pubescent Elmer Gantry."[3] Despite the grueling hours and whiff of carny exploitation in the escapades, Buchanan loved the limelight, and he caught the show biz bug.

His proselytizing talents so recognized, Buchanan was awarded a ministerial scholarship, slated to become a Baptist preacher. Sensing the stifling nature of a life of what he considered hypocritical piety, Buchanan instead let the fire in his belly dictate, and he hitchhiked to Hollywood. Finding work as a bit player, augmented by a wartime gig at Douglas Aircraft, Buchanan immersed himself in the electrifying atmosphere that was Hollywood of the late 1930s. Content for only a short time in being a bit player, Buchanan ached to make his own movies. Understanding that making it in Hollywood as a nobody was out of the question, he finally gave up the ghost and took a night train to New York City, then the hub of independent, or "poverty-row" filmmaking. By pure chance, the handsome Buchanan found lucrative work as a male model, including a famed *Life* magazine portrait by Irving Penn.

In 1951, Buchanan landed his first plum production role, as writer, musical director and performer on *The Gabby Hayes Show,* an early live-TV variety show starring the popular cowboy sidekick of B-Western fame. Each week, Buchanan and his Martin Dreadnought guitar would introduce and end the show with some classic tune, becoming television's first "Singing Cowboy." Soon Buchanan had accumulated enough experience to finagle production gigs with the Long Island–based Signal Corps Photographic Center, producing and directing short instructional films for the U.S. armed forces.

Thanks to pals such as actor Rod Steiger (*On the Waterfront,* 1954) and director Alex

Singer (*Glass House,* 1952), Buchanan soon found the Mecca of New York indie filmmaking: the Screen Building at 1600 Broadway, where hundreds of fledgling filmmakers were cutting and perfecting their first features. "Sixteen hundred" was abuzz twenty-four hours a day. Buchanan embedded himself in this community of struggling filmmakers, and this was where he observed, among others, neophyte director Stanley Kubrick agonizing over his first feature, *Fear and Desire* (1954). The resultant film, subsequently disowned by Kubrick, was wretched, but it garnered enough attention to warrant United Artists to back Kubrick's next film, *Killer's Kiss* (1955). This groundbreaking psychosexual noir quickie was a grindhouse favorite, and *The Killers* (1956), Kubrick's breakthrough feature, followed in short order.

Buchanan watched this mercurial rise of a superstar director with awe and admiration, realizing that the only salient rule to filmmaking was simplicity itself: make the damn film! The final portent for Buchanan came one fateful day, while he was watching Marcel Carne's stunning *Les Enfants du Paradis (Children of Paradise,* 1945) at the Museum of Modern Art's film library. Buchanan knew then that he must find a way to make his own pictures. Yet his Texas home was calling him, and he obediently returned. And Buchanan's beloved Lone Star State is where "TV's Singing Cowboy" would make his unlikely fortune, starting with a short subject called, appropriately, *The Cowboy*.

Much has been written about the revisionist trend in cultural studies. New books appear weekly which challenge accepted theories of current historical texts. In popular cultural criticism, a similar wave is growing. The baby boomer generation is reevaluating its art and taking a new look at the music, theater, fine arts and motion pictures it grew up with. In the area of cinema studies, this involves two primary trends. Firstly, artists generally considered to be "sacred cows," esteemed filmmakers like Jean Cocteau and Orson Welles, are being scrutinized in a light less obsessed and worshipful, and one more intent on uncovering underlying motives, cultural prejudices and other problematic areas of the artists' theses.

Even more exciting, cultural flotsam previously discarded as trash is being looked at with a loving, yet not uncritical eye, to see what is salvageable, valuable, even laudable, in this vast ocean of pop ephemera. One of the most exciting features of the revisionist viewpoint is that one can now, without guilt, appreciate artistic integrity and conscious motive in even the most heretofore unlikely places. Rewriting cultural history doesn't dissemble or cheapen the object under observation. It elevates and resurrects it, proves it worthy of respect, even adoration.

As an artist, Larry Buchanan fits well into this new trend in a very specific way. Many of his films deal with tackling alternative, or what might be considered revisionist, looks at popular history. Buchanan offers us few happy endings, but in fact many tragic ones, substituting something far better — a glimpse at a possible alternate truth, illustrated as engaging and provocative melodrama. Even venturing into the cinematic avant-garde, Buchanan took the screenplays of several black and white 35mm drive-in films, and refilmed them in 16mm color, with far less budget than the originals, as filler material for television. Buchanan's unique works stand as excellent examples of "filmic revisionism," a movement which has yet to take off as a recognized subgenre worthy of note and analysis.

Indeed, Buchanan stands tall as a guerilla film artist. The B-movie director, a.k.a. the cultfilm or badfilm director, is now accepted as a popular art icon. Cinematic luminaries such as Roger Corman, Edgar C. Ulmer and Sam Fuller were until quite recently thought of as talented craftsmen of no particular note. As time itself is the only true test of the enduring quality of art, it makes sense that out of today's crop of filmmakers certain ones will grow in stature as the years progress.

Larry Buchanan falls into a classification which might vaguely be construed as the "baby boomer" auteurs, postwar directors who worked during or shortly after the time of the Kubricks, Cormans, Ulmers and Fullers, whose work was widely seen but not critically recognized, being enjoyed at the time as mere throwaway entertainment. Other names in this short list might include Norman Taurog, William Asher, and Hugo Haas, among others. A thematic consistency imbues the work of all these filmmakers. More than just craftsmen, although many were working primarily to create commercial product and thus make a living, these film artists managed to craft not only merchandisable entertainment but identifiable work with a signature stamp and a unique perspective on the cultures from whence they came. Viewing an individual Larry Buchanan film, one is taken by how charming and entertaining it is, despite its overriding darkness. Overviewing his entire canon, one is humbled by the integrity and consistency of his vision.

A certain sense of classicism creeps into even the most unlikely Buchanan opus, giving the admittedly low-rent atmosphere a verifiable polish of legitimacy. Perhaps the biggest secret of Larry Buchanan is that he always thought of himself primarily as an art filmmaker. He manifested a lifetime of rare (even then) opportunities to make truly independent films under corporate sponsorship, and he managed to imbue even the lowliest exploitation vehicle with some vestige of high art. Buchanan gravitated toward art cinema with a fierce dedication. He adored Bergman, as witness his "high art" experiment, *Strawberries Need Rain* (1970). Yet Buchanan did Bergman one better. By crafting a powerful art film from something consciously designed and produced as commercial exploitation fare, he served two masters, one economic and one aesthetic. Ultimately, Buchanan's experiment was a test to see what a talented and dedicated person could make for a mass audience, with little money, yet offering as much production and entertainment value as possible.

Traditional auteur theory may not be the best way to look at Buchanan, as this theory tends to laud visual and aesthetic style over narrative or philosophical substance. Buchanan, in fact, may be an example of someone who best suffers scrutiny under a sort of "anti-auteur theory." Buchanan is first and foremost a storyteller, yet his stories always offer, in addition to entertainment, education and enlightenment. One could even say that Buchanan, from the aesthetically-anchored auteur perspective, has no recognizable style, and is almost the antithesis of someone like Alfred Hitchcock. Yet the powerful consistent themes which emerge in Buchanan's films illustrate that an intelligent artist was at the helm. Buchanan may be a prime example of an all-too-rare film artist whose works champion *substance over style*. As any glance at the bulk of films made in the last twenty years can attest, style has triumphed over substance in the filmmaking industry, that style being slick and gaudy, completely lacking dramatic substance.

Buchanan's unique childhood gives us the skeleton of many issues evolving in his films: A sorely missed mother, who becomes a martyr by her death, the engine for all the despair and mischief which follows and in some ways a sacrifice; a powerful father figure, working in a daring and dangerous field, who nonetheless rejects his offspring in an act both noble and cowardly. The rejected offspring, thrust into an evil corporate environment which punishes him for his individualistic views. A sense of isolation from his peers, a sense of rootlessness, a search for surrogate family and community. The institution, advertising love but preaching hate, a virtual conspiracy against the individual. The "rebel outsider," Buchanan trying first to escape then secondly to expose this corrupt gaggle of psychotics known as "organized religion," and its modern manifestations, the government and the corporation, i.e., any institution which enters a community promising salvation but delivering only destruction. But some say that "all earthly institutions are corrupt," and in Buchanan's case this appeared to result in a general mistrust of mankind, and institutions in particular. Yet underlying all this hard-won cynicism is an abiding faith in the healing sanctity of truth and fantasy, and in man's enduring potential as a redeemable creature.

Specific, consciously drawn themes abound in Buchanan's films, and many overlap into a generally cynical stew, within which burns the eternal spark of hope for mankind. One of the most prominent is the end of suburbia, as seen in the spiritual and ethical deterioration of middle-class America. In this, Buchanan's childhood orphanage community serves as a microcosmic blueprint for the generally faulty, often fatally corrupt communities depicted in his films. Many an artist throughout modern history has tackled bourgeois culture as a subject for study and criticism, but Buchanan takes specific aim at the American middle class of the postwar years and exposes much of its delusion, emptiness and moral decay, in real-life urban and suburban settings instantly familiar to his audience, which ironically is the very same middle class.

Often Buchanan's protagonist is a rebel or an outsider to a repressive community, a lonely, passionate soul persecuted for his beliefs or attempts to enlighten or infiltrate same. As an orphan, Buchanan was rejected by his birth family, so it comes as no surprise that many of his fictive characters spend a good deal of energy searching for a community to accept and embrace him, to serve as a surrogate father. Buchanan's heroes often confront a cold, calculating establishment on a quest for peace and justice. This juggernaut of anti-individualism is often the justice system, the military-industrial complex, the government in toto, or the entertainment industry, each of which actively conspires to thwart and suppress or exploit and abuse the protagonist at every opportunity. The evil institutions which inhabit Buchanan's film universe clearly evoke the ghost of his childhood orphanage, with its bureaucratic duplicity and scandalous underbelly.

On their journey, Buchanan's protagonists also search for some form of a god figure, some source of truth and trust. As Buchanan's heroes are undeniably fallible, their well-meaning but vaguely neurotic quest for a trustworthy authority figure has the tendency to ascribe untoward qualities to questionable imposters, and perhaps even honor false godheads. This exciting element in the protagonists' characters echoes Buchanan's search for the good father, unlike the one he believed abandoned him in childhood.

Aiding or abetting the hero in this quest is often a central female figure, likely a power figure, who aids the protagonist in his search for truth and justice. Often the female in a Buchanan film is martyred for her attempt at empowerment towards herself or protagonist, persecuted by society and yet often the emancipator of that same society. This frequent sacrifice of a heroic, even mythic female in Buchanan's films serves always to help the troubled community to heal and evolve. In this glorifying yet ambivalent representation of women, one recalls the loss of Buchanan's mother in infancy. This dearly missed matriarch, who became a martyr and hero to Buchanan by her death, surely became a symbol for the ideal, unattainable female role model throughout the son's subsequent life, and it is not surprising that she turns up as a powerful recurring archetype in his art. Thus, Buchanan's problematic depiction of women, simultaneously elevating and dispatching them, suggests a troubled depiction of the mother figure, who is elevated to god status by the surviving child, yet ritually dispatched, time and time again, to the black mysteries of death. This latter symbolic act is perhaps a function of the child's anger at the mother for leaving him, or a way to make the tragic death his own, to place it somehow under his control. Ritual matriarchal sacrifices aside, Buchanan clearly applauds and worships women in his films. In many instances he implies that the true hope for mankind as a whole lies with the empowerment of the female of the species over the brutish flaws of the male herd.

In addition to showcasing strong females, Buchanan also uses women as his mouthpiece, especially when he goes off on diatribes about equality, personal dignity and pacifism. Through women, Buchanan speaks of joy, longing and hope, but also of fear, depression, dreams shattered, lives unfulfilled. Buchanan's most powerful statements regularly emanate from a female protagonist, again underscoring his fascination with and belief in the power of women to participate significantly in the affairs of society.

As refreshing as is Buchanan's reframing of woman, he is not immune to carrying on certain male-oriented depictions of women. As Laura Mulvey has pointed out in her seminal essay on male-dominated cinema syntax, "Visual Pleasure and Narrative Cinema," traditional film tends to force a two-faced agenda towards women. First is undervaluation, in which the woman is degraded by narrative punishment. Buchanan's heroines, who often suffer a horrifying martyr's death, most assuredly fall into this camp. Buchanan is also guilty of overvaluing his female characters, which threaten at times to become pure fetish objects for the viewer.[4]

Buchanan surely underlines patriarchy's inherent authoritarianism and sadism towards women. He well illustrates the potential viciousness of masculinity, yet he doesn't wallow in the overt sadism to woman common to the exploitation film universe. In short, it is evident from the film texts that Buchanan respects women more than his peers do. In fact, he may go a bit too far. Buchanan tends to err on the side of idealizing his heroines, who often fall into certain classic "good woman" archetypes, including the naïve innocent and the tough girl with a heart of gold. There is, inherent in most of Buchanan's parables, the ghost of the Catholic "Madonna/Whore" complex, in which women are either saints or sinners. Buchanan's heroines tend to be good girls who are threatened with corruption by evil men. While this perspective is assuredly progressive, it might also be seen as ultimately sexist. Buchanan's "maleness" is evident not only in his worship of woman, but in his constant narrative threat to them, threats from which many do not survive.

The powerful male/female dynamic which energizes most of Buchanan's works usually sparks an ongoing dialogue between the couple, as they hammer out their inevitable differences to achieve both personal harmony and social progress. This dialogue essentially mimics a societal evolutionary process in microcosm, an evolution which is ultimately progressive but fraught with hazard, including argument, misstep and often tragedy. This dialogue is sometimes Socratic in nature, with one component eventually winning out over the other. Yet, just as often the dialectic is decidedly Hegelian in structure, as both sides bicker, bellow and battle towards an as-yet-unseen truth, forging at great personal cost a sorely needed, mutually beneficial synthesis. As frequent author of both sides of these illuminating dialogues, Buchanan plays the role of god-figure over his characters, an objective observer who effortlessly disseminates myriad relative viewpoints with equal persuasive fervor. Although this dialogue between couples is often philosophical or political in nature, there is always room for a lively discussion of more personal matters, and one finds engaging commentary on then-current sexual politics in many a Buchanan opus.

As progressive as Buchanan's "savior-couples" are in their self-sacrificing obsession to rescue a corrupted world, he also had the tendency to romanticize them. His recurrent proclamation that only a creative male-female coupling can save the world is, by definition, heterosexist. This glorifying of the bourgeois couple is likely a mythological construct of Buchanan's parents, who were denied by destiny the chance to remain together and forge a safe, happy world for young Larry and his siblings. To Buchanan, the specter of the dynamic heterosexual couple who could rescue prisoners of evil from corrupt institutions is, indeed, a paradise lost.

As Buchanan tends to rewrite accepted theorem in any given sociopolitical arena, one is tempted to call him a historical revisionist who believes in a subjective, often conspiratorial perspective on history. This general mistrust of recorded history may have an interesting genesis in Buchanan's birds-eye view of the hypocrisy of so-called educational institutions, in that in childhood he witnessed the painful discrepancy of adult institutions and their official credos compared with their vile and reprehensible actions. One might even say that an orphan is a child without a personal history, only a collective one, unless that child is able to manifest a worthy adulthood and create a living, ever-changing history for himself.

It is telling that Buchanan had two early brushes with regional, low-level fame, both as the teenage preacher and the singing TV cowboy, as Buchanan's later films become virtually fixated on "the curse of celebrity": the ironically illuminating, and crushing, burden of fame, which haunts the celebrity unto death. One entertains the notion that Buchanan, a talented and prolific filmmaker who never quite made it to the strata of fame and fortune of so many of his peers, had an ambivalent attitude towards fame, and the Hollywood system in general. Perhaps Buchanan considered himself an "outlaw rebel" of the film world, as his heroes were outlaw rebels of the worlds they inhabited. Buchanan occupied that excruciating netherworld of the "almost famous" throughout his career, and the attendant frustration fueled some interesting tracts on the subject.

An overweening presence throughout Buchanan's works is his adoration of, and constant referencing of, Western culture, and his beloved Texas homeland in particular. Certain Buchanan films are all but love letters to the Lone Star State, yet his three courtroom pictures present a highly critical but ultimately forgiving picture of Texas during the cataclysmic sociopolitical upheaval of the 1960s. In these films, and elsewhere, Buchanan consistently champions liberal, progressive racial politics in his films, an affirmation of his pacifist and egalitarian nature.

Yet underlying all of these varied themes, as encouraging as many of them are, is an understated but undeniable misanthropy, the quietly fatalistic outlook of one who, believing mankind to be, at heart, "no damn good," champions and nurtures its cause anyway, being a creature of love and forgiveness. However, the doubt and anger and mistrust of Man is there in every frame.

In weaving lurid and thrilling tales with these heady themes, Buchanan is still in essence both "the teenage preacher" of his youth and "the Singing Cowboy" of his acting days. He combines the entertainer-as-storyteller and entertainer-as-educator, regaling his audience with thrilling tales of man's fall from grace and mournful ballads of a lost innocence. Buchanan's films "sing" a sad, yet ultimately inspirational, story about a fallen yet redeemable mankind, about a culture in serious disarray, about the remnant hopes and formidable burdens of a mankind always seemingly at the crossroads of its own annihilation. The "Singing Cowboy," at least as composited in American history and myth, may be one of the first creatively endowed archetypes in modern male culture, that member of the male group who had creative talents other men did not possess, and who enjoyed entertaining the male group with these talents. Singing songs to the men around the campfire each night after a hard day of brutal reality in the plains of an untamed America, the singing cowboy both entertained and healed, salving the psychic wounds of the previous day with his ironic and humorous musical anecdotes. It may thus be helpful to see the "Singing Cowboy" as Buchanan's overriding spirit in his films. The audience are his "cowboys," and Buchanan's sad and soulful voice alternately attempts to amuse, entertain, educate, and even heal with his haunting tales of fall from grace, of corruption in high places, of proud men and heroic women doing battle against evil, of a world gone to pot and the flawed citizens who maintain their dignity in the face of it all.

2

Among the Missing

The Cowboy (1951)

Among all his hits and misses and unique experiments, Larry Buchanan shared the cursed luck of every prolific independent filmmaker in crafting works which were unfinished, unreleased, and, in at least one case, deliberately destroyed. The stuff of legend, these lost works in Buchanan's canon, and the stories behind some of them, are nearly as fantastic as some of his screenplays. Buchanan's inaugural film venture, *The Cowboy* (1951), was a short film which dealt with a subject near and dear to his heart: Western folklore. Performing as "the singing cowboy" on *The Gabby Hayes Show*, Buchanan had to put up with clichéd Western mythology weekly that was created by hacks "who had never been further west than New Jersey." Specifically, Buchanan was frustrated with the New York screenwriters he encountered and their ignorant perspective on the syntax and fashion of both the traditional and modern Cowboy:

> My worst peeve was writers' references to use of Western regalia and working clothes. Their expression for this wardrobe was "colorful." I don't believe they ever discovered that every garment the cowboy wore had a practical function. The large bandana was in reserve for a dust storm that might suddenly spring from the desert floor. The wide brim of the sombrero was for the unforgiving sun. The vest was for pockets to hold his makings for a cigarette, usually with Bull Durham tobacco. The leather chaps protected his legs from the chaparral shrub, a bothersome growth in the West. His high heels were to dig into the dirt when he was bulldogging a calf for branding and for locking his boots into his stirrups. Even the long duster coats, favored by Italian director Sergio Leone, functioned as an all-weather standby.[1]

Taking a hiatus from his New York duties, Buchanan returned to the Dallas, Texas, he loved and missed so much. With a World War II combat camera in hand, he filmed his short homage to the Old West under impossible conditions, including no money. The finished product, while likely an entertaining piece, found no takers. Short subjects were ubiquitous at the time, and usually added gratis by a distributor to a feature film program. Additionally, Western programming, so popular the decade before, was on the wane during the postwar period, with notable exceptions like *High Noon* (1950). Buchanan finally managed to sell the short to United Artists, who tacked it onto the tail of Arthur Miller's *Death of a Salesman* (1951). Buchanan recouped his production cost, which he considered a blessing.

However, the making of *The Cowboy* did offer significant advantages to the filmmaker. *The Cowboy* was Buchanan's first project working with the Jamieson Laboratories in Dallas, a professional relationship that would last virtually his entire career. More importantly, *The Cowboy* functioned as an important exercise for Buchanan, in that it was essentially a cinematic test in revising history. In this case, Buchanan desperately wanted to correct some of the errors and prejudices which the Eastern artistic establishment had about Texas, and its most popular and enduring product, the Cowboy.

Revising history, seen by some as dangerous and reckless, is at its best a noble and purifying act. One desires not to obfuscate the historical record where it is accurate, but to correct error. Revising history is *correcting false history*, and this is a cause about which Buchanan apparently felt strongly. Thus, *The Cowboy* stands as the archetype of much of Buchanan's later work, including his courtroom pictures and biopics, the spirit of which was to scrutinize, review and correct the faulty historical records of the protagonists in question.

Additionally, *The Cowboy*, and its iconic cultural archetype, suggests one plausible way of viewing Buchanan the filmmaker, that of the "singing cowboy," that is, the charismatic entertainer/storyteller. Buchanan *was* a singing cowboy, in a literal sense, having portrayed one on television and in his own inaugural film project. He is also, arguably, an *allegorical* singing cowboy, entertaining us with charming, intriguing tales of idyllic days gone by, of great social projects yet to tackle, of a beloved culture on the verge of collapse.

The cowboy is America's one true mythic hero, a historical fact yet also an undying legend, embodying desired national virtues of strength, wit and goodness. According to Duncan Emrich, "the cowboy is a symbol of what we as a people and nation have wished as our way of life. He is a projection of our hopes and desires, a projection of our best code of ethics, of our wished-for *mores*."[2]

The mythic stance of the cowboy, as national story-weaver and moral arbiter, will reveal much about Buchanan's ethical perspective as a filmmaker during the exploration of his films. Certainly Buchanan saw himself as a "good guy," someone upholding traditional values and promoting an ethical way of life. His protagonists, by and large, are good people, too, although circumstance often intervenes to distract and corrupt them. Their untoward actions are borne of ignorance, not malice. Like the problematic cowboy of old, Buchanan's heroes are thoroughly human, fallible, but ultimately redeemed by their higher aspirations.

Grubstake (1952)

Emboldened by the personal and artistic, if not financial, success of *The Cowboy*, Buchanan next attempted his first feature film, *Grubstake* (1952). Combining his paltry film rentals from *The Cowboy* with hard-won seed money from contacts in Manhattan, Buchanan crafted a Western which starred a young Broadway actor named Jack Klugman. Filmed in the remote Chisos hills outside Dallas under backbreaking conditions, the finished feature aired on local TV in the early 1950s, and was then consigned a curious destiny. The 1950s

Jack Klugman and Lynn Shubert commiserate in a now-lost first feature, *Apache Gold* (1952), aka *Grubstake*.

was the decade in which television came of age, turning virtually overnight from an obscure novelty to a omnivorous culture-machine. The nascent television industry soon became insatiable for product. In addition to the major networks, hundreds of local affiliates and independent stations sprung up, and filling these rapidly expanding broadcast days proved a challenge to the entire motion picture industry.

Like the B-Western of yore, which filled an immense number of theater screens from the birth of cinema until well into the 1940s, the Western television series, with its recognizable scenarios, recyclable stories and viewer-friendly hero figures, was a perfect product for the unblinking video eye. The Western TV series which dominated the small home screen during the 1950s owed a great deal to the Western cliffhanger serial, some of which were reworked and recycled into television filler. Independent producers, especially, were loath to mount an entire production crew to film new action sequences and melodramas, so they resorted to the use of stock footage, film shot for an earlier production, or taken at a location without any express production in mind, and now available for sale to the highest bidder. Stock footage libraries sprouted on both the East and West coasts during this time period. A most popular subject for producers was location footage of a Western nature: horse riders, panoramic vistas, cowboys and Indians, and anything of a vaguely "period" flavor. Along with many other ill-fated productions, Buchanan's beloved first feature was cannibalized for such stock footage, and likely ended up as filler for long-forgotten syndicated Western TV series. It is intriguing to note that these "seeds" of Buchanan's labors were sprinkled all over television during the period, laying the groundwork for his bursting on the scene a decade later.

Venus in Furs (circa 1957)

After the sobering experiences of *The Cowboy* and *Grubstake*, Buchanan became involved in commercial and industrial film production at Jamieson Film Labs in Dallas, where he would earn his meager bread and butter for years, and also meet many who would join his little film caravan on its circuitous trip to fame and fortune. Perhaps the most fascinating story of Buchanan's early career involves the ill-fated adult feature called *Venus in Furs* (circa 1957). Commissioned by a Texas oil baron, the film was to be a vanity piece for the entrepreneur's mistress, an aspiring actress. Buchanan was paid handsomely, in cash, to mount a production for this would-be thespian. Armed with a one-page script loosely based on the writings of the Marquis de Sade, Buchanan pulled off what sounds like a laudable example of the genre. As he had with *The Cowboy* and *Grubstake*, Buchanan once again thought he finally had his "breakthrough" film.

But fate was to deal Buchanan another cruel blow. After premiering the finished film to his producer, the oil baron took Buchanan and the film negatives, sailed out to the middle of Lake Dallas, and dumped the film cans into the briny deep. As it turns out, the tycoon's beloved mistress and star of the film had left him for a local disc jockey just the night before. One can easily imagine Buchanan's horror at having his newest creation drowned before his very eyes. This highly ritualistic destruction of a work of art surely had a profound effect on the psyche of the artist, and Buchanan's luck seemed to turn at that very moment. Soon, Buchanan would be rewarded with early exploitation hits like *The Naked Witch*, *Naughty Dallas*, and *Free, White and 21*.

Sam (1966)

In 1966, in the midst of Buchanan's churning out the Azalea telefilm series, a trio of Dallas lawyers approached the filmmaker and asked if he wanted to make a "modern" Western. Buchanan was thrilled — he hadn't made a Western in over a decade, since his beloved, lost *Grubstake*. Buchanan commissioned Jody McCrea from the American International stable of "Beach Party Boys" to star, and fashioned a loving Western melodrama, filmed on the border of Mexico. The film was called *Sam (or The Hottest Fourth of July in the History of Brewster County)* (1966). Buchanan even managed to meet his director-hero William Wellman (*Nothing Sacred, A Star Is Born*), along the way. Yet, in another of life's dirty tricks, the film was never released. It had been intended all along as nothing but a tax shelter for the conniving counsels-at-law. As Buchanan would intone many times, "sometimes life writes dirty scripts."

Comanche Crossing (1968)

A business associate approached Buchanan shortly after the *Sam* debacle and said "Let's make a real Western, and let's release it!" The eternally optimistic Buchanan again took the bait and produced *Comanche Crossing* (1968) between producing two of the Azalea telefilms. In a wildly radical departure for Westerns of the time, Buchanan cast Cynthia Hull and Anthony Houston as a sympathetic Comanche Indian couple. The completed feature was shown to a large group of Native Americans, who applauded it highly. Unfortunately, this historical revisionism of the Native American mythos was met with total silence at the box office, and was soon withdrawn from release. In this case, Buchanan's revisionist history was either ahead of its time, or too controversial, considering the subject matter; sympathetic Native Americans being depicted onscreen were still several years away.

Hell Raiders (1968)

One of the most intriguing of Buchanan's "lost" films is *Hell Raiders* (1968), the eighth telefilm contracted by American International Tel evision, and released under the Azalea Pictures banner. The only one of the Azalea films not of the science fiction or horror genre, *Hell Raiders* seems to have fallen off the face of the earth. This is slightly odd for a widely released television movie less than fifty years old. The World War II–themed melodrama starred John Agar and, according to Buchanan, "one Sherman tank." The film was shot at an old Dallas shopping center which had been designed like an Italian village. As in *The Naked Witch*, Buchanan uses an unusual real-life location to create a compelling period milieu which Hollywood would have crafted from scratch, at a cost of millions. And, as in *The Naked Witch*, *Hell Raiders* also turned modern America into "Olde Europe...."

The Rebel Jesus (1972)

Buchanan's unfinished labor of love, *The Rebel Jesus* (1972), gestated for thirty years, only to reside in limbo as *The Copper Scroll of Mary Magdelene* (circa 2004). Filming under backbreaking conditions in the deserts of Tunisia, on money borrowed from friends, Buchanan had high hopes for this film, which certainly foreshadowed such revisionist religious blockbusters as Martin Scorcese's lurid *The Last Temptation of Christ* (1988) and Mel Gibson's homoerotic *The Passion of the Christ* (2004). Buchanan's interest in the subject of the historical Jesus was piqued at an early age, and became a "frustrated obsession" throughout his life. *The Rebel Jesus* was his attempt to address his personal philosophy about the "man from Galilee":

> I believe that 2,000 years ago, in Judea, there lived a man who knew God. I do not believe his was a virgin birth, nor that he struck wine from water, nor that he raised the dead, nor that he experienced resurrection from his death. Rather he was an Essene who spent much of the period known as his "lost years" studying at Qumran by the Dead Sea and traveling to distant countries such as India and China. I do believe he gave his life to punctuate his mission and message: "There is one God; all men are brothers, love the worst of these." I was driven to make a film that explored what happened during those unknown years of Jesus' life between the approximate ages of 13 and 30. Thus was born *The Rebel Jesus*.[3]

Buchanan's loving treatment of the man from Galilee depicts Jesus as an exemplary spiritual teacher, nothing more, nothing less. The film follows Jesus' life during the so-called lost years, those between the ages of 13 and 30. Filming in Technicolor and Techniscope,

Top: Filming in Tunisia gave Larry Buchanan the opulent vistas he needed to fashion his biblical magnum opus, *The Rebel Jesus,* aka *The Copper Scroll of Mary Magdalene* (1972). *Bottom:* Jesus (Gene Otis Shane) instructs his disciples at the shores of Galilee in *The Rebel Jesus,* aka *The Copper Scroll of Mary Magdalene.*

on a budget of $170,000, Buchanan and crew filmed in Tunisia, creating a lush and evocative landscape worthy of any multimillion dollar Hollywood blockbuster. Buchanan even had the rare opportunity to work with award-winning composer Alex North on the project. Buchanan was sure he had a masterpiece on his hands, but, unhappy with the finished product, he withdrew it from release and noodled around with the film for many years. Buchanan eventually sold his interest, as well as all production elements of *The Rebel Jesus,* to another party several years before his death. The film has since been held from release by this individual. The predicament caused Buchanan considerable torment. He once lamented, somewhat resignedly, "[He] won't release it until it's 'perfect.'"[4] Buchanan later confided in an audio interview, '(He) keeps changing the ending...''[5] This is a sad coda to Buchanan's legacy. The film, in its finished state, would certainly represent a celebration of the director and his work, as it is undoubtedly his most personal work. It's to be hoped the completed film will be released in due course. It stands to be by far Buchanan's biggest work, a grand epic with a sweeping canvas and a unique perspective on the oldest tale of all. It is likely that Buchanan comes to terms in this production with the religious orthodoxy he both loathed and adored, and may well illustrate revisionist cinema at its finest.

3

That's Exploitation

Larry Buchanan shared the fate of most independent filmmakers of the period, producing lurid, hastily shot films for the exploitation film market. These films were produced to titillate and entertain the patrons of rural drive-in theaters and urban second-run or "grindhouses," venues which specialized in low-budget material of a sensational nature. As the urbanization of the U.S. progressed, and movie theaters proliferated to match the ever-growing population, demand for exploitation product grew as well, and some producers and directors mounted entire careers on the creation of this curious commodity of latter twentieth century America. Yet it is likely that Buchanan relished the opportunity to make films of any type, at any cost, and it is evident that even with these "little" pictures, he took care to produce something entertaining and moderately respectable, within severe financial and thematic restraints. Overviews of four of Buchanan's exploitation efforts follow.

Common Law Wife (1963)

Common Law Wife (1963) is a problematic film to discuss, as it is a hybrid, a common phenomenon in the world of the exploitation film. The film began life as *Swamp Rose*, a tale about rural love and betrayal. Larry Buchanan shot 16mm color footage for *Swamp Rose* in 1960, in the Caddo Lake swamplands on the border of Louisiana and Texas. According to Buchanan, the original *Swamp Rose*, budgeted at $18,000, was "beautiful and lyrical; it even had a theme song!"[1] Buchanan then departed the project, and the footage was sold to exploitation producer Mike Ripps (a.k.a. M.A. Ripps), creator of notorious drive-in fare such as *Poor White Trash Part 2* (1977). Ripps assigned Eric Sayers to shoot additional footage and merge it, somewhat arbitrarily, with Buchanan's footage. Ripps released the finished patchwork product to regional drive-ins in 1963 as *Common Law Wife*. The release prints of *Common Law Wife* were struck in black and white, so Buchanan's color footage was reduced to grainy monochrome. Even more egregious, Ripps and company decided to retain the main *character* from Buchanan's opus (Jonelle, played by Lacey Kelly), but replace the *actress* who played her. Thus, the lead character in this disorienting backwoods fable changes indiscriminately from one person to another, in some cases quite obviously, lending the finished product a certain schizophrenic air. As one might imagine, *Common Law Wife* comes across as a choppy and confusing experience, which is not helped by the fact that a great deal of the footage seems to have been shot silent and overdubbed hastily afterwards. In many cases, the original actor's voice was not used, and in certain instances the difference in the timbre of the voice with the character portrayed is significant.

Still, *Common Law Wife* is worth a look as an example of regional exploitation product of the day. The Buchanan footage, consisting primarily of scenes between Jonelle and the moonshiner Bull in the swamps, is nicely lensed and evocative, but few of the themes inherent in his earlier *The Naked Witch* are apparent. Title character Linda (Annabelle Weenick) is a strong central female character, a heroine of sorts, and she is sacrificed at film's end to correct things in the community, as in so many of Buchanan's subsequent efforts, but this appears to be more coincidence than design. Weenick (often billed as Anne MacAdams), an actress who would grace many of Buchanan's efforts with her austere beauty and penchant for tragic heroines, is terrific as the ill-fated "common law wife." Weenick often played a protofeminist character in Buchanan's films, and she is quite effective here, even under the guidance of another director. George Edgley, also effective as an absurd face of patriarchy in *Common Law Wife*, was used by Buchanan as "The Judge" in all three of his courtroom pictures. Lacey Kelly makes a sultry "Baby Doll," a.k.a. Jonelle, in the Buchanan footage that is extant. Buchanan said of Ms. Kelly, "Lacey was a real character! Totally independent, a true free spirit. She really took off in that speedboat during the swamp scenes; even the cops warned us a couple of times!"[2] The second, anonymous Jonelle who is featured in the majority of *Common Law Wife* is a pouty, baby-faced Barbie Doll clone with oversized eyes and a few studied and repetitious mannerisms, the complete antithesis of Kelly's natural charisma. Bert Masters, who plays Bull the moonshiner, was a real-life sheriff who took up acting as a hobby. Max Anderson, who plays Jake, the sheriff of Serenity, did a lot of voiceover and commercials work in the Dallas area. Libby Booth, who plays Jake's wife, also played the sultry Widow Witch in Buchanan's exemplary *The Naked Witch*. According to Buchanan, Booth enjoyed acting but never ventured out of the Texas area, happy to work in local theater.[3]

Buchanan was understandably bewildered when he finally caught up with *Common Law Wife*: "I thought I had made a low-country sex drama, in color, based on the writings of my role models Erskine Caldwell, Tennessee Williams and William Faulkner. What wound up on the drive-in screens of the southern United States was ... a grainy potpourri of out takes that I had rejected in my cut."[4] The sobering experience of *Common Law Wife* marked a turning point for Buchanan. He realized that he couldn't go on making low-rent regional pictures which barely covered costs and paid the rent. He decided to team up with longtime friend Harold Hoffman, advertising man-turned-attorney, and form a production company, attempting to mount productions that might be viable for the lucrative national theatrical market. The result was *Free, White and 21*, Buchanan's first true hit and breakthrough picture.[5]

High Yellow (1965)

Buchanan's 1965 potboiler, *High Yellow*, is an example of the filmmaker taking an exploitation-based assignment and using it to fashion something unique and engaging.

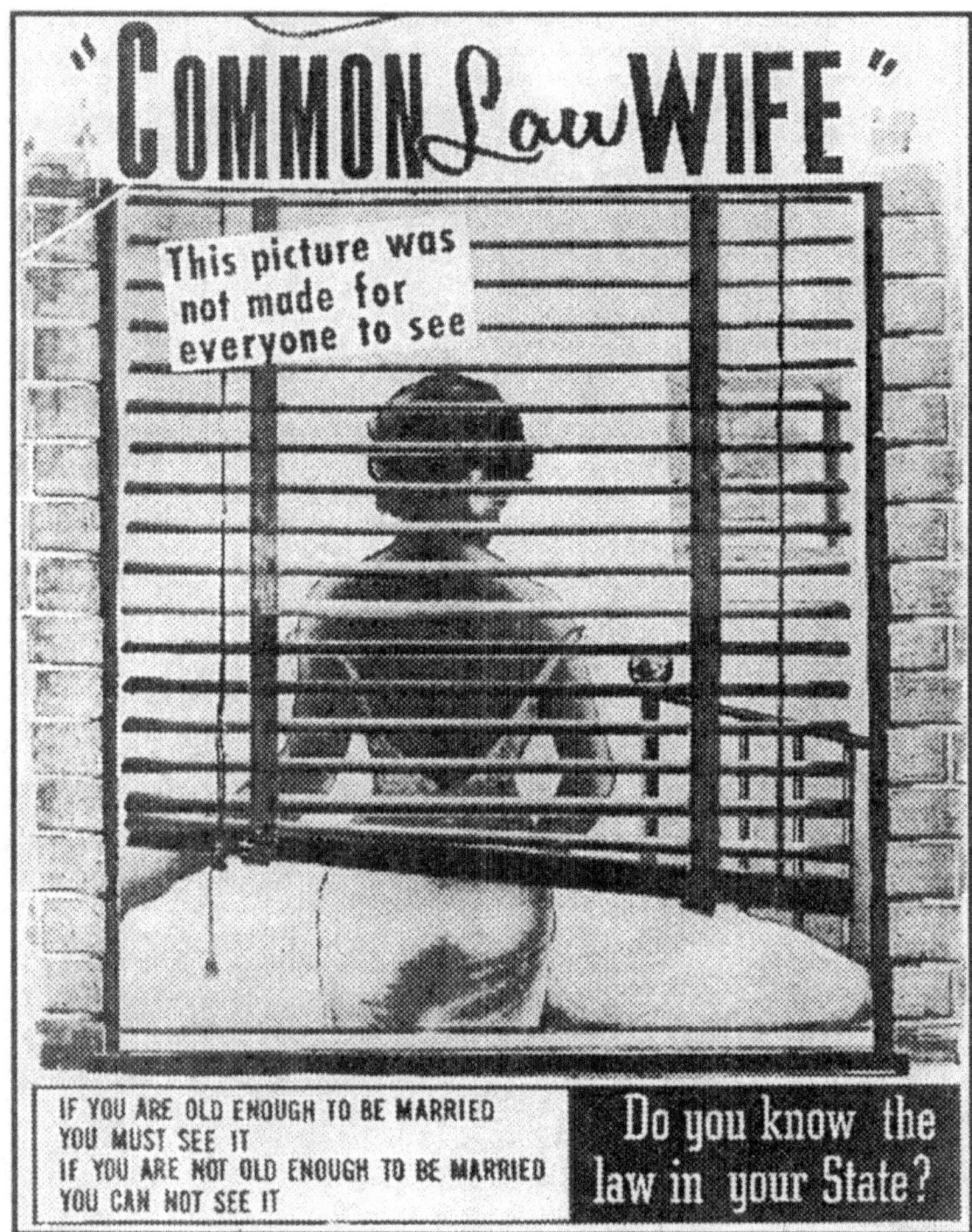

Swamp Rose (1960), Larry Buchanan's colorful homage to unrequited lust in rural Louisiana, was unrecognizable after other hands mutated it into the trashy black and white sexploitation potboiler *Common Law Wife* (1963).

Similar to how *The Naked Witch* (1961) was handled, *High Yellow* takes its sketchy, one-joke plotline and invests it with thematic and aesthetic material of substance. *High Yellow* tackles Buchanan's interest in progressive racial politics, a subject he explored in depth with *Free, White and 21* (1963), and fashions a lurid yet enlightening melodrama. Other films of the period which dealt with the then-hot topic of racial prejudice included *The Intruder* (1962, d: Roger Corman), *I Crossed the Color Line* (1966, d: Ted V. Mikels) and the box-office winner *Black Like Me* (1964, d: Carl Lerner).

The plot is loosely based on *Diary of a Chambermaid* by Octave Mirbeau, an author Buchanan greatly admired.[6] In the film, a seventeen-year-old black girl (Cynthia Hull) tries to pass for white. She gets hired as a maid for a rich white family comprised of a blustery patriarch (Warren Hammack), a spoiled matriarch (Annabelle Weenick), and a slutty teenage daughter (Kay Taylor), who is murdered by a sleazy caretaker (Bill Thurman). The black chauffeur (William McGhee) is falsely accused of the murder. The young lovers struggle to free the chauffeur against the efforts of corrupt police interests.

According to Buchanan, the filmmaker made *High Yellow* on the cusp of beginning his eight-film Azalea telefilms assignment, for he feared that the rigors of churning out cheap monster movies would take its toll on his creative side: "But I had one more kind of 'artistic,' if you will, film in me, before I could get down to business in earnest on Sam Arkoff's project. It was *High Yellow*, done kind of while Sam wasn't looking, and released as a big moneymaker for Dallas' Dinero Productions, and a picture that AIP could only wish it had latched onto."[7] Buchanan was unabashedly proud of *High Yellow*, and in fact considered it a rare example of his being able to function primarily as artist instead of hired gun on a film assignment:

> There's a lot of feeling in *High Yellow* and it's one of the few pictures of mine where my insistence on putting one special "day" of high quality and patience into every picture was actually stretched out over the entire production. For no matter how hectic a schedule or penurious a budget, every picture I'd shoot would have that one "day" in there somewhere that I'd declare to be set aside for a leisurely, artistic approach to what we were doing. My crew people got to where they called that practice "Larry's Day."[8]

Buchanan shot the film almost entirely in and around an infamous mansion in Frisco, a town north of Dallas. The "Frisco Mansion" purportedly had a grisly history of multiple murders, and when Buchanan leased it, it had been on the market for years with no takers. Buchanan professes to have had a supernatural encounter during a night of staying in the house alone. The mansion was chosen for use some years later in the TV series *Dallas*, but another "Southfork" was picked after cast and crew experienced other ghostly nuisances.[9]

High Yellow did extremely well in regional theater circuits, and garnered Buchanan the relief he needed for what would prove to be the most trying long-term assignment of his career, the Azalea telefilms.

The Other Side of Bonnie & Clyde (1968)

With *The Other Side of Bonnie & Clyde* (1968), Larry Buchanan tackles two of history's most notorious bandits, Clyde Barrow and Bonnie Parker, charismatic hoodlums with extensive Lone Star roots. Barrow and Parker were two of the more reactionary products of

WANT HER? TAKE HER!
..... she's big BOXOFFICE!

HIGH YELLOW

AN EXPLOSIVE STORY !!

A DINERO PRODUCTION

EXHIBITOR'S CAMPAIGN BOOK

Opposite: Other versions of the primitive, lurid theatrical poster for the racially charged *High Yellow* (1965) boasted "Two Men — One White, One Black!" and prominently featured stars Cynthia Hull and Billy Thurman in a potentially compromising position. *Top:* For added shock value, Larry Buchanan used gruesome clips from the infamous "death film" taken by U.S. marshals following the successful ambush of outlaws Clyde Barrow and Bonnie Parker in the exploitation quickie *The Other Side of Bonnie & Clyde* (1968).

the Great Depression which had settled on America in the late 1920s. The lover couple robbed banks, stores and individuals with equal enthusiasm. They had an especial loathing for law enforcement officials, and an astounding 80 percent of their murders were of lawmen, which made them popular with malcontents and anarchists, as well as the sworn enemies of peace officers everywhere. It was legendary Texas Ranger Frank Hamer who finally took it upon himself to track down Bonnie and Clyde in a massive manhunt which ended in a bloody, history-making shootout in Gibbons, Louisiana. Bigger in death than they were in life, the couple soon became an indelible American legend. Their "death car" and other artifacts toured the U.S. traveling carnival circuit for years.

Released in 1968, *The Other Side of Bonnie & Clyde* (henceforth referred to as *The Other Side*) seems to be less documentary or thrill-ride than a diatribe against another movie. A year earlier, director Arthur Penn had released *Bonnie & Clyde*, starring Warren Beatty and Faye Dunaway. The film was a critical and box-office smash hit, and is even today considered an example of an American "New Wave" in film, with its desolate landscapes, obsession with violence, and scattershot editing by Dede Allen. Others were horrified by the film and the way it depicted the criminal pair. History records that the real Barrow and Parker were demented, irredeemable sociopaths. Penn's romantic interpretation of the pair resulted in pretty-boy Beatty and cutie-pie Dunaway looking like poster children for hard-working proletariats. History's criminals became Penn's heroes, and their battle against "evil" lawmen became a metaphor for the little man trying to win out over an oppressive economic system. The heated debate about the film covered much territory. Film critics such as Pauline Kael lauded the film as a cinema landmark. *Time* magazine and others questioned the film and its cinematic brethren, and their role in glorifying violence and anti-social behavior for the nation's young.

Buchanan seemed to take this latter view. *The Other Side* is entirely in the service of depicting Bonnie and Clyde as lousy cutthroats, and not the lovable rascals of Arthur Penn's seriocomic fantasy. In Buchanan's opinion, "They were a dichotomy; they were a real weird couple."[10] The film is loosely based on the account of Texas Ranger Frank Hamer who, as mentioned, was the peace officer who hunted down and finally caught the elusive duo. Based on Hamer's 1968 autobiography, the film takes the viewpoint of the law enforcement organizations trying to locate and trap the pair, a viewpoint not without prejudice, as witness this quote from the book about Ms. Parker: "She was, begging your pardon, a bit of a female dog."[11]

The film is an hour-long overview of some highlights and lowlights of the spurious pair until their deaths by gunfire. Key scenes in the history of the pair are reenacted in sketchy fashion by a couple whose faces are never seen.[12] These scenes, while interesting, are not well-mounted enough to be narratively thrilling. The most effective of these recreates the infamous killing of two passing motorcycle cops by the thugs on Easter morning. More interesting are biographical facts revealed by the narrator of the film, popular actor and folk singer Burl Ives. Ives and Buchanan were longtime friends, and first met in 1946, when Ives was just beginning to forge a career as a folk singer in Greenwich Village.[13] As evidence of their friendship, Ives agreed to narrate this low-budget project for a fraction of his then-going rate. Ives' colorful narration, which evokes Buchanan's "singing cowboy" persona, reveals much about the lives of the star-crossed lovers Bonnie and Clyde, accompanied by photographs and newspaper clippings. There are also on display some grisly photographs of the Texas Rangers standing over piles of dead bodies belonging to bank-robbing gangs which then roamed the land. More information is revealed via interviews with persons involved in the Bonnie and Clyde phenomenon, including the wife of Frank Hamer, Hamer's son, a hostage of the pair, and a historian. This utilization of real people is highly effective. Hamer's widow, for instance, speaks lovingly and with amazing recall about her husband's trials and tribulations. Sofia Cook's recounting of her kidnapping by the thug couple brings to vivid life the terror of being in the presence of human monsters. She spins her tale of horror while peacefully knitting, calmly telling of the terrors and thrills inherent in the lawless South during this turbulent time period. Hamer's son shows off the Barrow-Parker arsenal, which his father was awarded as a bonus for gunning down the criminals. Each observer has a unique perspective on the pair, but the overwhelming opinion is a negative one.

Finally, the film recreates in abbreviated form the final shootout between Bonnie and Clyde and Hamer and assorted other lawmen. Punctuating this brief massacre is a sequence featuring the black and white "death film" taken after the actual ambush in Louisiana. It shows Ms. Parker, crumpled like a rag doll, in the front seat of the bullet-mangled automobile. *The Other Side* dissects the "death film" footage like a cinematic autopsy, running

Notorious Depression-era gangster "Pretty Boy" Floyd Hamilton, a free man after years of imprisonment, suffers one final indignity by taking an onscreen lie-detector test in the sensationalist docudrama *The Other Side of Bonnie & Clyde* (1968).

it in slow motion and holding for freeze frames to emphasize certain moments. Following this are several grisly morgue photos, including one showing Parker lying on the morgue slab, her bare breasts covered with blood, her bloated face contorted in agony.

One of the most curious scenes in the film features real-life gangster Floyd Hamilton, a.k.a. "Pretty Boy" Floyd, taking a lie-detector test onscreen to share what he recalls about compatriots Bonnie and Clyde. Buchanan's partner, Harold Hoffman, is the onscreen moderator of this sequence. According to Buchanan, Hamilton was found, down and out, working as a night watchman for an Oldsmobile dealer in Dallas, and after an initial refusal to discuss anything about his sordid past, warmed up to the idea and became surprisingly forthcoming.[14] As the sequence begins, the visibly embarrassed ex-gangster dutifully answers questions about Barrow, Parker, and their sometime-partner, Roy Hamilton, Floyd's brother. Clearly, the most painful revelation for Floyd is acknowledging that his brother Ray was not only a crime partner of Bonnie and Clyde but also sex partner to both. Yet something strange happens as the interrogation unfolds. After overcoming his initial shyness, Hamilton comes to life in the latter segments, even cracking a hard-won smile, creating a larger-than-life character who is no longer despicable, foreshadowing the mythic outlaw with which Buchanan would fuel his theatrical hit, *A Bullet for Pretty Boy* (1970). Overall, however, the Hamilton sequence is shameful and in poor taste. While Hamilton was no angel and was likely compensated for his participation, the sad sequence smacks of freak-show sensationalism, and cheapens the overall project. The fact that Hamilton was not allowed to be interviewed like the other participants in the film but was treated like a common criminal reveals a cynicism on the part of the filmmakers that diminishes whatever other, more noble purposes they were trying to serve.

If it was Buchanan's intention to de-romanticize Bonnie and Clyde with this picture, he succeeded. The film is as drab, artless and lackluster as one could imagine. Yet ironically, in exposing humanity's dark side, Buchanan inadvertently bared the darker aspects of his artistic self: sensationalist, morbid and bitter. Perhaps Buchanan had a bone to pick with Arthur Penn over his success with *Bonnie & Clyde*. For years Buchanan had been trying to get Sam Arkoff at American International to green-light a remake of *The Bonnie Parker Story* (1958, d: William Witney). Perhaps Buchanan felt that Penn's film stole a hit which he deserved. Surely Buchanan's version of the Bonnie and Clyde saga would have been light-years away from Penn's vision, aesthetically and philosophically. Buchanan even insisted that Penn's film stole a great deal of scenario from *The Bonnie Parker Story*.[15]

Ethical considerations aside, *The Other Side* is a slight curiosity, entertaining enough but not one of Buchanan's shining moments. It does, however, briefly touch upon two recurring themes dear to the filmmaker. The film is an example of Buchanan's penchant for historical revisionism and passion for setting the record straight. The film also conveys an avowed misanthropy regarding the film's subjects, and covertly shines an unflattering light on the human race for elevating these corrupt and depraved souls to folk-hero status. When it comes to seeing people as they really are, Buchanan's explorations into the dark soul of man are compelling, and *The Other Side* is a bare-bones example of this energy at work as it ponders the allure of evil men to a morally conflicted society as well as the community's curious penchant for transforming the villainous into the heroic.

Buchanan's traditional views of justice, and his continual predictable siding with the law as evident in this and other films, make sense, as his father was a peace officer who had extensive dealings with criminals, including peers of Bonnie and Clyde. Buchanan's deputy-father had a near-death encounter with "Pretty Boy" Floyd Hamilton, which makes Hamilton's appearance in *The Other Side* even more intriguing. Perhaps with this film, and Buchanan's soon-to-follow box-office hit, *A Bullet for Pretty Boy*, Buchanan was trying to understand his father's enemies, and thus make peace with the patriarch himself. For as much as Buchanan tries to de-romanticize the criminal element, neither is he immune to the dark allure of the outlaw, as witness his returning to these enigmatic offshoots of capitalistic society time and again. Always the historian, Buchanan uses *The Other Side of Bonnie & Clyde* not only to entertain, but to emphasize the potential of history to educate. As he himself stated, "We should learn from these things."[16]

Sex and the Animals (1969)

Buchanan and his partner, Harold Hoffman, returned to pure exploitation territory one last time, in 1969, with *Sex and the Animals*, a wildlife documentary depicting the mating rituals of nonhuman creatures. Produced by an uncredited Buchanan, and helmed by partner Hoffman under the pseudonym "Hal Dwain," *Sex and the Animals* is primarily a showcase for the research of Drs. Lorus and Margery Milne, a husband and wife research and teaching team who, according to the film's pressbook, wrote over 25 books on animals,

Dr. Lorus J. Milne and his wife, Dr. Margery Milne, award-winning biologists and authors, are prominently featured onscreen in *Sex and the Animals*, which was based on their best-selling book, ***The Mating Instinct***.

including *The Mating Instinct*, the best-seller on which *Sex and the Animals* is based. Although the intent was likely pure exploitation (the film was rated *R*), producer Hoffman adapted the high-handed approach of exploiters of old, insisting that the film was intended to be educational, and was even suitable for children: "We hope to banish man's guilt and fear about sex and make him realize that it is a normal, natural thing. In this way we can relieve a great deal of emotional and mental anxiety and illness. Although the film is presented on a college level, it is suitable for children of all levels."[17] Regardless of the spurious nature of the project, *Sex and the Animals* likely did well in its regional playdates. In 1974, Columbia Pictures released a similar documentary, with the focus again on animal mating rituals, produced by award-winning documentary filmmaker David L. Wolper. Called *Birds Do It, Bees Do It*, this film covered exactly the same territory as *Sex and the Animals*, and the advertising emphatically stated, "See it with your children." Even odder, *Birds Do It, Bees Do It* was released to weekend "Kiddie Matinees" populated almost exclusively by children. Surely these sexually oriented films aimed, at least secondarily, at the youth market represented a most peculiar cultural response to the then-burgeoning sexual revolution, combining some tamer aspects of the "adults only" genre with the popular, family-oriented "wildlife adventure" genre then in vogue thanks to blockbusters such as *Born Free* (1966).

As might be expected, the synopsis offered to distributors in the *Sex and the Animals* pressbook stresses the "educational" nature of the film, concluding with,

> Sex is nature's greatest marvel. The male and the female animal, the two sexes, make it possible to combine the heredity of a specie in every conceivable way. And in the fusion of the sperm and the egg, individuality is created ... each member of the specie becomes different, unique. This great variety of individuals gives a flexibility to the specie that helps it adapt to the changing world. And it is the versatile animal that shall inherit the earth ... not the meek.[18]

Aside from a somewhat ironic pre-credits teaser in which two turkeys do a mating dance to the sitar music of Ravi Shankar, *Sex and the Animals* is a straightforward documentary,

The newspaper advertisements for *Sex and the Animals* (1969), edited and produced by Larry Buchanan, emphasized the educational value of this risqué wildlife documentary.

lacking the tongue-in-cheek perspective one might expect in this type of film. The film is narrated alternately by both the male and female Milne, who also appear on screen, walking together through various natural landscapes. As might be anticipated, the wildlife photography is by and large of excellent quality, and serves the film well. The film follows the published press synopsis slavishly, following life from its primitive beginnings to the more advanced forms. It is somewhat unnerving to follow how the animal kingdom progresses until it looks uncomfortably like human beings, eerily familiar and yet starkly alien. Indeed, Buchanan stated that he tried to convince producer Hoffman to end the film with a short segment on human love during the sexual revolution,[19] but to no avail. Regardless of this impasse, this is definitely where the documentary seems to be leading, although one understands why producer Hoffman did not want to tread into the sexploitation minefield with this film.

Oddly, the most disturbing sequence in the film does not involve intercourse but shows a man wearing a long latex glove extracting sperm from a bull and then reaching deep into the cow's vagina to artificially inseminate it. Also strange is a sequence of three men, wearing cowboy hats and white lab coats, coaxing two horses to copulate. There is also some childbirth footage, of elephants and horses, which harks back to the childbirth footage which was a staple of the exploitation film over a decade earlier. Finally, the R-rated film gives the customer what he paid for, with frank scenes of zebras, hippos, rhinos, horses, elephants, etc., making love in shameless ecstasy. The film ends with scenes of primate mating rituals, including some surprising homosexual behavior, in the film's only black and white footage. Using science and education as exploitation was certainly a tradition known by the exploitation filmmakers of the past, although by 1969 the genre had all but faded from view due to the increasingly frank nature of sexploitation films.

It would appear that Buchanan's participation in the film was minimal and primarily centered around postproduction work such as collating and editing newsreel film from the many credited cinematographers. It is nonetheless interesting to note that Buchanan and Hoffman's Dallas-based film enterprise, Falcon International Pictures, was still creating product almost a decade after its formation for *Free, White and 21*.

4

The Naked Witch

When Betty Friedan's *The Feminine Mystique* was first published in 1963, it was a revelation and reignited debate over the role of woman in a patriarchal society. Significant changes were already underway during the first half of the twentieth century: women's suffrage and the right to vote in the 1920s and the influx of women into the workplace during World War II. In the post-WWII era, the punitive myth of the "happy housewife" was undergoing considerable discussion in American culture. One way this discussion was framed was in the archetype of *the witch*.

Males have been fascinated with the notion of the witch throughout history and in culture, ranging from demonic figures, magical whores, powerful nemeses, devouring vaginas, dominating mother figures, healing saints. Arguably the most famous witches in American popular culture appeared on American television in the 1960s: Samantha Stevens (Elizabeth Montgomery) on *Bewitched* (1964) and Jeannie (Barbara Eden) on *I Dream of Jeannie* (1966), precisely in the wake of *The Feminine Mystique*. Samantha and Jeannie epitomized the "good witch" as a beautiful magical helper who subordinated herself to the male and the patriarchal order (Jeannie continually referring to Major Nelson as "Master"); their husbands routinely discouraged their witch-wives from using their omnipotent powers, and when they did use them, it was only when necessary and for "good" (i.e., preserving the status quo). In contrast, the *bad* witch was a dangerous and vindictive woman who realized her immense power could wreak havoc on the established order — typified by sitcom stereotype Endora (Agnes Moorehead), the meddling mother-in-law on *Bewitched*. In the context of American culture in the early 1960s, the witch held potentially inappropriate, and, most importantly, uncontrollable power over man's domain and a patriarchal system: the good witch collaborated and was canonized; the bad witch rebelled and was a scapegoat, a convenient villain for all of society's ills. Even Freidan was stunned by the reaction to her feminist brand of "witchcraft":

> I became a leper in my own suburb. As long as I wrote only occasional articles most people never read, the fact that I wrote during the hours when the children were in school was no more a stigma than, for instance, solitary morning drinking. But now that I was acting like a real writer and even being interviewed on television, the sin was too public, it could not be condoned. *Women in other suburbs were writing me letters as if I were Joan of Arc, but I practically had to flee my own crabgrass-overgrown yard to keep from being burned at the stake.*[1]

In this context, *The Naked Witch* (1961), Larry Buchanan's allegorical fantasy of the supernatural, becomes a scathing and yet problematic sociological study of gender politics. Buchanan was approached by drive-in owner and exploitation film distributor Claude Alexander, who wanted to make "a drive-in picture with lots of nudity and very little dialogue and all I can spend is $8,000!"[2] Lured by Alexander's promise of total artistic freedom, Buchanan pitched Alexander a script he had written previously, wholly inspired by a real-life village which appeared in the finished film:

> I was inspired to write the story when I first visited the hills west of Austin, the capital of Texas. The little town of Luckenbach, among others, had been settled by Germans from the Old Country around 1936. Sparkling springs gushed from the limestone rocks. The flowers and climate reminded them of their homeland, and they cluster there to this day. They are an industrious and clannish people who hold annual holidays called Saengerfests (Singing Festivals) and Schutzenfests (Shooting Festivals). Their homes are such as you might see along the Rhine, and their lifestyles are almost Amish in their simplicity.[3]

Yet *The Naked Witch* is far from rural nostalgia, and is rather a crude stab at feminism from a male artist who had deep respect for women within the constraints of drive-in exploitation cinema. In fact, *The Naked Witch* starts out like any number of lurid exploitation films of the period, thanks to a hastily attached, postproduction prologue added by Alexander. Presumably added to pad the scant running time of the narrative, it also appears Alexander thought Buchanan's lyrical and empathetic melodrama was a bit "soft" on the exploitation angle, even sympathetic to the title character, expected to be a figure of lust or horror, or ideally *both*, to the grindhouse audience. This overwrought eight-minute prologue starts off with the title "Witches," accompanied by ominous horror-film music and abstract graphical backgrounds. The title crawl, also narrated, distinctly posits the witch in history as the evil, supernatural enemy of the male, a thing more monster than mortal. The viewer is shown horrific images by artist Hieronymus Bosch, including details from *Hell*, *The Hay Wagon* and *The Garden of Earthly Delights*, where witches are defined as demented creatures who have given their souls over to evil. These images are implied by the narrator to be depictions of true, ghastly events, as opposed to nightmares or dark male fantasies. This disingenuous viewpoint of women was consistent with traditional exploitation-film syntax, and one that becomes crucial throughout Buchanan's career as a filmmaker with a distinctly liberal political agenda, a feminist stance that was progressive yet provincial, working within the constraints, conventions, and demands of the B-movie genres in which he worked. With its hyperbolic narration and grim visuals depicting murderous rampages and perverse sexual debauchery, the prologue generates anticipation for a subsequent depraved melodrama as the narration finally turns back on itself with an odd disclaimer: "Modern man no longer believes in witches! Do these ominous creatures still exist? Let us see...."

The first shot of the film proper zooms into a graveyard, in the middle of which a marble cherub-angel prays to the heavens as a windmill rotates behind it. Aided by foreboding organ music, a different narrator (Buchanan) offers a quote from Shakespeare, also shown in graphic: "This is the very witching time of night when churchyards yawn and hell itself gives out contagion to the world." The cast is introduced onscreen one by one. First seen is a young blonde woman, described as "Jo Maryman as Kirska." Kirska slowly dissolves into a shot of Robert Short as "The Student." He is shown bare chested, naked, a "clean slate"—the impressionable "new man" of America whose destiny will be written

The lurid exploitational emphasis of the poster art for *The Naked Witch* (1961) belies the film's progressive sexual politics.

by experience and adventure. Finally, there is an extreme close-up of Libby Booth (as Libby Hall), the title character, appearing alluring yet angry, the archetypal erotic fantasy of the witch as both irresistible and dangerous. The opening shot and *dramatis personae* bear more comparison to silent films, expressionist cinema, and classic Universal horror than the often utilitarian exploitation film strategies, indicative of Buchanan's eclectic merger of various and sometimes disparate film influences which defined his filmmaking style. Moreover, the presentation of the three main characters constructs the classic "romantic triangle," which will be played out in surprising ways.

The Student, now the *third* narrator in the film, speaks: "There are those who say it was all a dream.... And there are few places in the whole world as lovely as central Texas in April, but this is not the Texas of cowboy lore..." Two issues are immediately raised. One is that the Texas the film takes place in is indeed not "the Texas of cowboy lore" but an isolated, antiquated town inhabited primarily by German expatriates, and still boasting a heavy Teutonic emphasis in architecture, costuming and custom: the Old World of Europe incongruously placed in the Texas frontier. As the film progresses, the Witch and the Student suggest a series of binary oppositions: the Student as America, the New World, rationalism, modernity, patriarchy; the Witch as Europe, Old World, the supernatural, tradition, and, above all, woman's revenge against patriarchy. Indeed, *The Naked Witch* offers many allegories which are profoundly political. The Student's car runs out of gas, and, now separated from the comfort, security and convenience of the machine age, he reaches the village of Luckenbach, where a group of schoolchildren are walking in formation back to school, dressed in authentic German garb and singing a traditional German folk song. The location not only appears to be a different country but a different time period. Revealing to the audience that his main reason for this journey is to write a thesis on the early Germans in Texas, the Student becomes much more than a mere tourist; he becomes an intellectual explorer in a world "about to take me back 100 years ... as indeed they soon would."

The Student soon meets an old innkeeper who speaks in German, a cultural anomaly in twentieth century America which reinforces the accruing cultural disorientation. Politely but firmly the innkeeper warns the Student not to speak of superstitions and witchcraft while here. Yet the innkeeper introduces the subject of the Student's quest, "The Luckenbach Witch," only to then withdraw the subject, refusing to speak further of her. The Miller's daughter, Kirska, also dressed in native German costume, is inquisitive, asking the Student what it's like "on the outside," as if she were a prisoner in this Brigadoon-like village out of time. Later that evening, the young and innocent Kirska, wearing a stark white dress, shows the Student to his room, a barren space with a large four-poster bed the only object of note. Kirska returns shortly with a pitcher of water, which she holds at crotch level, proudly proclaiming, "This water came fresh from the well," a blatant metaphor for unsullied sexual "waters." Oblivious of Kirska's sexuality, the Student solicits her for more information about the town and the mythic Luckenbach Witch. Kirska declines, citing, "You are what we call 'Fremptor.' You are from the outside," implying that outsiders are not privileged to know the community's sordid history, let alone study and pass judgment on it, an attitude prevalent in both rural communities and the American South during the era in which Buchanan helmed his film career.

The Student attempts to ease Kirska's fears and enlighten her: "In any age where there was widespread famine, sickness, want, you find an outbreak of women being denounced as witches." Befuddled, Kirska replies, "But what pleasure can you get from studying all

The pouty allure of Libby Booth (as "Libby Hall") combines elements of villainy and seduction in her role as *The Naked Witch* (1961).

this?" The Student then reveals his thesis: "To better understand the witch hunts we have today.... the medieval idea of witchcraft was replaced with things like race, and nationality." In effect, Buchanan draws an analogy between the witch hunts of medieval times with the modern day witch hunts: racism, Cold War jingoism, or feminists such as Betty Freidan who believed they were about to be "burned at the stake." To this extent, the Student embodies Buchanan's passion for "historical revisionism," which is explicitly not used in the current sense of the term, to reductively marginalize any questioning of history that falls outside perpetuating the status quo. In fact, Buchanan's historical revisionism is very much concerned with revealing the potential misdeeds and "dark side" of the official historical narrative; the enlightened man is the one who embraces the humanitarian task of spotlighting the failings of the past in order to remove prejudice, ignorance and persecution from the present. Indeed, "historical revisionism" becomes a dominant crusade of Buchanan, be it in examining possible government conspiracies in *The Trial of Lee Harvey Oswald* and *Beyond the Doors*, or demystifying American cultural myths of the outlaw (*A Bullet for Pretty Boy*) and Hollywood (*Goodbye, Norma Jean* and *Goodnight, Sweet Marilyn*).

As Kirska and the Student gravitate toward potentially unknown personal/political territory, they move closer to the bed. As the bed represents modern civilization's symbol and location for coitus, it becomes an appropriate site, as their discussion, as well as subsequent events, focuses on the "personal politics" of sexuality both between the couple and in the community. Kate Millett contended:

> Coitus can scarcely be said to take place in a vacuum; although of itself it appears a biological and physical activity, it is set so deeply within the larger context of human affairs that it serves as a charged microcosm of the variety of attitudes and values to which culture subscribes. Among other things, it may serve as a model of sexual politics on an individual or personal plane.[4]

Kirska sheepishly tells the Student that her grandfather—"the settler who built this inn"—denounced his poor mistress as a witch, which led to her death: "Schoennig denounced her in this very room, in that very bed." Conversely, a subtext of the Student's thesis is the emancipation of women, which parallels Kirska's own increasingly amorous interest in the Student, an interest outside the moral standards of the community (premarital sex). As they are poised to kiss, Kirska retreats, and informs the Student about an old book which might help his studies. Instead, the Student makes a clumsy pass at Kirska, but she deflects the advance, visibly shaken. The Student apologizes, saying, "I don't ever notice anyone until they get a little bothered, and light up like a candle." His double entendre could refer to either anger or sexual arousal, especially the latter when Kirska blushes. After the Student remarks, "You know, with your German good looks, set off in something simple and black, you'd look like a little cameo," Kirska leaves the bedroom only to return in a slinky black negligee. "You said something simple and black. Shouldn't you close the door?" Kirska's white dress (virginity) is replaced by black (coitus) as she is about to engage in the sexual transgression of premarital sex in the same bedroom where another act of transgression–adultery—occurred years before when her grandfather bedded and betrayed his mistress. In this almost perverse setting, the traditional power dynamics are reversed as well: Kirska becomes the sexual aggressor, and the Student now retreats in fear, babbling on about nothing. Kirska pouts, "Too much talk ruins it," gently mocking the Student for his loss of bravado, and leaves as the Student mutters to himself, "Well, I'll be damned." Instead, he picks up the history book, now seen as an emblem of his sexual failure, and brings it to bed as his surrogate lover.

As the Student begins to read the book entitled *The Early Germans in Texas: An Inquiry into Their Customs, Legends and Superstitions*, the prologue narrator begins a description of the events surrounding the "Luckenbach Witch." As the Student had theorized, the village was long ago struck by disease, famine, and death, and eventually succumbed to widespread hysteria regarding its survival. The town fathers needed a scapegoat for this devastating streak of cruel fate (a combination of natural disaster and government mismanagement). In true patriarchal fashion, they picked on the most disenfranchised person in town, the unmarried, independent woman. As the narrator explains:

> Remember that in the first year of the settlement, typhoid, sleeping sickness, and other bitter hardships, were climaxed by an epidemic that took the lives of 200 of the 600 settlers. The villagers looked for someone on whom to blame their troubles. What better subject than the widow who walked by moonlight, the widow who was too aloof to speak to the women of the village, the widow who caused the whispers about a clandestine affair with the innkeeper Schoennig. 'The widow witch,' they called her. Witch? It must be remembered that this was a time when any man of power could conveniently denounce as a witch any woman discovered with him in his bed. Such a man was Otto Schoennig.

Simultaneously, the viewer sees evocative scenes of the "Widow Witch" walking at dusk through the village to a sexual rendezvous with Schoennig. It is also possible to suggest that this flashback is infused with the Student's own sexual fantasies, in that the historical book he is reading is being projected onscreen and filtered through his sexually agitated thoughts after his failed encounter with Kirska. The film has now entered the other world completely, both historically and as a product of the Student's unconscious. The Widow arrives at Otto's room, and they discuss their irreconcilable differences around the same bed later used by Kirska and the Student, or, more correctly, the Student and his book. To no avail, the Widow pleads to Otto that he divorce his wife and marry her. Enraged, she demands he respects her: "What am I? A chattel to be used when convenient? To function where your wife cannot? To lie with, but not marry?" She also tells Schoening about the villagers' accusations of her being a witch, and accuses Otto of starting the cycle of slander against her. He not only confirms her allegations, but has summoned the village elders to take her away for execution for practicing witchcraft. Appeals to the irrational and community-sponsored punishment of scapegoats become a means for personal expediency and political practice: the hallmark of authoritarian politics and, in this sense, this microcosm of Germany in Texas, inevitably suggests another historical era — the Third Reich.

This exchange between the local figure of authority and his estranged mistress is a centerpiece of the film, again taking place on the battleground of the sexes, the marriage bed. The Widow, as the outsider, can be made the scapegoat for a patriarchal order and a "non being" to be persecuted and exterminated. As Edward Mullins suggests in *The Painted Witch*, the sexual woman is an easy target both for male desire and male hatred: "The primal sin of lust being laid at Eve's door, it became easy to dump upon women the responsibility for all manner of other sins and vices, each of them emanating from her supposedly indiscriminate appetite for sex.... The fantasy that women, and particularly beautiful women, are deadly dangerous and can usurp men's power, is among the oldest in our civilization."[5] Before she is put to death, the Widow utters a curse: "Death to all Scheonnigs!" and is unceremoniously impaled with "a post oak spire," the crudest, most violent phallic symbol imaginable, the Phallus incarnate of the village.

The scene returns to the Student. Whether intellectually or sexually stirred, the Student investigates the graveyard seen in the beginning of the film, where "hell itself gives out contagion to the world" and is about to be released: the historically oppressed force of the Woman and her revenge against patriarchal order. He claws desperately at the ground with his bare hands, and after removing a token amount of dirt he improbably uncovers the face of the Widow, seen as an unconvincing rubber fright mask. The Student wrenches the spire from her corpse, the Phallus of the community which killed her and, above all else, *kept her dead*. To his amazement, the Widow's face slowly reverts to its former beauty via crude stop-motion animation, evoking images of 1940s horror films of resurrected vampires. Taken aback, he flees with the spire.

The resurrected Widow rises from the grave and determinedly begins her mission. She is consciously eroticized with excessive makeup as she wanders naked, becoming the titillating title character promised to the viewer by the film's sensationalistic title. Yet her body is hidden to the viewer with a crude obstruction placed over the camera lens. A necessary strategy to self-censor the film given the era it was produced, it appears somewhat ludicrous today, yet also denies the viewer the opportunity to festishize the screen object due to the blatant obstacles placed between the naked woman, camera, and (male) spectator.

The Widow's first encounter is with the Student. She takes the phallic spire from him, which he clutches as he sleeps, suggesting attempts to "hold on" to his masculinity, put in question after his failed tryst with Kirska. More importantly, it is the Widow who now holds the Phallus, the symbol of power — and who can wield power — in the insular, provincial community. The Widow then enters Kirska's bedroom, and the viewer suspects she will be the first of Otto Schoennig's descendents to be executed. Instead, she strokes Kirska's black negligee and attempts to fondle her breasts. Kirska awakes screaming, and the Widow flees with *both* the spire and the negligee. In one respect, the scene smacks of a certain political stereotype: if she can be read as the force of feminism, it is because she is a lesbian whose actions are simply the result of penis envy (seizing the phallus) and man-hating. Yet the scene is more complex. In the circulation of signifiers that ascribe gender and sexual roles and conduct, the negligee is also a symbol of sexual control over women: the conversion of the woman from the man's sexual fantasy into an attainable object (the Student's suggestion that Kirska would look good in black) and willing servant (Kirska's sudden transformation from tentative virgin dressed in white to brazen whore dressed in black). *Both* the spire and the negligee are essential parts of Luckenbach's symbolic order of patriarchal control, and maintaining that control, and now *both* are held by the Naked Witch: one the sign of male phallic power and domination, and the other the sign of female sexual submission. Nevertheless, the theft of the negligee also serves a purely practical propose; the Witch dons the negligee, which allows Buchanan to avoid the exaggerated and necessary lengths he took to avoid full-frontal nudity (which was impossible at the time). Yet, by holding the community's twin symbols of patriarchal domination — spire and negligee, the Naked Witch becomes the classic "bad witch" archetype, the all-powerful woman who is both the seducer and destroyer of men; the antithesis of the "good witch" who functions as a sexual and social "healer," meaning a woman who uses her immense power to maintain the structures of her own oppression (*Bewitched*).

The Widow next encounters the Miller, another Schoennig, who she throws in the stream while chanting, "And one by water!" and then quite fittingly kills him with the phallic spire, using the Phallus against the patriarchal order, with the discharge of blood representing orgasmic disgrace, a common trope in the later sexploitation roughies where "blood rather than semen becomes the symbolic fluid of erotic expression."[6] The next day, the village elders meet at the inn to discuss the Miller's death. The Student narrates this somber scene, which unfolds in complete silence but for the curious sobbing of one disembodied male voice, a dark and cruel comment on the patriarchy's pathetic self pity. The town realizes its horrible secret has not only been revealed but has become a material force of revenge. With the terrified villagers shuttered inside their homes, the Witch locates her next victim, as she chants, "And one by fire!" and, of course, impales him as well.

Racked with guilt for unleashing the force of the Witch, the Student is now more than ever convinced that he may be "hexed" by this demon, and feels he must do what he can to destroy her. Again relying on books, he visits the local library and deduces the Naked Witch may be hiding in the caves downstream. Indeed, the Witch bathes in a lake and the Student is mesmerized, staring at the figure in the lake recalling both contemporary pin up photography and the voluptuous paintings of Rubens.[7] She immediately throws him in the water, submersing him in her sensual domain; the Student becomes her sexual slave. After a journey which takes place almost entirely in water, they reach a cave where the sexually hypnotized Student is seduced and dominated by the Witch (in this sense, water and the caves can be read in admittedly vulgar Freudian terms of female sexual arousal and vaginal orifices). The unseen sexual tryst is signified by a dissolve to a close-up of a burning torch. While the previous murders were underscored by water and fire, the Student's powerless seduction by the Witch is referenced to the ancient, antithetical elements of water and fire as a kind of Jungian metaphysical synthesis of opposites: male and female, fire and water, the *anima* and *animus*, the masculine and feminine essences that constitute Jung's gender-specific conception of the universal order (which will be returned to in the film's conclusion).

After the mystical sexual encounter, the Student lies comatose while the Witch studies a list of victims inscribed on the cave wall and repeats the mantra: "One by water, one by fire, but all shall die by the self-same spire." Kirska is next, the final Schoennig. Returning to the graveyard, the Witch hypnotically summons Kirska, who is dressed in black as she sleeps in a chair. (Again, the tropes are much more consistent with vampirism than witchcraft.) The Student fortuitously awakens and rushes to the graveyard as the Witch draws Kirska towards her open grave to replace her in eternity. The Student intervenes just in time, forcing the spire into the Widow's heart and sending her back to her grave, where she quickly degenerates to a hideous rubber-faced corpse. As the Student covers the Witch's grave, he pontificates: "My feelings were mixed. Here was a woman who had taken two lives, yet she had been denounced maliciously, and killed by the same stake. Was she Witch, or wronged Widow? It is not for me to say. I am only glad that her tempest is over, and she is returned to dear sleep." The Student and Kirska walk off together hand in hand to continue their sexual and spiritual journey in unity.

In this way, the conclusion of *The Naked Witch* is highly problematic. In one sense, Buchanan has presented a vivid and savage critique of provincialism and patriarchy which is nearly destroyed by its own past excesses and historical retribution. The Witch becomes the progressive feminist archetype, the woman who must be recognized as a vital part of society rather than its sexual object and scapegoat. As Friedan contended, "There is only one way for women to reach full human potential—by participating in the mainstream of society, by exercising their own voice in all the decisions shaping that society."[8] While Buchanan esteems and champions women throughout his film career, his feminism is ultimately rooted in a great deal of old-fashioned romanticism, if not outright Catholic parochialism—a social, political, and even metaphysical universe composed primarily of innocent yet curious virgins and sullied yet noble whores. Thus, the Witch as an avenging omnipotent force must be destroyed, and Kirska, as a helpful, productive woman—the good witch stereotype devoid of supernatural powers—is integrated into the order.

This reflects another tendency that is seen in Buchanan's subsequent films. Frequently protagonists are removed from familiar surroundings and enveloped in mysterious events, or inexplicable occurrences disrupt their normal and often mundane lives; as much as encounters with the paranormal or the extraterrestrial, they embark on a *spiritual journey* in which, through their tribulations, they gain some sort of insight into their psyches, and sometimes metaphysical mysteries. While Buchanan's films teem with Freudian symbolism and Lacanain subtext, Carl Jung's more mystical, metaphysical brand of psychoanalysis can be seen as a key influence on Buchanan's films. In numerous films (*Mars Needs Women* the primary exception) this journey is framed as much around the establishment of the heterosexual, "New Age" couple in the aftermath of the strange events, not only as a source of new, progressive social order (the young couple as the model for a new and better society in *The Eye Creatures*) but as the point of a metaphysical harmonic convergence (most overtly demonstrated in *Strawberries Need Rain*). The issue of *The Naked Witch* is that the title character—the historically revolutionary force of feminism—must literally be put back in the grave with the Phallus in order to construct the New Age couple as they embark on their unified journey: the Student and Kirska as the binaries of Old World–New World, modernity-tradition, and, of course, man and woman, towards a potentially utopian tomorrow with the cosmic convergence of *anima* and *animus*.

The Naked Witch almost never saw release when a Colorado film lab threatened to confiscate the early dailies as obscene material. However, when the film was released, it did exceptional business at regional drive-ins throughout Texas, bringing in more than ten times its cost to Alexander and company. For Buchanan, it was his first hit, giving him a much-needed boost of artistic self-esteem. Even more, he began to catch the eye of other quick-buck producers in the Dallas area, who saw in Buchanan not an artist but an alchemist who could turn celluloid crap into box-office gold. In any event, Buchanan's own long journey as a filmmaker was beginning.[9]

5

Naughty Dallas

Strictly speaking, the burlesque film was a filmed stage show, traditionally consisting of several women doing striptease acts, plus a peppering of musical and comedy performances — an adults-only "variety show." A subgenre of exploitation filmmaking that peaked in popularity in the early 1950s, this group of films brought regional burlesque show entertainers to a national audience via the grindhouse movie theater circuit. Two of the most famous burlesque films are pinup photographer Irving Klaw's *Strip-o-Rama* (1953) and *Varietease* (1954), legendary largely due to the presence of pop-culture icon Betty Page. Another style of burlesque film was the faux travelogue, such as Phil Tucker's *Baghdad After Midnight* (1954) and *Tijuana After Midnight* (1954). Filmed entirely on small sound stages in Hollywood, the two movies couched strip tease numbers around racist stereotypes of sexual exoticism. Other films such as *Naughty New Orleans* (1954, d: Sidney Baldwin) and *Burlesque in Harlem* (1954, d: William Alexander) were filmed in and around the regions specified and served as vanity pieces for business interests of the featured communities, as well as provided taboo entertainment to audiences outside the film's birthplace.

Larry Buchanan's *Naughty Dallas* (1964) falls into this last category of burlesque film. Released in 1964, it was filmed in and around Dallas, Texas, to extol the virtues of "Big D," where liberal philosophy battled with conservative religious influences to create a singular and unique cultural atmosphere of cosmopolitanism cohabitating with fundamentalism. *Naughty Dallas* may also have the dubious distinction of being the last burlesque film ever shown theatrically, as the burlesque film had long since become an anachronism in exploitation cinema. In 1959 the burlesque and nudist films that dominated the market in the 1950s were rendered obsolete by the narrative-fueled "nudie-cutie" formula largely invented by Russ Meyer's *The Immoral Mr. Teas*, which combined slapstick comedy with requisite pinup and strip-tease nudity. By 1964, the nudie-cuties were themselves replaced by "roughies," dark, sordid films of sexual immorality with Herschell Gordon Lewis (*Scum of the Earth*, 1963) and Russ Meyer (*Lorna*, 1964) among their prolific creators. As Doyle Greene observes, "If the nudie-cutie emphasized a burlesque and pinup view of American sexuality, the roughie offered lurid, sensational stories of moral decay and psychological studies of sex and violence. If the nudie-cutie was pop art and *Playboy*, the roughie was film noir and exploitation tabloid."[1]

After the success of *The Naked Witch*, Buchanan became something of a celebrity in Dallas, known as a local filmmaker who could turn a small investment into a lucrative cash cow. According to Buchanan, this reputation was a mixed blessing, as local investors approached him to use his filmmaking services to make them, or their charges, "movie stars":

> There were plenty of offers. The well-heeled oil tycoon caving in to his mistress who wanted a shot at the big time, the lavender-haired, oil-rich widow willing to spend an inheritance for a film about her late wildcatter husband, and a vast array of rich, bored wastrels who just wanted to get into the movies for the kicks. And then there were the kinkos. Nothing of merit was on the horizon.[2]

Envisioned as a quick, money-making film venture, Buchanan formulated *A Stripper Is Born*, an obvious and rather caustic allusion to the Hollywood ode to its own star-making machinery, *A Star Is Born*. Buchanan originally planned to star the infamous exotic dancer Candy Barr (a.k.a. Juanita Slusher) in *A Stripper Is Born* as a kind of burlesque biopic. Inarguably the most famous stripper who ever hailed from Texas, Barr's life story of sexual abuse, gangster companions and shady backroom dealings was the stuff of legend. However, as Buchanan recollected, "Certain mysterious forces were having none of it, as I confronted a series of dark threats. The persons making them ranged from city fathers who used go-betweens to contact me, on down to small-time Dallas hoods and even a spokesman for Hollywood mobster Mickey Cohen."[3]

Buchanan also intended to shoot *A Stripper Is Born* at Jack Ruby's Carousel Club, as the Carousel was the first club in Dallas to feature an Amateur Strip Night, where, as Buchanan noted,

> ... innocent young country girls would come into Dallas from small, dying and impoverished towns across Texas, Oklahoma, Arkansas, and Louisiana, hoping for a piece of the good life. Sadly, most failed and returned to Miseryville to marry mechanics and farmboys. A precious few, with minimal talent and blessed bodies, could earn handsome weekly bucks.[4]

The cramped quarters and low ceilings prevented the use of movie lights, which made shooting the film at the Carousel logistically impossible. Buchanan later admitted he was secretly relieved not to have extensive dealings with Ruby, as the club owner was universally disliked: "In fact, he was detested. He was cheap and a cheat, inarticulate, antisocial, a bully, a troublemaker, profane, and a pathological liar. He was a bisexual who loved to fistfight, constantly trying to validate his manhood."[5] Buchanan's solution was to import Ruby's headlining acts (Jada, Peggy Steele and Kim Athas) and shoot their performances at two other famous Dallas nightclubs: Abe Weinstein's Colony Club (with Weinstein playing himself in the film), and the Montmarte Club, owned by the Youras brothers, Jimmie and Don. To placate the egomaniacal Ruby, Buchanan shot some footage at the Carousel, including scenes of Ruby introducing two acts, playing the drums, and beating up three club patrons. Buchanan never intended to use this footage in the finished product, and later claimed the roll of 16mm color film was languishing at a Dallas film laboratory.

As *A Stripper Is Born* evolved into *Naughty Dallas*, Barr's replacement was Marilyn Pope as "Toni Shannon," a character emblematic of the young amateurs with "minimal talent and blessed bodies" who carved a niche in the Big D strip club circuit. Moreover, Pope invested money into the project and received an associate producer credit, and is exemplary of the "vast array of rich, bored wastrels who just wanted to get into the movies for the kicks."[6] Ultimately, *Naughty Dallas* became Buchanan's mordant satire on the local burlesque scene, the exploitation genre, and individuals such as "Toni" and Pope — the desperate farm girls and bored Dallas upper class seeking stardom in the momentary limelight of the burlesque clubs and the movies.

Naughty Dallas opens with a nighttime shot of Dallas, as a narrator, Buchanan, extols the virtues of the city, its surrounding hamlets, and, above all, its women: "It is often said that the prettiest girls in the world come from Dallas, Texas. What isn't said is that those girls come from small towns all across Texas. This is the story of one such girl...." *Naughty Dallas* established itself as a bluer version of *A Star Is Born*, as well as a send-up of the ubiquitous pulp-fiction scenario of a small-town girl coming to the big city to find fame and fortune, yet finding only heartache and misery and gratefully returning to her sheltering hometown universe. *Naughty Dallas* modifies this narrative template substantially for the benefit of the primarily male audience by framing its narrative within the dated, restrictive confines of the burlesque film.

The credits begin over a shot of a woman's legs as she sits next to a pink poodle, a sardonic icon of the nouveau riche in America and bourgeois cosmopolitanism reduced to kitsch "big city chic"— and a not-so-subtle jab at star and associate producer Pope. The camera swings up to reveal Toni. The attractive redhead picks up the poodle and cuddles him close to her face, suggesting the drive for stardom is rooted in a need to be admired and loved, either by a cherished puppy or a group of anonymous males. After the credits, the camera pans 8×10 glossy photographs of striptease artists, finally stopping on a marquee showcasing Toni Shannon, Buchanan continues:

> These are exotic dancers, these beautiful women who practice an art which has refined itself from the old "bump 'n grind" days of the striptease, to the refined and enchanting form of dance it is today. This is the story of Toni Shannon, who tonight has become one of the brightest stars in the glittering skies of show business. Tonight, Toni saw in the faces of the audience beyond the footlights that magic something that every entertainer lives for: the applause, the smiles, the curtain calls. The beginning, of her "dream come true...."

As the viewer watches Toni doing a final twirl in a striptease act that has just finished, she throws her beloved audience a perfunctory kiss. As *Naughty Dallas* will sardonically depict, "the magic ... that every entertainer lives for" is a compulsive thirst for public adoration, and stripping for indifferent, anonymous men and becoming "one of the brightest stars in the glimmering skies of show business" is predicated on a course of economic and sexual exploitation. It is a harsh critique of stardom that Buchanan subsequently addressed in his savage studies of the machinations of the Hollywood star system with *Goodbye, Norma Jean* (1976) and *Goodnight, Sweet Marilyn* (1989), savagely chronicling the construction and destruction of the cinematic icon "Marilyn Monroe" at the eventual cost of the person behind it, Norma Jean Baker.

Buchanan continues, "Toni's dream started in her little hometown in East Texas, just a whistle-stop on the main line." The film begins a lengthy flashback in order to chronicle Toni's journey from small-town girl to big-city stripper. Toni's childhood was happy and rewarding, a naïf safely nestled in the comfort of her socioeconomic cocoon: "Toni was con-

Opposite: In this poster art for the notorious ***Naughty Dallas*** (1964), popular Texas stripper "Jada" (aka Janet Conforti) points knowingly at the cartoon marquee for Jack Ruby's Carousel Club, a hotbed of political intrigue in the Dallas night-scene of the early 1960's.

tent in this sleepy town, until she grew up," a statement which targets puberty as the force which unleashes the unquenchable adult libido, with its potentially disastrous appetites. The narration shifts to Toni, who immediately pouts, "Gee whiz, life around here sure seems dead lately!" The scene shows a bouncy, teenaged Toni walking down a dreary Main Street in dungarees and blouse, waving at other bored teens, her appearance incongruous as she looks like a modern-day nymph somehow transported to the set of an old Western picture. Toni has outgrown her withering small-town environment: "I guess I've just been too restless since graduation for this little town." Presumably, Toni is referring to a recent graduation from High School, but she could just as easily be referring to her more crucial sexual graduation from child to adolescent.

Insisting that "the only exciting thing that ever happens around here is the County Fair," a sequence depicts the influence the carnival has on her growing disenchantment with small-town life and its constraints. The traveling carnival has served a powerful and salient function in modern society, a function by and large replaced by the movies. With its exotic sights and sounds, the carnival acts as an institutionalized outsider representing society's repressed but omnipresent libido, floating from town to town, inflaming the citizenry with all manner of lewd and dangerous cultural fantasy, titillating by design but never anchored long enough to take root in the community and contaminate it.

The experience-starved Toni enthusiastically sightsees, especially attracted to the exotic dancers: "Oh, how I envy these carnival people! What an exciting life they must lead! Traveling, and seeing the world. I know what! I'll become a famous sideshow dancer like those girls up there!" Meanwhile, in the footage shown, the dancers and carny barker appear absolutely miserable. Toni is fascinated with the idealized, superficial aspects of the carnival and not the struggles that are part and parcel of their nomadic lifestyle. Toni even ponders that she "could be a sword swallower, or a fire-eater"; here are two ironic double entendres which not only hint at repressed sexual curiosity but the unspoken code of Hollywood, that the road to stardom is paved with endless blow jobs.

The perfunctory scenes of dancers at the carnival are similar to the artless photography of the strippers in Dallas and burlesque films as a genre: long takes with little or no editing, creating the experience of watching a static theatrical stage show versus cinema. Moreover, this inattention to cinematic or artistic pretension echoes the agenda of female objectification in such films, as well as their carnival prototype:

> The exploitation cinema's collapsing of carnival and cinema to encourage a certain kind of looking at the female body is also apparent in the genre's visual conventions. While the abundance of long-shot compositions in exploitation films is both a hold-over from early cinema techniques and a budgetary constraint (less editing needed, less film used), the lack of close-ups also shows a different emphasis of these films. Since there were few real female stars in exploitation, women tended to be archetypal, a random collection of faceless T & A.[7]

When Toni returns home from the carnival, she goes to her bedroom and slowly undresses. This striptease is far more titillating than the staged performances which follow, as the film viewer watches Toni strip in a private space and not on the stage where the act of voyeurism in certified by economic exchange, the stripper being paid to take off her clothes. Watching Toni strip in her childhood bedroom becomes more forbidden, an act of transgression in that the voyeur is not authorized or even acknowledged by the object. As Toni removes her stockings, the perspective changes to watch her through a mirror, and she ponders how slim her chances are of succeeding in show business, and how likely she will have to become resigned to a stultifying life in her "crummy" little town (Buchanan's "Miseryville"). As Toni "bares all" in both the narration and in the mirror, it suggests Lacan's concept of "mirror-stage," in an admittedly simplified form: the initial moment the subject recognizes oneself in the mirror as a moment of narcissism and seeing the image of the Self as an image-ideal, and the moment of alienation as the subject sees oneself as an Other and how the world sees them as a sign in the Symbolic Order. This unsolvable schism underscores Toni's own desire for "stardom"—to displace the alienated image of the Other, *who the world sees* (and who the subject sees *as the world seeing them*) with the narcissistic image of the Self, the image-ideal *that they want the world to see*. In Buchanan's *Goodbye, Norma Jean* and *Goodnight, Sweet Marilyn*, his later bio-pics on Norma Jean Baker/Marilyn Monroe, stardom and Buchanan's use of mirrors as figurative tropes become even more pronounced.

While Toni takes a bath, she suddenly decides to head to Dallas and become an exotic dancer, and her first act is to study her dancing in a full-length mirror. The viewer sees both Toni and her reflection prancing about in unison, the alienated Other—the small-town girl the world sees—and the narcissistic Self—the exotic and erotic Dallas stripper Toni imagines herself to be—who will become an object of adoration, as well as exploitation.

The next morning, Toni steps off the bus in Dallas, entranced by the immensity of Big D, and surrounded by its skyscrapers as symbols of phallic power. Her first meeting is with Jack Cole, owner of the Jack Cole Theatrical Agency. An actual businessman and talent agent on the local Dallas club circuit, Cole assumes the narration, and candidly expresses doubts of her "making it" in show business. However, the allure of Dallas at night has a hypnotic effect on the disappointed girl, and she decides to take in a nightclub show before she catches the bus home. The city manifests the same forbidden allure as the carnival, and she wanders to the Colony Club and ponders pictures of the "glamorous" dancers. Toni spies a crudely drawn (and misspelled) sign stating "Amatuer [sic] Contest Tonite!" Toni tries to enter the contest, but Colony owner Abe Weinstein (as noted, playing himself) informs the enthusiastic starlet the show is booked for the evening. Nevertheless, he asks Toni to show him her legs, and she dutifully lifts her dress: the casual dynamic of sexual exploitation occurring in the sterile, cold space of an office is as brutal as the staged stripteases. Weinstein likes what he sees, encourages Toni to come back and enter the contest another night, and invites her to stay for this evening's program.

In this respect, this narrative scenario of *Naughty Dallas* allows the film to essentially recreate an evening at a burlesque club by featuring striptease and comedy acts supplied by mainstays of the local burlesque circuit and satisfy the exploitation film genre demands for scenes of women undressing. As noted, the burlesque shows are filmed in one static shot, with infrequent zoom work; they offer little in the way of conventional cinematic interest and instead become minimalist, existential vaudeville. The first number is Peggy Steele, hilariously billed as the "I Don't Care Girl." Ms. Steele, a buxom brunette in an evening gown, dances before a spare backdrop which crudely sketches the city at night, the lone woman as an object against an abstracted, sterilized patriarchal universe. As the sultry Steele slowly strips, she is finally left in tiny pasties which barely conceal her nipples, and bikini briefs, and summarily leaves the stage. This depiction of the strip tease is not unlike Roland Barthes' seminal essay, "Strip Tease" (1991), in which Barthes argued the act of stripping and the tease is the fundamental component in the act, the degree of dramatic suspense and power relationships that can be sustained from the moment the stripper comes on stage and the moment she is naked (or as naked as Dallas community standards allowed). The act of stripping is the essence of the striptease, and once the woman is naked, she is, as Barthes claimed, "desexualized."[8] Moreover, her performance is interrupted by crudely placed insert shots of a horny old drunkard (Buddy Raymon) who makes farcical, bulge-eyed faces at the performer, a sardonic metaphor of the crudeness of the male voyeur, both in the club and the film audience (a trope frequently used in exploitation films, including those of Herschell G. Lewis and especially Russ Meyer).

The scene shifts to sequences filmed at the Club Montmarte, a larger stage with garish red curtains, although the narrative suggests the scenes are the same location, creating either a glaring continuity error or a disorientating effect, depending on how charitable the viewer is towards Buchanan's filmmaking techniques. Instead of a striptease act, the viewer endures a vaudeville comedy routine by Bill Demar[9] (a.k.a. William D. Crowe), a comedian, who walks onstage wearing a red derby and vest, and carrying a banjo. In burlesque films, the comedy acts reveal as much or more about the cultural attitudes of the time as the strip acts. Demar regales the tipsy audience with off-color jokes and musical ditties that accurately reflect burlesque's strange mixture of adolescent fascination and Puritanical derision of sex and especially women, who were simultaneously "overvalued" as fetish objects and "undervalued" through coarse comedy.

After Demar finishes, he introduces popular exotic dancer "Jada" (real name: Janet Conforti), who was legendary in Dallas for her wild lifestyle, including brushes with the law and connections to Jack Ruby. As the band begins a bump 'n grind tune, the sultry redhead begins her routine by vamping in a "classy" sequined gown and fur wrap, and then changes into a cliché harem skirt and adopts some hammy dance moves — in essence, Buchanan's parody of the "sexual exotica" genre of burlesque films. The camera becomes more involved in Jada's performance than previously, following her closely and zooming in tight on several occasions as she become fetishized by the camera, yet this attempt at eroticism is negated when she lies on the stage and performs apathetic, mechanical gyrations which simulate coitus. With the dreaded element of actual sex act "thrust" into burlesque, the horny old drunkard makes a particularly painful grimace. Again, this act concludes with a desexualization of the dancer bordering on surrealism. The band's trumpeter walks upstage to join Jada, and plays a solo directly into her breasts as the dancer shimmies in an absurd mimicry of erotic arousal. Jada forces her breasts into the bell of the trumpet. The blustering male libido spews towards the woman via the (safe) phallic symbol as the musician blows his horn (or his "wad"). With this brazenly exaggerated sexuality occurring in a film otherwise devoid of any eroticism, Buchanan viciously mocks the exploitation film universe, which emphasizes the vulgar and debases rather than respects its primary subject: the figure of the Woman, often romanticized and canonized in Buchanan's films. It is hardly surprising that burlesque, one of the most misogynistic discourses in American popular culture, despite its apparently harmless mix of striptease and sophomoric comedy, endures an increasingly caustic and satirical critique by Buchanan.

Indeed, in a later striptease sequence, Jada and the old drunk directly interact when Jada removes her stockings and teases him with them, until they are brought together in the same shot, briefly eliminating the filmic barrier constructed between the performances and the reaction inserts. The drunk sheepishly grabs the taboo stocking from Jada, and scurries back to his seat, exposed in his infantile lust and cowardice. Jada reacts with victory, standing proudly and statuesquely on her prop hassock, a momentary superiority in this twisted world of female objectification. However, the burlesque formula necessitates the woman be demeaned and put back in her place as an object of debasement. This "correction" is achieved subsequently through an abysmal slapstick comedy routine featuring Jada and local comedian "Breck Wall."[10] Wall stands with a table full of pastry and announces a "pie drawing contest." Wall asks Jada to draw the winning ticket. The stripper, being only a sexual object incapable of thought, appears unable to read the winning number, so Wall grabs the ticket, and reads: "2–7–2–0-5." Not surprisingly, the winner is the horny old drunkard, who stumbles onstage just in time to receive his prize pie in the face, poorly thrown by Jada. Wall then throws a pie onto Jada's midriff. As she turns and starts to run offstage, Wall hits her on the ass with another pie. The drunkard throws a pie, the bandleader throws a pie, and a man dressed as a head chef throws a pie. With its aggressive physicality and surrogate seminal fluids flying about, it is nothing short of a metaphorical gang bang, culminating with bandleader Bill Peck throwing a pie directly into Jada's face. The stripper seems genuinely taken by surprise at what appears to be an unscripted act, and her studied theatrical grin changes into tangible anger. She shouts something which looks to be, "Not in my face, you bastard!" as the poor bandleader freezes in fright. She glares at him and the scene fades out, her complete ignominy manifest by the male collective — the flurry of pies a collection of symbolic "money shots" (to use porn film vernacular) with the all-important "climactic" one placed right in the face of the woman

Due to a cancellation, Weinstein informs Toni she can appear in tonight's program. Naïve Toni is thrilled, and runs to the dressing room as she gushes, "This is my lucky day after all! What a lucky girl I am! I'm in show business!" Toni's pure naiveté as she is being primed to essentially lose her stripper "virginity" in the dressing room is made even more unsettling by the fate of the first amateur contest performer, a scrawny young woman named Suzanna. Apparently from another rural "Miseryville" like Toni, Suzanna is visibly nervous and awkward, and often stares into the camera with abject fright. Finishing her highly uncomfortable performance, she runs offstage to be out of the oppressive male gaze, oblivious to the enthusiastic applause. Yet any appreciation for her performance by the male can hardly be as an object of erotic excitement, but sadistic pleasure purely derived from her humiliation and discomfort — yet another of the textual nails Buchanan puts in the coffin of the burlesque film genre.

Likewise, Toni's first burlesque is a far cry from her idealistic preconceptions. She struts tentatively, musing: "Oh gosh, look at all those people staring at me!.... If I could only relax, *and do as well as I do in front of the mirror at home!*" (emphasis added). The schism between the narcissistic self-image and the alienated object seen by others becomes irreconcilable as she begins to remove her dress and becomes increasingly uncomfortable, noticing "all those cold, staring faces," a montage of male patrons who are bored, angry, or both. As Toni is about to remove her bra and reveal her breasts to the indifferent herd, she runs offstage to mean-spirited laughter, inadvertently succeeding in accomplishing the goal of burlesque — the comical derision of women. Nonetheless, the film viewer is given the privilege of seeing Toni removing her bra in the dressing room while chastising herself for her cowardice. The film viewer, in effect, has access to her private, as well as public, humiliation.

As Toni starts to pack her things, she meets another exotic dancer, Kim Athas (often billed as "The Texas Tornado").[11] Through voice-over narration, the sultry, dark-haired beauty speaks to forlorn Toni, giving her a classic, and hilariously clichéd, "motivational speech" by a seasoned pro to a struggling novice, a template required in "success story" films (the sports film in particular). Athas (portraying herself) explains how normal feelings of fear and inadequacy are in the early stages of a stripper's career and what counts is "star quality"—having the courage of one's convictions and the persistence to conquer obstacles in order to reach one's goals: "A real artist just won't give up, and dancing *is* an art." The speech becomes one more component in *Naughty Dallas*' wicked satire of the very genres it is operating within, yet mocking: burlesque, exploitation, Hollywood melodrama.

Introduced as "a Turkish exotic from the land of the sphinx and the pyramids," and another parody of the racist "sexual exotica" stereotypes in burlesque films, Athas storms onstage in a fiery red cape with matching bra and panties; as the narrator explains, "'Athas' in Turkish means 'bold fire,' which describes Kim's dance perfectly!" As Kim gyrates, Toni ruminates on her good fortune in finding this dancing star as her personal mentor. Later, Athas instructs a group of women, including Toni, on the fine points of striptease and selects one to personally groom. Toni gushes, "When Kim told us who the lucky girl was, I almost fainted. She chose me!" Soon Kim announces that her protégé is ready to premiere. Toni walks from the dressing room wearing a red harem outfit remarkably similar to that of Athas, in effect becoming *her* mirror image. Toni is shown in a rare close-up, revealing painted eyebrows and dark lipstick, giving her a completely altered appearance. As opposed to the naive farm girl who came to Dallas—the Other she saw in the mirror back home—Toni is now becoming the image-ideal she longs to be and what the world will see her as: an image-ideal that resembles the proverbial Byzantine whore.

As Toni begins to dance, her back to the camera, the stage differs from the others in the film, looking more like the stage at a local high school. Toni's dance features more cutting and camera movement than in the other acts. As this was Pope's showcase as actor (and perhaps stipulated through her influence as producer), this staging of the grand finale as a "big" production number parodies the structure of the classic film musical, and the "chorus line to spotlight" films. While Buchanan parodied the burlesque film ethnic stereotypes with the other performances, Toni is presented as a new sexploitation stereotype: the all-American WASP whore when she discards her robe and is dressed in polka-dot bikini,[12] a subversive nod to 1950s kitsch Americana and the *Playboy* stereotype of the "girl next door." When Toni removes her bikini top, she finally reveals to the public the breasts that the film viewer was allowed to see privately back on the farm and in the dressing room. Toni's journey has come full circle. The image-ideal she conceived in her bedroom mirror is literally born onstage: *a stripper is born*. The private fantasy of the Self as the image-ideal becomes the Other—the public fantasy and fodder for the rest of the world to adore, idealize, idolize, and, above all, consume like any other product, and the person behind along with it (again, the central theme of Buchanan's subsequent indictment of the Hollywood star-machine, *Goodbye, Norma Jean*). In a fitting cutaway, Jack Cole and Abe Weinstein enthusiastically discuss their future trading of Toni's body to the highest bidder, Toni the stripper now a commodity in patriarchal-capitalist machinery. Toni finishes her inaugural act to enthusiastic applause, blowing kisses to everyone. Narrator Buchanan intones with what may be great deal of acerbic irony, "Tonight, Toni's star shines a little brighter, because her dream has come true, as will the dreams of many small-town girls, who have the nerve to try, and the heart to succeed." The end title bears the following caveat: "THE END: WE HOPE!!!" A tongue-in-cheek reference to a ponderous, pointless film that has finally ended, it also becomes Buchanan's *coup de grace* to the anachronistic sexual ideology of burlesque as *Naughty Dallas* satirizes and explodes the exploitation film. By 1964, with the dawn of a resurgent feminist movement and the sexual revolution, sexploitation was quickly becoming obsolete. While the quaint charms of burlesque and nudie-cuties made their sexism and misogyny more palpable, by framing it in a slapstick comedy narrative, the unbridled aggression of the roughies were far more honest and upfront in their gleeful hatred of women, often overtly misogynistic sex films where the (female) protagonist was unabashedly and repeatedly assaulted, raped and even murdered for the sin of sexual curiosity. Both genres share similar ideological agendas for women, one being simply more obvious about it. The power of *Naughty Dallas*, made precisely during the transition from nudie-cutie to roughie, is how Buchanan reveals the supposedly benign and gentle burlesque and nudie-cuties as implicitly vulgar and violent, and as punitive as any of the eventual roughies.

Buchanan and other sources list *Naughty Dallas* as having been filmed either in 1958, 1959, or 1960. The latter date is by far most likely, as the Carousel Club first opened in 1960. Other sources list *Naughty Dallas* as premiering in February 1964, in San Antonio, Texas. Why the film would have been shelved for almost four years after completion is open to speculation. As mentioned earlier, the burlesque film genre, which had peaked in the mid-1950s, was considered extinct by 1964, replaced by other permutations of the exploitation film genre. Surely releasing a film called *Naughty Dallas* a mere 75 days after a world-shattering assassination in said city seems either the world's worst coincidence or the height of opportunistic marketing. This latter possibility gains some credence from an unlikely source. The complete transcript of the Warren Commission hearings on the JFK assassination had been released, and one of those questioned at the time was William D. Crowe, Jr., who appeared in *Naughty Dallas* as Bill DeMar, the banjo-playing comedian. The testimony given by Crowe added another piece to the puzzle of the film's production dates.[13] His recollection certainly referred to *Naughty Dallas*, which was about a stripper in Dallas, and possibly even boasted this as a working title. Diamond Pictures is the outfit listed as the film's production company. Jada was the star of the film, and the club Crowe mentioned is surely the Montmarte, where Jada and his segments were filmed. If one is to take Crowe at his word, at least these final segments of *Naughty Dallas* were filmed on or around November 30, 1963, a week *after* the assassination of JFK. This suggests the disturbing possibility that Buchanan rushed to get *Naughty Dallas* into theaters as soon as possible after the national tragedy, to profit from the spotlight focusing on "Big D." If this ghoulish theory be true, *Naughty Dallas* is one of the most exploitative films in history, its makers taking bald-faced advantage of an immense crime for quick profit. Even worse is the possibility the participants were celebrating the downfall of one of their own, a local icon who figured prominently in the community but was universally despised: Jack Ruby. By the time of the purported filming, the club owner was behind bars for life. Indeed, everyone in *Naughty Dallas* seems to have been having a ball, especially Jada and Breck Wall, both of whom were having legal and financial disputes with Ruby during the time period in question.[14] Jada seems to have had special cause for celebration at this time, according to Gary Cartwright:

> Jack Ruby was having one of his customary feuds with an employee of his Carousel Club, but this one was serious. His star attraction Jada claimed that she feared for her life and placed Ruby under peace bond. Newspaper ads for the Carousel Club during the week of November 22 featured Bill Demar, a comic ventriloquist — hardly Ruby's style but the best he could do.[15]

If Ruby had threatened violence toward Jada, a likely assumption, as by all accounts Ruby was a violent man, then Jada would certainly have had reason to celebrate her freedom from this vicious man who all but destroyed her career even as he promoted it. A telling remark comes from Jada herself, when she was asked by a reporter if Ruby's murderous actions surprised her: "Frankly, no. Jack was that type of person. He loved to be the center of attention and thought that by doing this he would be a hero. Maybe he is."[16] This cool, calculated observation reveals no shock, grief or regret. The published Warren Commission report states that Jada had been fired by Ruby in October 1963, after numerous disputes, increasing the likelihood that Jada had positive feelings about her former employer's terrible fate.[17]

Its historical place notwithstanding, *Naughty Dallas* is a film which had no effective afterlife, being worthless to drive-ins, television and home video. It fell into obscurity after its brief 1964 run, and for years was more legend than fact, which is likely where the speculation about Jack Ruby's involvement started. It was thus something of a revelation when Something Weird Video unearthed a rare re-issue print of *Naughty Dallas*, with a replaced main title of *Life in the Raw,* in the late 1980s.

Larry Buchanan claimed that certain persons had insisted his footage of Ruby at the Carousel Club showed the owner speaking with Lee Harvey Oswald. Buchanan denied this claim, stating that the footage was filmed too early for the meeting to have occurred, and directly contradicting Bill DeMar's testimony. Perhaps Buchanan wanted to obscure the unseemly production history of his film. Finally, Buchanan reveals his particular perspective on the JFK assassination when he claims that there was much information available to investigators, information that was never solicited: "...many of the night people, who were sleepwalking through the underbelly and after hours life of Big D, were prepared to shed light on the Oswald connections. But the Warren (or more correctly the LBJ) Commission was having none of it. These revelations would not have fit the Johnson plan for cover-up."[18] The sinister implications of this statement are clear, and will haunt Buchanan's next film, *The Trial of Lee Harvey Oswald* (1964). To the end of his life, Buchanan maintained that anyone "in the know" in the Dallas community believed that Vice President Lyndon Baines Johnson was the *deus ex machina* behind the assassination of President Kennedy.

Naughty Dallas, indeed.

6

Free, White and 21 and *Under Age*

The move towards racial integration was one of the defining movements of the 1950s and 1960s, and sparked intense levels of acrimony; Alabama, under reign of Governor George Wallace, veered perilously close to civil war. Buchanan recounted the situation as being far different in his hometown: "Someday, sociologists and students of racial politics will turn to Dallas, Texas, of the early sixties and discover a noble experiment that worked: 'the bloodless revolution.'"[1] Dallas, dominated at the time by large business interests such as Neiman-Marcus, realized racial strife and all its attendant ills were not only embarrassing for a community, but, more importantly, bad for business. Buchanan cited Stanley Marcus, retail tycoon and founder of Neiman-Marcus, as being a major author of the progressive Dallas segregation statutes, and as a decree of "no more segregation" was declared by the city fathers, a great deal of suffering and bloodshed was spared as a result.

As Dallas made a relatively calm transition to integration, *Free, White and 21* (1963, referred to henceforth as *FW21*) originated as *A Question of Consent*, screenplay written by Larry Buchanan and Harold Hoffman (under the pseudonym "Harold Dwain") based on a 1961 court case involving an unidentified white British woman and civil-rights activist who accused a black man of raping her. The alleged rapist was Tony Davis, a black businessman in the Dallas area, as well as a popular disc jockey. A good friend of Buchanan's, Davis is described by the filmmaker as "a lovable, jovial con man who was fair in his dealings, a somewhat overweight bon vivant, a gatherer of bar tabs, a hustler with a heart, a man in love with life. *He was no rapist.*" In fact, Davis was the first black man in the history of Dallas County acquitted of rape charges filed by a white woman, largely due to legendary Texas defense lawyer Charles Tessmer, known as "the don of Dallas criminal lawyers."[2] Tessmer not only generated controversy with his hard-living personal lifestyle but with his unorthodox approach to presenting evidence: "Tessmer understood the spectacle of the courtroom, trying to re-create a crime scene not with two-dimensional photographs or scaled-down drawings, but with the actual crime scene itself. In the 1961 trial of Tony Davis, Tessmer brought the bed where the act allegedly took place into the courtroom."³ Certainly impressed with the famed local lawyer, Buchanan later enlisted Tessmer as the technical advisor on *The Trial of Lee Harvey Oswald.*

In contrast to the affable Davis, the British woman, as described by Buchanan in his autobiography and renamed "Greta Mae Hansen" in *FW21*, was a conniving, money-hungry opportunist:

> There were those who believed the "quiet revolution" was a sell-out for the blacks, but on the whole they were soon convinced and joined the sweep towards harmony. Yet there were outsiders who saw the climate as rich with opportunity for someone with a personal agenda and ambition. Such a player was Greta Mae Hansen. A stunning blonde from Sweden, Greta had organized an integrated bus tour in Mississippi and was following a carefully calculated route through the South and Southwest. Her final destination with her "brothers and sisters," black and white, was Hollywood. There she would cash in her publicity chips for a career in flicks.... As her bus lurched from town to town, she would inflame her audiences with a recitative of their plight and the "enemy." But on the long nights on the road, while the others slept, Greta Mae would stare out of the window. She didn't see the towns or the railroad crossing lights. She saw herself on every drive-in screen that flickered along the two-lane black-tops in Biloxi, Fayetteville, New Orleans, Texarkana, then Dallas.⁴

While Buchanan's stance towards the principals in the case is quite clear, it is rather surprising how *FW21* portrays the characters. Ms. Hansen (Annalena Lund) is presented as a rather sympathetic character whose manipulations are only implied. Moreover, defendant Davis — a friend of Buchanan — is depicted as a highly suspect rascal, and possibly a sociopath in the form of Ernie Jones (Frederick O'Neal). While it is possible to suggest Buchanan and Hoffman crafted their film so as to balance their own prejudices and attempt to turn an exploitation melodrama into a complex legal drama, there was probably a much more practical purpose: Southern white audiences in the early 1960s were much less likely to embrace a film blatantly siding with a black man accused of raping a white woman, regardless of its historical accuracy.

For the main skeleton of their screenplay, Buchanan and Hoffman relied on actual transcripts of the court case, which largely explains the dialogue's arid nature. The courtroom sequences contain minimal camera movement and infrequent cutaways, with characters sitting in sterile interiors and talking endlessly, in this respect suggesting a cross between *Perry Mason* episodes and the work of Michelangelo Antonioni (*L'Avventura*, 1960; *Il Grito*, 1961; *L'Eclisse*, 1962, *Il Deserto Rosso*, 1964). Antonioni's work of the era was characterized by laborious long takes and aimless conversations with characters as they became overwhelmed and secondary to the spaces around them, spaces which become devoid of picturesque qualities and instead became generic voids.

The courtroom in *FW21* becomes a similar such void, with the characters merely interchangeable "parts" in a mechanistic legal system — a central feature defining Buchanan's "courtroom trilogy" of *FW21*, *Under Age*, and *The Trial of Lee Harvey Oswald*. In *FW21*, the "plastics" of the courtroom setting, the barren walls, the stark furniture, even the dispassionate faces of the courtroom observers, constitute a sort of "dead space." The effect is even more striking as *FW21* shifts between stifling courtroom narrative and evocative, illustrative flashbacks of the sexual encounter, constructing a certain aesthetic schizophrenia which is quite disarming. The flashback sequences in *FW21*, concerning the illicit relations between a man and a woman, possess an undeniable voyeuristic quality, providing *FW21*'s combination of courtroom drama and art-film with necessary tawdry exploitation film titillation. (The flashbacks are the only sequences in the film to contain background music, much of it of a somewhat "sexy" ambience.) However, if provided to satisfy a drive-in or grindhouse audience, the sex in *FW21* will inevitably and ironically disappoint the viewer looking for cheap thrills. With their overbearing narration and complete lack of any overall sexiness, the film not only becomes a kind of Antonioni-like anti-drama, but, like *Naughty Dallas*, an exercise in anti-exploitation filmmaking.

The film opens with an establishing shot of the county criminal courts building in downtown Dallas, Texas. As a jazzy music cue plays, the main titles play over a freeze-frame of the defendant, Ernest Jones, as he walks into the courtroom. This freeze-frame gives the audience a chance to study the defendant: a well-dressed black man. Itself a provocative image in 1963, when African-Americans were rarely featured in starring roles, the freeze-frame also features a white court employee glaring at the defendant and frozen in a posture of prejudicial dismissal. Additionally, the freeze-frame manifests the ossified anti-drama of the courtroom action throughout the film, slowing down cinematic time to an almost interminable pace, again recalling Antonioni and foreshadowing the moment "frozen cinematic time" becomes a central focus with the trial's conclusion.

A disclaimer follows the credits: "The essence of the story you are about to see is true. Names, dates and places are fictional, and any resemblance to persons living or dead is a matter of coincidence," a disclaimer obviously untrue given the film was directly based on a case with which Buchanan was well acquainted. Inside the Dallas courtroom, the Judge (George Edgley) orders the witnesses sworn in, and gives them instructions on how to compose themselves. The attorneys are introduced: Mr. Atkins (Johnny Hicks) for the state and Mr. Tyler (George Russell) for the defendant. Jones enters a plea of "not guilty" to an unlawful "carnal knowledge" with Ms. Hansen, who is called as the first witness. As the shapely blonde slowly takes the witness stand, the camera zooms in to establish a voyeuristic relationship between her, the camera, and the film spectator. As Atkins questions Greta, a short biography is given: she arrived in the United States from Sweden two years ago, and had been staying in New York until recently, at an integrated YWCA, along with "members of the Negro race." She worked for the Congress of Racial Equality (CORE), and participated in a CORE protest in Jackson, Mississippi. She appears to be a typical archetype of the period: a young white woman dedicated to liberal racial politics. Yet, as a European with pretensions toward social progressiveness in a land not her own, her status becomes more suspect as an outsider not just to a community (liberals invading the South in the Civil Rights era to enforce their political agenda) but an entire country. One could argue that Greta represents the specter of "Old Europe" in the form of the Woman threatening the xenophobic and somewhat insular "new" nation of America, and particularly the provincialism of the American South, a reversal of *The Naked Witch*, where a modern American male becomes trapped in a supernatural version of Old Europe.

Arriving in Dallas, Greta found a job as a bank secretary, attended a Negro church, and also a meeting of the local chapter of the NAACP. She was subsequently asked to leave the YWCA for "associating with Negroes." Dejected and homeless, Greta moved downtown to the Ebony Hotel, and soon after met defendant Jones at the Comet, a local dance club. *FW21* leaves the stifling courtroom and begins a flashback of her version of events, or rather footage of events accompanied by her spoken narration and music. She explains Jones told her he was in the advertising business and could get her modeling work, and accompanied her to her hotel room, where he took measurements of her body for possible future modeling assignments. Jones touched Greta's leg, and she objected, countering that she

Ernest Jones (Frederick O'Neal) somberly enters a Dallas courtoom, preparing to defend his actions against the plaintiff, Swedish bombshell Greta Mae Hansen (Annalena Lund), in the courtroom blockbuster *Free, White and 21* (1963).

would rather measure herself, and was convinced to put on a bathing suit, to better see how she looked overall and to measure her thighs and hips. Jones then urged her to strike various poses on the bed as practice for the upcoming camera session. With a hand-held camera assuming Jones' point of view, Greta smiles sexily at the viewer while rolling around on the bed, a virtual recreation of a stag film loop, with the film viewer assuming the position of the person she claims later raped her. The sequence manifests one of Buchanan's prevalent themes: objectification of the woman as an idealized sexual fantasy, a source of male visual sexual pleasure (*Naughty Dallas*) and ultimately physical sexual conquest (*Mars Needs Women* and *Goodbye, Norma Jean*). According to Greta, Jones then made physical contact with Greta, pretending to brush her with "an imaginary powder puff." Greta refused this lewd advance, so Jones grabbed the struggling girl and threw her down on the bed.

Throughout Greta's description of the attack, the scene crosscuts between her describ-

Greta Mae Hansen (Annalena Lund) confidently enters the courtroom to defend her honor and give the attendees a lesson in subjective reality, in *Free, White and 21* (1963).

ing the action in the courtroom and the same events dramatizing the action shown as a flashback with her narration, continually increasing the tempo of the editing as the encounter veers towards the assault, a use of Eisenstein's principle of rhythmic montage to manufacture a physical sense of agitation–and arousal — for the film. Her account of the sexual incident ends with Greta breaking down on the witness stand, yelling, "God, take my life! God, take my life away!" The trauma of the rape is transferred from its original, dangerous setting of the Ebony Hotel — a racially black space — to the sterile, "safe" courtroom — a racially white space — where the spectators are visibly disturbed by the raw emotion of the outburst. Greta's obvious pain spoils the spectators' erotic investment in the narrative up to this point. In this respect, the scene encompasses two tensions that will dominate Buchanan's films throughout his career. One is the problem of objectifying women while providing a critique of voyeurism and its political implications in a patriarchal society. Buchanan attempts this consistently in his films, carrying on a long tradition of contextual schizophrenia in the exploitation film genre, which offered tawdry stories that appealed to the viewer's puerile interest while making strident moral judgments on the people and subjects in question — in order to make the lurid subject matter "socially relevant" in the hopes of subverting local obscenity standards that would frequently jeopardize the film's run. The underlying problem becomes Buchanan's claim that cinema was an art form that intrinsically "honored" women versus how cinema, as Laura Mulvey claimed in her pivotal treatise on women in film, "Visual Pleasure and Narrative Cinema," is a medium that undervalues women through narrative punishment and overvalues women as idealized fetish images. The second, related problem becomes Buchanan's "feminist" politics themselves, which despite their overtly liberal-progressive agenda, can be seen as containing more traditional, at times even parochial, attitudes towards women. Indeed, the day after the assault, Greta sought out the nearest Catholic church, where the compromised virgin asks forgiveness for her attacker, and for her own missteps which may have led to this tragedy, as the camera zooms into a statue of the Virgin Mary.

After the prosecution rests, Tyler begins his defense, first calling Dr. Alexander P. Sutton, assistant health officer for the county. Sutton relates the results of his examination on Greta, revealing that her hymen was ruptured, and the tissue around it was swollen and irritated. In addition, there were traces of male spermatozoa. Sutton concludes by saying that, in his opinion, Greta had indeed been a virgin before the attack. Tyler asks Sutton to define what a gynecologist is, and the witness briefly describes this specialist's duties. The questions which follow ("Did you find bruises or lacerations on her body or clothes?" "Is it possible for a woman to have relations with a man without rupturing the hymen?" "Likewise, a ruptured hymen does not necessarily mean that the woman has had sexual relations, correct?" "Is there any way to tell if spermatozoa is from a Latin, a White or a Negro?") are lurid to the point of absurdity, and the airing of these "gory details" in the sterile courtroom setting has a shock effect on the viewer. The segment is jarringly anti-erotic, painting sex as a clinically measurable body function that becomes central to *Mars Needs Women*. Similarly, Tyler calls the police officer in charge of the arrest of Jones and accuses the officer of performing a "botch job" of the investigation, and by implication accuses law enforcement of ineptness and obstruction, a theme prevalent in Buchanan's work (*The Eye Creatures, The Trial of Lee Harvey Oswald, Creature of Destruction, Beyond the Doors,* et al.). Tyler queries the hotel's night clerk, and his recounting paints the impression that Greta was "on the make" that evening, and not the injured innocent she is portrayed as by the prosecution. The court is recessed, and the scene fades out.

When the court reconvenes, Greta is again called to the stand, and Tyler questions her, asking if she was a member of the Swedish Club of New York. Responding in the affirmative, Tyler asks if Greta knew the manager of the club, Karl Bjorkman, and did she in fact ask Mr. Bjorkman to gather up all the newspaper articles regarding the rape case and collect them in a scrapbook. Greta, her head hanging, reluctantly answers yes, at which point Tyler pounces on her: "Isn't the real reason you did this is you wanted to create racial strife in a community where there was none, and where you do not belong?" Greta defends her actions by stating that she wanted to gather the news reports of the attack, especially overseas accounts, to see how much her family back home might have learned about her unfortunate situation. Tyler shouts at Greta, "When you were on that bed, and ole Ernie Jones was brushing you down with that imaginary powder puff, didn't it finally dawn on you that there was something rotten in Denmark, something sour in Sweden, and that there was a nigger in the woodpile?" This inflammatory remark is able to pass here because the incendiary use of the word "nigger" is attached to the colloquial expression "a nigger in the woodpile," long considered part of the slang lexicon of rural America. Still, it has a shock impact surely intended by the filmmakers, punctuated by prosecutor's Atkin's lone handclapping, which both applauds and mocks the prosecution's cheap theatrical outburst with Brechtian satire. Tyler asks Greta to reaffirm that she was raped that night, and cruelly asks her to scream for the jury like she screamed for her life that night, asking her in effect to relive the climax of the attack in public, for the voyeuristic benefit of the (male) audience by recreating the real-life "exploitation film" event directly into the courtroom. Again, *FW21* manifests a strange contradiction. On one hand, Tyler's defense is clearly racist and sexist and exposes the core of the defense's argument as American cultural xenophobia, especially prevalent in the South. Yet Tyler at this point essentially voices Buchanan's own opinions about the actual rape case: that Hansen was a publicity seeking opportunist and Jones was the true "victim" of her ploy.

Ernie Jones is called to the stand. Like Greta, a background of his life is provided; he dabbles in real estate, is a radio disc jockey, and runs a small advertising agency. Jones explains that, as an ad man, he "takes pictures of pretty girls and superimposes the products on the photos," to sell as advertising in local media. While Hansen is depicted as a cross between a freedom rider and the Virgin Mary, Jones is depicted through racial stereotypes: a con artist, a distributor of black music, and, above all, a black man on the make for white women. Moreover, Jones states that he often has freelance photographers doing the shooting, while he "directs" the picture. It is a commentary on the business of exploiting women, be it the advertising industry, the peepshow, or, of course, the exploitation film genre and the exploitation film Buchanan is "directing": visual culture that makes money on prurient male voyeurism. In this respect, Greta's Swedish heritage becomes an allusion to the American perception of a decadent, sex-obsessed country churning out many of the sex films of the era.

Another lengthy flashback begins with Jones recounting his version of the sexual encounter (which, to reiterate, is the one that Buchanan believed). These sequences superficially mirror the previous flashbacks of Greta's experience, but present a different history of the events in question. Taken together, the two sets of dramatized memories diametrically opposed to each other present a study of the subjective nature of memory, especially when memory becomes tied to advancing personal and even political agendas. In what becomes a key concern for Buchanan, history is not simply recounted, but *revised*. Indeed, *FW21* becomes the drive-in exploitation version of Akira Kurosawa's *Rashomon* (1950), in which conflicting flashbacks by various people (attacker, victim, witness) depict vastly different accounts of a rape.

Not surprisingly, Jones' version of events paints him as a god-fearing, altruistic businessman who was merely attempting to help a hotel patron in need, and paints Greta as a flirty, money-hungry tramp. In Jones' scenario, they met at the Comet Club, where she provided a sob story to get him to buy her dinner, conducted herself in an inappropriate manner by dancing flirtatiously, and solicited modeling work under the pretext of CORE fundraising. He "foolishly" agreed to join Greta in her hotel room, where Greta "sprawled herself on the bed" and confessed to Jones how disappointed she was in having collected a mere 40 dollars at the last CORE meeting. After providing some effective advice to help her fundraising efforts, Jones claimed she hugged him and the two kissed. Greta asked him about getting her some publicity towards her goal to become an actress, and Jones mentioned his modeling business and took some measurements "for purely professional reasons." When he challenged her if she looked as good in a bathing suit as in her dress, she offered

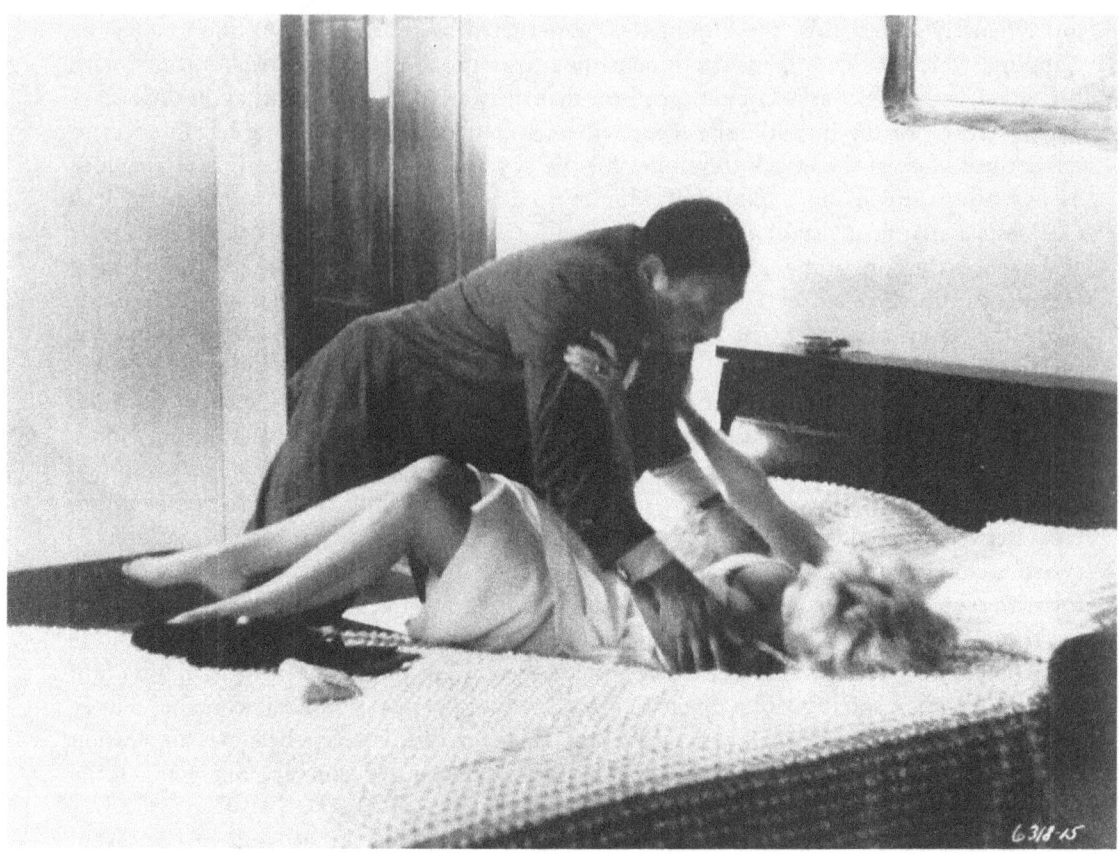

This unusual frame blow-up from *Free, White and 21* (1963) shows the pivotal event which leads to the court trial; it is difficult to tell whether it depicts a willing seduction or a forced attack, an ambiguity which underlines the importance of subjective memory and personal agenda in recounting any historical event.

to change her wardrobe. Greta reentered the room, twirling to show off her swimwear while Jones took more measurements, then in the classic romantic cliché, she wanted to "change into something more comfortable." She went into the bathroom, but didn't close the door as she changed. Jones then stated, "She wanted a couple of hundred dollars to fix herself up," and he promised that he could come up with the amount later in the day. In his version, Jones was not a rapist, but Greta was essentially a prostitute, and he finally confesses, "I was intimate with Miss Hansen, stupidly so."

After a dinner break, the jury listens to the closing arguments. The defense, under Tyler, goes first, and attempts to ingratiate himself to the jury with statements such as, "I live in this community" and "I believe in the individual's rights." He segues quickly into implication and accusation: "The prosecution believes that Greta was raped. It makes no difference that there were no marks, no evidence of any kind." Having cast doubt on the plaintiff, Tyler elicits sympathy for his client: "And where was ole Ernie? On his way to Mexico? Hiding out in the bushes, police dogs baying at his heels? No, he was at home." Tyler paints the plaintiff crudely, stating that Greta "is just white trash." Tyler qualifies this rude insinuation by claiming that the white trash of this country, "and thank goodness there

Greta Mae Hansen flirts with the audience in *Free, White and 21* (1963); is she thus inviting, and deserving of, a brutal sexual attack?

aren't too many of them," are not a threat to decent society as long as they "consort among themselves." While shielding his client from racist attacks, Tyler nonetheless feels confident in applying sexism and jingoism to his attacks on the plaintiff:

> Greta isn't even an American citizen. She comes to this country uninvited, an immigrant who asks the protection of our laws. Are we going to apply her customs of Sweden in this country? Swimming in the nude, free love, and all that? What was her real reason for coming here? We were solving our racial problems just fine. Was she specially trained, sent here to cause upheaval?... Maybe some wanted to see if a Negro, charged with rape, could get a fair trial in the South.

Tyler introduces the specter of paranoia in the jurors by hinting that other countries (read "Old Europe") may desire to thwart America in her attempts to harmonize the races. This fear on the part of U.S. citizens to be "contaminated" by European influences dates to the American Revolution, and the belief that America was not merely a break from Europe but antithetically opposed to Europe: class privilege and decadence. The depiction of foreigners as evil and even conspiratorial was applicable with the prevalent mood in the South of the early 1960s, which combined an intense mistrust of outsiders with an insular sociopolitical body and an almost incestuous desire to remain pure from outside influences.

Prosecutor Atkins follows with his closing argument, itself another mixture of racial, sexual, progressive, and reactionary politics rather than addressing the facts of the case:

> Greta Mae is a peculiar person, a stranger to our shores, twenty-two years old, still a virgin. While I disapprove, and you may disapprove, she cast her lot with the Negro race. She is a missionary, a crusader. She is carrying their banner, fighting their fight for freedom.... I believe in equal protection under the law, equal rights for education and work, but I don't believe the Negro and White races should mix socially.... Are you going to believe an ex-convict like Ernie Jones?.... Big Ernie Jones, the big-time ex-disc jockey, the advertising man, the expert on modeling.... Can you honestly believe that this woman carried her virginity around with her for twenty-two years, traveled all over Europe, and in this country, and picked out you, Jones, to surrender her virginity to.... Are you going to punish Jones for what he has done to this woman, to his race, to his community? Or are you saying that if a white woman is in a Negro hotel, she is fair game?

With the closing arguments and their political agendas in place, the judge reads the long-winded charge, specifying that the indictment being decided today is "rape by force, which means the carnal knowledge of a woman without her consent obtained by force." The scene changes to a close-up of an institutional-type wall clock. The voice-over by a solemn narrator provides instructions to *FW21*'s other jury, the film audience:

> Ladies and gentlemen, you are the jury. When you entered this theater, you were given a subpoena, a summons that put you in the jury box in the case of The People vs. Ernie Jones. The judge has charged you to render a verdict of guilty or not guilty on a question of consent. Greta Mae Hansen was free, white and twenty-one, the age of consent. If she did not consent, then it was rape, and Ernie Jones is guilty. If she consented, then Ernie Jones is not guilty, and should leave the courtroom a free man. Now, weigh your conscience. Follow the instructions on your summons. See if your decision coincides with the actual verdict brought in by the jury in and for the State of Texas. You have approximately three minutes while the management polls you, the jury.

The static shot of the clock remains for four minutes. During *Free, White and 21*'s theatrical release, the audience-jury filled out "ballots" and handed them to ushers, who would collect them. From this ballot-taking and the film's promotional campaign, it was subtly implied that the audience was actually involved in the outcome of the filmed trial, but as the narrator states, the ballot-taking is just an exercise to see if the audience's feelings on the matter coincides with the actual verdict. The ending is predetermined, and not subject to the audience's verdict. Buchanan possibly borrowed the idea from the B-movie horror legend William Castle, who used a very similar audience participation gimmick with his 1961 film, *Mr. Sardonius*; two endings were supplied to theaters and the audience could vote on whether the title character lived or died in a "Punishment Poll." (Castle soon quit supplying the ending where the character lived because audiences always opted for his death). In *FW21*, exploitation gimmickry and political discourse merges in a most unusual sociopolitical stew. Moreover, viewing the clock scene on a video or television screen has a curious effect, not intended consciously by the filmmakers. The clock ticks away, while ominous xylophone music plays, becoming a purely existential segment, as the second hand obediently revolves and the minute hand slowly reaches its incremental goals. Originally designed to disengage the audience and kill time while the ballots were collected in the theater, here cinema itself becomes an exercise in time management, a moment of interminable waiting literalized on the screen by a clock in real time.

At exactly the four minute mark, the clock scene fades out, and the verdict is announced: "Not Guilty." Echoing the results of the 1961 trial, *FW21* ends in a revelatory coda which radically revises much of what has been presented in the trial. Again, it bears mention that Buchanan was a friend of defendant Davis and firmly convinced of his innocence and of the ulterior motives of the defendant. By constructing a trial largely composed of racial and sexual politics, with the audience being forced to choose sides, the film audience becomes the prosecutor, defense, and jury and are no longer spectators but participants in a trial where they have to address, or admit, their own racism, sexism, and xenophobia.

After the courtroom empties, only Atkins and Tyler remain, sitting at their respective tables. They eye each other warily, then break into weary laughter. One tosses a coin, and the other "calls it." The winner agrees to buy drinks for the two. The two former "enemies," once standing on two diametrically opposed sides of a societal argument, are revealed to be on the same team after all: the machinations of the U.S. justice system versus plaintiffs and defendants. Specifically, in a trial between a black man and white European woman, the two apparent rivals, working for the same ultimate master, are both white males. Preparing to adjourn to a local diner, the two see Greta standing alone with a single suitcase, boarding a departing bus in exile. Then Atkins poses a shocking and provocative question to Tyler: "Is it that we love Negroes more, or that we like intruders even less?" The apparently progressive verdict becomes black comedy, not a statement of justice but a political

In this newspaper advertisement for Larry Buchanan's second courtoom melodrama, *Under Age* (1963), the racial theme of the drama is downplayed in order to emphasize the possiblity of sexual perversions revealed.

Annabelle Weenick dramatically denies forcing her daughter into a life of sin in *Under Age* (1964).

juggling act between the lesser of two evils in the American South in the early 1960s.

Upon completing the film with the title *A Question of Consent*, Buchanan and Hoffman received a call from Samuel Z. Arkoff and James H. Nicholson, heads of prolific B-movie factory American International Pictures. Using their clout as owners of MovieLab, the Hollywood film laboratory where Buchanan and company still had unpaid negatives in storage, AIP managed to get "first refusal" for the picture, meaning they optioned the right to accept or pass on the film before others were offered it. After agreeing to distribute the film, the first thing AIP did was change the title to *Free, White and 21*, over Buchanan's objections: "I thought we had an art picture, but we had an exploitation picture. We were learning."[5] Nevertheless, the film did remarkable box office, covering its production costs in the first week of release. By the spring of 1963, it was one of the top-grossing films in the United States. Buchanan attributed *FW21*'s success to his belief that the film touched a nerve among moviegoers, being one of the first sympathetic and honest portrayals of black-white relations to come to the screen. Yet the power of *FW21* as an objective anti-drama was completely lost on mainstream critics. Eugene Archer at the *New York Times* stated of the film:

Judy Adler and Roland Royter are cast as young lovers who wind up in court in *Under Age*, the probing story of parental delinquency.

"No attempt is made to take sides in the case, with the result that both protagonists emerge as unpleasant and unsympathetic. Possibly some socially conscious spectators will find the subject matter significant enough to overlook the film's unconvincing dialogue, awkward acting and total absence of cinematic technique."[6]

Nevertheless, *Free, White and 21* allowed Buchanan and Hoffman to begin a long and fruitful association with American International Pictures. For their next project, Arkoff commissioned the Dallas team to recreate their success with *FW21*, asking bluntly, "When can we have another one?" The only demand AIP made for this next picture was to cater to their primary market, American teenagers. Again using an actual court case to fuel the screenplay, Buchanan and Hoffman relied on a case involving Wanda Duckworth, who was accused of conspiring against her teenage daughter by encouraging the fifteen-year-old to have intercourse with a Hispanic male of seventeen years, hoping that the subsequent scandal would ensure financial security for her and her daughter. The plan backfired, and Duckworth was indicted, charged, found guilty of rape, and sent to prison. The result was *Under Age* (1964), which was essentially less a sequel and more a remake of *FW21*. The judge, prosecutor Tyler and district attorney Adkins return and are played by the same actors, reinforcing the idea that the legal system is an unchanging machine circulating plaintiffs and defendants, with the added benefit of sexual scandal. *Under Age* similarly used a mixture of objective courtroom footage and subjective flashbacks, with characters who were thinly disguised versions of the actual people involved. Buchanan later described *Under Age* as a competent courtroom drama with the added attraction of race relations as in *Free, White and 21*, but it generated disappointing business. Buchanan and Hoffman vowed never to make another courtroom picture after *Under Age*. World events soon altered that decision.

7

The Trial of Lee Harvey Oswald

Guilt is never to be doubted.
— Franz Kafka, *In the Penal Colony*

A political coup occurred in the U.S. on November 22, 1963. In his book *Blood, Money & Power: How L.B.J. Killed J.F.K.,* Barr McClellen states, "The emotional shock to the nation had never truly gone away. There simply had been no closure because there was no national consensus that justice had been done ... the evidence and the conclusion just did not fit together. In addition, we could not balance Johnson with what we had lost and the grief we had suffered."[1] The shocking murder of President Kennedy in Dealey Plaza, Lee Harvey Oswald's nationally televised murder, and the subsequent Warren Commission report that produced more questions than answers fomented a collective feeling in America combining anger, disillusionment, and sorrow.

In this context, Larry Buchanan produced the third installment of his courtroom trilogy, *The Trial of Lee Harvey Oswald* (1964, henceforth referred to as *Trial*) mere months after the world-shattering events of November 1963. According to Buchanan, *Trial* was rushed into production in the early months of 1964 in an attempt to capitalize on the heated debate going on at the moment, and revealing classic exploitation film strategy as well — to be the first film to address the national tragedy by maximizing controversy and potential box office. Controversy was certainly achieved, but Buchanan received some foreshadowing of the film's eventual fate early on: "The city fathers felt it was unwise to do this so quickly after the death of Kennedy. I felt that it was important to get it out as soon as possible."[2] According to conflicting reports by Buchanan, *Trial* had its world premiere at either the Warner Theater in Milwaukee, Wisconsin, or the Apache Drive-In in Dallas. The film was also well received at a press screening at Southern Methodist University, and was slated for general release shortly thereafter. American International Pictures originally offered negative pick up for *Trial*, but it is unclear if AIP subsequently distributed the film during an all too brief theatrical run. Buchanan never explicitly accused specific agencies or interests of suppressing the film, but did pointedly suggest, "It did very well until we were squashed...."[3]

Buchanan and Harold Hoffman were working on the screenplay for what would later become *Mars Needs Women* when they heard reports of the president's shooting on the radio. Buchanan, for one, never believed the official story: "A charismatic president, terribly flawed and tragically ill, slumped from a frontal bullet to the head. The patsy, Lee Harvey Oswald, was arrested for firing diversionary shots from an ancient building along the fatal route."[4] When Jack Ruby killed Oswald two days later, Buchanan and Hoffman devised a radical idea for a film: "We wanted to give this man [Oswald] the trial that he was denied by the bullet from Jack Ruby." Labeling the new project *The Trial of Lee Harvey Oswald*, they enlisted the professional aid of their friend and colleague, famous Dallas trial attorney Charles Tessmer, their legal technical advisor on their earlier box-office success, *Free White and 21*. Tessmer, even more skeptical about the real forces behind the murder of JFK than was Buchanan, not only wrote much of the lawyer's courtroom arguments but appeared in the epilogue to the film.

Buchanan and Hoffman wrote the script for *Trial* in two weeks, and built the set "literally overnight." According to Buchanan, the strange courtroom benches were actually pews borrowed from a local church (a most ironic mixture of church and state). Although the film was rushed into production, Buchanan was careful not to sabotage the film with hasty on-location shooting: "We can't shoot it in a barn this time, we need to build a sound stage and do it right. The voices were so important in this one."[5]

Buchanan also retained the services of several of the actors from *Free, White and 21* and *Under Age*. George Edgley returns as "the Judge," a character not given a proper name and a perfect symbol of the stony face of the American justice system.[6]

George R. Russell returns as "good old boy" defense attorney Tyler, and Arthur Nations replaces Johnny Hicks as prosecuting attorney Atkins, named "Adkins" in *Under Age*. By having unchanging characters in the three pivotal roles of prosecutor, defender and judge, Buchanan depicts the U.S. legal system as a vast machine, a faceless juggernaut in which defendants and plaintiffs come and go indiscriminately as its machinations grind away. Moreover, the witnesses who take the stand in *Trial* have no names, and instead become archetypes of modern American life: the boss, the doctor, the psychiatrist, the coworker, the neighbor, the innocent bystander, the cop, etc. This reinforces the sense that *Trial* takes place in a dehumanized and dehumanizing generic space, the "justice machine" where citizens wander in and out as highly interchangeable ciphers, mere pawns in a rigged institutional chess game. In this respect, *Trial* is structured identically as the previous two courtroom films. They are remarkably similar visually, almost indistinguishable, and the sum of the trilogy becomes part of a powerful treatise on the American justice system.

Although Buchanan had very specific ideas regarding the person(s) behind the assassination of JFK, there is no overt reference to conspiracy in the testimony as given in *Trial*, but it is implied in the film's construction. First and foremost, there is a recurring montage of shots (literally, camera shots and gun shots), used three times during relevant testimony by witnesses. The three exterior shots focus on Elm Street, the location of the murder, and zoom in on the place where the president's motorcade was positioned when the fatal shots rang out. The first shot comes from the far right of the street. The second shot comes from further up the road and at a higher elevation. The third shot comes from behind, and from a high angle. As each shot zooms in, there is the sound of a single gunshot. Buchanan visually recreates the three shots that killed JFK with point-of-view shots *from the viewpoints of the shooters and from three different points of view*: the bushes near the grassy knoll, an overpass near the grassy knoll, and the sixth-floor book depository window. The astute viewer can easily assume Buchanan's subversive intent with this clever, virtually subliminal montage.

Trial also contains a brief clip of amateur home movie footage as average American citizens — men, women and children — flee for their lives, and a burly, leather-clad Dallas police officer nervously fumbles with his motorcycle. As chilling as any footage taken in lower Manhattan on September 11, 2001, an American city becomes a dark theater of the apocalypse that will permanently define America "before and after" the event — be it JFK's assassination or 9/11. Finally, *Trial* contains actual footage of Lee Harvey Oswald being escorted by Dallas police detectives through some institutional corridor. Buchanan was proud of this footage, likely shot by his cameraman Ralph Johnson: "That's our footage of Oswald, that's our man with an Eymo camera, one hundred foot load."[7] While not shot on that fateful day, it clearly evokes the basement of Dallas Police HQ on November 24, 1963, when Jack Ruby materialized and shot the accused killer dead with one mob-style hit to the abdomen. Oswald seems ironically bemused in the Buchanan sequence as he is surrounded by an anonymous crowd of sullen, suit-clad lawmen. It again reinforces the depiction of the nameless, faceless, officious American justice system of suits as it smothers and devours its only recognizable face, subsumed with the only recognizable figure: Oswald, patsy and victim.

The opening credits sequence begins with the Dallas cityscape dominated by the skeleton of a mammoth unfinished skyscraper, a metaphor that Dallas will be stripped to the bone over the course of *Trial*. The scene shifts to the courtroom, where Tyler argues with the judge over jury selection. After attempting to dismiss single members of the jury without success, Tyler finally resorts to one last plea: "I request this entire jury be dismissed. Nine members of the jury have already informed me that they have formed an opinion in the case. Some of the jury have actually seen physical evidence displayed on TV, have heard a captain of detectives say 'that's the man who killed the president, we have a cinch case!'" When Tyler essentially points out that a trial for Oswald is a pointless formality in order to convict him, the judge turns sternly to the camera and addresses the jury — and also the film's audience:

> I have asked you individually, now I ask you collectively. Could you put aside anything you may have seen or heard or read about this case and decide it solely on the basis of sworn testimony, coming to you from the witness stand and from the charge given you by this court? If you cannot answer yes to this question, speak now.

This technique of "breaking the fourth wall" was frequently used by Buchanan, where characters directly address the film viewer and pose questions to them regarding what they will see and how they will form a political opinion on the situation. The very idea of conspiracy in American politics suggests an affinity to the work of Bertolt Brecht, in which the spectator is no longer allowed to passively watch, but is asked, even told, by the characters to make critical judgments on what is being presented and how it is being presented. In fact, Tyler turns towards the camera, and gives the jury/audience what amounts to a dirty look, positing another direct challenge to the film audience: whether they can approach *Trial* objectively and critically. Certainly, Tyler does not believe any jury — or film audience — could be impartial, due to the magnitude of the crime and its collective, traumatic impact.

The Texas Schoolbook Depository on Elm Street in Dallas, early in the morning, with no sign of life. This theatre of murder and deceit becomes a ghostly urban "dead space" in *The Trial of Lee Harvey Oswald* (1964).

The defendant is brought into the courtroom and a group of faceless persons, backs to camera, crowds into the frame, obscuring the viewer's view of Oswald's entrance. As Oswald is seen entering from an oblique angle, he is framed so that a clear view of his face is never seen. Other than several extreme close-ups of eyes, which convey so little they might even be called "anti-closeups," Oswald's face is not seen during the entire film. The protagonist is literally, as well as metaphorically, faceless, a generic subject of civilization, a modern "everyman" doomed to persecution by society. Oswald, as a character trapped by conspiratorial circumstance, almost inevitably recalls the "hero" of Franz Kafka's *The Trial*, another scapegoat or "patsy" of the massive and duplicitous bureaucratic system of the law, guilty of crimes that are never fully explained. While the particulars of Buchanan's own conspiratorial take on JFK's assassination will be addressed later, *Trial* suggests a broader conception of conspiracy: the individual who is only the lynchpin of the crucial event functioning simply as an interchangeable cog in the conspiracy machine. Oswald becomes a real-life Kafka character, a pawn in the juggernaut of industrial society, its bureaucracies and legal machinations. While certainly not considered guiltless (Buchanan's belief that Oswald fired "diversionary shots"), Oswald is conspired against by society, with total strangers implicating the bewildered man as the "lone gunman" and architect of the most infamous crime in twentieth century America. The charge is read, and Tyler declares that the defendant, in

Authentic home movie footage taken on November 22, 1963, shows the blank chaos of the moment in *The Trial of Lee Harvey Oswald*.

an appropriately Kafkaesque gesture, "Stands mute," before adding "not guilty by reason of existing insanity."

According to Buchanan, many of the witnesses were played by the actual people they portray, but the cast list does not reveal any matches to people who testified to the Warren Commission. They were likely listed under pseudonyms for personal security. Much of *Trial* is made up of witnesses, who, one by one, testify as to various particulars of the assassination in order to form a collective web of Oswald's guilt: bystanders, the surgeons who operated on JFK, Oswald's fellow employees at the Dallas Book Depository, his neighbors, police officers, forensic experts. The final and twentieth (!) witness against Oswald is an announcer for a New Orleans radio show, who had Oswald as a guest on the program in August of 1963. The radio personality has brought the taped transcript of the program in question, and it is submitted into evidence and played for the court. Cutting back and forth from a close-up of the Revere reel-to-reel tape machine to reaction shots of various people in the courtroom, the jury and audience hear the actual voice of Oswald as he nervously and awkwardly tries to explain his philosophies and actions to a hostile interviewer. Among the topics discussed are Oswald's "secret" political organization, "Fair Play for Cuba," and the ambiguous status of his American citizenship, including the following:

INTERVIEWER: Are you now, or have you been a Communist?
OSWALD: Well, I had answered that prior to this program, on another radio program.
INTERVIEWER: Are you a Marxist?
OSWALD: Uh, yes, I am a Marxist.
INTERVIEWER: What's the difference?
OSWALD: Well, the difference is that, primarily, the difference between a country like Ghana, Guyana, Yugoslavia, China, or Russia. Very, very great differences.
INTERVIEWER: I'm curious to know just how you supported yourself during the three years that you lived in the Soviet Union. Did you have government subsidy?
OSWALD: Uh, well, uh, well, I would answer that question directly then, since you will not rest until you get your answer. I worked in Russia. I was under the protection of, that is to say, I was *not* under the protection of the American government, but that I was at all times considered an American citizen. I did not lose my American citizenship.... The United States government, through certain agencies such as the state department and the CIA, has made monumental mistakes in its relations with Cuba.

Oswald does sound mentally disorganized as he communicates in fitful starts and spurts, combining moments of clear paranoia with statements of arrogant bravado. As the audience hears Oswald's fragmented mind unreeling, the camera focuses intently on a close-up of the unspooling tape reel, an apt if simplistic metaphor of Oswald's deteriorating mental state. Like the static clock in *Free, White and 21* and *Under Age*, history unfolds here in stark, existential real time. Buchanan claimed he obtained the actual transcription of Oswald on the radio program through contacts and payoffs. Sometime later, the entire interview was released to the general public on an LP record entitled "Self-Portrait in Red." Indeed, the final, damning evidence against Oswald is his political beliefs rather than conclusive evidence of a crime.

The taped interview ends, the prosecution rests, and the defense calls its first witness: rather than contest the evidence, Tyler's strategy is to provide evidence for an insanity plea. Two psychiatrists are brought to the witness stand to paint a psychological portrait of Oswald through a history of antisocial behavior, his maladjusted childhood without a father, their diagnosis that Oswald is a schizophrenic and therefore not legally culpable for the crime he is *presupposed* to have committed. In Buchanan's legal scenario, the prosecution relies on circumstantial evidence and highly subjective character assassination to ascribe guilt. Yet the defense presents a similar character assassination in depicting Oswald as a "lone nut" who committed the crimes but was not rational at the time. Oswald's guilt is produced by his own defense, and Oswald continues to "stand mute" by not testifying. The mythic Oswald of American political history is reduced to a voiceless and largely faceless enigma in the courtroom (save for the occasional close-up of his eyes), a cultural construction of second-hand sources, each with their own agenda, an existential character who cannot even speak for himself and ultimately the product, or composite, of other people's perceptions and conceptions which have largely been predetermined before the trial — in other words, the perfect Kafka-esque patsy.

After a brief fade-out, the judge again reads the charges, accompanied by a rare full-pan shot of the entire courtroom audience, revealed to be an eclectic cross section of American citizenry. Defense attorney Tyler's arguments are spoken directly to the camera and film audience. Tyler begs the jury to judge Oswald fairly and objectively, regardless of the horrendous nature of the crime. He reminds them that all the evidence is circumstantial, and thus inconclusive. Tyler believes that Oswald is now, and has been for the bulk of his life, under the spell of a disabling mental illness, and not accountable for his actions, concluding, "If he was insane, he must be acquitted and committed to a mental institution." Building to a crescendo in his impassioned plea for forgiveness, Tyler exclaims, "Isn't it time we give this man, Lee Harvey Oswald, the treatment and care he was entitled to eleven years ago? Isn't it time society makes room for those who suffer the tortures of the damned?" This dramatic declaration is accompanied by a final close-up of Oswald's haunted eyes.

Prosecutor Atkins presents his closing arguments, also directed at the film audience, insisting that "murder is murder," and that the killer should not be excused for the act simply because it falls under his "warped political philosophy." Continuing, Atkins declares that "If Oswald killed, and then tried to hide behind a plea of insanity, I call that the greatest crime of all." Atkins insists that Oswald did kill the president, and all evidence points "conclusively and overwhelmingly" to this verdict. Atkins then unreels the bulk of the circumstantial evidence, and again ends his prosecution by trying Oswald's political beliefs: "Oswald is a Marxist. What do the Marxists say about killing? Well, they say it is perfectly alright to kill a man if he stands between them and their objectives (a philosophy ironically similar to the brand of legal morality known as "Texas Justice" or "Bubba Justice"). Discussing the rifle, Atkins grabs it from the table and vigorously thrusts it towards the audience in what is the most violent gesture in *Trial*. "If such a man is insane, God help us all!" The judge asks the jury to retire to the jury room to render a verdict, as the scene fades out.

Instead of returning to the courtroom with a verdict from the jury, *Trial* ends with a coda featuring legal consultant and Dallas attorney Charles W. Tessmer. After being introduced by Buchanan, Tessmer offers his own thoughts on "the trial you have just seen." This segment features the first and only mention of defendant Oswald's shooting by assassin Jack Ruby, who nonetheless remains unnamed in the film. Tessmer briefly describes the inherent difficulties in conducting a trial such as this, one surrounded by such publicity, notoriety and emotion. Tessmer adds a historical footnote by stating that past presidential assassins were invariably found guilty and executed, "despite strong insanity pleas by some." Tessmer ends his speech with a terse comment: "Perhaps a valuable lesson may be learned from this case, that one accused of a crime, regardless of the seriousness of the charge, should be tried in the courts, and not in the newspapers and in the news media," a telling indictment of the mass media, its whitewashing of the assassination, its unconditional following of the government line, its desire to sacrifice Oswald as the "lone nut" and effectively squelch all other possible lines of inquiry. *Trial* ends on this bitter, obscure note, with no verdict reached, and thus, no closure to the case of Lee Harvey Oswald versus America. This frustrating anticlimax eerily echoes the real-life frustration surrounding the actual assassination and the obfuscation of other possible lines of investigation. Buchanan's refusal to provide a pat answer to the sea of unanswered questions is far more effective than the approach Oliver Stone took in *JFK* (1991), an engaging and eclectic, but ultimately haphazard and self-sabotaging collection of conspiracy jumble that may have unwittingly reinforced the conservative Warren Commission agenda, rather than shedding new light or opening up avenues of further investigation. Indeed, *The Trial of Lee Harvey Oswald* is a dense, disturbing and even distraught work, somber to the point of despair, and completely lacking in any pretense of conspiratorial titillation. Save a melodramatic theme over the main credits and a syrupy anthem during Tessmer's epilog, there is no music in *Trial*, adding to the film's desolate feel. It is a bleak, despondent "anti-docudrama" about the assassination of JFK and its symbolic murder of the

A nameless judge (George Edgley) directly challenges the audience in one of several startling fourth-wall moments in *The Trial of Lee Harvey Oswald*.

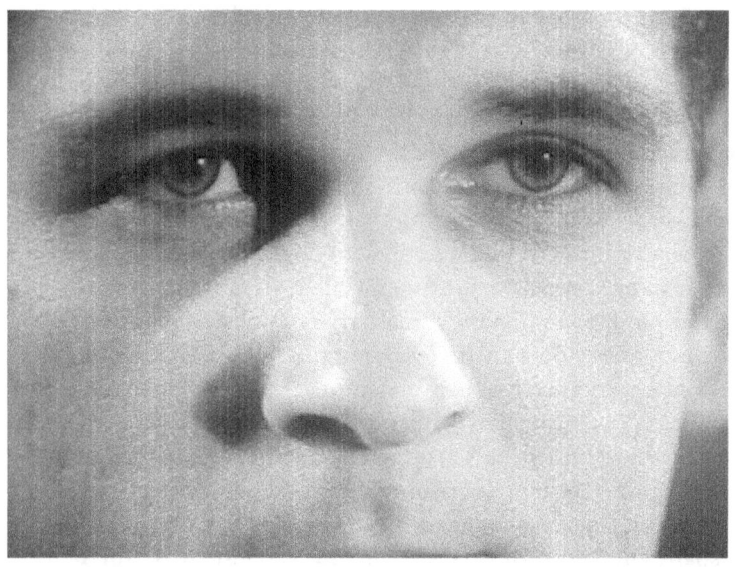

Lee Harvey Oswald looks on helplessly as a parade of strangers pronounce him guilty of one of the great crimes of the 20th century in the bleak *The Trial of Lee Harvey Oswald*.

American Way. This collective trauma would reverberate throughout the political chaos of the 1960s, indeed by Buchanan himself with one of his final films, *Beyond the Doors*, a film which invites another comparison to Oliver Stone and his own *The Doors* (1990). In *Beyond the Doors*, Buchanan devised a U.S. conspiracy for assassinating key rock stars that would outrun Stone's wildest dreams and offer a damning indictment of Nixon's America, while Stone was content to recycle the anachronistic myths of the 1960s counterculture.

It does bear reiterating

that *Trial* does strongly hint at conspiracy, particularly in its "three shot montage" that underscores the film's testimony, enough of a smoking gun that the film was, as Buchanan stated, "squashed." Speaking thirty years later, Buchanan declined to reveal the identities of those who threatened him about the film, or how these threats manifested themselves, saying only, "It was difficult, because we were harassed, we had the usual threats from those on the Dallas scene, or elsewhere, we don't know."[8]

Regarding JFK's assassination, Buchanan unequivocally stated, "It took us many years to accept the fact that there was the 'grassy knoll' shot. And Oswald? No way. He was a patsy. He was to be taken out. It had to be a marksman, working out of that manhole cover on the grassy knoll. That's the only thing that works."[9] Ultimately, perhaps the reason for *Trial*'s suppression, and Buchanan's own hesitation to discuss the matter, stemmed from his belief that LBJ was the driving force behind a coup d'etat.

Buchanan's fear and loathing of then–Vice President Lyndon Baines Johnson does not come from mere prejudice, as he knew the man well: "Bill Moyers and I wrote a lot for him [LBJ], a lot of speeches. People do not know this man. He was so clever, a very brutal man when he wanted something."[10] Buchanan believed that LBJ was capable of anything in his rise to power, including murder: "Texans take their politics very strongly. That's why they make a big noise in Washington, and they get elected. They get things done, but they get things done by 'unapproved means,' you might say. And that goes to the highest level."[11] In *Blood, Money & Power,* McClellan echoes this assessment of traditional Lone Star ethics, sometimes referred to as "Texas Justice" or "Bubba Justice":

> The roots of the crime rested in that violent cauldron of cold-blooded murders and atrocious lynchings that permeate Texas history. Lyndon Johnson and his personal attorney, Edward Clark, were dedicated to an awful objective based on primal emotions of greed for absolute power and, particularly in Johnson's case, of a fear that became a stark necessity for survival. Their crimes against our nation were deemed necessary and sufficient by them to protect their very personal sense of superiority and destiny mixed with a very profound fear of loss of power, one that would be followed by prosecution, by conviction, and by loss of all they had achieved.[12]

In Buchanan's opinion, LBJ's incrimination in events leading to the murder of Kennedy is strong, and reinforced by many factors: the strange inability of doctors to save the president's life ("If anybody could have been saved, it would have been Kennedy"); the theatrical placing of the "magic bullet" on Kennedy's stretcher; the implausibility of the awkward and distracted Oswald having fired clear shots with a cheap rifle ("It was such a defective instrument. No way he could have shot that man, from that distance, with that rifle, and his abilities")[13]; the rushed, almost panicked way in which the vice president was sworn in as president: "He [LBJ] really put that together very quickly. Johnson just ordered it, he said let's do it. Nobody checked what is the protocol, he just said let's do it and they did it. When Johnson said do something, nobody checked with the rules or the law. [He was a] lawless, difficult 'Texas gunslinger.'"

Ultimately, *The Trial of Lee Harvey Oswald* became another victim of Texas Justice.

8

The Azalea Pictures

With the eight telefilms collectively known as the Azalea Pictures, Larry Buchanan took a huge leap as a filmmaker. Here, Buchanan exercised ever-increasing creative control and expanded his audience significantly. How these films came to be reflects not only Buchanan's growth as an artist, but the culture's insatiable need for generic entertainment. By the mid-1960s, TV packagers such as American International needed features to flesh out their television syndication packages for the quickly expanding baby boomer demographic. The number of TV stations across the country was growing rapidly, and many of these stations were gearing up for 24-hour color broadcasting, making the need for program content nearly boundless. Film historian Kevin Heffernan describes the phenomenon succinctly: "It was the same in television markets all over the country: television syndication had become a highly lucrative sellers' market for distributors of feature films, and program suppliers at all levels of the industry attempted to exploit the shortage of feature films for American TV broadcast. Two technological trends, the rise of color TV and an increasing number of UHF stations, accelerated this process."[1]

In addition to purchasing inexpensive foreign films (primarily Japanese monster movies and European crime thrillers), AIP sought out filmmakers such as Larry Buchanan to craft original features for essentially the same price as the purchase of U.S. TV rights to similar foreign product. AIP also solicited producer Roger Corman who, with the help of young California filmmakers such as Francis Ford Coppola, Curtis Harrington, Stephanie Rothman and Peter Bogdanovich, took foreign genre films and "Westernized" them for U.S. audiences by shooting additional scenes for the TV market. The resultant features (sometimes referred to as "hybrids") such as *Voyage to the Prehistoric Planet* (1965), *Track of the Vampire* (1966) and *Voyage to the Planet of Prehistoric Women* (1968), are colorful patchwork sketches of genre formula which still retain their European flavor despite all attempts to homogenize them into bland U.S. fare.

As one might anticipate, AIP wanted the new telefilms "fast and cheap."[2] Larry Buchanan was originally solicited to create a dozen feature films in black and white. The filmmaker countered by offering to shoot the films in color. In exchange for this budgetary addition, he would take control of any theatrical rights. AIP agreed to this, although, as far as is known, Buchanan never exercised his right to market the telefilms theatrically.

Buchanan dubbed his telefilms project the "Azalea Pictures," based on the name of the street where his creative partner, Harold Hoffman, held offices in downtown Dallas.[3] The budgets for the features were shockingly low, even for that time period. According to various sources, including Buchanan himself, the Azalea films were produced for between $20,000 and $30,000 apiece.[4] Comparing this with an average production budget for a low-budget theatrical feature of the day, approximately $388,000,[5] one understands why the Azalea telefilms have an unshakably low-budget aura. They are some of the least expensive features ever produced for a mass audience. Even compared to the source films which inspired them, such as *It Conquered the World*, which was produced in 1956 for approximately $100,000, one can see that Buchanan was able to craft impressive works with extremely limited resources.

Buchanan's contract with AIP budgeted the films in groups of three, and stated that the filmmaker could opt out after each three-picture sequence.[6] Originally contracted for a total of twelve pictures, Buchanan produced only eight Azalea telefilms, so AIP presumably considered the theatrical *A Bullet for Pretty Boy* (1970) as the completion of the third and last triad of films. The eight films which Buchanan crafted consist of four remakes of previously filmed American International properties, plus three films based on original screenplays: *The Eye Creatures* (1965) is a remake of Ed Cahn's *Invasion of the Saucer Men* (1957); *Zontar, the Thing from Venus* (1966) is a remake of Roger Corman's *It Conquered the World* (1956); *Curse of the Swamp Creature* (1966) is an original production[7]; *Mars Needs Women* (1967) is an original production; *In the Year 2889* (1967) is a remake of Roger Corman's *Day the World Ended* (1955); *Creature of Destruction* (1967) is a remake of Ed Cahn's *The She-Creature* (1956); *Hell Raiders* (1968) and *It's Alive!* (1969) are original productions.

AIP was purportedly thrilled with the results of the first production contract with Buchanan, consisting of *The Eye Creatures*, *Zontar, the Thing from Venus* and *Curse of the Swamp Creature*. According to Buchanan, AIP offered *Zontar* to ABC affiliates nationwide in 1967, and returned an astonishing two million dollars in rentals over the course of several years, a record for syndicated television product at the time.[8] Based on this positive response to Buchanan's little pictures, AIP readily agreed to finance a second group of films. This trio of pictures also consisted of two remakes (*Creature of Destruction*, *In the Year 2889*) and one original production (*Mars Needs Women*).

The third and final trio of telefilms consisted of all original productions, which suggests that Buchanan was winning a greater share of creative control over his product, in a most difficult commercial film field. This is something of an accomplishment for any filmmaker, and reinforces the notion that AIP had been financially successful with the previous telefilms. *Hell Raiders* (1968) is the only film in the series which is not a science fiction thriller. It is a World War II-themed adventure film set in a small Italian village. Starring John Agar and Richard Webb, *Hell Raiders* is currently considered a lost film. *It's Alive!* (1969) is a brutal, cruel and reckless thriller, by far the angriest film Buchanan ever made. The ninth Azalea telefilm eventually became Buchanan's theatrical box-office hit, *A Bullet for Pretty Boy*, released in 1970.

The number of feature films produced specifically for national television syndication during the 1960s was an infinitesimally small number, so the Azalea telefilms stand out as something of an anomaly. It would be several years before national broadcast networks started to regularly program movies expressly shot for television and advertised as such. It seems likely that the major TV networks were aware of the success AIP had with syndicating original productions such as *Zontar* and *Mars Need Women* to ABC networks and affiliates, and that this success led the networks to aggressively seek feature films for television, a trend which eventually led to the popular "Movie of the Week" format which predominated in the 1970s.

The Azalea telefilms offered Larry Buchanan a unique experimental laboratory in which, within admittedly severe budgetary restraints, he could pursue numerous cinematic avenues with relative creative freedom. The resulting films prove that Buchanan did just this. The Azalea telefilms are brimming with interesting and unusual examples of narrative structure, montage and verisimilitude. The Azalea telefilms are, at root, anchored in traditional narrative structure, yet they contain many experimental and even avant garde techniques. They are a unique hybrid, combining the dramatic syntax of "Old Hollywood" with distinct elements of new wave cinema. The results, even within the strict guidelines of genre convention and finite resources, are a unique and striking body of work which owes equally to the look of both commercial film and art film, and the philosophies of both mainstream and underground cinema. Although they may have ostensibly been created by a filmmaker who wanted merely to work in his field and get compensated, the Azalea telefilms hold together as a powerful and consistent body of work, and come across as examples of a society, and an art form, in the midst of significant upheaval. Their strange and compelling atmosphere seems both hopelessly quaint and dangerously modern.

From a strictly historical point of view, the Azalea telefilms are probably the "smallest" (most primitive or low-budget) films ever to reach a mass audience, and this "cheapness" or "shoddiness" greatly enhances the dramatic impact of the films. In short, the Azalea telefilms brought the dark, raw and experimental disciplines of independent cinema aesthetic into the cultural mainstream, right into the living rooms of America. The films combined the most entertaining elements of poverty-row exploitation pictures with a large portion of underground/experimental technique. For many baby boomers, the Azalea telefilms were probably the most *unusual* films they had seen to date. As such, they opened up a whole new world of viewing experience, and to the neophyte filmmaker, an area of great inspiration. Both due to severe budget restraints and Buchanan's unique reading of classic narrative structure, the Azaleas adhere to and yet subvert traditional "monster movie" syntax, creating something familiar yet alien, neorealist yet abstract. Buchanan undoubtedly understood that in this abstracted and alienated format the Azaleas could therefore safely be used as vehicles for many subtle cultural messages both artistic and political. Buchanan used this opportunity to craft what come close at times to art film. With the Azaleas, Buchanan brought both narrative and cinematic daring into a relatively new field, the made-for-television feature, and reached a far larger audience than the average independent filmmaker of the day. Buchanan's financial compensation surely increased significantly during this time, but likely more exciting for the artist Buchanan was knowing his audience had grown exponentially. To many artists, this would represent complete success.

The source films used for the four Azalea remakes were all high-concept exploitation films with relatively big budgets. What Buchanan did with these screenplays a decade later was not to "bring them up" in stature, but to "bring them down," to deconstruct them thoroughly, almost clinically, to virtually documentary level. The complete and conscious primitivism in Buchanan's telefilms give them a compelling, hyper-real quality not seen in much film of this vintage. The narrative structure intact, thanks to Buchanan's taut and vivid screenplays, the films are free to wander into the worlds of creative montage and stylistic experimentation.

The Azalea telefilms come across as somewhat of a cross between a staged reading and a dramatic production filmed in an arty way, a theatrical melodrama captured via a generic style. This is why their many fans have gravitated to the Azaleas with such fierce devotion since their initial release, and why others simply cannot endure them. They are strong and vivid and unlike any other low-budget feature films of the period. For better and worse, the Azalea telefilms are haunting. This has been observed by both admirers and detractors. As the word suggests, it signifies the presence of an overriding spirit in the films, that spirit being Buchanan himself. Ironically, the Azalea telefilms are also memorable in their conspicuous and relentless lack of flavor or strong personality. Many key dramatic scenes are played out in medium or long shot, thus subduing the action, and making it both more theatrical and less intimate. This is one of Buchanan's most interesting aesthetic quirks. Though the cause may be budgetary, the effect is impressionistic, as moments of high drama are filtered through the lens of distance, indifference, perhaps even aloofness. Drama takes a back seat to theatricality, and the filming of this act of theater then becomes more alive, more than a mere story, more like an "event." Watching an Azalea telefilm is often less like watching a movie, and more like participating in filmed theater.

The Azalea telefilms were, almost without exception, filmed on location, in recognizable, generic American settings such as suburban homes and shopping malls, wooded areas at the edge of urban sprawl, even such lackluster locations as parking lots and alleyways. The Azalea films brought the beloved science fiction genre literally home to middle-class America. By setting these fantastic melodramas in the familiar landscapes of Suburbia (homes, hotel rooms, country clubs, etc.), Buchanan took the identifiable geographic icons of the audience, and made them fantastic, romantic, even mythic.

Buchanan primarily used local theater actors in the Azalea films, performers with an avowed Texas spirit to them, who give broad readings to their characters, as many came from community theater. Among these were many recurring faces, actors who Buchanan would call upon time and time again: Bill Thurman, Anne MacAdams, Enrique Touceda III (as "Anthony Houston"), Patricia Delaney, George Edgley, William McGhee, Byron Lord and others. With their identifiable regional accents and somewhat overwrought performances, these actors would help turn the Azaleas into what might be called a national filmed theater. Adding to this is the "box-office appeal" of faded B-movie stars in the lead roles, professionals with large resumes and name appeal who would give the films a dash of respectability. John Agar, Les Tremayne, Tommy Kirk, John Ashley, Paul Petersen all lent an air of professionalism to one or more Azalea, and the resultant performances help to make the films adhere to the traditional narrative mold which American International was likely trying to achieve for the films.

Considering the "throwaway" nature of the Azalea telefilms, it is impressive to find that the films as a group share a powerful and undeniable thematic consistency, and a very dark one at that. The Azaleas all feature protagonists living in an isolated locale, both trapped and seduced by the evil designs of man's worst self, drowning in cultural and moral decadence. Enveloping these heroes is a universe that is bleak, melancholy, depressed, creating a sense of psychological disturbance and spiritual upheaval which augments the dramatic tension in the melodramas. There is an overriding sense of existential despair in the Azalea telefilms. Few other independent filmmakers of the era fashioned a spirit of gloom and doom so consistently in a body of work as Buchanan did with this series of films. Due to location shooting and budgetary restrictions, much of the drama in the Azaleas takes place in deep shadow, lending a literal metaphor to the darkness of his films.

As hinted at in several earlier Buchanan films, this despair has a specific source, for the Azalea telefilms illustrate the loss of American innocence launched with the trauma of President Kennedy's assassination in 1963 and ricocheting through the 1960s in myriad, violent and desperate ways. They dramatize through fantastic metaphoric scenario the loss of national hope, the very crumbling of middle-class American society, suburbia in upheaval and its inhabitants engaged in cultural, political and sexual war. The films present ludicrous yet compelling melodramas of the average man caught up in fantastic happenings, occurring literally in his own backyard, triggering spiritual and political upheaval. The Azalea telefilms mourn not only the loss of hope and innocence in a once-great land now fallen, but fear for the very survival of the nation. In addition to the screenplays, the pervasive mood of dolor in the Azaleas is enhanced by the generally lackluster settings of the films, the bleakness of much of the cinematography, and the decidedly mournful selections for the stock-music scores, much of it by prolific composer Ronald Stein.[9]

The Azalea telefilms mock and dissemble bourgeois ideology (the home, the family, democracy, etc.), often with extreme prejudice, yet they just as often fixate upon and even worship these very same assaulted values. They reflect the political and psychological turmoil of America during the turbulent, self-searching mid-1960s.

There are moments of revelation, apotheosis and hope in all the Azaleas, yet the overriding message remains dark and unyielding: despair at man's accumulated misadventures, pessimism regarding man's potential for lasting change, and a cynicism which borders on unshakable misanthropy. The Azaleas also address another salient topic of the period, that of spiritual alienation. The much-vaunted "death of God" during this period, and its attempted replacement with Science, is a theme addressed consistently in the films, along with Man's neurotic, dangerous quest for false gods.

Addressing all of these important issues of the American middle class, the Azalea telefilms reveal themselves to be not only cheap monster movies, but cheap home movies about the intended audience, primarily the baby boomer generation, the first in history which grew up almost entirely by experiencing life vicariously through its most sacred and abused sensory unit, the eye, and its modern electronic counterpart, television. The films express lucidly the suburban malaise of the mid-1960s, the alienation attendant to a culture in psychic paralysis, a feeling the viewer might have previously thought was his despair alone, but could subsequently see as being ubiquitous to the culture in general. The four Azalea remakes of earlier films suggest something equally grim: are the films' audience "remakes" as well, shoddy replicas of greater parents? With these films particularly, Buchanan seems to slyly suggest that the baby boomer audience, the psychologically crippled children of "The Best Generation," are little more than cheap knockoffs of their parents. One of many impressions noted when watching an Azalea remake is a sense of time frozen, of evolution stayed, a cultural reflection of arrested development.

One of the most notable icons in the Azalea canon is the "beast" or "creature" seen, with some modification, in every film. The most familiar "creature" in the Azalea canon is the one seen in *Curse of the Swamp Creature*, *Creature of Destruction* and *It's Alive!* and in a modified version in *In the Year 2889*. (*The Eye Creatures* and *Zontar* feature original creations although each utilizes the humanoid suit and fanciful headpiece design.) This beast primarily consists of a scuba-diving wet suit painted green and adorned with layers of vinyl "fins." The headpiece evokes a vaguely amphibious creature, with a slight nod to the creature design of Universal's *The Creature from the Black Lagoon*. The most prominent and oft-noted feature of the beast's head are the eyes, which appear to be Ping-Pong balls with slits in them. Also, the mouth features some rudimentary fangs, making the whole headpiece look amusingly like a Halloween mask that one might purchase at the local costume shop. This absurd, frightless beast is in many ways the "perfect" cheap monster, blatantly using the cheapest construction possible. In a certain light, it comes across as "impossible" and somewhat surreal. Buchanan himself considered the Azalea beast to be more of a parody of the traditional B-movie monster than any attempt to homage same. Ultimately, it may been seen as a somewhat reckless "pun" on the beloved cultural icon known as "the cheap monster." As Buchanan deconstructs the traditional horror thriller with the Azaleas, he also deconstructs and demythologizes the horror-movie monster with his patently fake creation.

Yet the "beast" in the Azalea telefilms acts as a pivotal symbol of Man and his monstrous inner self, as a masked character representing Man's unruly and insatiable libido. This highly metaphorical beast, like the mask-icons of ancient Greek tragedy, portrays something larger than itself. In *The Eye Creatures*, the beasts are uninvited voyeurs, and represent Man's loss of privacy in the age of mass communication. In *Zontar*, Zontar is an absurdly false prophet, mocking Man's infantile, neurotic need for a God figure and his blind faith in anyone who claims that title. In *Curse of the Swamp Creature*, the beast is a symbol of Man's suicidal desire for immortality through reckless procreation. In *Mars Needs Women*, the beast is the Martian Dop, looking suspiciously like a humanoid Halloween beast in his scuba suit. He represents Man's fear of being conquered, and having his possessions, including his women and sexuality, stolen. In *Creature of Destruction*, the beast is woman's rage manifested in a search for long-delayed justice. In *In the Year 2889*, the beast is man's guilt manifest, specifically his despair at being unable to harness his intelligence to a compassionate morality. In *It's Alive!* the beast represents the old world of patriarchal domination, murderous and ancient and begging for extinction. In addition to its specific roles, the beast also universally punctuates Buchanan's underlying philosophy in the Azaleas, profoundly pessimistic and undeniably misanthropic, which could be paraphrased thusly: "Man is a cheap monster, and Life is his cheap monster movie."

For the casual viewer or the cultural studies maven, the Azalea telefilms offer a treasure trove in dramatizing many facets of the struggle between men and women, by showcasing many sexual topics of the time. Although they ostensibly adhere to the adolescent entertainment medium known as the monster movie, the Azaleas contain much adult thematic content, and are abundantly awash in sexual politics. At the heart of each Azalea telefilm is a man and a woman, and the drama largely involves the couple's struggles to either come together or stay together amidst both internal and outside forces which threaten their romantic harmony and often their very existence. Although a heterosexual "couple logic" may predominate in the Azaleas, it is decidedly in the service of progressive, egalitarian politics.

The male of the species in the Azalea telefilms is most often depicted by two men with opposing agendas and viewpoints, a warring duo who engage in an ongoing battle which has all the elements of a Hegelian dialectic, positing one thesis against its antithesis, towards a mutually acceptable synthesis. In the forefront of all the Azaleas stands an empowered female character who attains some form of apotheosis through enlightenment and sacrifice. Women figure significantly, even pivotally, in all of Buchanan's films, and are both the victims of evil and its vanquishers, alternately passive and proactive, in the Azalea telefilms. To Buchanan, the female is undoubtedly the bright side of humanity and the only hope for the future. In constant battle against the murderous, ego-blinded male, the female is the only power capable of fighting evil and bringing the notion of "civilization" back to society. Evil is destroyed via the sacrifice of one of its members, so that the new age may dawn. Ironically, the sacrifice is often a woman. This certainly doesn't suggest that Buchanan is, at heart, a feminist, but it does emphasize that Buchanan sympathizes with and even worships women.

The Azalea telefilms all feature harshly critical views of the American military-industrial complex, a subject Buchanan was likely familiar with since the powerful cabal was born and bred in Texas, in corporations such as Brown & Root (later Kellogg, Brown & Root), General Dynamics, and Halliburton. In four out of the seven Azalea films, the military is ruled by a small cadre of amoral megalomaniacs, secretive and with delusions of grandeur, who have their diabolical orders carried out by armies of dysfunctional lackeys. The allusion here is crystal clear: the U.S. military is the repository of society's lunatics and perverts, sad fools who have no business lording over a nation, a virtual criminal class who by some ungodly twist of fate have been put in charge of the asylum. As it stands in Buchanan's thesis, it is fortunate that the military is by and large incompetent, for if it were as efficient as it is demented, the world would have long ago vanished in a mushroom cloud. Although the presence of the military in low-budget science fiction genre is by no means unusual, the Azalea telefilms brought the military-industrial complex into sharp critical focus during the peak years of its massive growth, as well as society's increasing disenchantment with it, and this is one of the Azalea films' more politically significant achievements. In short, the view of the military in the Azalea telefilms is one of conspiracy, secretiveness, censorship, and reckless decision making.

From a marketing standpoint, the Azalea telefilms represent an interesting contribution to a curious cultural trend of time, that of the American consumer accepting a cheaper brand of product, one distinctively inferior and conspicuously so, instead of the more popular, higher-quality one (for instance, purchasing a lower-priced "house brand" of a staple such as margarine instead of a pricier "name brand" of creamery butter). The Azaleas acted as a cultural reinforcement of the notion of a "generic" brand of any given product available on the market. Instead of a classic horror film on the lines of a *Frankenstein* or a *Dracula*, the Azaleas offered the insatiable mid–1960s television audience cheap but lovable substitutes in films such as *Zontar* or *Creature of Destruction*, films which had their inherent inferiority displayed prominently in their parodic, tongue-in-cheek titles, and proceeded to entertain the audience with their rough-hewn charms. One might call the Azalea telefilms the "Brand X" of monster movies.

The cultural phenomenon known as the remake has a long and august tradition, even outside the motion picture industry. In the world of serious music, remakes are ubiquitous and well received, known primarily as "paraphrases" or "variations on a theme." A famous example is the mournful Gregorian chant melody from the *Dies Irae*, which was appropriated by composer Hector Berlioz for his *Symphonie Fantastique*, and later by Franz Liszt for

Totentanz, a symphonic piece for solo piano. Also, Johannes Brahms composed many variations on themes from previous composers such as Haydn and Handel.

In the world of the visual arts, more common than paraphrasing another's work are the innumerable artists who continually revisited favored themes and subjects. Perhaps the most recognized example is the painter Edward Hicks, who painted over one hundred works based on the biblical parable *The Peaceable Kingdom*. Each painting revisited the very same content and setting, with wildly varying results. Van Gogh's inexhaustible series of sunflowers and Monet's ubiquitous haystacks also come to mind. Additionally, certain schools of art borrow from one another and refine or clarify another's work through their own particular sensibility. In each discipline, by letting the audience experience a similar source material from a wholly different perspective, the artist creates opportunities for meditations on thematic subjectivity, artistic appropriation and cultural revision.

The Azalea remakes are not attempting to be faithful reproductions of film classics. They are cheap imitations of cheap products, and they wear this badge of honor proudly. Although Buchanan often worked very closely within the expositional confines of the source film's screenplay, he was never trying to make a "copy" of the previous film. More accurately, Buchanan was "sketching" the source film, and adding his own thematic and aesthetic touches to it to make it his own. This is more in the tradition of the fine art and music "paraphrasing" mentioned earlier, a noble tradition and one from whence enduring art may emerge.

The Azalea remakes instill a haunting sense of déjà vu to the average viewer, who has seen the source film from which the remake sprung and may wonder where they have seen it before. This awareness lends itself to contemplation of the film genre represented, but more importantly, of the culture in general, and its evolution over the course of a very turbulent decade. The Azalea films were many baby boomers' initial firsthand experience with the peculiarly postwar phenomenon of recycling. Stumbling on a film such as *Zontar* late at night on television in the late 1960s must have come as something of a shock to first-time viewers. Presumably, the audience would not have known at the time that the film was an authorized remake of *It Conquered the World*, so one could easily deduce that the Azalea remakes were some sort of primitive, unauthorized, "outlaw" pictures. Yet it was something almost celebratory at the time to discover that a cultural artifact as disposable as a cheap monster movie was aesthetically and economically important enough to warrant an homage or remake, even if that remake stood as little more than a metaphor for industrial society in decline, one which has taken to cannibalizing its own product for an insatiable, undiscriminating consumer culture.

9

The Eye Creatures

The Eye Creatures (1965), the first telefilm created by Larry Buchanan under contract to American International Television, is in many ways the most interesting, as Buchanan was in unknown territory. Producing an 80-minute color feature film in 16mm for under $30,000 is in itself a daunting task, but Buchanan managed to create a most engaging genre feature with *The Eye Creatures*, and introduces some themes which occur in much of his work. Under the agreement with AITV, Buchanan based *The Eye Creatures* on the screenplay from a former American International film, *Invasion of the Saucer Men* (1957) (henceforth referred to as *Saucer Men*), to fashion this color remake, and enlisted AIP contract player John Ashley as the lead in the film.

Saucer Men is one of the more hip and intelligent of the late-1950s drive-in pictures produced primarily for the drive-in/youth market. Boasting a title like a tabloid headline, *Saucer Men* offers a satire of the flying saucer mania of the day and its effect on suburban youth. *Saucer Men* is a fairly sophisticated entry in the SF film genre, with crackling dialogue, moody cinematography, a haunting score by Ronald Stein, and well-choreographed, brisk-paced action which jumps seamlessly from comedy to fantasy-thriller. The fanciful title creatures, literally "bug-eyed monsters" straight from the pages of pulp fiction stories, are the creation of Paul Blaisdell. Scenes featuring the title creatures are effectively spooky, despite the somewhat ludicrous nature of the aliens. One scene, featuring an alien's severed crawling hand, introduces some light gore into the proceedings. The year 1957 heralded the introduction of gore into mainstream cinema with this film and others, including *Attack of the Crab Monsters* and *X—The Unknown*. After retaining a tense melodramatic flavor for most of its running time, *Saucer Men* returns at the last minute to light comedy, with narration by the grifter, who confesses the story was all part of a book he's just written, and may or may not be true. This odd framing device was abandoned by Buchanan, who fashioned *The Eye Creatures* as a straightforward science-fiction thriller with political overtones. Indeed, Buchanan took the screenplay and added much of his own material, especially focusing on the sinister machinations of the military-industrial complex. The resultant film is in some ways a recognizable remake of *Saucer Men*, but in other ways is a unique and provocative thriller in its own right, illustrating that Buchanan was using this unique artistic opportunity to experiment with independent film narrative in ways quite unusual for the time.

The very first image in *The Eye Creatures*, and in the Azalea telefilms universe, shows an anonymous man in a dark suit walking down a hall and carrying an attaché case. This iconic image of the postwar business man is made significant by the fact that the man is handcuffed to the briefcase, suggesting that man in the mid-1960s was not only a *slave* to his burdens and efforts, but a veritable *prisoner* of his accumulated past and its secrets. The man passes by a smirking soldier (Bill Thurman) who is wearing a shiny, toy-like helmet, a figure both sinister and childlike, menacing yet silly, very much in keeping with certain views on the military of the day. Inside a threadbare conference room, the handcuffs are removed, the case is opened, and the "secret" is revealed to be a 200-fool spool of 16mm motion picture film, which a military elder carefully threads onto a movie projector. Over an extreme close-up of the military man snaking the mystery film through the cogs and wheels of the projector, the main title is superimposed in a graphic meant to mimic the outline of a human eye. The viewer notes with irony that he is watching a movie about watching a movie, a revelation which might lead to a feeling of self-consciousness, a feeling which will resonate throughout the following film, for *The Eye Creatures* is, first and foremost, a treatise on voyeurism, a film about *watching* and *being watched*, and even about paranoia, *the feeling of being watched*. It is a short jump from these themes to another which features prominently, the invasion of privacy, both individually and collectively.

The military man summons a Lieutenant Robertson (Warren Hammack) to the room, and briefs him about the top secret nature of the project, dubbed "Project Visitors." The film is viewed by all parties. It depicts, through crude miniatures work, sightings of UFOs in earth's atmosphere, as a narrator describes the Air Force's latest surveillance on the foreign spacecraft. The first shot, of two model spacecraft, features one vaguely hubcap-like vehicle which was created new for the film by special effects man Jack Bennett. The orbiting U.S. space station, however, is an off-the-shelf plastic model hobby kit, the "Star Probe Space Station," put out by the Lindberg Corporation in the early 1960s, utilizing the popular "donut" design of rocket designer Willy Ley. This mass-produced toy icon of childhood would likely be recognized by many viewers of the film, some of whom undoubtedly owned the model in question, thus bringing the Azalea film universe intimately close to a large portion of the audience. The effect of spotting such ubiquitous mass-culture product in a "professional" film must have had several significant effects, among which was the assumption that this film must indeed, be very cheap, but also making the Azalea universe identifiable to the audience, familiar and contemporary.

What is most telling about this introductory scene, however, is the revelation that the military *already knows about* the existence of craft from outer space, and has told no one outside of a small circle of privileged members. Thus, in the first five minutes of the Azalea telefilm canon, the U.S. military-industrial complex of the mid–1960s is set up as a villain, a place of secrets, cover-up and conspiracy. To punctuate this dark agenda, the General threatens Robertson: "It is *imperative* that no public information be released at this time." The General declares that the UFOs are most likely headed to "Security Sector Six," and he ends his edict with a cryptic reference: "I want those infrared scanners manned every minute!"

The General bids Robertson adieu, and the scene changes to another military location, where two goofy soldiers (one played by Enrique Touceda III as "Anthony Houston")

Low-level military personnel abuse their sanction to conduct surveillance by peeping at teenaged lovers in *The Eye Creatures*, a treatise on the watched, and the watchers, in an out-of-control technocracy.

raptly watch two video monitors. These are supposedly the "infrared scanners" mentioned by the General, and the soldiers are thus assumed to be watching for unidentified objects in the vicinity. One soldier named Culver barks, "Got anything? Get it on the scope!" and the viewer sees what the soldiers see on their monitor: groups of teenagers necking in cars in the woods. As one soldier coos, "Ain't science wonderful?" the other soldier zooms in on the erotic action, adjusting the scanners to an extreme close-up of a boy and girl kissing. The soldiers, watching private citizens in intimate activity without their knowledge, are voyeurs of an avowedly Orwellian nature, using advanced technology not only to invade another's privacy, but to achieve erotic arousal.

This line of sinister thinking continues, and the girl who is being watched suddenly feels a chill. She tells her paramour, "Somehow, I have the feeling that we're being watched." Although the boy dismisses the claim, the girl exhibits the classic symptoms of paranoia, and she even insists, "But Harold, I just *know* they're watching us." Woman's intuition tells the viewer that all is not right with the world, because the viewer, who is also watching the girl, knows that her hunch is correct. As the girl further insists, "No, the feeling I have is like someone *out there* is watching us," the scene changes to show the two soldiers grinning like idiots at the images of the lovers. Robertson enters and browbeats the soldiers for spying on civilians. Briefly he sits down and joins the enlisted men in their visual subterfuge, demonstrating that aside from pretending to maintain a code of ethics, the military is corrupt and complicit in wrongdoing *all the way to the highest level*. The shocking and amoral misuse of technology by the military-industrial complex could not be portrayed more simply, or with more effect, and as these scenes are new to *The Eye Creatures*, Buchanan must be credited for crafting something far more original, and darker, than a mere remake of an old thriller.[1]

As the voyeurs ponder the fate of these innocent teens, the scene cuts to a local tavern, the White Rock Terrace, where teenagers dance (and where the original *Saucer Men* begins). A waitress walks over to two grifters, who flirt crudely with the woman. The men, Mike Lawrence (Chet Davis) and Carl Fenton (Bill Peck), plan to exploit the town in some fashion. The scene cuts to the nearby woods. Next is inserted a quick stock f/x shot of a flying saucer landing behind a hill, taken from the fantasy thriller *Invaders from Mars* (1953, d: William Cameron Menzies). Teenagers parked in cars in the woods see the strange craft landing. The scene reverts to the military spies at their infrared scanners. They are so busy watching teenage sex on their video monitors they completely miss the landing of the alien spacecraft, thus painting the military not only as sinister, lawless and conspiratorial, but incompetent.

Back at the White Rock, three teenaged males, including the star of the film, John Ashley, discuss seeing the ship. Elsewhere in the cafe, military man Robertson eats alone. Overhearing the teens' discussion of UFOs, Robertson intrudes, angrily denying the existence of flying saucers. After all, his principal duty as "information officer" is to obscure the truth. Next, grifter Carl drives deep into the woods to try to locate the strange thing he saw in the sky. He drives by an old house, from which Bailey, a cranky old farmer, runs outside with a shotgun and sputters, "Another carload of them blasted smoochers on my property." Eventually Carl locates the spaceship and drives back into town.

Elsewhere in the woods, two attractive teenagers, Stan Kenyon and Susan Rogers, sit in their car and make out. Stan is played by John Ashley, a charismatic actor who would grace many a B-movie in the late 1950s and 1960s before becoming a successful movie producer. (According to Buchanan, Ashley was in the midst of a traumatic separation from his wife, actress Deborah Walley, during the shooting of the film.)[2] Susan is played by Cynthia Hull, a stunning beauty whom Buchanan would feature in the same year's *High Yellow*. As Stan and Susan chat, two key plot points are revealed. First, the loving couple plan to elope this evening, making the subsequent events highlighted as a journey towards adulthood. Secondly, Susan reminds her beau that her father is the city attorney, connecting her with the establishment, a fact which will soon become significant. Stan teases Susan by giving her a glimpse of her wedding ring, and they head back to town.

Back in town, grifter Mike is sleeping in his rented room when Carl enters and regales him with his fantastic story of a "real, live flying saucer." Mike is unconvinced, and goes back to sleep as Carl leaves angrily. The relationship between grifters Mike and Carl, transplanted almost verbatim from similar characters in *Saucer Men*, is an odd one. Aside from possible homosexual allusions, the two aimless drifters represent eternal adolescence arrested in intellectual and moral development, leading to unfulfilling lives void of true purpose. Although the grifters are played primarily for comedic effect in both films, they are tragic figures.

The scene with the grifters is followed by a similar scene, this time involving Air Force

Lt. Robertson, and an unnamed Colonel. These men also come across as tragic and pathetic creatures. Career adolescents one might call them, and as is revealed by their actions, their ethical framework is rotten to the core. Lt. Robertson arrives at the house of an Air Force Colonel and discusses the present situation: there are reports of a UFO landing outside of town. As the Colonel finishes his toilet, the two plan their next move. The Colonel asks Robertson if his infrared scanners had spotted the saucer before the local citizenry did, but Robertson avoids this embarrassing question. The Colonel browbeats Robertson, reminding him that in civilian life he was a successful publicity man with an assignment to spread information, while in this instance his job is to prevent a possible nationwide panic by *keeping* information from the public. The Colonel contemplates, "I figure a public information officer is about the *last* thing we need." Robertson reassures the military man of his qualifications for the job. Even better than his prototype in *Saucer Men*, Robertson in *The Eye Creatures* well illustrates the dark truth that the genius of the PR man is not the dissemination but *modification* and *obfuscation* of information for public consumption.

Back in the woods, Stan and Susan drive the road back to town with their headlights off in order to avoid attracting attention. Suddenly, Stan's convertible hits something. As lightning strikes, Stan and Susan look down upon the ugly face of an Eye Creature, a monstrous being with a gaping black mouth and a face full of bulbous eyes. The alien's dis-

An "Eye Creature," emblematic of the Orwellian traits of advanced industrial culture, has a multitude of orbs with which to spy on humanity in *The Eye Creatures*.

membered hand falls off the car's fender, and crawls away under its own power. The hand deflates one of Stan's tires with its claws, disabling the car. Stan and Susan walk down the road to Farmer Bailey's as another Eye Creature watches them. At this point, it can be safely assumed that any event occurring in *The Eye Creatures* is being watched not only by the audience, but by a third party in private.

Stan and Susan arrive at the farmhouse, but Susan is afraid to enter. Stan convinces her there is nothing to fear, and the teens enter the house, committing an invasion of privacy in its most elemental form. Stan calls for Farmer Bailey, but he doesn't seem to be home. Susan opens a closet door and screams when a stack of boxes falls out. Stan chastises her, and lectures her to "leave the opening of strange doors" to him, in a blatant reference to their highly anticipated wedding night. In the next sequence, Susan spots a telephone on the wall just as Stan opens another closet door. The two playfully continue their argument about sexual roles as the viewer sees a dreaded Eye Creature peeking out from the blackness inside the open closet. Stan then closes the door without either teen seeing the threat so close to them. In this added bit of business by Buchanan, the audience is privy to something none of the protagonists are, and as such become intimately involved in the proceedings. The Creature in the closet also reinforces the film's paranoid thesis, that someone is always being spied upon, that is, *watched in secret*. Stan telephones the police, but the cops hang up on him, reinforcing the populist notion of law enforcement as being largely ineffectual. The lights go out, plunging the teens into darkness. Farmer Bailey returns home, gun in hand, and catches the teens. At gunpoint, they attempt to explain their actions, but Bailey chases the teens off and Stan and Susan continue towards town on foot.

Meanwhile, Carl the grifter happens upon Stan's T-Bird and the dead alien. Deciding the monster would make a good source of quick cash, he wraps it in a tarpaulin. Elsewhere, Farmer Bailey prowls the woods. Unbeknownst to both parties, sinister Eye Creatures stalk their every move. Carl enters Bailey's house, unsafe from all intruders. He calls Mike, and begs him to clean everything out of the refrigerator, in anticipation of the alien. Mike gets out of bed, wearing an old striped dressing gown, and begins to empty the refrigerator. Showing Mike dressed in old-fashioned, effeminate nightwear reinforces possible homosexual alliance between the pair.

Farmer Bailey returns home in time to see another city boy running out of his home in complete disregard of the social contract. Carl returns to the woods to retrieve the alien, but a group of Eye Creatures ambush him. This first good look at the Eye Creatures shows them to be impressive man-in-suit creations, easily the most elaborate creature used in any of the Azalea telefilms. F/x man Jack Bennett manages to get a maximum of otherworldly ambience out of what was likely latex and foam-rubber construction.

Elsewhere, Robertson, the Colonel and another military man (director Buchanan as uncredited extra) arrive at the saucer's location. Faced with the unknown, the Colonel becomes paranoid: "Somebody may be *watching* us right now!" He decides to solicit the aid of National Guard engineers. When Robertson questions this decision, the Colonel insists that in cases like this one needn't think but merely resort to "standard operating procedure," perfectly encapsulating the entrenched mediocrity of the military.

Meanwhile, Stan and Susan continue towards town. On the way they spot an Eye Creature hammering away at the fender of Stan's car. Soon, a police car races towards the scene of the accident, and the teens follow, innocently believing that the police will take over and protect the community. At the accident scene, the corpse is taken away in a hearse.

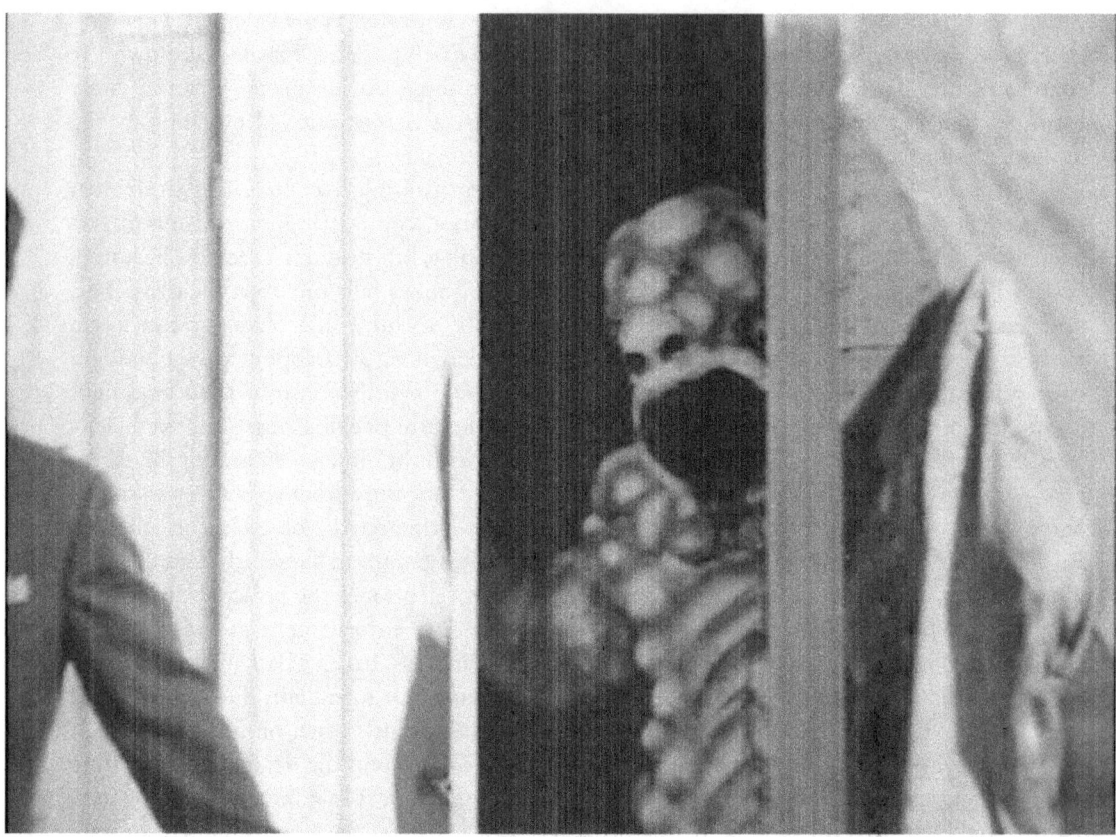

Monster in the Closet: Even in the supposed shelter of the postwar middle-class home, no one is shielded against unwitting surveillance in the paranoid *The Eye Creatures*.

Stan and Susan tell their story to a police lieutenant, who doesn't believe them. The police take Stan and Susan back to headquarters, where they try to coerce Stan into signing a confession of murder. Stan refuses, and Susan demands to see her father, the city attorney. Still not realizing that this evening represents not only her wedding night, but more importantly a highly symbolic journey for her and Stan's maturation into adults, Susan still acts and thinks as a child by relying on her father, the symbol of the entrenched patriarchy and representative of the previous generation. Susan's father arrives, and vows to do what he can for Susan. Susan's father despises Stan, and leaves him to work out his own evolution.

Back at the saucer site, a solider suggests shooting at the craft to try to get "some sort of response," and the Colonel readily agrees to this reckless and hostile action, again underlining the military as essentially adolescent (ignorant, impulsive, destructive). The ensuing shots elicit no response, so the Colonel orders his men to attack the saucer with acetylene torches. Back in town, the police escort Stan and Susan to Oneal's Funeral Chapel to identify the person they supposedly hit. It isn't the alien but Carl the grifter who lies on the stretcher. Stan and Susan are in shock, and insist that poor Carl isn't the "thing" which they hit.

Back at police headquarters, Susan's father explains the gravity of the situation to the teens. Seeing that Stan is in trouble, Susan lies and declares that she was driving the car when the grifter was killed. Susan has taken a big step towards adulthood with this loving sacrifice, becoming one of Buchanan's heroic females with this act. Susan now understands that her father, as well-meaning as he may be, represents part of a corrupt moral establishment that must be abandoned or overthrown in order for justice to prevail.

At the saucer site, engineers apply torches to the spacecraft. The torches ignite the saucer, which explodes. The explosion is heard in town, and the police leave to investigate, leaving Stan and Susan alone in the interrogation room. The teens try to piece together what has happened, and conclude that the aliens have framed Stan for the murder of the grifter. Stan and Susan realize that their foe is clever and deadly, and that they are *on their own*. It is clearly time for them to grow up. The teens sneak out the back door, and head back to the woods in a stolen police car. This daring theft, also in *Saucer Men*, is highly symbolic. Stan and Susan understand how corrupt and useless the institution known as local law enforcement has become. They must take matters into their own hands, and, more significantly, *appropriate the tools* of the fallen authority figures in order to put them to better use, a good example of maturity in action. This theme of the empowerment of youth is addressed in similar fashion in *Saucer Men*, and was certainly a major theme in cinema of the 1950s, including *Rebel without a Cause* (1955, d: Nicholas Ray).

At the military base, the two spy-soldiers are still monitoring their infrared scanner units. One chastises the other for failing to spot the flying saucer while spying on the teenage lovers, but soon they are again haunted by the lure of forbidden erotic images and scan the woods for more smooching youngsters. The first image they receive, however, is a shocking close-up of an Eye Creature. Shocked and revolted, one protests, "I think I have some weird monster film on TV! Nothing as ugly as that could be for real!"—a nice bit of self-parody by Buchanan. The two soldiers bet against each other that the "film" is coming to an end. On cue, an Eye Creature falls off a cliff-side. Here is yet another male couple, like the grifters and the military leaders, who feed off each other's arrested psychological development to form a negative bond with destructive potential. Each male dyad represents in extreme microcosm the essentially noxious nature of a male-dominated, i.e., patriarchal society.

Back in the woods, Stan and Susan drive on in the stolen cop car. They return to the scene of the accident, trying to find evidence of the aliens. Unbeknownst to them, the alien's dismembered hand crawls slowly to the police car and hops in, hoping to ambush them. It is obvious in this scene that the crawling hand is a fabricated piece attached to a human arm, filmed closely and cropped off at the wrist, an amateurish cheat which brings the scene to seriocomic level. The teens return to the car, and drive back to town, as the alien hand slowly makes its way up the back of the front seat, trying to reach the pair. Stan tries to put his hand on Susan's shoulder, but Susan shudders and says she's just not in the mood. It is interesting to note that Susan rejects Stan's attentions, as symbolized by his "crawling hand," just as the alien hand also seeks union with the virgin. One could see these attacking members as metaphorical for a most particular kind of invasion of privacy, sexual intercourse. This appears to be exactly what is on Susan's mind, as she ponders their curious fate this evening and laughs: "I expected to be frightened on my wedding night, but nothing like this!"

The monster hand finally reaches Susan, who shudders and screams. The teens ditch the car and watch in horror as the hand tries to escape. Stan realizes that the hand is the evidence they need to convince the elders of their integrity. Forgoing the untrustworthy police, he decides to enlist the aid of Carl's roommate, Mike. At the rooming house, Stan and Susan convince Mike to call the police, who confirms that Carl was indeed killed in a hit-and-run accident this evening. Mike pretends to be angry when the police confess that the suspects have escaped police custody, shouting, "I've been living in a fool's paradise! I thought the police were alert!"; this is yet another nice jab at police incompetence.

Mike joins Stan and Susan, but Susan's convertible won't start. Stan and Mike push the car while making sexist cracks at Susan's expense, all taken from *Saucer Men*. Most odd is the revelation that Susan named her automobile Elvis, after Elvis Presley. When asked to elaborate, Susan explains, "She shakes and shimmies a lot, but she can really go!" This corny reference might have made sense in 1957, when Presley was a pop superstar, but it seems sorely dated almost a decade later.

At the saucer site, a police car arrives, and the cop asks what is happening. Robertson lies to the cop, saying they are just cleaning up after an Air Force jet crash. The cop shares his gathered information about saucer sightings, but the Air Force man feigns ignorance with a studied poker face. In this most corrupt "adult" world, even lying institutions lie to each other. After the cop leaves, Robertson assures the Colonel of the efficacy of his disinformation campaign. When the Colonel presses Robertson on this obfuscation of reality, Robertson boasts of previous success in the private sector by stating intact a line from *Saucer Men*: "Colonel, you're talking to the man that made the papers believe that forty-five-year old b-girls were teenage maidens!" Presumably, the sexist message here is that anyone who could convince the public that old women were young girls has to be clever. The Colonel gushes on about how successful the cleanup effort was, and how proud he is to be on a team that can obscure evidence so completely. He boasts, "Think of it; nobody but this special unit, and the president of the United States, know what really happened here tonight!" Again, the military-industrial complex not only lies and cheats and obscures truth, but revels in these dark acts. Robertson responds, "You mean, you think *we* know what happened?" Continuing this line of paranoid thinking with choice dialogue from *Saucer Men*, Robertson continues, "This top-secret security business is like scratching, Colonel. Once you get started, it's hard to stop." Attempting to clarify, Robertson continues, "Did it ever occur to you that there are other things being hushed up by other units, just like ours?" As the Colonel looks up worriedly at the sky, his security shattered, he realizes that the inevitable flip side of secrecy is indeed paranoia.

In the woods, several Eye Creatures attempt to rescue their brother's hand from the police cruiser. However, they scurry when Stan, Susan and Mike arrive. Stan shines the car's spotlight on the police car, and Mike finally sees the ugly monster hand. Mike fantasizes about the fortune he could make if he had twelve of these self-propelling hands to play piano and drums, performing as "The Fingers." Mike grabs a camera and attempts to take a flash picture of the hand, which promptly vaporizes from the light of the flashbulb.

The trio decide to return to town for help as more Eye Creatures watch them, but the car won't start. A group of Eye Creatures advance slowly upon the three. Stan tries to confuse the monsters by shining the car's spotlight on them, and is thrilled when the bright light makes one of the monsters explode. However, the battery gives out and the spotlight dies. The Eye Creatures continue their forward advance. Mike hops out of the car and runs into the woods, where the monsters corner him. Another Eye Creature slowly approaches the car. Stan remembers the effect the flashbulb had on the monster hand, and by using the camera manages to stall the monster long enough to escape. Stan and Susan return to Farmer

Bailey's and phone the police. They are surprised to learn that they are no longer suspects, as an autopsy has revealed that Carl died of alcohol poisoning. The lieutenant chirps sardonically, "The exertion and the liquor were just too much for his ticker," cleverly revising the original line from *Saucer Men*: "The exertion and the alcohol were too much for his ticker."

Alone again with the monsters, Stan and Susan try to enlist the aid of the other teens still necking in the woods. They have trouble convincing the kids, who would prefer to continue their carefree adolescent activities. They finally coerce the others to follow, and an impressive caravan of big American cars ensues. Back at the saucer site, the cleanup campaign has been completed, and the Colonel looks on with pride at his suppression of significant world history. Seeing the Colonel's joy, Robertson smirks coyly, "Aren't we regular devils!" as a curious admission of narcissistic self-loathing.

Meanwhile, the Eye Creatures stalk the dark woods as Stan instructs his peers. The teens are to assemble at the clearing near an old ice plant and wait for the monsters to converge. When Stan honks his horn, the motorists are to put on their headlights, which will dissolve the beasts. The cars assemble at the clearing, illustrated by a fetishistic montage of headlights, fenders, hubcaps, and grills. At Stan's cue, the headlights come on and the aliens explode in flash-powder clouds. Soon, Stan and Susan find Mike, who is not dead, just stunned by the aliens. The group's attempted celebration is preempted by a gunshot from Bailey, who still thinks the teens are just goofing off on his property.

Sometime later during this long evening, Stan and Susan sit in the front seat of a friend's car, pondering the previous fantastic events while their friends, Ralph and Sheryl, kiss in the back seat. Susan ruminates on the possibility of yet another invasion, or even of other aliens *watching them right now*. Stan brings Susan's attention back to the present by pointing at their pals and remarking, "Y'know, being young *does* have its compensations." Stan asks Ralph to be his best man, and Susan asks Sheryl to be her maid of honor. The two heartily agree to the surprise wedding. As Stan and Susan continue to embrace, the scene cuts to a shot of the rising sun. It is the dawning, literally, of a new day for all. The film's parting shot offers a close-up of the two heroes ruminating on their good fortune and the exciting road ahead and finally embracing with a passionate kiss. The scene cuts to black, but the film doesn't end. There is a full twenty seconds following, wherein a rocking instrumental cue continues over a pitch-black background. This primal void of filmic space suggests two things. Stan and Susan have finally earned the right to go from innocent petting to passionate lovemaking, an act which is private and taboo to the viewer (and the film's various "voyeurs"). It is the only act which should not be watched, as it is sacred. Also, Stan and Susan have grown up, literally overnight, their evolution to maturity containing both mystery and certainty, both the unknown and the familiar; so another one of Buchanan's beloved yet problematic heterosexual savior-couples is born.

Thus *The Eye Creatures* offers an allegorical journey from adolescence to adulthood. Although they wish aloud throughout the film for adult assistance and supervision, Stan and Susan have become adults through their increasingly responsible actions, have evolved to maturity through the cleansing fire of a life-and-death crisis. They will realize this ascendancy to adulthood only after the sobering perspective of a new day and the glorious promise of their hard-won sexual reward, a lovely allusion to sexual awakening as intellectual evolution.

As sobering counterpoint to Stan and Susan's inspirational example, *The Eye Creatures*

As the dawn of the day shines upon them, Stan Kenyon (John Ashley) and Susan Rogers (Cynthia Hull) celebrate their hard-won apotheosis into adulthood after a soul-searching night of terror in *The Eye Creatures*.

contains three male couples who have a decidedly negative impact on the proceedings. The message of these microcosmic templates of patriarchal society is pessimistic: male-dominated groups tend to feed off each member's adolescent tendencies, and often conspire to maintain silence over their faults and misdeeds. They thus have a primarily destructive impact on the community. On the other hand, a balanced society where men and women work together with equal liberties and power, and can feed off each other's significant and unique creative energies, manifests a mature and progressive society.

From a political point of view, Buchanan suggests something profound to his audience. Just as Stan and Susan learned in the film, Americans in the mid-1960s needed to learn how to evolve, how to "grow up" on their own, with the help of only each other, foregoing the dubious help of formerly trusted authority figures and institutions that had proven themselves obstructionist and incompetent (law enforcement) or conspiratorial and malevolent (the military-industrial complex). *The Eye Creatures* offers a tough lesson of encroaching conspiracy by diabolical institutional enemies, but also hope for victory by using courage, intelligence and camaraderie among one's peers to conquer virtually any threat from without or within.

The Eye Creatures, even more than its predecessor, is about watching and being watched. The film obsesses on the invasion of the average citizen's privacy, from people sneaking into one's house to folks spying on one's private activities to otherworldly monsters watching one's every move. The handmaiden to being watched and invaded, of course, is paranoia, the *feeling* of being compromised. The irony in *The Eye Creatures* is that everyone who thinks they are being compromised *is* being compromised, leading one to entertain the dark notion of paranoia as being not as far from reality as one might like to think. To paraphrase novelist Jack Kerouac, "Paranoia is reality; it is the nature of things." Even the title is more likely symbolic than literal. The "eye creatures" are those who watch, as well as the technologies which aid the watchers: cameras, televisions, spy satellites are all "eye creatures," designed exclusively for the watching of others.

To further erode the viewer's sense of well-being, the police are seen as being completely ineffectual, and unable to protect the community they are sworn to protect. The final insult to this shattered sense of community is the dark realization that the military is actively engaged in covering up and repressing events of historical import, and offering instead well-crafted lies that were heretofore considered only the harmless antics of the advertising industry. Indeed, Buchanan shines a most cynical eye on the woefully conspiratorial nature of the military-industrial complex in *The Eye Creatures*, going so far as to suggest that one of its primary societal goals is the ongoing suppression of truth.

Considering the pessimistic nature of the proceedings, it is not surprising to find *The Eye Creatures* a somewhat melancholy experience. The first Azalea telefilm to feature the music of Ronald Stein, many of the cues used in the film are of a mournful nature and add to a notable sense of loss and despair in the film. These music cues were all taken from previous film scores by Stein, including the film's prototype, *Saucer Men*, and others, including *It Conquered the World* and *The She-Creature*. The cinematography, by longtime Buchanan associate Robert Johnson, features many moody scenes shot in murky, dusk-lit woods. As convoluted as the interweaving occurrences in *The Eye Creatures* are, it is worth noting that the entire scenario unfolds in the space of about ten hours, a temporal feat Buchanan will perform again in *Mars Needs Women*.

As successful as *The Eye Creatures* is, TV viewers circa 1965 were likely not ready for a narrative film so ostensibly crude and threadbare nor one with more dark and troubling undertones. Yet other factors contributed to make the film resonate among fans of the genre. The years 1965 and 1966 witnessed an immense increase of reports of UFOs and "Flying Saucers" worldwide, but especially in America. Likewise, interest in paranormal phenomena such as extraterrestrial spacecraft increased manifold, leading to heated debate as to the relative truth behind these observations. Even illustrious astronomer Carl Sagan chimed in on the subject: "The possibility of life beyond the earth evokes today strong and partisan emotions."[3] Thus a "new" movie about flying saucers would be of interest to fans of the subject, as well as underlining society's current preoccupation with same. Regardless of one's position on this most controversial subject of alien life spying on planet earth, one can readily agree that the sightings of and belief in UFOs during this period of time reflected a deep disturbance in the American psyche. The flying saucers certainly represented our fear of a collective invasion of privacy, as well as the dread of being watched by sinister, otherworldly others. Whether true or fictious, this mass fear of being observed would likely be diagnosed by a psychologist as a textbook case of paranoia, surely a sign of psychic disturbance on a mass level. *The Eye Creatures* thus not only fueled the culture's appetite for pleasant and thrilling entertainment but also offered vivid illustrations of some of the dark psychological fears, and even darker political forces, which haunted American society at the time.

10

Zontar, the Thing from Venus

Larry Buchanan's second assignment picture for American International Television was *Zontar, the Thing from Venus* (1966, henceforth referred to as *Zontar*). Buchanan's unusual paraphrasing of Roger Corman's oppressive monster movie, *It Conquered the World* (1956), explores new vistas within the formulaic but flexible framework of B-movie structure. With *Zontar* Buchanan drew attention to himself as a filmmaker, offering to late-night television audiences some of the possibilities available to the clever micro-budget filmmaker.

Zontar's source film, *It Conquered the World* (henceforth referred to as *It*) is an impressive cold-war thriller, and prolific independent producer-director Corman gives the film a flawless Hollywood polish which belies the film's tight budget (approximately $100,000). Intended primarily as a "quickie" drive-in picture for the fledgling American International Pictures, *It* comes across as an accomplished and accessible film, due in no small part to an insightful screenplay by Lou Rusoff, itself a reworking of the screenplay for *The Day the Earth Stood Still* (1951, d: Robert Wise).

Creating a smothering, hopelessly paranoid universe, *It* focuses primarily on the political ramifications of the mass takeover of man by otherworldly socialist baddies. The Venusian creature who tries to take over the world using lurid polemic and mind control techniques works well as an adolescent's idea of the alien, vaguely demonic threat of the Soviet Union. Functioning both as simplistic political allegory and terrific pulp science-fiction thriller, the hour-long *It* unfolds at breakneck pace due to Rusoff's screenplay and Corman's efficacious pacing. The mournful score by composer Ronald Stein, some of which was also used in *Zontar*, adds much to the atmosphere of dread.

As to comparing the creatures themselves, It and Zontar, it is somewhat unfair to pit the two space demons against each other, as they were design projects born from different time periods, budgets and intended markets. *It* was, first and foremost, a monster movie for teenagers at the drive-in, so the monster had to be memorable, which it was, thanks to the brilliant design and construction skills of Paul Blaisdell. The Venusian in *It*, nicknamed "Beulah" by its creator, is a fanciful creation, very much influenced by the school of science-fiction artworks designed for pulp books and magazines, and with a hint of surrealism thrown in for good measure. The beast, alternately labeled a giant cucumber, carrot, or ice cream cone, is a weird, grimacing Moloch, with lobster claws, glowing eyes and bull horns, a true amalgam of various pulp-fiction nightmare creatures. Movie monsters of the 1950s often had a human face, and these creatures represented the disembodied rage of man himself, out of control in the nuclear age. Thus the drive-in screens of the late 1950s were haunted with grotesque animated vegetables, crustaceans, leeches, trees, rocks and other nonhuman objects, all with scowling mortal visages, appearing to the teenage audience perhaps like demented, angry authority figures or else the libido gone wild.

Zontar, on the other hand, is a simpler creature, seen more briefly than It. The reasons for this are not purely economical, although Zontar is not as handsome a creature as "Beulah." Zontar is meant not to be a monster per se, a dramatic focal point of the film, but a *dues ex machina* of events, a catalyst for conflict and change between the two protagonists. Zontar, the most complex creature design of any in the Azalea telefilms, is a humanoid demon looking somewhat like a giant bat, with a mottled, vaguely human face and large, enveloping wings. Zontar sports three eyes, the third eye an emblem of malevolent psychic ability. In terms of Zontar's figuring in the proceedings, one could also say that it looks like an angel of death, for this is largely the role it plays in the film.

Whereas Rusoff's screenplay for *It* ruminates more on paranoia, madness, and political aspects of the threat from the outside, Buchanan gives his screenplay an injection of high melodrama and eliminates everything which doesn't further the pivotal Socratic dialogue which is *Zontar*'s heart and soul. At some points a literal shot-by-shot remake, at others a wildly divergent "sketch" of the prototype, *Zontar* is a prime example of what a filmmaker can do with an existing property, honoring its essential message while creating something entirely unique.

The very notion of the movie remake suggests for the audience a unique, somewhat disorienting parallel universe experience, in which certain scenes and dialogue, as well as thematic constructs, seem familiar and yet not immediately identifiable. This creates a sense of déjà vu, not unpleasant but unsettling in that it cannot be specifically recalled. Buchanan took this sense of temporal and aesthetic disorientation and painted some interesting pastiches with it. In some cases, the Azalea remakes mimic the source material slavishly, reenacting dialogue and scenario with a literalness which borders on homage. At other junctures, Buchanan sketches the landscape broadly and lets the viewer wander far enough away from the original blueprint to experience the sense of wonder accomplished by expanding upon an aesthetic and thematic universe.

In *Zontar*, Buchanan takes the claustrophobic psychic landscape of *It Conquered the World* and distorts it just enough so that the events which transpire become mythic yet familiar. There is also a subtle but profound shift in location. *It* takes place in a Hollywood façade of postwar America, whereas *Zontar* takes place in small-town suburbia. This significant change in setting is one of the things which makes *Zontar* such an icon to the baby boomer generation.

The heart of *Zontar* is its Socratic dialectic between the two rocket scientist friends, Keith and Curt. A sensitive and emotional person, Keith's thesis is a well-intentioned but impulsive reading of events which leads him to fall into the emotional trap of "worshipping false idols." According to Keith, Man is a blithering idiot and a dangerous fool well on the way to destroying himself. Luckily, a wise and omnipotent super-being from the stars has contacted him and generously and gregariously offered to save Mankind from himself.

Cool and rational, Curt's antithesis is twofold. First, Man, although flawed, is capable of significant improvement, and more importantly can and must do this work himself. Second, if foreign entities actually do exist, a debatable proposition at the film's start, it is unlikely they want to help Mankind. It is more likely they want to exploit the species. *Zontar* also paints a melancholy picture of the impending end of middle-class America, the death of Suburbia, as triggered by the inherent ideological contradictions in modern man, his dangerous and unstable duality, made visible by the wildly shifting polarities of certain main characters, and their disastrous actions.

As in many of Buchanan's films, there is a central female figure who sacrifices herself in order for the community to be healed. This female, sketched lightly on the feminist model of the times, speaks her mind, demands a voice and, unable to manifest change through normal (read: patriarchal) channels, takes matters into her own hands and forges change through self-sacrifice. Finally, *Zontar* offers echoes of the major philosophic debate between the two main characters, with occurrences of bickering among couples, another dramatic archetype which places the drama squarely in a middle-class suburban setting.

Zontar starts off with a prologue in which a man and a woman in a bare-bones scientific installation argue over a stray airliner which has wandered into the flight path of a satellite about to be launched. Although the location is militaristic, the bickering man and woman already set the emotional space as middle-class America. Dr. Curt Taylor (John Agar) enters, worried, from a small anteroom, and wonders if things have gone awry. The aircraft is identified and Curt ruminates on the significance of this historic satellite launch. No sooner has he stated his thesis, the ascendancy of rational, technological man over the forces of nature, when his bubble is burst by a voice telling him that his friend, rocket scientist Keith Ritchie (Enrique Touceda III, as "Anthony Houston"), has come on a mission of "utmost urgency."

An agitated Curt returns to the small anteroom, where Keith paces nervously. The scene switches to the smaller room with the two men, and the camera changes angle completely, switching the left-right positions of the two main characters. Keith begins to speak. He warns Curt to halt the launch before it's too late. His antithesis to Curt's optimism maintains that man is puny and stupid and greater forces than he rule the universe. More specifically, he is certain that aliens from other worlds will do something to stop man from venturing into space. Curt counters that, although he is well aware of Keith's theories on the subject, he has never provided enough evidence of this alien threat to have it taken seriously.

The two geniuses argue back and forth, throwing thesis against antithesis in a Socratic dialogue which will stretch to the final frame of the film. Ritchie makes one final plea. Curt waits until the satellite has launched and states, "The problem has just become an academic question." Ritchie somberly replies, "For your generation, yes." Curt's disclaimer, "The problem has just become an academic question," appeared in *It*, whereas Keith's enigmatic reply, "For your generation, yes." is new to *Zontar,* suggesting that things taking place in the current time frame may well have ramifications far into the future. This opening sequence of *Zontar* is quite similar to that of *It* in terms of dialogue, but in *It* the two main characters are not placed together. They speak through a middleman, represented by military brass. In *Zontar*, Buchanan wisely cuts out the middleman, and puts Keith and Curt together to battle out their philosophical differences *mano a mano*, *Zontar* thus initiating the philosophic dialogue which is the film's centerpiece.

Over the credits, a rocket blasts off to the heavens, in grainy stock footage shot off a television screen. This clever use of a televised image, refilmed, gives *Zontar* an important abstraction. The self-reflexivity of the scene reminds the viewer he is watching a movie on TV, and also triggers a familiar memory of the time, as the watching of NASA space launches on television was a ubiquitous national pastime of the period. This narrative conceit places *Zontar* into an identifiable cultural setting and helps launch the ensuing narrative into the realm of mythic allegory.

The saucer-shaped satellite floats high above the earth. The scene shifts to Keith Ritchie's home, an attractive modern duplex nestled in the woods outside of town, placing *Zontar* in the very heart of Suburbia.

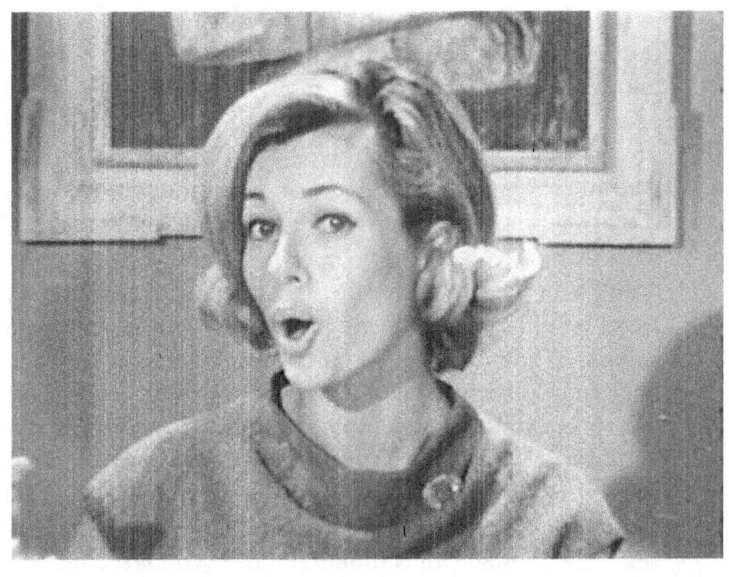

Martha Ritchie (Pat Delaney) is a bemused, self-deprecating prisoner of middle-class servitude in *Zontar, the Thing from Venus* until she learns to manifest her own power and thwart her oppressors, both human and nonhuman.

The Ritchies and the Taylors are finishing a nice dinner, sitting together at a small dining room table. Curt's wife, Ann (Susan Bjurman), asks Keith's wife, Martha (Patricia Delaney), if she baked the wonderful pie they just shared. Martha, who will prove to be the hero of *Zontar*, quips in self-deprecatory fashion, "Oh, sure, an old family recipe my grandmother sold to the bakery." While this line is borrowed intact from *It*, how Buchanan frames it in *Zontar* is different. While the question is being asked, the camera focuses on a primitive portrait of a woman. The camera pans down to Martha, who is the subject of the portrait. What is curious about this scene is that the woman in the painting *has no eyes*. Her eye sockets are vacant, making her inhuman, soulless. This is a chilling prophecy of Martha's destiny, a spooky portrait which reflects her martyred psyche. As Martha speaks, it is as if she is mourning not only her suburban laziness but the very loss of tradition the extended family entailed, a tradition lost in the sterile postwar community. There is also the suggestion of grief, perhaps for the loss of traditional women's skills, such as home baking. Suburbia, to the modern woman, is both sentence and prison, and Martha is merely one of an army of prisoners. Curt asks Keith why he seems so content and happy this evening, not his usual, agitated self; he quips, "You look like a man who's just inherited a major portion of the world!"[1] Against his wife's fervent pleading, Keith decides to reveal a secret to his friend. Keith has broken a sacred vow to his mate, and broken the social contract.

The subservient women clean the dinner dishes. Martha wears a blue dress, and Ann a red one, which seems fitting given their husband's political leanings, as Keith is the wide-eyed liberal and Curt the down-to-earth conservative. The two men wander across a sterile living room to a strange compilation of electronic equipment, hidden behind a folding screen. In *It* the radio set was nestled behind a curtain. In both cases the allusion to the false god standing behind the curtain in *The Wizard of Oz* (1939, d: Vincent Minelli), hiding behind a cheesy façade while barking out authoritarian orders, is clear. Keith turns on his special radio receiver and, soon, odd noises fill the room. Keith reveals that the strange noises are emanating from the planet Venus, a thought which Curt finds absurd. Keith presses the issue, asking Curt to listen carefully: "I don't mean the static. Can't you hear it? The other thing? Listen to it, Curt, listen to the voice!" Curt appears to strain to hear something, then he dismisses the notion. Keith confesses to Curt that he has been in contact with this "space voice" for "over two months" through some from of telepathy which he dubs "hyperspace hypnotism." Keith tries desperately here to have Curt "buy" his thesis, based on circumstantial evidence which Curt dismisses. What Keith has, and Curt lacks, is faith. While in some circles faith may be a good thing, it may more often that not lead one astray, promoting a tendency to overinterpret chance events.

It is significant that Zontar's voice, and his power, reach Man through a radio set in a suburban living room. It trivializes something as potentially revolutionary as alien intervention to the level of mere mass entertainment. Keith appears to virtually fetishize the squeaks coming out of the radio set. The seductive, curiously intimate notion of Zontar coaxing his disciple thus should not be overlooked. Yet the ultimate effect may be to abstract content and diminish importance, similar to the fate of the grisly newsreel footage of the wounded and dead in the Vietnam War shown nightly on television during this time period. In both cases, this "filtering" of information through a mass communications machine makes it easy for the experience to be abstracted, to seem unreal, and, most importantly, apolitical. Americans did not, until much later, take the bloody carnage seen on nightly TV seriously, and Keith Ritchie does not see the evil implications behind the seductive voice which speaks to him in soothing hums and whispers. It is easier to avoid the sinister implications of an eventuality if presented through a highly abstracted medium.

Curt mocks his friend, but Keith holds firm. He insists his Venusian "friend" has big plans for the planet Earth. Additionally, Keith states, "although his name is untranslatable into any known earth language, it would sound *something like* Zontar!" It seems that Zontar's name is intended to be more metaphorical than literal. Reminiscent of the biblical superstition, "Speak of the devil and he will appear," at the precise moment Keith murmurs the name to Curt in a kind of trance, the atmosphere of the film changes dramatically. A spooky musical cue, comprised of harpsichord, flute and bongos, punctuates that something creepy has just happened. The telephone rings, with the dread news that the satellite has disappeared.

The scene shifts, with the camera again reversing the positions of the main characters. With Curt and Keith, the "dominant" men looming in the foreground, Ann and Martha, the "little women" enter the frame, small and diminutive in the background, each wife close to their husband in the frame. The "conservative" Taylors now occupy the left side of the scene, the "liberal" Ritchies the right side. Perspective and loyalties have become thoroughly mixed up in this new, sinister reality. Curt now secretly fears the worst. The Taylors make a hasty exit. Keith, however, is in ecstasy. His god, false or not, has come to Earth.

Later, Keith plays elevator music on his reel-to-reel tape deck (a most ostentatious sign of suburban affluence), and tries to relax. Martha enters the room, and watches her husband from a distance. Soon Keith sees his wife and walks up to her. The two hold hands as Martha expresses her disappointment in Keith in betraying her and expressing his ideas, which she thinks are delusional. She pleads, "Please come out of it; please come back to

Keith Ritchie (Enrique Touceda III, as "Anthony Houston") is so obsessed with the promises of his false messiah in *Zontar, the Thing from Venus* he is blind to both the abundant physical charms of his wife (Pat Delaney) and her compelling emotional arguments. In short, he has become a religious nut, a slave to false dogma, slated for extinction.

me...." The couple embrace and kiss. The scene fades out with the impression that the two are going to make love, "make-up sex" being a last-ditch effort of a relationship on the rocks.

Some time later, Keith "speaks" with Zontar, and awaits further instructions. Martha enters, now dressed in a sexy yellow negligee, and implores her husband to join him in the bedroom. Keith, however, is obsessed with his new playmate. Martha pleads with Keith to give up this "fantasy" and be her lover, but Keith is adamant. He will stay by the radio all night, awaiting his master's orders. Summarily rejected by her husband, Martha covers her breasts in shame and slowly retreats to the loneliness of the marriage bed. By covering her breasts, Martha admits failure in utilizing sex as a tool (or weapon) to lure her husband back to the sanctity of their marriage. She is thus forced to evolve to another level to attain action, a level which involves increased participation on her part. But the act is also a symbolic death, as she crosses her hands over her chest like the pose of a corpse in repose.

The next morning Keith is dressed in a snazzy yellow blazer, which alludes to a yellow blanket given him by his wife the night before. He speaks to Zontar, who has arrived on Earth and is nestled in a nearby hot springs. Keith excitedly calls Martha, and tells her the "good" news. She, however, is horrified. His "mental illness" seems to be out of control, and she looks on aghast as he rants on. Martha runs off to do some shopping, fearing the alienation between her husband and her may be beyond repair. Martha will act, later on, in heroic fashion not only to save the world but also her marriage.

A montage follows, of trains stopping, phones going dead, machines not working, the electrical grid gone silent, the whole industrial world come to a baffling stop. This montage is structured in a similar vein to one in *It*. The halting of power, primarily its implications to transportation and supply, is an effective symbol for the loss of fuel energy, the lifeblood of Suburbia, instrumental to its existence. Without fossil fuels and its analogs, Suburbia is paralyzed.

Elsewhere, the Taylors are driving home when their car, too, mysteriously stops dead in its tracks. As Curt checks under the hood, Ann notices that both her watch and the car clock have halted at exactly the same moment, a curiosity if not an impossibility. The intuitive Ann protests, "I've got a premonition!" But rationalist Curt refuses to hear.

Back at the house, Keith gives Zontar the names of the townspeople who will need to be "controlled," including his friend Curt. The two discuss the Venusian's control devices, named "Injecta-Pods." The absurd name chosen for these control devices suggests a playful mockery of U.S. consumer culture, and its obsession with cheap gadgetry with silly names. During this shot, in which Keith willingly endangers members of his community as well as his friends, the camera moves around him, so that by the scene's end the viewer is literally looking at him from a completely different angle, seeing him "turn traitor," as it were.

The scene next shows Zontar, in several quick zoom shots, and an Injecta-Pod clinging childlike to one of the monster's immense wings. Zontar's horrible face stares at the camera with its hideous third eye. The citizens of Jackson evacuate on foot in near panic. This mini-apocalypse looks like home-movie footage of real people fleeing their homes in terror, a visceral and accessible document of the great American nightmare: invasion of the homeland. Keith runs through the panicked crowd, eventually finding Martha and taking her to their car, which still functions.

The Ritchies arrive home, and Keith tries to explain to Martha why they have power when no one else on earth does. To disprove his theory, Martha turns on the garden hose and threatens to squirt him with it in an elemental switching of sexual roles. The Taylors eventually arrive at the Ritchies' house, and, they all relax with a drink. Curt grills Keith about the day's events, but Keith beseeches him to be patient, assuring him that "There will be ample time for explanations, perhaps time even for understanding...." Keith utters this line directly to the camera, almost smiling as he says it, in an effort to engage the audience.

The next scene, a striking visual non sequitor, shows a picture of a sexy pinup girl floating disembodied in space. The effect is somewhat disorienting. The audience's understanding of events is rendered impotent, for emphasis now shifts to the military, specifically to the enlisted man. The bored sentry at the tracking station is looking at the girly picture in a peepshow viewer when a scientist from the tracking station comes out to chat and report that things are still "snafu" inside. As in *It*, the military in *Zontar* is depicted entirely as comic relief and the "enlisted man" is painted as little more than a good-hearted ignoramus. The audience suddenly understands why a crafty Venusian could come to Earth and take it over so easily. Mankind, by and large, is idiotic and easily duped. The military especially seems prone to ignorance and error.

Back at the Ritchies, Keith patiently explains to his friends what's been happening. Curt still refuses to believe and challenges Keith: if this fantastic story is true, why isn't Keith fighting it? Having been thus challenged to defend his very thesis, Keith explains himself, in a most revealing close-up. Facing stage left, Keith speaks to Curt as he defends his actions. He then turns and faces in the opposite direction, stage right, as he speaks to the women. To them, he boasts in self-congratulatory fashion about how brilliant he was to manifest an encounter with this creature-savior: "I was his first contact, and I contacted him!" Suddenly turning somber again, Keith then turns back to Curt and continues about the selfless aspects of this other-worldly adventure: "I believe he's here to save us from ourselves, not to dominate us, as you have so quickly concluded."

What this scene offers is a vivid sketch of the two faces of man. On the one hand, there is the higher self, the spiritual one of lofty goals and altruistic purposes, the self he is proud to share with his intellectual peers. On the other hand is the ego-fueled, lower, animal self, whose highest goal is to conquer, feel important, and impress those whom he covets or desires. These two selves, constantly warring with each other, are what make up the complex and usually neurotic modern man, a creature whose highest ambitions are often clouded and thwarted by his baser lusts and animal drives. This also well describes Janus, the Roman god of mythology, whose two faces staring in opposite directions represent the dichtomy between the savage and the civilized.

Later, Ann and Curt discuss the possibility that Keith's wild assertions might be correct. The sensitive, intuitive Ann seems to be convinced, but Curt valiantly, even doggedly, recites his rationalist theory to her. He has been so badly miked in this scene, however, that his words are virtually unintelligible. At times, his voice is a mere whisper. His argument, therefore, is literally weak and without power. Faced with a new, horrific reality, Curt is starting to lose his intellectual nerve.

At the Ritchies, Keith receives new orders from Zontar, who commands his flunky to sit tight and wait for further orders. The disciple responds reverently, "It will be done," alluding to the Lord's Prayer ("Thy will be done"). Keith is obviously in the throes of a religious hysteria. Meanwhile, a distraught Curt runs into town to find some answers, leaving his wife alone at home. This mistake on the part of realist Curt is emphasized by a slow zoom into Ann's forlorn face as she now faces the world alone.

Elsewhere, a military group walks through the woods on a forced march. An Injecta-Pod flies overhead and one of the soldiers declares, "I saw a funny-lookin' bird!" His superior officer ignores the comment, marking yet another missed opportunity for the military to take charge of the situation, and be proactive in service to the community.

Curt returns home and grabs his bike. He tells Ann to stay home, but she begs him to stay. Curt leaves anyway, leaving his vulnerable mate alone once again. When Curt abandons his wife the second time, against her pleading, he commits his only real sin in the film and it is a sin of ignorance. Still, he suffers for it, for his innocent wife is now an unprotected target for Evil.

The community's authority figures are soon all under Zontar's control. Keith stands alone on his balcony, binoculars in hand, hoping to spot an Injecta-Pod, some visual verification of his increasing dementia. He describes the creatures to a disgusted Martha, who asks, "How do they control the victim?" Unsurprisingly, emotions must be removed from people in order for this new society to function without greed or hate or love, exactly the "mass society" which observers had long warned about arising from the Suburban phenomenon. Keith takes Martha in his arms, and Martha asks why he is holding her. He exclaims, somewhat surprised, "Why? Because I love you!" Martha corrects him: "But love is an emotion!" Keith still will not understand. He storms off, perturbed by his wife's intellectual courage and emotional fervor.

Curt pedals to the tracking station on his bicycle, looking small and helpless, rendered very much a child by his "loss of power." He is met at the gate by General Young (Neil Fletcher), who offers to take him back home in a jeep. Curt spots a control device clinging to Young's neck, and understands that he has been controlled. He knocks him out and takes the jeep. Curt races to Keith's house and expresses anger for allowing this awful thing to happen. The two hash out their differences and attempt a workable synthesis of their antithetical philosophies. Keith insists that Zontar must be good, because he is so smart and omnipotent. Intelligence and power cannot be evil, according to Keith's underachiever worldview. Curt reminds him that this benevolent "master" of Keith's has caused untold havoc, including over a dozen murders, in his attempt to "rescue" mankind. Keith is nonplussed, suggesting to Curt that history proves that human evolution is not pretty. Curt counters that the changes he speaks of were made *for* humans *by* humans. Assistance from another being changes the equation entirely. Curt also reminds his deluded pal that revolutions, plagues and wars have also resulted in a number of regressions, suggesting that violent overthrow in itself offers nothing of value. This dialogue frames a consistent assertion in the films of Larry Buchanan, that history is a living and mercurial thing and must be constantly challenged and revised. It is painfully easy to take a piece of the historical record out of context and use it for one's current agenda. An objective, far-reaching view of history is needed in order to use it wisely. Curt rises, indignant: "And you actually think I condone this reign of terror?" Keith is moved, but cannot change his opinion. An enraged Curt leaves, calling Keith "the most diabolical traitor of all time!"

Martha enters, informing Keith that Curt had a gun and had intended to shoot him. Keith is disturbed by this news, the first time his fantasy revolution has threatened his personal world. His thesis is not holding up to reality. Keith takes Martha in his arms and mutters unconvincingly, "Don't worry — we know what we're doing." Zontar calls for his assistant, and Keith obediently runs to the radio, leaving the forlorn Martha clutching her breast. The disoriented Keith finds the courage to tell his master, "Zontar, I'm troubled. I must see you." The alien puts him off. Keith insists that Curt must be controlled. He wants to keep his friend, apparently at all costs. Still intellectually naive, Keith desperately desires to save Curt, that is, incorporate his friend-as-antithesis into Keith's shaky thesis.

Curt returns home to a dark living room. Ann walks in, her hands hidden behind her back. She asks coyly, "Guess what I've got?" and unleashes an Injecta-Pod to chase Curt around the room. Ann leaves the house to take a walk. Curt manages to fight off the winged monster with a fire poker in one hand and a lit cigarette in the other. He spears the beast, and the phone rings. Zontar has instantly communicated to Keith that Curt has disabled the last control device. Keith requests Curt's presence. Curt picks up a gun, saying he will be over after he "takes care of something." Ann returns and, assuming her husband to now be under Zontar's control, tells him that they must wait for orders to take over the world. Curt asks his wife, "And we'll be like this always?" As she murmurs yes, Curt shoots his wife. This apparently cold-blooded murder was necessary because Curt knows at a logical level what Martha and others have intuited and what Keith seems unable to grasp. Life without emotion is slavery, a living death not worth preserving. Mass society, perhaps enticing on paper, falls apart in the testing ground of individual human needs.

Soon night has fallen, and the soldiers rest, looking for "suspicious activity." The sentry reminds his sergeant that he "seen a funny-looking bird" earlier, but the officer merely corrects his bad grammar. Protocol being more important than activity in the military, the momentous incident goes unreported, reinforcing the tenet that the armed forces are at best ineffective and at worst obstructionist. As in other scenes featuring the military, characters speak with their backs to the viewer, obscuring clear communication and suggesting secrets and duplicity.

At the Ritchies, Martha follows Keith around, enraged at his irresponsible behavior. She ridicules Keith's childlike loyalty to his demon-god. Martha insists that his "god" must be both a coward and a charlatan: "Hiding in a cave, away from the light? Earth must be of no use to him except for a place of conquest!" Brainwashed completely by Zontar's religious dogma, Keith mutters, "I must have the courage of my convictions." Yet Martha sees clearly the flaws of Keith's thesis. She runs to the radio set and calls Zontar the manipulating coward that he really is. She promises to kill him. As in many Buchanan films, patriarchal society fails and a visionary female must intervene, even at her own peril, to correct things.

Curt drives to the Ritchies to confront Keith. Martha sneaks out unseen, taking a revolver. She steals Curt's car and races off to confront the evil Venusian. Curt pleads with Keith to destroy the monster, and clarifies the inherent contradiction in Keith's thesis: this "savior," who wants to rescue Mankind from doom by removing all of the supposedly "negative" emotions, was able to lure Keith as a satellite only by exploiting his own "positive" emotions of pride and altruism. This suggests at least hypocrisy, and likely duplicity. Keith, still possessing the rudiments of an open mind, is visibly moved by this glaring example of flawed logic.

As the two men argue, Martha races toward her destiny, willing to sacrifice her safety to save her husband from this deadly philosophy, and her community from this deadly surrogate father figure. Nearby, the soldiers hear the car and ponder its significance, as all vehicles have been disabled by Zontar. Meanwhile, Curt keeps chipping away at Keith's fatal delusion by painting the demigod as the crafty, manipulating creature he really is. Through astute cross-cutting, Martha and Keith approach their destinies simultaneously.

Curt pulls a gun on Keith and threatens to kill him. Martha walks through the dank caverns of the hot springs, spies the horrible Zontar, and screams. As the radio set is on, Curt and Keith hear Martha's scream. Martha tries to escape, but Zontar sneaks up behind her. Martha unleashes her feminist rage on the father-beast: "Zontar, you're slimy! Horrible!" Martha shoots, but the revolver jams, and Zontar kills the brave martyr. At Martha's death scream, Keith sighs, "Oh, Lord!" His god is now revealed to be a demon. Keith shows Curt a recent invention, a laser beam gun which may well be able to destroy Zontar.

Curt arrives at the tracking station just as the possessed General and technicians finalize their plans to assassinate the President with a briefcase full of explosives. The death throes of Suburbia threatens to bleed out into the world, to engulf whole nations. Curt shoots all three of Zontar's zombies. Elsewhere, the Sergeant decides that he'd better investigate the caverns after all, and sends some men into the caves. Keith is stopped by the Sheriff on the road to the hot springs, and destroys him with his laser gun. Keith continues his journey on foot, and reaches the caves along with the military. Keith runs through the caves, and eventually faces the horrible face of his master. Keith tells Zontar how wrong he was to trust him, and moves forward to destroy him with the laser gun. As he does, Zontar opens his immense, angel-like wings, embraces his misguided disciple, and both of them die together.

Zontar ends in a revelatory coda. From a distance, Curt runs towards the Sergeant. Curt and the Sergeant next enter a scene in close-up, their positions reversed. Curt, as a character, has come full circle. The Sergeant tells Curt that Keith and his wife are dead and ponders, "He acted like he knew that thing." Curt articulates the hard-won synthesis derived from his life-changing encounter, in a touching soliloquy to his fallen friend:

> Keith Ritchie came to realize, at the loss of his own life, that man is the greatest creature in the universe. He learned that a measure of perfection can only be slowly attained, from within ourselves. He sought a different path, and found death, fire, disillusionment, loss. War, misery and suffering have always been with us, and we shall always try to overcome them. But the answer is to be found from within, not from without. It must come from learning. It must come from the very heart of man himself.

The speech is punctuated by shots of the satellite launch, the dead sheriff, the dead Martha, a revolver, and a burning car, a simple collage of Suburbia, postmortem. Finally, the camera focuses on the dead traitor-general in the rocket lab, then pans up to an electric arc generator commonly known as a "Jacob's Ladder," which generates a dancing, ever-ascending spark between its two poles, a spark which rises towards the very heavens themselves. The End.

Zontar has much to teach. Man's evolution is best given over neither to rash superstition nor cold rationalism but to a learned, compassionate humanism, which can best embrace and balance the awesome potentials of both human heart and human mind. It isn't the one "pole" or the other, the one person, philosophy or perspective which owns the truth of existence. The truth is the brilliant, mercurial, empowering tension that jumps endlessly between two opposing energies. The secret of *Zontar*, like the secret of the universe itself, is the life-giving energy generated by opposites, the very heart of this Socratic dialectic turned Hegelian, as well as the enduring spiritual principle of Yin and

General Young (Neil Fletcher) serves his current evil master, Zontar, as unthinkingly as he served his former evil master, the military-industrial complex.

Yang. *Zontar* is essentially a treatise about the attraction of opposites, the debate between opposing theories, the antagonistic dualities within man, and the awesome power of this creative fission, a power with the potential to either heal or destroy. This is played out in two basic scenarios, the first being the ongoing debate between Keith and Curt. The ongoing tension between the two men and their wives, what might be loosely termed domestic quarrels, makes up the counterpoint to this primary thrust. If Buchanan can be accused of applying heterosexual "couple logic" to many of his film tracts, in *Zontar* that logic is distorted and shattered beyond repair.

To augment this obsession with opposites, *Zontar* contains several dizzying 180-degree flips in perspective, in which characters switch places without rhyme or reason. In this chronic shifting of polarity, dramatic focus changes radically and tends to momentarily disorient the viewer. Thus, a key theme in Zontar is the notion of relativism, as illustrated by a frequent change in visual perspective. Arguments subtly switch emphasis as reality itself undergoes chaotic metamorphosis. Reversing the cardinal "Director's Line of Sight" intentionally in dramatic sequences serves at least two purposes. It signals a major shift in dramatic emphasis, and also makes an aesthetic statement, tagging the film as structurally revisionist, making everything from point of view to the character's perspective open to reinterpretation.

Curt's claim that "Man is the greatest creature in the universe" at first seems an arrogant, egotistical boast, implying that Man is the *best* creature in the universe. But rather, *Zontar* suggests that Man is the *most powerful* creature in the universe. There is no one above him in an evolutionary sense. Man has only himself to lean on, and it is his intelligence *and* emotions, working together, which makes Man redeemable. The implication is clear: *there are no gods*. Man is alone in the universe, completely responsible for his own fate. This atheistic claim at first seems a contradiction, as *Zontar* seemed in some sense a spiritual parable. Yet the spiritual journey is the journey within, to discover the potential of Man when he draws from the vast resources contained within himself. The perilous and doomed spiritual quest is one which leads outward, one which depends on outside forces to dictate one's actions. To Buchanan, the constrictive and unyielding dogma of organized religion always leads one astray, oftimes to disastrous results.

Zontar is hard on religion, and with good reason. Buchanan saw organized religion as a threat and a danger to the free-thinking spirit of Man. Dogma is death to Buchanan, a theme which turns up in a majority of his films. Buchanan's idea of religion turns well-meaning men, even men of valor and brilliance, into drooling, homicidal idiots. Only men can solve Man's dilemma; no supernatural beings will help us. Indeed, any self-proclaimed "gods" who seek to help are evil. The title offers another clue; *Zontar, the Thing from Venus*, sounds less like satire, more like mockery of science-fiction titles, meant to ridicule, not elevate its subject. In line with the film's overriding religious metaphor, the title may be a subtle mockery of Christianity, along the lines of "Jesus, the Thing from Heaven" or "Satan, the False Messiah."

During its initial run on late-night TV in the late 1960s and early 1970s, *Zontar* developed a sizable cult following, and was, according to Buchanan's own observations, popular among college students who were studying the hard sciences or theology. This is understandable when one considers the film's endearing fixation on both subjects. If *Zontar* is little more than a cheap monster movie, it is assuredly a thinking man's cheap monster movie, its deep intellectual base making it accessible to many segments of an audience.

Zontar, the Thing from Venus is a masterpiece of budgetary creature design by Jack Bennett, evoking the Christian "Angel of Death."

In spite of the film's stark histrionics and lurid undercurrent, the overriding mood in *Zontar* is one of melancholia. The viewer is constantly aware that something is dying (Suburbia and intellectual naiveté) and that something unhealthy threatens to take its place. This indelible mood of despair is greatly augmented by the music score, largely comprised of reused cues from earlier scores of composer Ronald Stein.

Anthony Houston is powerful as Keith Ritchie. Utilizing overwrought histrionics as an aid to characterization, Houston's portrayal of the alternately deranged and charismatic scientist deftly expresses the warring elements within Man. Ostensibly a scientist, Keith falters when he resorts to faith over reason. His faith is well intentioned but ill advised, the result of faulty reason. His "worship" of the god-figure Zontar is decidedly irrational. As Zontar's slave and flunky, Keith becomes a pathetic, tragic figure. He has succumbed to evil due to unchallenged naiveté. Keith is the failed romantic, the Utopian thinker who is blind to reality. Significantly, Zontar is portrayed entirely through the mouthpiece of Keith, his ardent fan. All communication regarding Zontar comes in the form of translated messages spouted by Keith. One might intuit that Keith has some megalomania lying dormant, and is abetting this ally in some part to fulfill his own dreams of world conquest.

Houston's eventual wife, Patricia Delaney, is also powerful as Martha Ritchie. Martha well embodies the middle-class wife of the day, an amalgam of fierce independence, largely repressed, and dutiful devotion to a troubled man. Her struggles against her husband's deadly delusions are mythic, and her eventual sacrifice, so common in the films of Larry Buchanan, is not merely a gift to old, patriarchal gods, but a selfless offering of love to a wounded community in the throes of painful but emancipating evolution.

11

Curse of the Swamp Creature

After completing two remakes, *The Eye Creatures* and *Zontar, the Thing from Venus*, Buchanan tackled an original production which adhered to B-movie tradition while injecting doses of topical social commentary. *Curse of the Swamp Creature* (1966), the third Azalea telefilm, melds two horror-film genres. Firstly, a "mad doctor" attempts to create ungodly life and is punished by forces both natural and supernatural. Secondly, a community of blacks use occult ritual to protect their community from evil. In these plot templates, *Curse of the Swamp Creature* (henceforth referred to as *Swamp Creature*) owes something to previous genre films, most significantly the Halperin brothers' *White Zombie* (1932). Several basic plot elements of *Swamp Creature* are remarkably similar to those of *White Zombie*, although it would be unfair to call *Swamp Creature* a remake of the previous film. Likewise, although *Swamp Creature* boasts certain similarities to an AIP drive-in picture of the previous decade, *Voodoo Woman* (1957, d: Edward L. Cahn), the differences overshadow any superficial comparison.

In *Swamp Creature*, Buchanan changes his setting to contemporary Louisiana. The main theme in *Swamp Creature* is White Evil, as embodied by Science. The mad doctor in *Swamp Creature* lords over a microcosmic patriarchy, an abusive male-dominated power structure which enslaves and abuses its members until they rise up and revolt for their freedoms. *Swamp Creature* simultaneously champions black empowerment and female emancipation, two key social movements of the day, continuing the racially progressive agenda Buchanan addressed in *Free, White and 21* (1963) and *High Yellow* (1965).

Swamp Creature opens with a brutal prologue. A doctor, Simon Trent (well played by Jeff Alexander), yells to a creature shown only by a scaly monster hand convulsing in a mist-filled vat. Trent shouts "Breathe! Breathe! Live!" to the hand, in a desperate attempt to impart life to the monstrous thing. The attempt fails, as Trent carries a sheet-covered corpse to an enclosed pool of alligators and tosses the failed experiment into the milky water, where the reptiles devour it. Disappointed at this failure to create life, i.e., "procreate," Trent trudges towards his plantation-like mansion when a young black man runs up to him and demands, "I'm looking for my brother!" In this highly metaphorical statement, the black is asking the white where lies their mutual bond, their commonality, their hope for progress as men of good faith. Ignoring the youth, Trent is attacked by the distraught young man until another, older black man named Valjean intervenes and stabs the younger man to death in order to protect his white master. Trent sneers, "You want to join your brother? You shall!" Trent orders Valjean to feed the youth to the alligators, a racist allusion to non-whites being closer to the "lower" animal kingdom than whites. A close-up of Trent which follows depicts him to be a stereotypical, almost caricaturist, "egghead" scientist. With his large, virtually bald head, high forehead, pasty skin, pouty childlike facial features and comically oversized glasses, Trent represents white power as somewhat farcical but nonetheless deadly, like a monstrously overgrown infant. Trent rants on to Valjean, "Keep all strangers out of my swamp!" He thus reinforces the selfish, childish (and entirely patriarchal) illusion that this is *his* land, *his* kingdom, *his* world, over which he desires complete control.

The opening credits unfold over a slow zoom into an angry-faced totem pole in a jungle-like setting, implying that the story will unfold in a most brutal human jungle, one still haunted by fear and superstition. The scene changes to a dingy rural hotel called the "Fly-N-Fish," a popular tourist destination on the Louisiana/Texas border, which gets its coy name from the small airstrip which leads to the front door. Inside the dismal bar, a geologist named Driscoll West (Bill Thurman) enjoys a late afternoon drink. A woman, Brenda Simmons (Shirley McLine), enters and flirts with West, shamelessly pumping him for information. West reveals that he is in the oil business. A young man, Ritchie (Cal Duggan), enters the bar but gets nonverbal signals from both Brenda and the bartender, Frenchie (Roger Ready), and leaves suddenly, revealing the universe of the Fly-N-Fish to be entirely conspiratorial. Ritchie enters what is presumably West's hotel room, carrying the theme of invasion of privacy over from *The Eye Creatures*, and snoops around. He finds an attaché case and rummages through it, looking for secrets hidden within another fabled American "dead space," the faceless hotel room. At the bar, West is about to retire but is detained briefly by Frenchie with the lure of a complimentary drink. West becomes suspicious and heads back to his room. Entering, West sees Ritchie pilfering through his documents. A fight ensues and West knocks the youth unconscious. As West prepares to pick him up, Ritchie jumps the older man and stabs him to death with a knife, painting rural America as a brutal, amoral environment where justice and compassion are absent.

Ritchie, Brenda and Frenchie gather in the room and discuss their fate. This lawless gang frets not over their actions but on how to effectively obscure them, in true conspiratorial fashion. It is revealed that West was expecting another geologist named Rogers, soon to arrive. Brenda decides to play the role of "Mrs. West" in a desperate attempt to fool the approaching visitor. They enlist the aid of another local, "Rabbit," and use his stump-cutting machine to get rid of the body. West's corpse is unceremoniously dumped in the nearby swamp, where the horrible cutting machine, with its giant, claw-like blades, does its grisly work, looking very much like a monstrous metal alligator devouring its prey. It is also revealed at this point that Brenda and Ritchie are a couple, a fact which makes her liaisons with Frenchie, West, and soon Rogers all the more suspect.

Soon a small airplane arrives at the Fly-N-Fish, and Barry Rogers (John Agar) disembarks. Rogers registers at the hotel, speaking briefly with the desk clerk (Anne MacAdams). Rogers enters the bar, and Frenchie informs his partners that their new "mark" has arrived. Frenchie introduces himself to Rogers and explains the duplicitous mix-up with the Wests. Rogers is puzzled, but accepts the woman as his companion for the upcoming surveying trip. In the hotel office, Brenda introduces herself to Rogers as "Mrs. West." The two make plans for the next morning and Rogers retires. Brenda and Frenchie go over their dastardly plans again, and reveal that they, too, are lovers, suggesting that this triad harbors conspiracies within conspiracies, and enemies within their own ranks. The two coldly agree to "take care of" Ritchie after he has finished serving them by helping steal the oil secrets from Rogers (whom they presumably plan to kill as well). *Swamp Creature* takes place in a completely corrupt universe, and Brenda is a particularly amoral woman, a character type not frequently seen in the films of Buchanan. She solicits romantic exchanges with four males in order to further her own greedy agenda. She is unable to relate to the fifth power figure, Dr. Trent, only because he is impotent, too far gone to be considered a virile male.

Next morning, Rogers and "Mrs. West" head out into the dismal swamps with Robbie and Ritchie. Via an evocative montage of the swamp, laced with effective lap dissolves, the film enters a primeval, dangerous world. Buchanan filmed these striking scenes in the swampy Caddo Lake area on the border of Louisiana and Texas, an area used as the backdrop for his aborted pet project, *Swamp Rose*, released as *Common Law Wife*. The use of swamplands as the primary setting in this woeful tale of greed, savagery and homicide nicely mirrors the sense of devolution, of narrative and psychological regression to a former, prehistoric world previous to any social contract, where brute force rules the day. The scene changes to show a young black girl running into a dilapidated house and informing a young black man of the approach of strangers. The young man runs to a kettle drum and starts to beat a rhythmic communication to his peers. Elsewhere, the white entourage continues on their way, clearly unsettled by the sound of the "native" drums, another sign that they are entering savage territory.

Evil egghead Simon Trent (Jeff Alexander) pouts like a small child when he doesn't get his way in his little kingdom specializing in racial and sexual slavery in the angry *Curse of the Swamp Creature.*

The scene changes to Dr. Trent's mansion and his pool, where hungry alligators lie in wait for their next meal. Trent and his assistant, Tom (Enrique Touceda III as "Anthony Houston"), walk to the pool and continue an argument begun earlier over ethical considerations, while Trent throws fish to the 'gators. It is revealed that Trent is using human subjects for his unorthodox medical experiments, which Tom finds highly objectionable. Trent professes to welcome Tom's questioning, but there is a look of pure malice on Trent's face as he tosses more food to his "pets." Trent closes the discussion by didactically stating,

"The best study of *man* is man himself," but Tom is unmoved. Trent orders his subordinate to continue as dictated, and Tom reluctantly agrees. Trent adds threateningly, "I'm the one who says if someone has had enough," over an extreme close-up of an alligator's mouth chewing food. Trent assuredly fancies himself the totalitarian ruler of his little domain, where associates are treated more as slaves than peers. Sadly, Tom acquiesces to this brazen dictate and retreats silently. Trent then intones, "Tom, I can see that this work is going to be too much for you." Trent looks down at his alligators and then up at the canopy above him. He notices a tiny salamander walking across the covering, and smiles sinisterly at the vulnerable reptile. This battle of ethics has been won, as in the jungle, not by logic or compassion or negotiation but by brute force. This is the hierarchy of patriarchal systems, in which the "boss" can tell the "employee" what to do, even if it is objectionable. The subordinate can either obey or quit. He cannot negotiate with his superior, illustrating one of the fatal flaws of labor's relationship with management in any capitalistic economic structure, a structure which still has many of the punitive, restrictive aspects of the "slave/master" relationship of yore. As Trent's argument becomes more bitter, scenes of alligators eating raw fish-flesh become more vivid and bloody, as Buchanan playfully suggests that bosses, rulers, kings and governments are essentially reptiles in cheap suits, and their workers mere bait for their insatiable gullets.

Trent's bouncer, Valjean, reenters, and informs his white master that strangers are approaching. Meanwhile, Rogers' group finally goes as far as they can by boat. They continue their fateful trek into the swamp by foot. The scene dissolves into an idyllic wooded landscape, which turns out to be a painting hung on a wall. The camera zooms back to reveal a beautiful young woman (Francine York) sitting on a couch and reading a book. Trent enters the room, as a ceiling fan swirls menacingly overhead. Trent tells the young woman, apparently his wife, about the impending visitors. The woman seems excited about the possibility of having visitors, as she has seen "no one for so long." She seems lonely and depressed. Trent threatens his wife to keep their troubled relationship a secret should visitors arrive. The deferential woman reluctantly agrees. The painting of the outside world is the sad woman's only window to this world. She is a prisoner of her husband, a tragic heroine of the old school, and one of Buchanan's iconic New Age females struggling to escape abusive patriarchal bonds.

Trent meets Tom in the lab, where the assistant has just completed a successful gill transplant. Tom ruminates on how Trent could win worldwide acclaim with his work on mutating alligators into prehistoric fish, but Trent is unimpressed: "Acclaim? that's nothing! To create life, to move it at will up and down the evolutionary scale, that's something! Something I don't think you appreciate, Tom...." Trent sends Tom away, and starts to bark commands to the thing in the tank: "Awake! The sound of my voice is your master! Get up! The world awaits you as my first citizen!" The thing expires, however, and Trent is shattered. Trent desires to create life solely in order to rule the world. He, like all other megalomaniacs, seeks immortality through the ruling of kingdoms. He wants personal offspring at his command. The allusion to sexual impotence here is clear. Unable to relate emotionally or physically to his beautiful wife, Trent seeks to procreate via artificial means, to achieve a legacy through the cold, loveless promise of science.

At the lab, Trent has diagnosed the reason his artificial progeny keep dying: "acute congestion" (an allusion to "acute emotional repression"). Trent dumps the failed surrogate child into the alligator pool, then prepares a hypodermic needle and injects assistant Tom while the poor man sleeps. This truly "mad" doctor is so desperate for someone to carry on his evil seed he will risk the lives of even his most trusted associates. Trent carries Tom's drugged body into the lab, cradling it as one would a child. He injects him with the evolutionary serum and places the body in the methane pool, which Trent uses as an artificial womb-chamber, his wife being off-limits.

At Trent's house, Valjean warns his master that the local citizens are becoming upset about recent disappearances. The father of the young man whom Valjean murdered asks Trent for the whereabouts of his missing son. Trent lies and insists he has never seen him, but the old man knows better: "We are poor, but not blind in the swamps." The old man leaves, and Trent chastises Valjean for the unpleasantness. Trent returns inside as Valjean grimaces and spits on the ground. Rebellion is brewing in this rapidly imploding patriarchy, and Trent's abused "right-hand man" will figure prominently in the empire's swift decline. The father of the murdered youth stops at the edge of Trent's property and sets up a primitive religious altar, presumably for future occult-oriented activities against this evil overlord. Albeit through primitive means, the shattered and abused community is finally addressing their own empowerment, beginning to take matters into their own hands to reject their corrupt rule and save their community from this despot.

Later, Trent's wife sneaks into her husband's laboratory, for she has had enough of his deceit and secrecy. She stares into the methane tank, into the horrible mechanical womb her husband has fashioned in her emotional/sexual absence, and is horrified to see the comatose body of Tom floating in the murky liquid, like a drowned infant. The woman screams, which brings Trent running. Trent browbeats his wife as Valjean assaults a guard named Tracker, whose duty is to guard the lab. Trent leads his wife into her tiny bedroom and they argue. Trent insists that Tom is not dead and that he volunteered for "the final experiment," but his wife is no longer fooled by his feeble lies. As Trent argues, the viewer sees two images of the evil man, one in the room and one in the mirror, a simple but effective illustration of split personality. Trent slaps his wife, who challenges him to kill her, but Trent says he

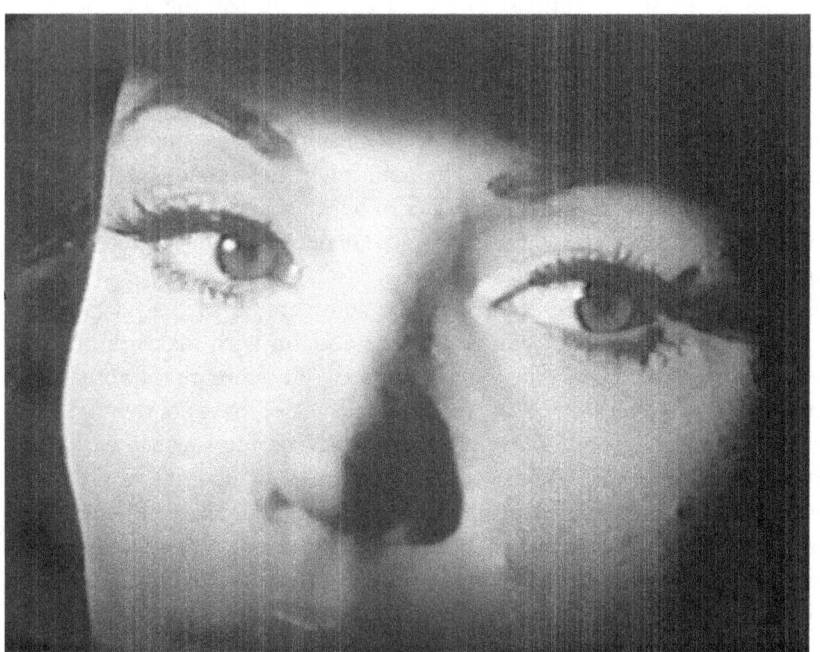

Clinically depressed Mrs. Trent (Francine York) waits passively in a closet, prisoner of her evil husband; the audience won't even learn her name until the final moments of her enslavement, in the brutal *Curse of the Swamp Creature*.

has other plans and leaves the abused woman locked in her cell. Mrs. Trent is a seriously depressed, repressed and neglected wife in a loveless marriage to an evil, bullying male, the prototypical pre-feminist which Betty Friedan outlined in *The Feminine Mystique*. She is a veritable prisoner of her rural Suburbia, a domestic environment seen by some as an elaborate, coded prison system of entrenched postwar American patriarchy. A classic non-self, Mrs. Trent will not even have her own name until the final moments of the film.

Valjean returns with Tracker, turning him over to the rages of his white master. Valjean runs through the swamp until he reaches his village. He instructs Mora, the young black girl seen earlier, to prepare the others, saying, "It is time, time for gathering." Valjean, ostensibly the flunky to white master Trent, turns out to be a pivotal figure in the unraveling of Trent's evil empire, and thus fits well into the historical archetype of a ruler's "right-hand man," a significant power figure who often manifests his boss's overthrow even as he pretends to be his fiercest advocate. Mora, apparently deaf, answers Valjean in sign language and runs off to warn the community. It is significant that Buchanan creates with Mora a character who would traditionally wield very little power in any male-dominated community (a poor, disabled minority female) and uses her as a central power figure in the proceedings against the corrupt phallocentric system in which she and her neighbors have been held as economic and emotional prisoners.

Trent returns to the lab, and speaks with the mutated Tom-creature, who apparently can still hear him. Trent prattles on about Tom's great contribution to science, and then gives the poor assistant his supper: a live turtle. As the viewer hears horrible crunching noises, Trent looks down at his ungodly creation with true compassion, as if looking down upon a newborn infant's angelic face as he sleeps in a crib. A quick shot of Trent's gloved hand passing the wriggling reptile to the waiting creature hand aptly punctuates the sad devolutionary aspect of these two characters, as they sink together into psychological and genetic states of true despair.

Elsewhere, Tracker guards the room where Mrs. Trent is held prisoner. The woman pleads with the guard to help her escape, but Trent enters and orders the guard to locate the intruders. When Tracker leaves, Trent speaks tenderly to his wife through the emotional barrier of the door, promising her that "Everything will be much better, very soon." Tracker soon finds the travelers, and escorts them to Trent's house. Inside, Trent prepares to move Tom, his "indestructible fish-man," from the womb-machine, all the while instructing Tom on his duties to his "father." Trent twice intones, "Obedience is the key to survival," a phrase which could serve as the motto for any patriarchal or totalitarian regime in history.

Soon Rogers and company sit in relative splendor in Trent's living room, pondering why a successful man would isolate himself in the middle of a creepy jungle. Trent enters and introductions are made. Rogers reveals the expedition's goal, to find surface indications of oil reserves in the area. Trent comments, "You're looking for the results of the evolutionary process, and I'm investigating the evolutionary process." Trent brings up the subject of his wife, another mute subject in his banana republic, and prepares the visitors for her imminent arrival by stating, "She's not well. She contracted a fever in the tropics which she never quite recovered from," a feeble attempt to explain away her depression. Trent invites the group to stay overnight, offering "Mrs. West" the guest room and the men the living room floor. Rogers gratefully quips, "Anything's better than that cold, cold ground," an overt death reference which prompts Trent to respond with overwrought laughter. Rogers may intuit Trent's mental instability and murderous inclinations. As Trent shows the guests down the hall, Rogers sees a lock on a door, and Trent explains that it is his wife's room and he locks the door because "she walks in her sleep and could hurt herself." Rogers finds this statement odd, as the viewer realizes that Trent has not only emotionally but physically imprisoned his wife, making her an actual as well as metaphoric slave. Mrs. Trent hears the men talking, however, and meekly inquires about it. Trent peeks his lizard-like head inside her room and orders her to dress for dinner, "with guests." The sad woman smiles wanly, probably for the first time in many years.

Later, Rogers asks Trent about his work. Trent counters by asking Rogers if he has ever heard of the "Oceana" theory of evolution, which posits that most land-based life forms originally evolved from sea creatures. Trent adds that he is particularly interested in the evolution of human life from reptile life. The allusion is that Trent's attempts at procreation, at conquering the "ocean" of his wife's fertility, have gone terribly wrong, and his life's work is a fanatically misguided attempt to recapture that lost union. At that moment, Mrs. Trent enters the living room, wearing a bright peach-colored dress. She is introduced to the men only as "my wife," still not earning a first name or an identity outside her male-owned prison-world. The sad woman apologizes for being such a shy hostess, and retires to see how the maid is doing, more comfortable in the company of other subservient females, i.e., slaves. Rogers compliments Trent on the depressed woman who has just left, and Trent sighs, "I'm afraid she made a bad bargain when she married me," alluding to Faustian deals with soulless monsters. Trent adds, "If at times she seems preoccupied, you must excuse her," as the scene dissolves to an extreme close-up of a human skull, surrounded by a huge black snake, the bare skull of existence encroached upon by evil, ancient phallocentrism.

Deep in the swamp, the drums have started again. At the ceremonial space, a magic snake dance commences in scenes which harken back to the many voodoo-oriented genre films of the 1930s, as well as African-based documentaries of the same time period. Mora is the lead dancer, wielding more power in the community than originally perceived. In the background can be seen an effigy hanging from a tree, featuring a round, pink head and a white lab coat. It is a symbolic representation of Trent. White male patriarchy is represented here by the most elemental, disdainful symbol imaginable, a mocking caricature of the male body itself, and its "uniform" of presumed power. A man wearing a demon mask tosses spears into the effigy, which swings pathetically, flaccidly, from a pole. Ritchie watches from behind a bush, an amoral white voyeur to this attack on patriarchy.

At Trent's house, Rogers, Brenda and Mrs. Trent finish a late-night conversation. Mrs. Trent approaches Rogers after Brenda retires and tells him about her insane and dangerous husband. She invites Rogers to look into Trent's laboratory, but the naïve Rogers defends the male code by insisting that he cannot interfere with another man's business, thus preserving the patriarchy for the interim. The viewer may wonder where Mrs. Trent finally got the strength and courage to speak out about her abusive situation. It might have been the fateful arrival of the visitors, or perhaps some effect of the locals' magic rituals. Either way, the radical shift in the community and in her immediate environment has emboldened the heroine to take daring risks to preserve her life. Mrs. Trent excuses herself and enters Trent's lab by herself. She decides to rescue Tom from his fate as her mad husband's surrogate reptilian offspring, and disconnects the life-support systems. If the Tom-creature is seen as an attempt at summoning artificial offspring by Trent, Mrs. Trent's act is assuredly then a maternal one, a mercy killing, the woman acting as a mother figure by rescuing a doomed "infant" from a life of undeserved pain and horror. As she finishes this courageous act of love, Trent enters, enraged at his wife's nascent autonomy. Mortified at the death of his surrogate child, Trent tosses his wife into a small closet in a final act of abusive power. First a prisoner of her bad relationship with a bad man, then of his house, and finally of her own small living space, Mrs. Trent now finds herself in a tiny cell, virtually an upright coffin, and understands all too well that patriarchy is not satisfied until its subjects and enemies are confined absolutely and have no freedom, becoming non-selves.

At the ceremonial site, the ritual cleansing of the stricken community continues. The leader continues to mock the effigy. At the lab, Trent speaks to Tom's corpse and orders it to breathe. Yet the summoning is a failure, and the Tom-creature dies. The community's magic is already working, and Trent admits defeat. Trent yells at his wife in the closet, "You've succeeded! He's dead!" Mrs. Trent counters, "You mean *it's* dead!" She is referring not only to the poor creature, but Trent's little kingdom, their shattered relationship, and Trent's worthless penis. After throwing Tom's corpse to the alligators, Trent prepares another hypodermic needle and sneaks into the guest room, where he injects Brenda as she sleeps, in ever more reckless attempts to foster life where there is none. Trent carries the drugged woman into the lab, stating, "You are a perfect subject for the new derivatives, Mrs. West! I believe you will be a perfect subject for instant transmutation!" Mrs. Trent listens helplessly to the fate of her sister-in-peril.

At the ceremonial site in the jungle, the ritual continues, as the leader intones, "The evil doctor is now afraid"; he extols the assembled, "You must become the instrument of revenge! Go do what you will, you are now protected!" The community is finally empowered to rise up against their oppressor, and they run off to confront their personal devil. Ritchie, watching all along, now decides to assault Mora. Valjean returns to his room. He is the archetypal "right-hand man" of historical consequence, working alongside the boss while orchestrating his destruction. Tracker sneaks up on Valjean and stabs him to death, tossing the ceremonial mask to the ground. This murder is obscure, as Tracker and Valjean were victims of the same despot. Perhaps Tracker harbored a grudge against his superior for the verbal and physical abuse he had taken in the past. Perhaps Tracker saw Valjean as a traitor, abandoning his race in an attempt at personal gain. Finally, perhaps Tracker intuited that Valjean had the potential of becoming yet another evil ruler of the community, replacing Trent.

Mora walks towards her house with Ritchie stalking her, a lesser white evil but despicable nonetheless for preying on a vulnerable member of the community. Mora reaches her bedroom and is shocked to see Ritchie right behind her. Unable to communicate her crisis, Mora pretends to acquiesce, but when Ritchie grabs her, she flips him over on the bed. An enraged Ritchie chases Mora through the woods. She runs to a conveniently placed quicksand pit and pushes Ritchie in. Ritchie begs pitifully for help as the muck pulls him back to prehistory, but Mora just watches him drown, both relieved and remorseful to have ended this sinful life.

At the lab, Trent looks with admiration at the new, reptilian Brenda, as his wife begs to be released from her prison cell. Outside, a posse of locals approaches the Trent mansion, and shoots Rabbit as he walks out the door, a shocking act of black-on-white violence that eerily echoes the previous year's race riots in Watts. Rogers hears the gunshot, runs outside and finds Rabbit's body. Inside, Trent also hears the gunshot and looks out a window. He is distressed to see his entire enslaved community standing outside his door with murder in their eyes. Trent runs to his new monstrosity, and orders it to get up, plead-

Dr. Simon Trent (Jeff Alexander, right) tries to reason with his ungodly creation in a hasty, futile effort to turn it against his wife (Francine York) and a colleague (John Agar), in the climax of *Curse of the Swamp Creature*.

ing, "My enemies are here!" He then shouts, "Obey me!"—which sounds at first hearing like "A baby!" This declaration reinforces the idea of Trent's desire to spawn offspring through diabolical means. Due to his estrangement from his sexy and compassionate wife, Trent must attempt to achieve immortality through any means possible. In short, the childless and loveless Trent is faced with extinction, like the animal species he so assiduously studies, unless one of his "monsters" lives long enough to carry on his tradition of totalitarian domination of the community. Facing primitive justice from the mob outside, Trent desperately desires to achieve some sort of assurance that his evil spirit will live on in one of his hideous creations. As Mrs. Trent listens in horror from her prison cell, Brenda rises. The creature emerges from the house, to the horror of the assembled lynch mob, and heads for the alligator pool. Trent follows his creation with a combination of fear and fascination. Rogers finally locates the imprisoned Mrs. Trent, and frees her. She in turn fills him in on her husband's insane designs.

Trent orders Brenda to attack the mob, as Rogers and Mrs. Trent enter the scene. Mrs. Trent communicates, telepathically as well as verbally, with the she-creature, who seems confused and forlorn. Finally, Mrs. Trent pleads, "Brenda! It's me, *Pat!*" This stunning, long-awaited revelation of the abused woman's first name, her *real* name, is her first step towards freedom and personal autonomy, towards an *identity*. This attempt at female solidarity seems to have a profound effect on Brenda. Now finding her long-suppressed voice, Pat tries to convince Brenda to realize what has happened to her, and, more importantly, *who is responsible.* A desperate Trent tries to mollify the sad she-creature by using a hackneyed political tack. He insists, "She hates you because you have more *power* than she does!" Pitting members of an underclass against each other is an old patriarchal trick, and one which has met with some success, but here it seems destined to failure. Trent insists that Brenda kill his wife, revealing himself to be completely without heart or conscience. Pat counters, "He's only *using* you!" This is perhaps the most salient line in the entire film. Brenda responds to this revelation by taking a good long look at her hideous reptilian features and then looking angrily towards Trent. She, and the audience, have finally seen the connection between the rule of a totalitarian patriarchy and the immanent threat to one's self and well-being. Now ironically given the brute power to change her fate, Brenda grabs Trent and tosses him to his pet reptiles, who greedily devour their cruel master and show him to be, ultimately, lower than even these "lowest" of creatures. The doomed she-beast, preferring to end her life rather than continue as the mutant freak of an evil regime, lets herself also fall into the pool and be taken back, as food, into the natural chain of life. Later, Rogers escorts Pat onto his private plane, and the two fly off into the skies, hopefully to begin a new life together, far away from the barbaric, primeval world they have just barely escaped. Rogers and Pat, Buchanan's increasingly obligatory heterosexual savior-couple, are in *Swamp Creature* thrown together only at the film's end, via this sketchy coda, which suggests that their "career" of saving civilization has only just begun.

Much more than a "cheap monster movie," *Swamp Creature* is a surprisingly mature melodrama, touching on several significant themes, including the overthrow of totalitarian leadership, the use of cold science as a replacement for failed human relationships, and the emergence of female emancipation and black empowerment as leading social movements of the day. Indeed, the film's title refers more to Trent, the ruling patriarch, and the community of blacks who take power into their own hands than the "monster" itself.

Trent is portrayed as a fitting emblem to an overbearing patriarchy. In the specific geographical and racial setting he occupies, he could easily be seen as a modern-day incarnation of the white plantation master who ruled his army of black slaves with an iron hand. Using science as a vehicle for exploiting and destroying his non-white victims, Trent's crimes even include racial genocide. Trent is an advocate of plantation capitalism, ruling his kingdom as absolute monarch. Everyone else, including peers, associates and loved ones, are slaves to him, as are the local citizenry. As the villain is a white overlord who threatens the entire community with mad notions of immortality, *Swamp Creature* is also a curious diatribe against white procreation. The stereotypical desire to create life in the mad doctor film essentially conveys a metaphoric desire to *pro*create, to continue one's own bloodline, and by extension one's race. The mad doctor, representing science, is thus somehow suggested to be rejecting nature, and by inference is rendered sexually impotent. He then needs science to help him create life he can no longer create naturally.

Pat is an exemplary example of the New Age female archetype, a woman who is almost fatally compromised by an evil patriarchal regime until she stands up for herself and rebels against sexual and political tyranny. This basic template is addressed in many Buchanan films, and revisited almost verbatim in the final Azalea telefilm, *It's Alive!* As for why Pat and Tom offer little or no resistance to their rule by tyranny by Trent, the answer is two fold. Firstly, the characters are ostensibly stereotypes of the horror film genre, in which the dominant male(s) must by definition have passive subordinates to exploit and bully. Also, Pat and Tom are individuals who have formed partnerships with Trent and thus are presumed to be within the bounds of an assumed social contract with him. As for Pat, the marriage bond is sacred, at least in theory, and the woman likely had no reason to suspect that her husband would devolve into this godless beast over the course of their emotional journey together. Likewise, Tom probably entered into a professional relationship with his mentor while at university, and imagined the highly ordered conduct seen there would continue into the private sector. The shattering of this faith on Tom's part is well illustrated by one of Trent's caustic comments: "This isn't an ivory tower," reminding the forlorn associate how far from the safety and order of the academic environment the two had fallen. Ironically, victims of tyranny often feel defeated as well by their own sense of guilt and complicity in the failed relationship. The domineering and manipulative party often exploits this self-doubt to further feelings of self-loathing in the individual, reinforcing their sense of despair and hopelessness. This feeling of powerlessness, combined with a sense of isolation, helps the controlling party to "divide and conquer" their subordinates and colleagues.

Likewise, the community of blacks, through focused and determined effort, bring justice back to their land. By accessing their belief in the powers of magical religious rites, they are able to overpower their evil master. Regardless of the subjective efficacy of the "magic" rituals performed, the ceremonial amassing of mutually afflicted souls triggers empowerment of the community by unleashing its *faith* in its aggregate might. As well, the powerful energy unleashed by the group's abiding belief in righteousness in their quest for freedom acts as a powerful force for social change. Alternately, rural (white) America is depicted in *Swamp Creature* as evil, conspiratorial, even homicidal, represented both by the grifting gang at the Fly-n-Fish motel and the assuredly Faustian Dr. Trent. As opposed to the blacks, the white community has become fragmented, isolated and competitive, and there is precious little community strength to draw upon. It is literally "every man for himself" in modern middle-class white America, a jungle more regressive than any overtly primitive environment.

John Agar has a fairly lackluster role in *Swamp Creature*, and throughout seems confused and unfocused. A fine actor with many memorable roles to his credit, Agar can be pardoned for his lack of energy here because it was surely a "coming down" to be involved in such a threadbare production, which to the star of Hollywood blockbusters like *She Wore a Yellow Ribbon* (1949, d: John Ford) must have looked like an elaborate home movie. Agar is considerably more animated and engaging in *Zontar, the Thing from Venus*, as his role there had far more energy and life to it.

As were the other Azalea telefilms, *Swamp Creature* was filmed in familiar locations such as murky swamps, banal hotel suites and dreary living rooms, each one a generic American icon of the period, which placed the film firmly within familiar middle-class confines. The film combines a lurid and intricate scenario with that essentially documentary ambience which makes the Azalea telefilms so uncanny and haunting. The titular "Swamp Creature," played by Buchanan regular Bill Thurman, is sketched primarily by the facial design which utilizes facial putty, Ping-Pong ball eyes and dime-store fangs, foreshadowing the

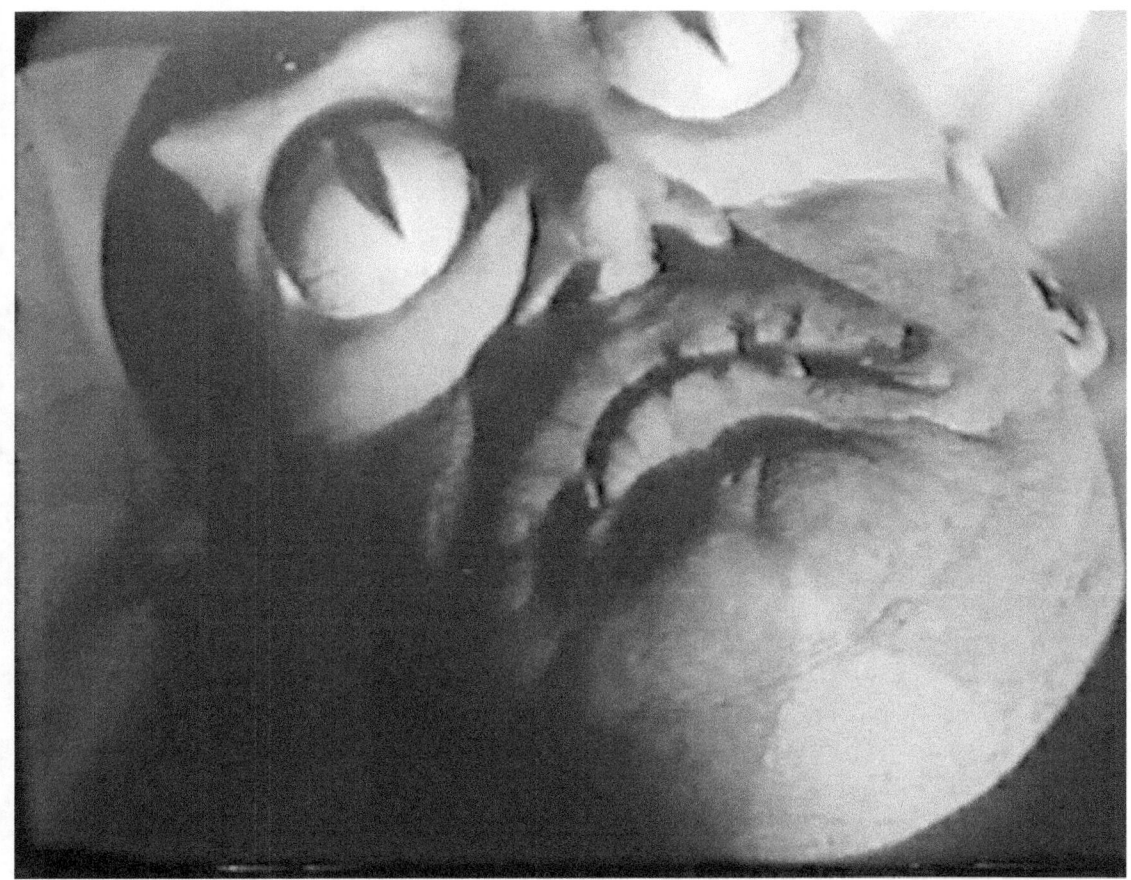

Bill Thurman wears makeup by Jack Bennett to become the titular beast in Larry Buchanan's ode to evil procreation and male impotence, *Curse of the Swamp Creature*.

more elaborate headpiece used in the later Azaleas *Creature of Destruction* and *It's Alive!* As in the other Azalea telefilms, the creature represents something larger than itself. Here, Trent's creation illustrates that the mad desire for male procreation *without the tempering emotional input of a compassionate female* can create nothing but soulless monsters.

12

Mars Needs Women

In 1967 American International Television released Larry Buchanan's *Mars Needs Women* to U.S. television. *Mars Needs Women* (henceforth referred to as *Mars*) is an affable science-fiction parable with more than a few nods to European New Wave cinema, which in addition addressed one of the most prominent social movements of the later twentieth century: the sexual revolution. At the center of *Mars* is one of Buchanan's most colorful and clearly drawn new-age heterosexual "savior-couples." Dr. Marjorie Bolen (*Batgirl* star Yvonne Craig) is both a feminist figure — bright, independent, nonconformist, even rebellious — and a classic male-held stereotype of the sexy bookworm. Her partner is a man literally "out of this world": Dop, played by former child actor Tommy Kirk. Buchanan had some initial reluctance in using Kirk in the part, indicated by a judgmental recollection from his autobiography: "When Kirk stepped off the plane in Dallas in 1966 to start production, I knew three things about him; he was a disciplined actor, he was into drugs and he was a homosexual."[1] Although Buchanan qualified his opinion by stating, "I was totally unfettered with the mindset that is uncomfortable with homosexuality, or the narrow hypocrisy that some have toward the alcoholic,"[2] and had nothing but praise for Kirk regarding his work in *Mars* ("I do not recall ever having to do a second take with Tommy"),[3] one senses by his declaration of low-budget filmmaking-as-therapy that he considered Kirk's sexual identity, like his drug addiction, something to be corrected and cured, if possible. In contrast, his feelings about Yvonne Craig can only be described as unabashed adoration, indicative of the privileged if romanticized status of women in Buchanan's work: "Yvonne embodied the totality of what woman can be when approaching perfection. She combined an incredible face and body with great attitude, camera sense, talent, humor, and, most importantly, sensuality coupled with quiet intelligence, a rarity in film."[4]

In *Mars*, Buchanan addresses the profound shifting of sexual roles and activities sweeping the nation in the mid-1960s, a movement dubbed "the sexual revolution." Sparked in part by the shocking revelations in the Kinsey Report about sexual preferences and activities in men and women, topics now brought into the public area for discussion and practical examination included frequency of sexual activity, extramarital activity, promiscuity, self-gratification, and homosexuality. The resultant increase in sexual activity and experimentation, which intersected into the civil rights and counterculture movements, had far-reaching repercussions on not only sexual mores but also on politics. Buchanan was apparently less than enchanted with this radical resifting of traditional sociosexual structure, which to him threatened the tradition of long-term, monogamous heterosexual relationships which dominate his films, *Hughes and Harlow: Angels in Hell* (1977) being the prime example. In *Mars,* Buchanan astutely, even cynically, suggests that this so-called revolution was less about the liberation from sexual taboos at all and more about *failed* attempts of people to connect emotionally. Ironically, this epidemic of furious physical coupling actually *increased* loneliness and despair, and adds to *Mars'* palpably desolate air. *Mars* is ultimately concerned about humankind's inability to connect emotionally, thus politically, to form vibrant and healthy societies, from a Freudian perspective, the battle between Eros (life, love) and Thanatos (death, aggression).[5]

Mars begins with a prologue in which three separate women, all involved in pleasurable activity, vanish into thin air: a tennis player disappears while her partner's back is turned; a woman out on a date in a restaurant evaporates while her date fetches a pack of cigarettes; a sexy young woman vaporizes while she takes a shower at home. As the title forewarns, these women disappeared due to some machination from otherworldly sources. Moreover, all three were spirited away while not only involved in some measure of pleasurable activity, but of personal empowerment. The tennis player had just gained a point over her partner; the woman on a date is having a good time being single and playing the field; the showering girl was engaged in a pleasurable and potentially autoerotic activity. The Martians plucked these women at singular moments of personal apotheosis, suggesting a theme common to Buchanan's films: the excesses of masculine power, frequently used to subordinate exceptional women.

Via a colorful swish pan, the scene changes to follow a black limousine, accented by two American flags, driving to a military installation with an escort of police motorcycles. The car stops at the front door of "USDS — United States Decoding Service — NASA Wing," and a uniformed man, Colonel Robert Page (an always-simmering Byron Lord), shown by a sign to be the head of this project, enters the building; along with him the audience enters the heart of the military-industrial complex. Inside, Page's subordinate reveals the content of the message from space they have just now decoded: "Mars needs women!" This cuts to the main credits over a montage of a toy-like spaceship flying through space. "The Martians" and "The Women" are given special, separate billing, while the earth men are listed generically, almost as an afterthought. The credits immediately situate the important power figures in this strange scenario: Martian men and Earth women. As the credits conclude, a news reporter enters a lackluster room as Buchanan's writing and directing credit appears. The reporter, a man named Stemmons, from a fictional wire service (portrayed by frequent Buchanan player Roger Ready) speaks directly to the camera as he sets up the ground rules for what is revealed to be a news conference between him and Colonel Page. Buchanan, the writer and director of the film, is explicitly connected to the reporter, the journalistic "truth seeker," in an information war with the government which boils down to "play by our rules or we'll kick you out of the loop." Colonel Page grudgingly offers Stemmons some trivial facts about the message from outer space, but will not reveal the content of the message. The two men, who speak to each other from different rooms separated by a window, spar with each other in ways alternately coy and bitchy, in an exchange that borders on sexual flirtation. Stemmons is skeptical from the outset about receiving anything valuable from the perturbed military man; he even ponders out loud the chances of his getting "anything in the national interest?" Page angrily retorts, "I don't have to be reminded of the ground rules, Stemmons!" in another allusion to sexual flirtation. Finally, Page "cuts off" Stemmons from further information, who seems both shocked and hurt by the rejection, reinforcing the curious sense that the exchange was in some ways a failed homosexual pick up attempt. Stemmons even whines, "Did you cut me off?" The double entendre has potential sexual implications, especially given the curious set up of the exchange. Both men are isolated from each other by plate glass, a set up which alludes to the ubiquitous sex-culture phenomenon, the "peep show," where men watched naked dancing women through little glass windows, both privy to and yet hopelessly distanced from their objects of desire.

Page next visits the secretary of state (Neil Fletcher) in "the war room." The secretary asks Page, "Is the security lid on tight?" and then requests, "Well, take it off for me!"—two statements with excellent double entendre potential. So far, every governmental male-male encounter hints at homosexual flirtation. The irony is especially apparent in that this encounter takes place in the war room probably referenced from Kubrick's military satire of male-bonding and Thanatos in action, 1963s *Dr. Strangelove)*. Mars was the Greek god of war, and homosexuality was a standard sexual practice in ancient Greece. Mars, as the film quickly explains, is becoming an almost entirely male planet, and the lead Martian is played by Tommy Kirk, who was in real life a homosexual.

Soon Page receives startling new information: a Martian announces he will materialize at USDS headquarters, but only if the earth men agree to stay three yards away from him, a curious reinforcement of the tradition of emotional distancing between males (and the paradox that most closeted homosexuals are outwardly the most homophobic). Via a simple jump-cut, a Martian materializes, and introduces himself as "Dop." He explains that his "fellows" are medical missionaries from the red planet; a critical recession in the Y chromosomes of their race has resulted in a preponderance of male births over females, in a ratio of 100 to 1, leaving the Martian race an all-male planet dangerously compromised for future generations. Dop dispassionately asks for five earth women to volunteer for their breeding program (as opposed to any specifically erotic, pleasurable purposes). His request flatly denied by a shocked (and disappointed?) Page, Dop vows to finish the project "with or without earth's help."

A montage conveys the world's reaction to the Martians, seen as "the world's first common enemy." A reporter declares that the Martian's ship is even now "hurtling toward the approximate vicinity of Houston, Texas." An X-15 rocket plane is launched from a B-52 Superfortress in an attempt to engage and destroy the enemy. (The X-15 was a famous test rocket designed to break the sound barrier. The inaccuracy of attaching this footage to what is being presented in the narrative would have been obvious and amusing to the astute viewer.) As Page and his men listen to the pilot's commentary over a wall-mounted loudspeaker, the X-15 searches for the Martian ship. However, the pilot announces that he is paralyzed at 40,000 feet, and is unable to climb higher or reach the location of the Martian craft. The pilot jettisons the useless craft, and the X-15 lands safely home via remote control. The Strategic Air Command next sends up more planes to intercept and if possible destroy the alien ship, but their instruments go haywire as well. Defeated, the F-16s return to base. This entire battle is concocted using stock footage, reaction shots of the principals and various close-ups of the loudspeaker from which the various pilots relate information. As well as revealing information, the camera's obsession with the Fedtro-brand

A female passenger glances casually at reports of the utter upheaval of Western civilization in *Mars Needs Women*.

loudspeaker turns it into a fetish-object. There is even an extreme close-up of the device, which reveals the corporate logo to be the symbol of the deadly atom, and thus the Atomic Age. The loudspeaker becomes, in essence, a character in itself, a symbol of man's technology, particularly technology's tendency to *distance* men from each other even as it purports to bring men closer. All the tension in the scene comes from the voice which crackles through the loudspeaker, the loudspeaker thus becoming the "action" of the film. The sadly isolated human characters can only stare and react in counterfeit dismay to the disembodied drama unraveling before them.

Later that night, another male couple, consisting of two fishermen (Pat Cranshaw and Bill Thurman), sit on a lakeside pier, sharing beer and camaraderie. They see a spaceship landing behind an abandoned ice plant across the lake. With its huge, phallic smokestack piercing the night sky, the skeletal ice plant perfectly symbolizes one male-dominated planet which the Martians, as members of another male-dominated planet, intend to invade and conquer: cold, dead, majestically phallic yet impotent in that the ice plant has long since "ceased production." Inside, the Martians emerge from a tiny porthole on top of their ship, as if emerging from a womb (mother-as-machine). They wear uniforms consisting of modified scuba-diving suits, with orange ear-pieces on their heads, and sporting heavy-duty flashlights. Dop's suit is accented with a stripe of silver duct tape, to form a *V* (as in

Churchill's "V for Victory"). Inside this skeleton of fallen industrial society, Dop and his fellows go over their plans for "Operation Sleep Freeze." Martian #2 (Warren Hammack), a doctor, seems optimistic about the earthlings' eventual turnaround, but surly Martian #3 (Enrique Touceda III, as "Anthony Houston") seems skeptical and wants to be more aggressive to attain their goal. Deciding they need earth apparel, earth money and a map of the city, they plan to filter into Texas society like everyday bourgeois tourists. Martian #3 next materializes in front of a Phillips 66 gas station, and immediately violating his superior's orders knocks the service station attendant unconscious with a well-placed judo chop. The Martian extracts cash and a map from the establishment, and disappears once again. Martian #4 (Larry Tanner) steals an unlocked Oldsmobile from the parking lot of Houston International Airport. Martian #5 (Cal Duggan) uses an "air knife" to gain entry to a local men's clothing store, and obtains cheap suits for his fellows. Dop's narrated insistence that his partner successfully garner "the right size" and style for their earth-wear perhaps reveals how insecure and conformist even these highly evolved beings are. Their very survival depends on "blending in" as average, middle-class American males. Moreover, when they return to the ice plant, now dressed in suit and tie and looking like everyday businessmen, Dop sputters, "These ties serve no useful purpose! The red planet abandoned the use of ties over fifty years ago as *useless male vanity*. It simply reveals the environmental naiveté of the earth men!" (Emphasis added). The ties could also be seen as a phallic symbol of "male vanity," with "no useful purpose," that the Martins have renounced.

With only twenty hours to locate, research, and abduct five earth women, the Martians head towards Dallas in the stolen car. Martian #5 is let off on Main Street, where he glances in befuddlement at a giant theater marquee advertising *The Fortune Cookie*. He seems especially unnerved by a giant picture of a grinning Jack Lemmon, which stares down menacingly at him. (*The Fortune Cookie* was a classic Walter Matthau—Jack Lemmon "buddy film," a genre with distinct homoerotic overtones.) Elsewhere, Martian #3 is dropped off at the Athens Strip Club, where popular exotic dancer "Bubbles" Cash is set to perform. As the stripper dances before anonymous, goggle-eyed men, the Martian observes one of the strangest rituals regarding earth men towards women, the striptease, an odd combination of worship and loathing, adoration and objectification, chaste reverence and shameless exploitation, issues explored deeply by Buchanan in *Naughty Dallas* (1964).

Dop and Martian #2 visit the downtown Holiday Inn and attempt to get a room, but the pretty desk clerk apologizes that there are no rooms, due to the current hysteria over invading Martians. She explains, "It's this Martian scare. Every newsman in the country must be here! Imagine, they want to take us earth girls!" The delicious irony in this scene is that while the clerk is confessing an almost perverse fascination with being "desired" by otherworldly creatures who happen to stand right before her (and who need women as reproductive stock rather than sexual enjoyment), the two Martians could be homosexuals seeking a room for a sexual encounter, an implication which reaches a stunning conclusion shortly. The Martians venture to the upstairs bar to wait for a room cancellation. A newscast informs them that Dr. Marjorie Bolen—"a stunning brunette who wrote her thesis on space medicine, and won a Pulitzer Prize for her book on space genetics"—will be part of a high-level meeting regarding the Martian threat, to take place at the very Holiday Inn where the Martians wait. Dop knows immediately that Dr. Bolen will figure prominently in their plans, although he is not aware yet on how personal a level. The Martians leave the bar, return to the hotel lobby and read the poster for Bolen's upcoming presentation, hilariously entitled "Sex and Outer Space," an ironic self-reference to the expected exploitation elements of *Mars* that the film's title promises but largely — and intentionally — fails to deliver.

The Martians decide to pose as reporters to gain access to the upcoming press conference. Posing as "Mr. Ross" and "Mr. Miller," the Martians cleverly learn the identity and location of a real reporter staying at the hotel, a Mr. Fast from the Seattle *Sun*. Dop goes to Fast's room, and gains entry via a white lie. Dop prowls the room while Fast (Chet Davis) tries to reach his family back home on the telephone. Soon Dop stands at the window and Fast joins him. As Dop and Fast stare down into the compelling reflection from the hotel pool, Dop begins to hypnotize the earth man. This exchange bafflingly turns into a failed gay seduction:

> DOP: Have you seen the view from this room?
> FAST: View? View?
> DOP: Are you afraid of heights, Mr. Fast?
> FAST: Heights? Heights? I don't follow you.
> DOP: Of course, we're only three stories high, but if you look down, you will see that heights have their own power of persuasion....
> FAST: *Really, Mr.! It would take more than that!*
> DOP: Persuasion, Mr. Fast, persuasion. Suggestion. Making you want to do, deeply, do my will. My will, Mr. Fast. You will do as I say. You will do my will.
> FAST: Will. Yes.

Throughout *Mars*, whenever two or more men stand together there is a palpable sexual energy (which becomes especially remarkable considering Buchanan's ambivalent attitude towards Kirk, a homosexual, portraying Dop). As Dop continues his psychological seduction of Fast, he edges physically closer to the man, finally standing so close as to allow Fast to feel Dop's breath on the back of his neck. After extracting the details of his itinerary and his press card information, etc., he releases Fast from the trance. The clearly embarrassed earth man looks at Dop, and then down at the pool: "Yes, it is a lovely view...." Martian #5 joins the two men in the hotel room, and apologizes for "the mix-up"; the clearly befuddled Fast mumbles deferentially, "It was my fault, all around." Realizing that he has "lost" his press card, he philosophizes to the two Martians that he "won't need it anyway, *unless you know some out-of-the-way place*?" Shocked at uttering yet another brazen sexual overture as a kind of Freudian slip, and unnerved by the Martian's lack of response, Fast mutters, "No, I guess you wouldn't," grabs his suitcase and exits the hotel room as fast as humanly possible. This remarkable scene clearly suggests that beneath the well-ordered consciousness of the average heterosexual family man lies a barely repressed homosexual curiosity, accessible by the slightest suggestion by other males.

After Fast's quick (or quickie?) departure, Dop and Martian #5 set up their radio equipment and attempt to contact the others. At the airport terminal, Martian #4 looks about for available females. He checks in with Dop via a radio wristwatch, and relates that he has "an excellent lead" as a blonde stewardess (Donna Lindberg) walks by in her cute little uniform. Dop attempts to contact Martian #3, but he is currently mesmerized by "Bubbles" Cash and her sultry performance at the strip club. "Bubbles" finishes her act, and Martian #3 follows her backstage to her dressing room, where he approaches her menacingly, like any garden-variety, earth-bound male predator. Dop prepares to meet his test subject, Dr. Bolen, downstairs, but Martian #5 decides to retire for the evening, because

Dop, the Martian (Tommy Kirk, left), puts poor newsman Fast (Chet Davis) under a hypnotic trance which has all the trappings of an erotic seduction, in Larry Buchanan's wild treatise on the sexual revolution, *Mars Needs Women*.

"coeds are early risers." His test subject is apparently going to be a local college girl. In the hotel conference room, the gathered reporters taunt the defensive Dr. Bolen with sexist comments such as "The girls they take to Mars are gonna have it great, aren't they, Doctor?" and "One hundred men to every woman, ha ha!" Bolen fidgets uncomfortably, trying to maintain her professional demeanor over the crude remarks. Bolen chastises the newsmen for their impertinence, and threatens to end the interview. Dop, having infiltrated the press conference, offers a question about the relationship between genetics research and the history of animal mutations, which piques Bolen's interest, as she answers enthusiastically. After the press conference ends, Dr. Bolen approaches Dop and thanks him for offering the only intelligent question about her research. Bolen suggests the two take a walk. In a melodramatic take on the sexual revolution, the female makes the sexual/romantic overture to the male, who takes a clearly subordinate role. They wander to the local planetarium, where the newest exhibition, "Trip to Mars," is slated to start. The planetarium director (George Edgley) shows the couple to their seats; just as they sit down, the empty auditorium is filled with the screams of dozens of schoolchildren. (It may be either ironic or regressive that Buchanan surrounds this avowedly New Age couple in a veritable ocean of fertility symbols via the swarm of school kids which invades the lovers' space.) A planetarium attendant starts a Buckingham reel-to-reel tape recorder, and the narrated program begins (the narration being voiced by Buchanan). It describes a fictitious trip to Mars, accompanied by stock footage of rocket launches, space travel, and sun spots, another self-reflexive commentary about the status of *Mars* as low-budget film where action is largely composed of stock footage, especially when the tape breaks and the room (planetarium, movie theater) is plunged into silence. Dop assumes the narration from Buchanan, describing life on his home planet and ending his exposition with a sad accounting of Mars' breeding problems. The assembled children applaud enthusiastically and depart, nicely accenting the barren sterility of the red planet.

As suggested, the sexual revolution ultimately increased loneliness rather than eradicated it, and exacerbated the emotional distance between people, and as the Martians begin their conquest of earth women, their "pickups" are little more than disguised sexual abductions that take place in what might be called "dead spaces" recalling the emptied urban landscapes of Michelangelo Antonioni. *Mars* strongly recalls Antonioni as American urban settings circa 1967 become such "dead spaces": gas stations, waiting rooms, parking lots, strip clubs, museums, hotels, airports, stadiums — places where masses of people gather *but do not connect emotionally*. When the film returns to the airport, Martian #4 continues his surveillance of the sexy airline stewardess. He follows as she boards an automated moving sidewalk towards her destination. This Antonioni-like scene depicts the paradoxical loneliness of crowded public places, a ubiquitous social phenomenon of the urbanization of modern culture as people pass closely and yet remain complete strangers. The public arenas such as transportation terminals are designed ostensibly to move people and machines efficiently from one destination to another but in reality distance the masses, thus reconstructing the individual as a *part* of something larger, not a separate entity unto themselves. The stewardess floats by on the moving sidewalk, looking more like a machine or a statue than a human being, silent and stiff. Martian #4 follows her to an elevator, and finally approaches and hypnotizes the woman. This sublime scene conveys the dark truth that since men want women, but women are silent, aloof and unavailable, the men become desperate animals who stalk, assault, and capture women for breeding their progeny.

The scene changes to another iconic American "dead space": a football stadium, where Martian #5 scouts for his test subject as the game commences. As the Martian overlooks the huge mass of people, he realizes that here there are, ironically, *too many* females to choose from and that finding the proverbial "Miss Right" as a "face in the crowd" is problematic. The halftime show soon begins, led by a marching band and a small army of cheerleaders, leading to the big event of the day: the crowning of the Homecoming Queen. To the Martian's delight, the announcer declares that today they will choose "the ideal woman!" The announcer goes on to define what earthlings consider a prime specimen: "Good looks, good health, good deportment, and personality! In short the good woman, as we know her in the twentieth century!" Thus the female ideal in a phallocentric society is presented: a sexually desirable creature in good health, and, most importantly, with a good attitude, which can of course be translated as deferential and male-worshipping. In fact, the announcer could have as easily been describing the criteria for choosing a dairy cow as much as a human female: Earth and Mars *both* "need women" as objects of sexual passivity. As the Martian watches excitedly, the winner is brought out on a ridiculous float. The Queen, a.k.a. Brenda Noland (Sherry Roberts), is described thusly: "A really popular girl on campus, a senior, with her major in journalism! She looks for a career in mass media communications!" After Ms. Noland returns to her Delta Gamma sorority, Martian #5 poses as an FTD florist, brings a box of roses to the front door, and hypnotizes and abducts her. This is soon followed by a final abduction: Martian #3 sits under a large reproduction of Rodin's *The Thinker*, literally pondering his next move, when he encounters a young artist (Pat Delaney) outside a museum and uses an impromptu painting lesson to hypnotize and abduct her.

Later, at a "Monitor One" meeting discussing the dire situation, the similarities between all four abductees are noted: "All lovely, built like goddesses, and none married!" In fact, the women the Martians abduct epitomize stereotypes and sexual fantasies of American womanhood: the stripper, the stewardess, the Homecoming Queen, the urban sophisticate. As one man mentions, "One more to go," the scene cuts to Dr. Bolen: Dop's target, and as noted, another stereotype — the sexy bookworm. The military men eventually pinpoint the Martians' base of operations to the old ice factory. Bolen explains that "sleep freeze," more commonly known as "suspended animation," is what the Martians would use for their subjects, and why the chemical inventory at the ice factory (ammonia, salts, lime) would make it a perfect operating base for them. The term "sleep freeze" is laced with irony, not only suggesting the "coldness" of casual sex without romantic involvement that defined the sexual revolution but that women in sleep freeze are literally "frigid" and made sexually passive.

That evening, Dop joins Dr. Bolen on a date. Bolen reveals that her interest in genetics was inspired by her own father's research, which she greatly admired. She asks Dop, "Would you like to meet my father?" The suggestion, a traditional sign of serious romantic interest, changes the scene to the Museum of Science and History, as Dop and Bolen walk through "The Bolen Wing," dedicated to Dr. Bolen's illustrious father, Gustave Bolen. An automated narrator, describing herself as "The Talking Woman," details the many fascinating exhibits, among which are anatomical models of women, including visible reproductive organs. Whether aroused by the inspirational words of the Talking Woman or the representations of women as a collection of internal organs, Dop and Bolen passionately kiss, and she unwittingly reveals her secret information to Dop about the plan to raid the ice plant. This disturbs Dop, who bids Bolen a hasty farewell and runs out to the car. The irrepressible Bolen follows Dop and hops in the car anyway. The two drive on in awkward silence, like an average American couple who just had a squabble at a cocktail party.

A ravishing stewardess (Donna Lindberg) is put under a hypnotic spell by a Martian as she makes her way to work, but she has also cast her spell of unearthly splendor on the hapless alien, and the audience, in *Mars Need Women*.

Meanwhile, at the ice plant, the Martians have prepared the female specimens for space travel. Laid out on stretchers with white sheets over them, the women look like corpses, or "dead lays." Dop rushes in and informs the others about the impending attack, and instructs them to abort the mission. He then declares that he is staying behind to be with Dr. Bolen. The other Martians remind Dop that this rash decision will mean certain death for them once they return to Mars. Martian #3 snidely suggests that they take Bolen with them, as their token test subject, while Martian #5 explains to Dop that either he or Bolen must accompany the Martians back to the home planet, and the decision must be made immediately. As armed soldiers surround the plant, Dop tearfully explains, "The word 'love' was removed from our vocabulary over one hundred years ago, but whatever 'love' is must be what I feel for you." The ill-fated lovers embrace as the military begins their attack. The Martians quickly board their ship as Martian #5 explains to Dr. Bolen that the other women "are under mild sedation; they'll come out of it shortly with no ill effects." Bolen runs out of the ice plant just as the Martian ship takes off. Colonel Page runs up to Bolen and asks her to reveal everything she has learned about the invaders, but she can only stare up at the heavens in awe and sadness, now acutely aware of the great chasm that will always exist between the sexes.

Tragically, but inevitably, the two star-crossed lovers Dop and Dr. Bolen do not end up united, unlike many Buchanan films in which unification of the heterosexual, New Age couple is a first step towards reestablishing social normalcy (*The Eye Creatures*) or even a metaphysical convergence (*Strawberries Need Rain, It's Alive!*). In *Mars*, the primary concern is the growing *lack* of a libidinal connection between men and women, not only with its personal, social consequences — the Freudian binary that a weakened Eros can only result in a strengthened Thanatos — in three distinct ways. One is the threat of the breakdown of the traditional heterosexual couple, privileged in Buchanan's films and heralded by the sexual revolution, with sexuality in America becoming defined as an industry of anonymous picks up between the sexes. Second is the subordination and objectification of women into purely utilitarian functions — sexually idealized stereotypes and breeding stock. Finally comes the establishment of what are not only male-dominated orders but *exclusively* all-male orders — both on Earth and Mars (the military–industrial complex, the press, and the virtually womanless "red planet"). While *Mars* strikes a precarious balance between homoeroticism and homophobia, in this context it reflects Buchanan's most prevalent themes: the idealization of the Woman, and conversely how a patriarchal order allies within itself to define the Woman as the Other: to exclude, to exploit, and even expunge (depicted particularly viciously, albeit problematically, in *The Naked Witch*). The brutal irony of *Mars Needs Women* is that "the world's first common enemy"— the Martian — is identical in every way to the middle-class American male.

As remarkable as *Mars Needs Women* is, it has generated legions of fans over the years. The film claimed devoted fans beginning shortly after its original worldwide television release, according to Christopher Jarmick: "In the early 1970s, Larry was interviewed at Cannes by journalists excited to talk with the director of one of the most popular television movies in Israel. It turned out that *Mars Needs Women* had been dubbed into Yiddish and was extremely popular...."[6] The eminently lovable film has also spawned many a cultural homage. The 1987 film *Fright Night* featured a TV horror movie host introducing a film entitled *Mars Wants Flesh!* At least one alternative rock band has appropriated the film's title verbatim as their name, with others, such as "Mars Needs Cigars," modifying it to suit their particular marketing agenda. Buchanan claimed that *Mars Needs Women* was one of his most popular properties:

A genius (Yvonne Craig) and a man from Mars (Tommy Kirk) bicker and pout like any middle-class couple on their way to a social engagement, in the final reel of *Mars Needs Women*.

Several real power players have optioned the underlying property for either a remake or a sequel. The most interesting proposal was for a Broadway musical. At this writing, the latest to option *Mars* has been the team that successfully brought *Fried Green Tomatoes* to the screen, Jon Avnet and Jordan Kerner. It was to be a Universal Picture. The option was renewed several times before they passed and the property reverted to me.[7]

Buchanan was terribly fond of *Mars*, and considered it the jewel in the Azalea telefilms crown.[8] Up until the days before his untimely death in late 2004, Buchanan was working with a new production company on a direct-to-video sequel to *Mars*, under the working titles *Mars Still Needs Women* and *Mars Needs Women Too!*

13

In the Year 2889

Of the four films which Larry Buchanan eventually remade in his own fashion, the toughest act to follow was Roger Corman's *Day the World Ended* (1956), the prototype for Buchanan's *In the Year 2889* (1967). Released approximately ten years after the U.S. bombing of Hiroshima, Japan, with atomic weaponry, *Day the World Ended* (henceforth referred to as *Day*) is a powerful B-movie apocalypse, and one of Corman's strongest early works.[1]

Buchanan filmed *In the Year 2889* (henceforth referred to as *2889*) with a script copied almost verbatim from Lou Rusoff's screenplay for *Day*. Buchanan eschewed the exploitation sensibilities of Corman's noir thriller, and fashioned instead something akin to a postmodern biblical parable. The somewhat peripheral bible references in *Day* become almost an obsession in *2889*. The sanctuary in which the protagonists struggle elicits much of the utopian mythos of the Garden of Eden, and surely the sinister woods which harbor unseen evil suggest the ancient "forest primeval" in ways more polarized than similar settings in *Day*. Robert Jessup's cinematography, which utilizes bright sun and deep shadow to brilliant effect, accentuates the dichotomy between light and dark, good and evil. Even Jessup's "signature" shot over the main credits shows a blazing sunburst pouring over a bank of tall, dark trees, a visual clue to the underlying philosophy of the piece.

2889 by and large foregoes the horror atmospherics of *Day* to concentrate on the immediate human interest story and its underlying philosophies. As such, *2889* works best as character study and allegory, and falters somewhat when it tries to saddle itself on some of the outdated sci-fi elements. In both *Day* and *2889*, there is no mention of enemies or politics regarding the atomic holocaust which has sealed the fate of the characters. This signifying event is used merely as a preface to setting up a microcosmic society thrust into a life-and-death survival situation in an isolated, socially regressive setting. The title, *In the Year 2889*, is meant to be taken as lyrical and poetic, not a literal statement of setting, as the film obviously takes place in the present day and not nine hundred-odd years into the future. The allusion to biblical language ("In the year of our Lord, etc.") punctuates the religious fixation of the film.

The only Azalea telefilm to lack one, *2889* does not feature a prologue. The main credits roll over stock footage of A-bomb blasts, followed by time-lapse footage of cloud formations passing over mountainous landscapes, an effective budget-conscious optical trick meant to convey waves of atomic mist. An older man and a young woman sit on a sunlit patio and listen to the radio. A newscaster named Ted Johnson (Roger Ready) tells of an atomic war ended "only 15 hours after the first nuclear bomb fell on Formosa," with "three billion people murdered by a thousand nuclear bombs." The man, John Ramsey (Neil Fletcher), and his daughter Joanna (Charla Doherty) discuss the dire situation, and the glaring absence of a third party, Joanna's fiancé Larry, who is missing and feared dead.

Joanna and her father go inside the house, and Joanna glances at a photograph of her beloved.[2] There is a knock at the front door. Against her father's orders, Joanna opens it, thinking it is Larry finally returning. Instead, a strange man stumbles in and falls to the ground, bearing horrible facial wounds. Shortly, a handsome young man enters the house as well. He introduces himself as Steve Martin (Paul Petersen), and explains that the sick man on the floor is his brother, Granger. Again ignoring her father's edict, Joanna offers the strangers the hospitality of their home. The world-weary John sits staring at a portrait of his dead wife which hangs ominously on the foyer wall and looks down on him, either judging or forgiving her mate for his failures.

Soon, two more strangers enter the house by shooting past the now-locked door. It is a seedy gangster named Mickey (Hugh Feagin) and his sexy girlfriend Jada (Quinn O'Hara).[3] Again overruling her father, Joanna invites the couple to stay with them. Finally, an old cowboy, Timothy Henderson (Bill Thurman), arrives, carrying a jug of booze. He wanders into the Ramseys' yard, and is startled to see Jada combing her hair in an upstairs window. Timothy hides his moonshine underneath some bushes and approaches the house. Jada sees Timothy peering at her and screams. Steve tackles Timothy, but the two make peace and Steve invites the drunkard inside.

Babyboomer heartthrob Paul Petersen makes a grand entrance as the quintessential New Age male in the biblically–attuned atomic apocalypse *In the Year 2889.*

Later, the assembled group sits at the Ramsey's dinner table, as he explains the unfortunate situation. John declares himself to be the undisputed leader of the group. It is revealed that the assembled may in fact be the last six people on earth. John explains their particular luck in being trapped in this valley, where the radioactive mist is unable to penetrate due to unique meteorological conditions. As he describes the unique geography of the region, the viewer sees an impressive tabletop diorama of the house and surrounding area. The model also punctuates the microcosmic aspects of this little society, a "toy" society perhaps; it leads the viewer to think of the group as more savage than civilized, a "tribe" of sorts lost in a primitive jungle.

After the meeting, Steve takes food to his brother Granger, but John insists that Granger is ill with radiation poisoning and not worth the waste of food. Joanna counters that they are all still human and that they should act that way. John counters, "That's what I'm afraid of; we're all human." Two generations with completely different philosophies convey two diametrically opposed views of humanity, optimistic and pessimistic, each aware that only one can predominate. As in *The Eye Creatures* and *Beyond the Doors*, *2889* paints a largely pessimistic view of the "generation gap" of the 1960s, in which each group is not merely antithetical but confrontational towards the other, considering the other an enemy in need of redress or extinction.

Steve takes the food to Granger, who seems uninterested in it after all. He insists that he needs raw meat from the irradiated world "out there." Later, Steve sits with Joanna at the piano, presumably a comforting connection for her to the memory of civilized culture. Joanna informs Steve about her lost fiancé, and at that moment gets a strange sense of being communicated to telepathically. Steve joins John outside, and reveals that he is a geologist for an oil company. He and his brother headed for the valley after the attacks, knowing of its peculiar properties. John reveals that he was a navy man, and was in charge of a ship carrying various species of animals which were used for experimentation at the "Matsuo H-bomb tests." He alludes to horrible aftereffects on some of the creatures. Meanwhile, deep in the woods, a horribly mutated human prowls the eerie night, echoing John's disturbing reference.

This interesting reference, which is taken verbatim from *Day the World Ended*, is in some ways a smoking gun, and Buchanan was canny in including the reference in his updated film as a possible case of suppressed history deserving further study. Although the mentioned "Matsuo Tests" are fictitious, similar tests did occur, of course, the most famous being the three-pronged A-bomb test collectively known as "Operation Crossroads" carried out in the summer of 1946 at a lonely Pacific atoll called Bikini. A joint effort of various branches of the U.S. military, the first Crossroads test,

Neil Fletcher evokes the world-weary visage of patriarchy in decline as John Ramsey in Larry Buchanan's *In the Year 2889*.

code-named "Able," did indeed use a veritable zoo of live animals as unwitting test subjects to study the effects of A-bomb blast and subsequent radioactive fallout on living organisms. According to author Jonathan M. Weisgall, "In fact, an entire ship, the Navy attack transport *Burleson*, was deployed in late June to bring out to Bikini 200 pigs, 200 mice, 60 guinea pigs, 204 goats, and 5,000 rats."[4] According to Weisgall, when the navy's intention to use animals as test subjects was first made public, there was significant public protest of this most heinous use of animals for what was surely a horrible death, leading to over 7,000 official letters of protest; the outcry alone from dog lovers led the navy to remove canines from the roster of test subjects.[5] Even more disturbing was the navy's cover-up of the eventual fate of the animal subjects after the blast. The sole survivor of the "Able" blast, a sow tagged as "Pig 311," made worldwide headlines, and purportedly the cover of *Life* magazine, by emerging from the blast intact and healthy, and living for months afterwards, albeit unable to bear offspring. Other than a few vague references to the eventual deaths of all the other test subjects by lingering (and excruciating) radiation poisoning, there is precious little documentation available to the public to this day on the exact nature and procession of the animals' atomic road to death.

Three weeks pass. John, Steve and Joanna discuss Granger, who continues to live, even with the apparently deadly dose of radiation. He sneaks out at night and doesn't return until early the next morning. Steve counters that the group would benefit from studying his fallen brother's behavior. Steve walks Joanna to the garden, which looks suggestively like a middle-class redux of the biblical Garden of Eden. Buchanan clearly frames the pair as a New Age incarnation of the biblical Adam and Eve archetypes, even more so than Corman did in *Day*; they are another in a long line of Buchanan's heterosexual savior-couples. The two young people profess their feelings for each other and begin to kiss. However, Joanna is distracted by the allure of the telepathic impulses, dark connections still tempting her from the old, dying world. Later, Granger sneaks out of the house and into the woods. He locates a rabbit which has been caught in a trap. As he prepares to eat it, he sees something approaching, and runs away. In an effective p.o.v shot, the camera becomes "the other," the Mutant, which ambles slowly towards the trapped rabbit. The viewer sees for an instant what it might be like to be a soulless brute in a godless jungle, reduced to seeking freshly killed sustenance in a treacherous and brutal environment. Steve and John enter the woods and locate a pile of still-moist animal bones, shown via an unconvincing close-up which depicts what looks like leftover chicken bones from a tourist's picnic. They discuss the likelihood that Granger is a freak of this new world, a horrible mutation of radioactivity. They realize, too, that they may be mutating even as they speak, the good inevitably contaminated by surrounding evil.

John asks Steve what they should do, and Steve suggests finding solace in the Bible. Through one of Buchanan's lyrical lap dissolves, the scene changes to picture John sitting in his easy chair, reading passages from the good book. The camera pulls back slowly to reveal that John is reading not to himself, but to all the others, like a good father would to his children. Timothy and Mickey play cards, while the women rest and Steve keeps watch. This is another of Buchanan's noted "art shots," scenes he took time and care to create, even under the torturous shooting schedules he had to suffer with his cheapjack TV assignments.

Steve and John discuss the threat of rain as thunder rumbles ominously in the background. They ponder the possibilities of forging a new civilization should they survive. Steve seeks and locates Granger, who crouches, childlike, on a tree limb. He is terrified of the impending rain for some reason. Steve tries to connect with Granger, but the doomed man runs off into the woods. Meanwhile, Joanna and Jada take a refreshing swim in the pool, an act which clearly reenergizes both women. Jada warns Joanna not to steal Mickey from her, because the thug is the only friend the insecure woman has in the world. Joanna clearly has no interest in the hood, and seems taken aback by the suggestion. As if to reinforce her previous commitments, Joanna receives more telepathic messages from the Mutant, who spies on the women from the dense woods. Joanna correctly intuits, "Somebody's watching us, I can *feel* it." The women get spooked and run back to the house. The Mutant reinforces the paranoid sense of being watched, the ascendancy of the invasion of privacy so prevalent in modern culture, and a theme dear to the entire Azalea telefilm catalog.

In yet another trip into the woods, Steve and John discover more carelessly discarded chicken bones on the ground. John insists that Granger be destroyed, but Steve reminds him that his survival is the only way to see what they are up against. Steve thus also reminds the elder that the weakest elements in society are not only the responsibility of that society but a vital link between the creative and destructive forces within that same society, and

"The Buchanan Beast," crafted from meager resources by low-budget f/x guru Jack Bennett, always represented something larger than itself in the Azalea telefilms; in *In the Year 2889*, the undead survivor of atomic holocaust haunts the still-human survivors as a manifestation of their collective guilt and a foreshadowing of their dire destiny.

an invaluable key to its ever-fragile balance. John counters by bringing up, yet again, the elusive "Matsuo Tests." At this point, it almost seems that John, the elder, is *teasing* Steve, the younger, with this precious information. He keeps mentioning it superficially, but never reveals the information he possesses. In this way, he maintains power over his younger ally, and the desired information becomes sacred. By passing the "sacred text" to other members of society it not only empowers them but also lessens the importance of the elder member. Perhaps John knows that once he passes this information to Steve, he is no longer needed as leader, and is thus slated for extinction.

Steve meets Joanna at a nearby stone bridge, a safe yet provocative location which seems both a literal and figurative "bridge" between the sanctity of the idyllic garden and the horrors of the black jungle beyond. Joanna is forever haunted by telepathic messages, temptations from the death-world, and she mentions this problem to Steve. It is clear that Joanna cannot successfully embrace her role as a New Age Eve until this psychic umbilical cord to her old, decaying world is once and for all cut. Steve, however, has his own issues to bear and is more concerned about Joanna's emotional distancing from him. Still ruled by remnants of machismo ego, Steve cannot clearly see that Joanna is imprisoned by old patriarchal forces and needs a cathartic and absolute break from them before she can evolve. Joanna even concedes to Steve that she is in no mental condition to begin a new relationship, considering all the unfinished business which swirls around them. Unbeknownst to both of them, that symbol of the old, machismo-bound order, Mickey, watches silently from across the water, a parasite even to their thoughts. Joanna finally rejects Steve, at least temporarily, in a murky and despairing long shot which lasts for several seconds, showing the fallen "Adam" slinking slowly off the bridge and out of frame. This striking shot conveys the sadness and coldness of emotional rejection successfully. Through another evocative lap dissolve, Joanna appears in close-up, alone with her confusion and despair. Like a demonic imp, Mickey suddenly appears next to Joanna, startling the woman. The opportunistic brute tries to force himself on the wounded female, but she resists his loveless embrace, screaming, "You belong to Jada!" Mickey spits back, "I belong to me, get it? Me!" In so doing, he declares the patriarchy's intractable, infantile self-absorption.

Elsewhere, Timothy extracts his moonshine jug from a creek. Jada joins him, and learns about the drunkard's stash. Timothy shares his prized liquor with the sexy woman, and the two lonely souls share some innocent flirting. As Jada spits out her first taste of the rotgut, Timothy tells her, "The first taste is never good, Miss Jada. It's that second, long one that puts hair on your chest," and in a nutshell, shares the dark secret of the alcoholic.

Granger stumbles deeper into the radioactive woods, while Steve follows him to where the atomic vapor threatens. The scenes of the atomic vapor are created economically, via judicious camera cropping and a prolific fog machine, and are adequate, although no match for the impressive fog sequences in *Day*. Steve tells John more about his brother Granger. These revelations apparently make the stranger seem more human to John, for he finally shares his knowledge of the "Matsuo Tests." Seeing Steve's overwhelming humanity in the face of crisis, John is ready to turn over the reins of power to the courageous young man. John reveals that he was the captain of a ship which carried various animals into a test area which was then exposed to one of the first hydrogen bombs. As the ship's captain, he was privileged to see the results of atomic radiation on these poor creatures as he towed the ship from "Ground Zero." According to him, the majority of the animals perished, but several lived for a few days, in horribly mutated form. A chipmunk, coyote and monkey all mutated rapidly into grotesque renditions of their former selves, with skin toughened into a leather-like substance. He now pondered whether the same thing was happening to animals and humans out there in the radioactive woods, including Steve's brother Granger.

Finally relieved of this horrible burden of suppressed history, John tells Steve how much inspiration he has been to him in this most trying time, and in so doing, passes the torch of responsibility on to him. John then reveals his plan to repopulate the earth by using Joanna and Jada as breeding vessels for the men. It is almost as if John is offering his daughter to Steve as a present for taking over leadership of this microcosmic society, a patriarchal gesture both tribal and universal.

Sometime later John reveals his breeding program to Joanna; he thinks that she and Steve, and, oddly, Jada and Mickey, should propagate immediately in a reckless attempt to repopulate the earth. Joanna is at first horrified by the thought of arranged marriages in this atomic hellhole. She truly believes that her old flame Larry still lives out there somewhere. Realizing at some level the foolishness of this sterile and unfounded faith, as impotent as faith in an unseen god, Joanna eventually concedes to marry Steve in a week if the situation has not further deteriorated. Elsewhere, Jada strolls through the gloomy woods and meets Mickey, who is trying to fashion a key to get into the storeroom; this defective, deluded being still wants to gain access to decent society by any means possible. Mickey obsesses on virginal Joanna, and Jada gets angry. Mickey slaps the woman and tells her to get lost.

Later, Timothy and Jada again get drunk on moonshine, with not a care in the world. Admitting their own weaknesses yet refusing to condemn the other, Timothy and Jada illustrate the mercy for self and others prevalent in characters who become both survivors and victims in life. Jada tells Timothy to come back with her to the house. She wants to reward his kindness. The two stumble towards the house and spot John standing solemnly on the balcony. Jada mockingly salutes the ex-military man and requests permission to enter his domain. John, becoming aware that these weaklings are the victims of forces beyond their control, responds in character, "Permission granted, sailor!"

Inside, Jada performs her trademark striptease for the assembled group, dancing to a jazz record. She describes the charm she held over the audiences during her nightclub routine, who would often be reduced to dumb silence by her erotic performances. Jada tells of a time early in her career when she got nervous and decided to leave the stage, but Mickey forced her back. Thus is described a moment in time when a weak person teetered on the verge of a life-changing decision, but was coerced by the brute force of peer pressure. Jada coos ominously to Mickey, "I'll have to return the favor someday." Jada begins to remove her stockings in front of Timothy, who grabs lustily at her. However, John enters the scene, grabbing the record and breaking it over his knee. This act of violence brings the group to sobriety. John next breaks Timothy's liquor jug, to the cowboy's utter dismay. Jada and Timothy both run out of the room crying. To John's surprise, Steve and Joanna also leave the room, each throwing a judgmental glance at him. John now realizes he has been too harsh on the weaker elements in his little kingdom.

Later, John watches the perimeter of his land with binoculars. His well-ordered society is swiftly crumbling beneath him. Steve joins John and wonders about the whereabouts of Timothy. John apologizes for breaking Timothy's jug, confessing, "I had no idea he was an alcoholic," finally acknowledging the imperative of extending mercy to the weak. The alternating sequences which follow, showing poor Timothy stumbling through the woods while John ruminates over his history of rigid, moralistic behavior, deftly illustrates the paradox of moral wisdom: it is important to hold people up to a certain standard of behavior, but more important is realizing that this standard is an *ideal*, and some members of any societal construct simply cannot function at the high moral level you may assign them. This juxtaposition of two diametrically opposed character types which nonetheless share some striking similarities comprises one of the best montage sequences in the film.

Timothy happens upon a mutant, and runs for his life. John searches for the old cowboy, and soon stumbles upon Timothy's discarded hat. Steve ventures to the patio, sees the patriarch's chair uncharacteristically empty, and ventures into the woods as well. Timothy continues to run for his life, eventually reaching the edge of the valley. He climbs over the ridge, through the atomic fog, into the unknown territory. The wounded animal, in a final act of courage, removes himself from his community in order to die alone. John has followed, and calls out to the cowboy, but he sprains his ankle, and so loses Timothy in the deadly mist. Soon, Steve catches up with John, who is now fatally contaminated. On their way back to the house, the two men find Granger, dead on the ground, their human guinea pig finally taken from them.

Elsewhere, Joanna sits alone at the stone bridge, throwing pebbles in the water. Mickey sneaks up to her and forces himself on the poor girl. As he is about to assault Joanna sexually, Jada appears and commands Joanna to run home. Mickey and Jada argue. Jada tries to make up with her man, but the gangster hates her and sends her away crying. Jada runs off to take a dip in the pool, but Mickey follows close behind and meets her at the poolside; pretending to help her up, he instead drowns the poor woman. In *Day*, the gangster tosses his girlfriend unceremoniously off a cliff. Jada's death, though horrific, is certainly more meaningful and significant, as she drowns in the very life-fluid which in another world might have revitalized her.

Later, John lies in bed, beginning to feel the effects of radiation poisoning. He pleads with Steve to kill Mickey before it is too late, before the "bad apple" really does spoil the bunch, but the honorable Steve simply cannot kill in cold blood. That night, Joanna awakens when she receives more telepathic messages; they compel her to walk into the woods wearing only her nightgown. The sleepwalking virgin is soon confronted by the Mutant, who can now be assumed to be her fiancé, Larry, in monstrously altered form. Joanna faints upon seeing her dear beloved in such a state, and the Mutant carries his betrothed deep into the woods, perhaps to consummate the nuptials denied him by atomic holocaust. Joanna's screams awaken Steve, who rushes to the living room. As John nears death, he becomes sensitive enough to feel some telepathic connection to his daughter; he is certain that the Mutant has Joanna in his clutches. John instructs Steve to get a 30-round Luger out of the storeroom and search for the abducted virgin.

As John rests fitfully, Mickey finally manages to steal his revolver; he reveals his selfish plans to take over the house and Joanna once John dies; with God-figure John dead, Eden is certainly vulnerable to being overrun by Evil. Suddenly, ominous thunder claps and the dreaded rain begins to fall, accentuating the dire fate of John's "tribe." The Mutant carries Joanna deeper into the woods, with Steve in hot pursuit. Suddenly, at the pond, the Mutant becomes afraid and drops Joanna. Joanna senses his fear and runs into the water. Steve joins Joanna in the water and they embrace; the New Age couple now feels both protected and empowered by the healing qualities of the water, as both symbol of female sexual energy and enveloping fluid of an earth-womb. Emphasized in *2889* even more so than in *Day* due to Buchanan's impressionistic, textural framing of the water, this scene shows the pond as striving to first heal and then birth this sacred pair, who portent a new hope for all mankind. It begins to pour rain, and the Mutant runs frantically, trying to escape the rain which to it is a purely destructive, even judgmental, force.

At the house, John asks Mickey to go outside and get a sample of the rainwater to test for radi-

Joanna Ramsey (Charla Doherty) suffers a near-fatal telepathic connection with denizens of the old order in *In the Year 2889*.

ation. While Mickey is occupied, John retrieves another revolver, hidden under his pillow. Mickey returns, and John discovers the water is pure, safe from contamination. The tribe has passed their survival test and can now benefit from God's showering of love and healing. John now realizes that the one thing atomic mutants cannot stand is pure water. In the woods, the Mutant is overwhelmed by the falling rain and sinks to the ground, only to dissolve into vapor. Steve and Joanna emerge from the healing pond and head back home. Joanna notes that with the death of the creature, the telepathic messages have stopped. At the house, Mickey informs John that he is going to shoot Steve as he returns. John waits until Mickey is taking aim and shoots Mickey in the back, a dishonorable but vital act for the survival of the tribe. Joanna and Steve break into a run at the sound of the gunshots and the film ends with a freeze-frame of the two lovers holding hands over the title "The Beginning." Significantly, Buchanan leaves out the death of the father, which comprises the dramatic coda in *Day*, preferring to leave the ending ambiguous and patriarchy's role in fostering a new egalitarian society more implied than stated.

At first appearing quite similar, *In the Year 2889* is markedly different from its prototype in many ways. For instance, Buchanan does a better job than Corman of painting the space surrounding our heroes' "Garden of Eden" as a threatening, primordial void straight from fairy tale mythos, a forest primeval of macrocosmic proportions. And by centering the narrative within the confines of a typical suburban home, the decay of the community within presciently mirrors the simultaneous crumbling of middle-class life in America.

Most of the exterior action in *2889* is filmed in the woods, a recurrent setting in the Azalea telefilms, a setting which figures prominently in the entire series but for the strictly urban *Mars Needs Women*. While filming in wooded areas is a low-budget film staple, providing a natural setting with abundant backgrounds and free lighting, Buchanan took the significance of this iconic American space one step further. The woods at the edge of Suburbia represent a primal space, a missing link between the urban and the rural, perhaps the last token "wild space" available to the urbanized middle class, a connection between its agricultural past and technocentric future. As such, it is a space of beauty and memory, danger and mystery, utterly nostalgic yet frighteningly unknown. Untouched by human progress, it is many ways a modern "sacred" space. It is a familiar and beloved environment, especially for the postwar baby boomers who were the Azalea telefilms' target audience. The Suburban woods are, in essence, *everyone's* backyard. Scenes filmed there come across as universal and familiar, yet another way in which Buchanan tied his films intractably to his target audience.

The characters in *2889* are more fleshed out, given room to grow beyond the attractive yet clichéd portraits seen in *Day*. John, well played by Neil Fletcher, encapsulates the harsh, rigid patriarchy with stunning clarity. His raspy voice, wrinkled visage and rigid demeanor portray perfectly the elder world in decline, perhaps even in its death throes, yet still determined to control its environment as long as possible. Given his strict moral structure, it is something of a revelation when he manifests the courage to kill Mickey, knowing that the new order cannot hope to survive until its mortal enemies are vanquished. Steve and Joanna are one of Buchanan's archetypal New Age couples, a dyad which appears with increasing frequency as Buchanan progresses, and achieving perhaps its purest invocation in *Hughes and Harlow: Angels in Hell* (1977). Battling, escaping and eventually abandoning the old order, these duos plow ahead to forge the beginnings of a new, pacific and egalitarian order from their own example, and with any luck, from their subsequent works. While admittedly romantic and heterosexist, these warrior-couples nonetheless appear in Buchanan's films as wholly progressive and egalitarian, emerging from a crippled middle class to wage war not only on the tribal, patriarchal father, but also on the corrupt institutions of their peers.

As opposed to Steve and Joanna, who represent the hope of a new world of resurrected and corrected middle-class values, gangster Mickey and his moll, Jada, signify both the lower classes, and thus the older world which is so brutally to die out. As Mickey and Jada are done in, finally, both by their low morals and their limited vision, so is the world surrounding them desolated by society's inability to apply strict moral precepts to applied knowledge, so well (and often) represented in genre cinema by orgiastic nuclear holocaust. Yet, ultimately Jada is a redeemable character, while Mickey is not. Jada deserves salvation because she acknowledges her low behavior and accepts redress from the community; several times throughout the film she solicits intervention from other members of the group for a betterment of her situation. Mickey, on the other hand, is blinded by idiot egotism and, more importantly, is completely unrepentant. His stance is not helped by the cruel murder of his lover, a sacrifice which makes Jada all the more dear, and perhaps even saintly, by her absence.

The alcoholic Timothy, played with grim pathos by Bill Thurman, is an interesting modification of the similar character in *Day*, an elderly gold prospector. The prospector, whose presence immediately recalled the mythos of the old West, and more specifically the B-Western movie genre which was in rapid decline at the time, carried with him as his constant companion and familiar, an old burro tellingly named "Diablo." The animal served as a diabolical anchor to the old man, fatally chaining him to the poisonous old order and making it impossible for him to establish healthy rapport with the new community and the younger generation. In *2889*, the donkey is replaced by "Demon Rum," and its owner/companion is most assuredly done in by his poisonous relation to the cruel substance. Timothy, knowing himself to be irretrievable and hopeless, mercifully isolates himself from the community, refusing to contaminate others with his illness. He is rarely seen in the home setting, but is often skulking the periphery of the woods, knowing that he is more of the dark world than of the light.

One of the highlights of *2889* is the presence of popular entertainer Paul Petersen in the lead role. Petersen, known at the time as the TV son of Donna Reed on the long-running *The Donna Reed Show*, also had successful careers as a recording artist and novelist. An affable, charismatic actor, Petersen reprised the role played in *Day the World Ended* by Richard Denning. Whereas Denning played the male lead in traditional B-movie style as a macho ex-soldier, Petersen updates the character to a composite of the "New Age" male and the All American "boy next door," a significant shifting of the male icon's identity and, ultimately, purpose and motivation. Wearing white chinos and a brown turtleneck through most of the film, and endlessly smoking cigarettes, Petersen's character Steve embodies an updated archetype of the sensitive, compassionate male. But for the ill-advised smoking, Steve succinctly embodies one of Buchanan's New Age icons, a courageous and kind soul who just might be able to rescue a diseased patriarchal society from complete annihilation.

In his autobiography, Buchanan stated that while shooting *2889* all cast and crew were distracted by the zany antics of sexy Quinn O'Hara, who apparently played Jada the stripper a little too realistically:

> Quinn O'Hara, through no fault of her own, was sabotaging the show. Quinn was a stunning sexpot with a comic temperament. While the crew should have been focused on the horrors of the nuclear story, they were in stitches from Quinn's antics and mesmerized by her measurements. We were at an impasse.[6]

Buchanan claimed his "solution" consisted of changing the script so that Quinn's character was killed off early, letting the production continue unfettered by her presence. Truth be told, however, Jada dies at exactly the same point (although not in the same manner) where her prototype did in *Day*, and the alterations claimed by Buchanan seem minimal, if indeed there were any.[7]

14

Creature of Destruction

Creature of Destruction (1967), the sixth Azalea telefilm, is a shoestring-budgeted color remake of Edward L. Cahn's *The She-Creature* (1956). *Creature of Destruction* (henceforth called *Creature*) is a film of impressive cinematic structural experimentation which ruminates on some of the darker aspects of sexual politics. In some ways, *Creature* is a follow-up text to *Mars Needs Women*, in which certain observations of the current state of sexual affairs are contemplated. Eschewing the issues of sexual promiscuity and identity, *Creature* focuses specifically on the problematic aspects of the middle-class heterosexual couple, and the destructive, potentially diabolical forces which such a dynamic can unleash within individuals, in essence the antithesis of Buchanan's beloved heterosexual savior-couple. The "Master-Slave dialectic" of Theodore Adorno is noted in *Creature*, and the film as well obsesses on the subjects of emotional repression and female rage.

Creature's source film, *The She-Creature*, is a most unusual entry in the mid-1950s drive-in thriller genre. The screenplay by Lou Rusoff centers primarily on the political and sexual intrigues between two couples, and how these persons intermingle with each other to largely disastrous effect. The sophisticated scenario suggests that this early AIP production was intended more for a general, mature audience than the subsequent "monster movies" which AIP fashioned directly to the teenage/youth market; it is by far the most "adult" film AIP released during this period.[1]

Larry Buchanan and Enrique Touceda took the screenplay for *The She-Creature* and radically transformed it; although the essential plot line remains intact, the settings, characters and philosophical impact of *Creature of Destruction* are far removed from its prototype. Buchanan eschews the carnival and beachside settings of *The She-Creature*, and bases his entire scenario at a seedy vacation resort in Suburbia, thus shifting the focus of the piece to the heartland of America. *Creature* showcases the key hypnosis act by placing it at the beginning, as it conveys essential information about the Master-Slave power dynamic which is pivotal to the film. This places *Creature* well in the tradition of the classic exploitation film, and the carnival atmosphere which the tacky enterprise evokes. The love triangle which develops between Andrea, Lombardi and the Psychiatrist, turning *The She-Creature* into predictable, steamy melodramatic fare, is downplayed in *Creature*, to focus more attention on the relationship between the evil hypnotist and his unwitting subject.

Creature weaves three sexually oriented themes, all intrinsically connected and each echoing the others in remarkable ways. Firstly, *Creature* is specifically about the exploitation of women, illustrated in a manner far more conscious and concise than its source film. The protagonist, Doreena, is the symbol for that exploitation, and her trials describe this systemic gender-based abuse in three major ways. Firstly, Doreena's "forced labor"

Doreena (Pat Delaney) slumps in her ersatz throne like a rag doll, an unwitting slave to her lord and master, Dr. Basso, in Larry Buchanan's treatise on female exploitation, *Creature of Destruction.*

mirrors in microcosmic form the ubiquitous exploitation of woman's labor by patriarchal society. Secondly, Doreena's psychic rape and humiliation, performed almost nightly and most significantly *in public*, echoes the exploitation of woman's suffering and performance as entertainment for the jaded bourgeoisie, with clear allusions to pornography and the sex industry. Finally, Doreena's conscripted performances echo the use of woman's suffering as *product*, a commodity made tangible and marketable. This aspect has uncomfortable allusions to the endemic exploitation of the animal kingdom by the food industry. Doreena's past life experiences, extracted against her will by a cruel master, reminds one of the hen in the factory farm, forced into producing eggs for the gluttonous masses until she has literally reproduced herself to death. All of these "uses" of the enslaved female have been used throughout history to make men (not women) rich and famous, in itself a final abuse and insult.

Allied with this theme, and essential to its existence, is the need for the dominating class to continually and effectively suppress Woman's identity, personality, and self. Basso's success is predicated on the assumption that Doreena is a mute, exploitable non-self, and will remain so indefinitely; her repression is responsible for society's ongoing supply of both entertainment and commerce. It goes without saying that for Doreena to sabotage this involuntary social contract with her masters would seriously thwart, and perhaps destroy, a community dependent upon her ill-gotten labors.

In response to this oppression, the third theme which dominates *Creature* is that of female rage. That this rage is expressed in *Creature* via violent, bloody means implies that emancipation is a revolution of sorts. This may have been what Buchanan had in mind when he conceived a more righteous "sexual revolution" than the confused, stumbling mass orgy going on during this time period. Buchanan's point seems to be that no matter what the subject and object, any revolution worth its salt is at its core *political*, and of necessity violent.

The opening shot of *Creature* features a superimposed quotation, attributed to sixteenth century French philosopher Michel de Montaigne: "There is no monster in the world ... so treacherous as man." This starkly misanthropic declaration flows into a bizarre, freeform montage which owes more to experimental cinema than mainstream narrative tradition. Loosely constructed, with alternate takes of a scene which occurs again later in the film, *Creature*'s prologue departs from expected narrative convention to emerge as a somewhat surreal collage, haunting and metaphorical. In the prologue, silent but for a music underscore, a goofy monster stalks and finally assaults a frightened man. Close-ups of the frightened man cut to close-ups of the monster, revealing both their synchronicity and essential sameness. As the monster catches up with the man on a dry-docked yacht, the man screams silently. The man rings a bell for assistance, but the bell's ring is silent to the audience, and thus to the world. The improbable beast claws the man to death, before looking directly up at the audience, as if to imply, "You're next!" Completely detached from any back-story or semblance of narrative anchoring, the scene becomes entirely cinematic. The beast can be interpreted any number of ways, but, as the man being chased looks both haunted and guilty, one assumes that in some ways the attack was deserved. The beast then suggests man's guilt of sin, hounding him to death, or justice, following the guilty to their final sentence. Most cinema monsters can be interpreted as a metaphor for death haunting the mortal soul, and *Creature*'s beast certainly represents Death to this man, and perhaps Man in general. Standing as an elemental metaphor for the life of Man, it reveals in simplistic relief the existential truth that throughout his short and desperate life, Man is constantly haunted by the shadow of Death. Facing Death, doomed Man rings the bell of Salvation, but for naught, as he knows all too well for whom the bell tolls. The villain of the piece, recognizable as a heavy because of his stereotypical attire (top hat and tails), appears at the start of the prologue and could be seen as a malevolent God figure, orchestrating this universal chase and watching bemusedly his creation's pathetic attempts to escape his fate.

Following this revelatory opening, which segues into a jaunty AITV logo, the main credits roll, starting over a low-angle, point-of-view shot of the camera on a lake and moving swiftly towards land. Accepting this body of water as symbolic of the feminine principle (female empowerment and libido), *Creature* starts from this point of view and is sympathetic to this principle. The camera quickly approaches land, the emphasis shifting to the earthly, male principle, which will figure significantly, if negatively, in the ensuing story. Finally, the film's title is superimposed over an extreme close-up of the goofy beast of the film, in order to clarify the metaphorical nature of the beast.

At the popular Tanglewood Lodge on the edge of Lake Texoma, near the Texas/Oklahoma border, the guests are not only treated to a smorgasbord of outdoor activities but a varied assortment of indoor nighttime activities, including nightly performances from popular entertainers in the Tanglewood Lounge. Tonight's performance features Dr. John Basso (Les Tremayne), the world-famous hypnotist. Basso claims that through hypnosis he can regress his beautiful assistant, Doreena (a sorrowful Pat Delaney), to a past life. Doreena, a haunting beauty, sits passively in a large upholstered chair, seemingly asleep or in a trance. The crowd applauds, and the arrogant impresario smiles smugly, starving for cheap adulation.

Basso intones, "What is the ultimate science can offer? Truth! One of those truths is this: that hidden within each of us is not only the capacity to love and to hate, but to take that final step, to become not only a creator but a destroyer, a mad, unreasoning killer! That final breakdown of our manners, morays, customs, that takes us away from the millions of years of civilization, to the animalistic, to the monster, that lies within each of us!" Thus is stated the philosophy of the movie in original dialogue written for *Creature*. This cynical, misanthropic, even apocalyptic perspective is a radical departure from the subtler mood of *The She-Creature*.

Whereas Lombardi's performances in *The She-Creature* are purely for financial gain and self-aggrandizement, in *Creature* Basso's talents seem focused on one goal from the outset: murder and mayhem. Indeed, no reference to the "past lives" aspect of the act is mentioned in the first performance. It exists only so Basso can shout, "The prognostication is Murder!" Basso's gleeful misanthropy is thus stated and further comparison to the prototypical character in *The She-Creature* can be dropped. Basso is a unrepentant sociopath, an architect of death, a "creature of destruction." Even his "uniform," an anachronistic hypnotist's outfit consisting of top hat and tuxedo, paints him as a vaguely comic caricature of domineering male power.

Buchanan's naming of his villain as Basso is inspired. In music, especially opera, the "basso" is the male singer with the lowest vocal range. As it applies to Dr. Basso, this implies three things. First, his overt theatricality is addressed in the allusion to opera and the performing arts. Second, his surname punctuates the fact that he symbolically and emphatically represents the male of the species. Third, the fact that the "basso" in musical terminology refers to the lowest of male voices, the choice of name might also be meant to imply that Dr. Basso is among the *lowest* of creatures, morally speaking.

A uniformed military man enters the auditorium to off-screen applause (which is notable, as he will turn out to be the hero of the piece). This is Dr. Theodore Dell (a deadpan Aron Kincaid), an air force captain and psychiatrist specializing in the studies of parapsychology and combat psychosis. As Dell steps into the room, he pauses long enough to frame himself on the right-hand side of the sitting Doreena, as Basso stands on the left. The scene thus framed clues the audience as to the three main characters in *Creature*, the central figure being the woman and the two men providing both positive and negative influences on her; this framing also alludes to another Socratic dialogue, a narrative device which worked well in *Zontar, the Thing from Venus*.

The scene changes to the outside of the lodge, at a stone grotto where a group of teenagers dance to the music of Texas pop star Scotty McKay. McKay warbles a song about comic-book superhero Batman, an ill-written knock-off of the classic Neal Hefti theme from the hit ABC-TV series *Batman*. The scene serves the plot briefly by introducing the audience to Dell's fiancé, Lynn (Suzanne Roy).

Back inside, the owner of the Tanglewood, Sam Crane (a curmudgeonly Neil Fletcher), and his lovely wife, known throughout the film only as "Mrs. Crane" (a long-suffering Anne MacAdams) share a drink on the lobby couch, in one of those dreadfully lackluster, generic middle-class settings Buchanan mythologized by inserting them into bigger-than-life scenarios. Mrs. Crane, a student of all things occult, is concerned about Basso's prediction of murder on the beach, but Crane laughingly chimes in, "That wasn't a demonstration; that was an *act!*" This modern entrepreneur is a cynical unbeliever, although not above exploiting other people's fears and superstitions, as will become evident.

Outside, Dr. Basso stands proudly in his "uniform," staring out at the water and trying to will a murder into existence, misanthropy personified. Simultaneously, Dr. Dell and Lynn are discussing Basso, and, surprisingly, Dell does not dismiss the man's claims of psychic regression. Suddenly a woman screams; the murder has occurred, just as Basso predicted. As Dell runs to locate the origin of the screams, the viewer is confronted with the possibility that the murder was indeed desired, and possibly engineered.

Dell runs into a nearby cottage as Basso watches from the shadows. Inside, a young man sits on a bed, apparently in shock, but when Dell touches the man, he falls over dead. A horribly mangled young woman slumps in the corner. The killings occurred in the "Honeymoon Cottage," so the murdered couple were likely newlyweds. The murder thus takes the role of a ritual sacrifice, symbolically attacking the institution of marriage and its attendant emphasis on procreation and the perpetuation of the species. Basso is thus revealed to have not only a misanthropic but apocalyptic agenda, as only the destruction of the entire world will satisfy his thirst for death.

The police arrive, and an investigation of the crime commences under the watch of Lieutenant Blake (Roger Ready). Blake interviews various members of the Tanglewood community, and Mrs. Crane posits the possible connection between the horrible murders and Dr. Basso's uncanny prediction of death the night before.

Basso returns to his rooms and speaks with Doreena, who is still in a hypnotic trance. Basso begins to bring Doreena out of her involuntary slumber when Blake and Dell join him. Both ask questions of the cagey hypnotist, who seems more amused than concerned. He reveals to the shocked men the actual identity of the killer: "She is a huge, indestructible creature who comes out of the beginning of time." Basso is cognizant, even at this early stage, of the gender of his pet "Creature of Destruction." Basso taunts the humorless pair by predicting that the killer will come ashore again soon.

The men leave, and Basso finishes bringing Doreena back to waking "life." The pouty Doreena mutters, "You've had me in deep hypnosis! I asked you not to do that!" and Basso apologizes, very much like a bickering married couple hammering out a domestic dispute. This exchange also illustrates the position of the postwar female, as she was used by the male, for cooking, cleaning and childbearing, unless she came out of her "deep hypnosis" and attempted a liberation. Doreena continues to communicate her hatred for her master/lover/boss, expressing also shame at her own inability to become autonomous. She sighs, "Here I am, sitting here like a piece of clay," a sketchy allusion to tales of "God" using dust or clay to fashion Man (and by extension Woman, solely for Man's service).

Basso confesses that Doreena is not only important to him as a scientific experiment and money maker but also as a romantic partner. Doreena is visibly repulsed by this recollection of her sexual servitude to this monster, and vows once again to leave him at the first opportunity. However, as Doreena tries to rise out of her chair, Basso easily deflates the woman with a wave of his hand, a sparkling illustration of the abusive male's effortless diabolical power over the female in entrenched patriarchal culture. To reinforce this power dynamic, and the woman's necessary low esteem in order to participate in this cruel sociopolitical dynamic, Basso taunts Doreena by reminding her, "What were you before I found you?" In response Doreena sadly whispers, "Nothing." In a hateful patriarchal culture where misogyny is essential dogma, Woman is nothing except in relation to Man. This has always been true in spirit, and in many cases in legal fact, as history shows numerous societies in which the woman, from a legal and political perspective, literally did not "exist."

As Dr. Theodore Dell (Aron Kincaid), a psychiatrist, comes to rescue Doreena (Pat Delaney) from her hypnotic servitude to mad hypnotist Dr. Basso in the misanthropic *Creature of Destruction*, one wonders if Dell's interest is purely altruistic — or is there a hint of lust in his sympathetic glance?

As Basso continues his attempt to seduce Doreena back into passive obedience, he caresses the throne-like chair on which Doreena rests, even fondling it suggestively. This reveals yet another side to this odd dynamic: Basso controls Doreena's mind, body and soul, and obviously desires her physically, *but he does not touch the woman*. It can be safely assumed that Basso is terrified of a woman's body, and probably can be claimed sexually impotent.

The next morning, Dell and Crane discuss Basso, and the horrible murders. Crane thinks there is big money in Basso's act when the lucky coincidence of the murders is thrown in. In the murderous regime called capitalism, death is not lamentable or even excusable, but an essential exploitable byproduct of this ghoulish, predatory system which sees profit in everything, including (perhaps especially) in the blood of innocents. Crane presents to Dell the idea that they could make Basso a worldwide phenomenon, with attendant fame and fortune, if augmented by Dell's official "stamp of approval" as a respected member of the scientific community. Dell is repulsed by the idea and excuses himself.

Crane visits Basso in his room, and goes into his proposal about going national with his "act." Basso retorts, "I have no act; I have *knowledge*," a statement simultaneously delusional and accurate. Mercenary at root, Basso acquiesces to the crude businessman, and Crane and Basso strike an uneasy deal. As Basso reluctantly shakes the entrepreneur's hand, they become a microcosm of that unholiest of alliances, the merging of government and business which creates the most tyrannical of political systems: Capitalism, or, to paraphrase Lenin, Fascism-in-training.

Basso runs to Doreena to tell her the "good news"; he oddly believes that she will be delighted at what is essentially the solidifying of their abusive bond in perpetuity. Basso whispers, "I will touch you, and you will awaken." In a startling fourth-wall occurrence, as Doreena slowly comes to consciousness the viewer can clearly hear director Buchanan whisper, off-camera, "Okay wake up. Now look up at him. Good!" Whether by accident or design, Buchanan here conveys the dark truth that all men are manipulators; indeed, even he, the filmmaker, is a Svengali of sorts, giving orders to his "puppets."

That evening Basso and Doreena again perform before the usual audience of vacationers, plus representatives of the mass media. As Basso and Doreena enter the theater, Dell gets his first good look at Basso's beautiful slave and he is entranced. He stares ceaselessly at Doreena, and the viewer senses that there is a definite psychic connection between the two. An enthusiastic Crane introduces Basso, who intones, "It has been my very good fortune to find in this young lady, the perfect hypnotic subject!" In other words, Man is grateful to have found in repressed Woman the perfect slave. Emboldened by his newly-found financial support, the arrogant Basso bleats, "In my hands has been given a power given to no other man!" revealing that he thinks himself more god than man. Basso taunts the audience with, "She will come out of the lake again, and she must kill."

Basso begins to put Doreena into her trance, but notices rebellion on Doreena's part and invites Dr. Dell up to observe the hypnotic regression. Dell politely refuses, but Crane bullies the young doctor into coming onstage to participate in the exploitation of this sad soul. Basso restates his philosophy to the audience, that "life is eternal and endless, and that the soul lives on from incarnation to incarnation." He could thus be seen as a symbol of organized Religion, another repressive political system in which the subjugation of Woman has always been a primary goal.

Basso continues to put Doreena into trance as Dell observes. The framing of this scene again shows Doreena in the middle, with Basso flanking the left and Dell the right. Here, Basso and Dell look amusingly like the little angel and devil figures that have sat on the shoulder of many a cartoon character, trying to convince them to choose either good or evil. Basso gives Dell permission to question his woman, giving him over to her figuratively as well with a sarcastic, "She's all yours, Captain!"

After Dell questions Doreena, Basso regresses her and she soon changes personality entirely, becoming a smiling, winsome young Cockney girl named "Marion Rhodes." During Doreena's metamorphosis into "Marion," the camera tracks in slowly, cautiously fascinated by what this picture of an emancipated woman might look like. Indeed, "Marion" does appear to be Doreena's healthier, happier alter ego, for the only time Doreena smiles is as "Marion." Dell dispenses more questions, all of which "Marion" answers flawlessly.

Basso ends the act by stating, "There are still more frontiers to be explored," at which point Doreena faints dead away. Basso ends the performance and escorts the exhausted Doreena offstage. Dell looks on, haunted by this astonishing woman. His fiancée, Lynn, notices Ted's interest in this new female and walks off, rejected. This scene paints well the sheer exhaustion, as well as humiliation, inherent in forced public performance, the act of baring one's soul for the passing amusement of complete strangers, again with clear allusions to the entertainment and pornography industries.

Dell walks onstage to confront Basso. The two stand opposite each other, with a lit candle standing between them — a referent to the healing light of knowledge, the abiding energy of truth, and symbol of the just-departed woman. Ted asks, quite candidly, if he could "borrow" Doreena for "my own examination." In requesting to join in the time-honored male ritual of passing the woman from man to man, Ted reveals himself to be, although progressive and surely not the drooling misogynist which Basso is, still a man, and not above some exploitation of the desired female object.

Basso responds, tongue firmly in cheek, "In the interest of science, I am more than willing." Basso then blows out the guiding light of the candle and announces, "Now if you'll excuse me, I think I'll go out and get some air," and walks off-screen while smiling smugly and fondling his moustache. He has won, for the moment; the forces of evil have duped the forces of good into appropriating the captured female object to their own purposes which, although ultimately altruistic, are ostensibly exploitative in nature.

The next day, after the creature has killed pop star Scotty McKay, Lt. Blake again confronts Basso and shows him a police composite sketch of the creature based on an eyewitness at the beach. The fairly accomplished sketch shows the head and right hand of the grimacing beast, thus codifying the implausible man-in-suit creation as iconic; as always, the beast in an Azalea telefilm is more than it appears to be, more symbolic than literal. Blake suggests that the witness hallucinated the creature, but Basso counters that the creature is "the soul of a living woman, transmigrated to her first, primitive body." An angry Basso excuses the cop abruptly.

Again alone, Basso looks out the window and notices Doreena uncharacteristically outside, sitting by the poolside. Panicked at this atypical show of independence, he rushes out to abort this display of autonomous behavior. Doreena sits at poolside, eyes covered in sunglasses, seemingly at peace. A military fighter roars overhead, foreshadowing Doreena's rescue by air force captain Dell, which she senses swiftly approaching. Basso reaches Doreena first, however, literally obscuring her sun-drenched face with his sinister black shadow; he reminds her of their malevolent pact. Doreena again pleads with Basso to free her from this domestic hell of spiritual and physical slavery. Basso asserts his will over Doreena,

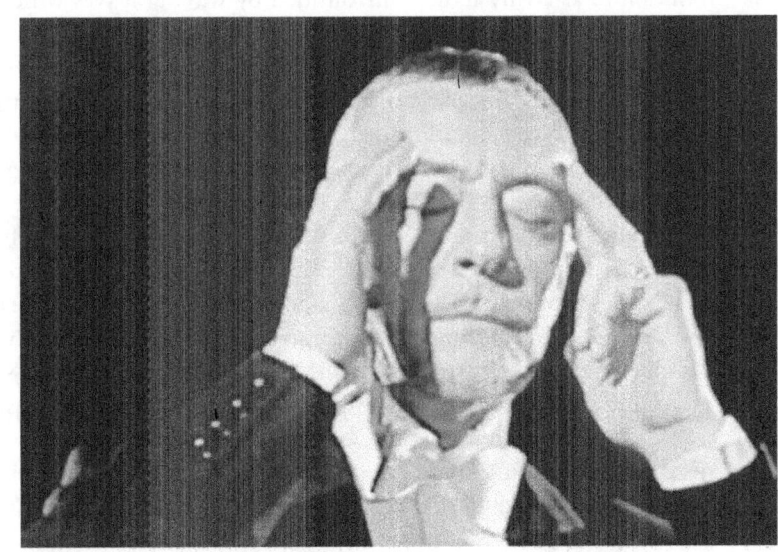

Dr. John Basso (Les Tremayne) focuses his powers of concentration to summon a hell-beast from the depths of the collective unconscious to actualize his desire for the complete destruction of civilization, in *Creature of Destruction*.

putting her into a passive somnambulistic state, ordering her to resist Dell's entreaties: "He is our enemy. He is trying to destroy us." Basso then whispers, "Your beauty must not be destroyed; it is *mine*, to do with as I will," in a frank declaration of abusive misogynist agenda.

Basso sees Dell approaching and bids a hasty farewell. Dell sits next to Doreena, loosens his tie, and quips: "You certainly picked a hot spot for our first session." He seems nervous, as if trying to impress a first date. There is definitely a sexual content to his intellectual query, but he is nonetheless empathic for that flaw. Foregoing hypnosis, ostensibly due to the heat, Dell reveals himself to be more merciful than Basso; he also has the power to manipulate this woman against her will but chooses not to. He thus offers Doreena a much-needed equalization of the maladjusted gender power balance.

Noticing how cold and aloof Doreena is, Dell queries, "You've been instructed to resist me. You must understand, I want to help you, I want to get you back to a real life. You've been living in a shadow." Doreena is sending mixed signals here. Is she under her boss's spell even now, or playing coy with her new love interest? The scene ends unresolved via a suggestive lap dissolve; it is as if Doreena is saying to Dell, "I like you, doctor, and moreover I trust you. Do what you will to me. It can't be worse than what the last guy did...."

Crane holds a meeting with Basso and informs him that their partnership has met with success: a book contract has been signed, along with a lucrative newspaper syndication deal. Emboldened, Basso insists that the contract be revised in his favor financially and Crane reluctantly agrees. This scene nicely illustrates the strained, ever-fragile dynamic between business and art, manufacturer and distributor, that corrupt liaison between the producer and the promoter in advanced industrial culture. Ironically, the commodity they are negotiating is the labors of Woman, who is not even acknowledged, being truly a non-self.

Dr. Basso, again dressed in his "uniform," walks along the beach in an arty shot which frames him as a tiny figure, surrounded by waving leaves which dominate the foreground, suggesting that though evil men try to conquer and exploit Nature, they are dwarfed by Nature's awesome power, which will triumph. Elsewhere, a young couple park along the lakeside, but they are soon attacked and murdered by the Creature. It seems evident by this time that Basso can manifest the Creature at will, with or without Doreena's intrinsic assistance, and that Basso murders at random as a way of releasing tension, painting him as a psychopath of the most diabolical kind, as is the patriarchy he represents.

Soon Dell questions Doreena again, who verifies that, before the murders, Basso puts her into a deep trance from which she cannot awaken. As she puts it, "It's like I was dead," a useful description of the non-actualized female of the day. She continues that she felt "very tired, as if I've been doing something very strenuous," certainly the voice of a woman who has given her labors to an ungrateful man, under the trance of servitude, for her entire life.

Dell goads Doreena by implying that someone who rested that much should feel refreshed upon awakening, but Doreena confirms that she always awakens from her marathon sleep sessions feeling more enervated than before. This is a classic description of chronic depression, in which a person can do little but sleep, and yet feels ever more fatigued and drained of life energy. Chronic depression, of course, was endemic to the middle-class postwar woman of Suburbia, where she was trapped in a pasteboard hell and given nothing to do but breed and serve males.

Dell insists that for Doreena to survive, both physically and mentally, she must leave Basso once and for all. He asserts that it will not be easy or painless, and compares abandoning her master thusly: "It'll take time; it's like getting rid of an infectious disease," a marvelous description as to not only how repulsive and negative this sociosexual dynamic has become for woman, but also how hardy the parasite, how deep the roots. Doreena asks Dell, "Why are you wasting your time with me?" Dell replies coyly, "Am I? Wasting my time?" in what is likely a romantic allusion. Doreena responds sadly, "Yes." This is not a rejection, but an admission of the woman's terminally low self-esteem, another sinister tool of the patriarchy to keep women enchained.

Blake enters and asks for the couple's input. He again states his belief that Basso is the killer, and paints the performer as a textbook sociopath: "Yet I know Basso hates the whole world and everybody in it, except himself. I believe he'd set a match to the whole thing if he could," a lyrical statement which could serve as a misanthrope's credo. Blake pleads with Dell to conduct a full scientific investigation of Basso, replete with experts in the field. Dell refuses, uncharacteristically obstructive to the cop; is it because he doubts the efficacy of the operation, or does he, indeed, like Basso, secretly desire Doreena all for himself, and will endorse nothing that might take her away from him?

Blake forces the issue, and even threatens to subpoena Dell, who reluctantly agrees to examine Basso. Blake tells the doctor that everyone, including Basso, has been informed of the impending critical investigation and concludes, "The rest is up to you." As he says this, Doreena, who has been sitting silent the whole time, bows her head in shame, as the two men turn to look at her. Again, a discussion of events which rely on Doreena's labors and, ultimately, her fate, is conducted entirely without her permission or input, *even in her presence,* yet another telling sketch of the blind, hateful misogyny of patriarchal culture.

Crane visits Basso, who plays solitaire, illustrating the inevitable loneliness of the misanthrope. Crane is nervous about the killings, and ruminates over his and Basso's futures as he gives Basso the revised contract. Crane is also nervous about the upcoming investigation of Basso, which he is sure will reveal the hypnotist to be a fraud. Basso, however, is excited about the scrutiny, which he believes will reveal him to be the spiritual giant he fancies himself. Crane laughs at Basso's self-importance, which angers the hypnotist, who glares at Crane in what appears to be an attempt to hypnotize him. Crane is incredulous and finally explodes and reveals what he has always thought of his partner-in-crime: "You know what I see? I see a cheap fortune teller with delusions of grandeur!" Crane tries to apologize, but Basso is now enraged. As Crane reveals that there will be television coverage of tonight's important performance, the two part company, aware that their tenuous bond has shattered.

The meeting for the scientific community commences. Doreena sits in a dark corner of the conference room, while Blake, Basso, Dell and two unnamed scientists observe her as is she were a laboratory animal, mere voyeurs being entertained by a gender-centric curiosity. Dell confirms the validity of Marion Rhodes' purported historical facts, but the scientists are unconvinced and mock Basso; the insulted man tries to retain his composure, but his constant facial twitching reveals deep rage ready to burst. Basso finally pleads with the scientists to take him seriously: "As men of science you know anything that will shatter a long-held concept is usually rejected." He again insists that he can take his muse back almost indefinitely, even "to the moment of her soul's creation," a remark with religious implications. Lt. Blake then sneers: "Can you turn her into a maniac that goes around the beach killing people?" Basso is incensed, and the scientists depart, rejecting Basso's claims.

Later, Dell and Crane argue yet again over Basso. Dell thinks the man is dangerous, and suggests that Crane get rid of him. Lynn enters, and is sad to see her fiancé walk haughtily out of the room; she now knows she has lost him for good. As interested as Dell is in Doreena's welfare, he is nonetheless guilty of treating his fiancé like dirt. Outside the lodge, Basso escorts Doreena to their quarters. Basso tells Doreena that they are going to leave the country tomorrow, but Doreena counters that she intends on staying with Dr. Dell. Basso is upset by this news. The tables have turned, and Doreena has achieved her first step towards empowerment with the announced intention to break with the abuser. This touching scene, shot outdoors at dusk, features Doreena walking through the world in flowing white veils, looking like an earthbound angel seeking apotheosis.

Inside the hotel lobby, Basso first threatens, and then begs, Doreena to reconsider her decision, but she is steadfast: "I've found the strength to resist you." Basso counters feebly, "You are mine, and I am yours!" Crane intervenes, and takes Basso off to meet some prospective investors in their ill-fated joint venture. The camera now closes in on Doreena, who stands as still as a statue, yet with a certain pride in her face which was not there before. Dell enters the scene and speaks with the woman. Standing close to her, Dell insists that Doreena find the strength within to resist her master. Dell paces around the woman, getting closer all the time, finally whispering in her ear, "If you can resist him publicly, he'll have to let you go." His altruistic intentions aside, the exchange still has many elements of seduction ritual to it. Dell promises to link his thoughts with hers at the night's performance, helping her to overcome the hypnotic sway of Basso. This interesting confession suggests that Dell, after all, does believe in this parapsychology stuff, although he has maintained a poker face on the subject throughout the entire film. The viewer might then wonder if Dell has always believed, or if Doreena's abiding presence in his life has radically modified his cold, scientific worldview.

Basso renters, and drags Doreena off by the hand as Dell looks on in anguish. The night's performance begins. Doreena sits stock still in her chair-prison, still at this late date the good domestic servant. As Basso faces the camera, he oddly declares, "I trust that those of you who have witnessed my demonstrations realize that the purpose is education, not entertainment," a line which could easily be coming from the filmmaker himself, imploring the viewer to look beyond the cheapjack entertainment he offers and to locate something deeper, timeless and instructive. Basso attempts to put Doreena into her submissive trance state, but she successfully resists his attempts. Basso fidgets, and apologizes to the audience; he then follows Doreena's gaze over to Dell, who stares at her longingly. Basso smiles, recognizing his enemy, and proceeds and fails yet again to put Doreena under. Doreena glances over at Dell, and this enrages Basso, who is now at an impasse; his power has not only been taken, but taken in a public forum, an event both humiliating and potentially dangerous in exposing him as being impotent, thus worthless to patriarchal culture. Basso's public exposure of impotence might even be seen as dark voyeuristic entertainment akin to the "peep show" aspects of Doreena's systemic public humiliation.

Finally, Basso gives up, and apologizes to the audience: "My subject is disturbed tonight; her world is disturbed." Basso suggests that there is a terrible menace afoot, and advises the audience to leave Tanglewood immediately and return home. This suggestion, of course, enrages proprietor Crane. The viewer may wonder if this plea for evacuation was based on a real fear by Basso that his "creation," now out of his control, might become even more destructive than he would prefer, or if it's just an act of anger and sabotage towards Crane, merely putting "the screws" to his business partner. Certainly one could entertain the assumption that this evil man, having lost control of his female subject, thus fears powerful, deserved retribution. The mass evacuation begins, with Lt. Blake orchestrating this microcosmic apocalypse. Back in the auditorium, Dell runs onstage and orders Basso to bring Doreena out of her soulless half-death. Basso refuses and leaves the stage, giving Doreena one final glance of disgust.

Crane exits his compound with a loaded revolver, as police patrol the beachside. Soon, the Creature rises from the lake and attacks the armed guard. As the film nears its completion, the scene which comprised the film's prologue repeats itself: Crane, revolver in hand, runs terrified into the boathouse, afraid for his life. The viewer wonders if he is more afraid of the Creature or Basso, but now the viewer knows *why* he is so terrified and guilty; he has been the engine of the ongoing exploitation of this woman, thus every Woman, and fears divine retribution, which will surely come. As before, the Creature stalks this greedy entrepreneur, finally cornering him in the boathouse. Crane fires at the beast to no avail. Crane runs to one of the boats, and attempts to start the engine. As the Creature finally corners Crane in the cabin of the boat, strange heavy breathing is heard on the soundtrack. This disembodied voice may equally represent the creature, the man, or even the audience. Crane rings the boat's bell in desperation, but his empire has crumbled and its occupants have vacated, so he is really ringing only to the heavens, announcing his own demise. As the symbolic murder occurs in a decrepit warehouse in which boats are dry docked — piles of giant, iconic toys of the middle class sitting still and useless — the setting suggests both the essentially corrupt, jaded nature of the bourgeoisie, and its subsequent desolate and amoral character. As well as this aspect, boats removed from bodies of propulsive, buoying water are paralyzed, without a purpose and the hope of progressive motion, as is Man without Woman.

Aside from the stunning effect of déjà vu which viewing this scene for the second time triggers, Buchanan offers the viewer a sketch of his working thesis on the remake as being an opportunity to revisit and embellish an earlier work. Within this remake of his is a remake of an earlier scene, structurally and thematically different. The first occurrence of the scene was without narrative context, and thus came across as symbolic and cinematic. The second time the scene occurs, it is augmented by the narrative content which preceded it, and the context of the scene shifts profoundly. Yet there are undeniable similarities within each, not the least of which is visual, with Buchanan in effect saying that, differences acknowledged, there is much in common between the narrative and the nonlinear. As Dr. Basso can predict the future, so the film itself performs a "trick" of narrative premonition, by showing the viewer the last scene in the film also at the outset of the picture. This avant garde twist makes for the curious sense of temporal dissociation in *Creature*, a winning trademark in other Buchanan films as well.

This duplicated and repeated scene also reminds one of similar events replayed in Buchanan's courtroom trilogy. In a film such as *Free, White and 21*, a pivotal event is recounted by more than one person, and visualized for the audience. The shocking differences in each retelling well illustrate the subjective nature of the memory of events, and thus history. Depending on the memory and agenda, i.e., perspective, of each observer, an event may pass into history with radically modified elements. This is the purpose behind the revisionist history trend, to seek out alternate views of historical events, in an attempt to weed out falsehoods, and come closer to an objective truth. In *Creature*, Buchanan offers the viewer a little experiment in revisionist theory, by showing the same event twice, each crafted in ways subtle yet profoundly different.

Back at the lakeside, Blake instructs his men to scour the area thoroughly. Suddenly, the Creature rises once again out of the lake, and Blake ignorantly shouts, "There *he* is! Get *him!*" The officers shoot at the beast, who stands on the shore, waving away the useless phallic projectiles. At the lodge, Dell hears gunfire and takes Doreena in his arms to carry her to safety. As Dell enters the theater lobby, he spots Basso, who stands across the room, holding a revolver. The mad hypnotist orders Dell to place the woman on a nearby couch, and in a sweeping pan shot of the lobby, Dell does so.

The three main characters are once again framed as at the opening of the film, with Basso at stage left, the always-comatose Doreena dead center, and Dell at stage right. Basso announces his intention to kill Dell, and Dell tries to talk him out of it. Doreena, sensing the urgency of the situation, finally comes out of her stupor and sees that this sleepwalking life of hers is not merely a passive, waking nightmare, but a struggle for life and death. Doreena runs into Dell's arms just as Basso shoots him; Basso therefore inadvertently shoots and kills his slave and thus his reason to live. Dell, horrified, places the murdered woman gently on the couch. At the same instant, the Creature at the lake falls to the ground and fades into nothingness. Its job accomplished, female rage expressed and exploitation extinguished, the metaphorical beast fades into oblivion.

Basso crouches over Doreena's lifeless body, and bemoans his actions: "In this ugly world, you were all that mattered to me," finally confessing that he was just a bitter, lonely misanthrope all along, worthless without his muse and "cash cow." Basso kisses Doreena gently on the forehead, as a doting father would a sleeping child. Basso points the revolver at himself and shoots. The gun falls to the ground, spinning around several times on the floor, suggesting both "Russian Roulette" and "Spin the Bottle," both highly allegorical games of chance. The patriarchy, its exploitable product taken from it, has no further reason to exist, and so kills itself rather than facing up to its actions. Dell looks on, resigned to this tragic yet inevitable resolution, in which Woman once again sacrifices herself so that Mankind may evolve.

Dell ruminates on the preceding story, in a coda similar to one in the previous year's *Zontar, the Thing from Venus*. Over shots of the film's highlights, primarily centered around the various deaths, Dell narrates:

> I'd like to believe that I got through to her. We'll never know. One way or another, she destroyed the Creature. She knew that the Creature was some sort of physical link to her past. In destroying herself, the Creature could not exist. She searched for freedom, and found violence, terror, destruction, greed! Was Basso right? Is there a monster lurking within each of us, waiting, waiting?

This coda is structurally identical to that which ended *Zontar*. In addition to padding the film's running time with extant footage, these codas efficiently recap events and tie up certain thematic threads, and close the film on a high dramatic note.

Creature ends by repeating the quote from Montaigne which opened the film: "There is no monster in the world ... so treacherous as man."[2] Buchanan seems determined in *Creature* to strike home the point that "Man is Bad." A pure, even simplistic misanthropic stance, Basso's character seems to effectively mirror Buchanan's thematic spirit throughout the film. *Creature* is certainly the darkest of the Azalea telefilms, and possibly Buchanan's angriest work ever. *Creature's* overarching message is that the real "Creature of Destruction" is Man himself, particularly the male of the species; from the greedy entrepreneur to the self-righteous psychiatrist to the megalomaniac hypnotist to the arrogant police detective, there is nary a justifiable male character in the entire film. Although there are murders of two females in *Creature*, more emphasis is placed on the deaths of pivotal, symbolic male figures, whose numbers make up the majority of the killings. For Basso, the murders may serve as the removal of rivals and competitors, but for Doreena-as-Creature, the killings are a violent but essentially creative expression of her rage at being repressed as a human being in an abusive relationship, and suppressed as a member of an oppressed gender.

As counterpoint to the relentless misanthropy of the film, *Creature* also continues a discussion of the sexual revolution as it manifested itself in the mid–1960s, a discussion begun in *Curse of the Swamp Creature* and carried through *Mars Needs Women*. *Creature*'s Doreena does not follow the example of the independent, autonomous, emancipated female as represented by Dr. Marjorie Bolen in *Mars Needs Women*. Nor, finally, is she as helpless as Pat Trent in *Curse of the Swamp Creature*. The character of Doreena sketches the dark side of this revolution, of how a repressed and abused female may emancipate herself indeed, but in a violent and ultimately self-destructive way. The combination of Basso's entrenched power over his victim, combined with Doreena's enervating low self-esteem, makes her situation all the more perilous, and her triumph, albeit tragically self-negating, all the more laudatory. One might successfully argue that Doreena's apotheosis was inevitable, even preordained, but her "acting out" of aggression on the abusive power males in her community had the spirit of the biblical apocalypse about it, a holocaust which eventually swallowed her up as well, as selective holocausts are rare. In this darkest description of the radical upheaval of traditional sex roles, the ubiquitous "Master-Slave" relationship seen in Adorno can be glimpsed as an overlay which has the ominous scent of sadomasochism to it, this dynamic also well illustrating the endemic Patriarchal exploitation of Woman throughout history. Still, as an allegorical expression of pent-up female rage, *Creature* can be seen as a wholly feminist tract, and it is this perspective, curiously, which may well attract the largest number of fans to this extraordinary film. *Creature of Destruction* could even be seen as Buchanan's valentine to the nascent women's liberation movement. One might consider the screenplay for *Creature,* penned by Enrique Touceda (a.k.a. Anthony Houston), as a gesture of love and devotion to his beloved wife, Pat Delaney, who is featured prominently, even mythologized, in *Creature* as the tragic figure Doreena; Houston had costarred with Delaney in *Zontar, the Thing from Venus*, and had became her husband by the time *Creature* was shot.

The "Creature" (played by Buchanan stock player Byron Lord) is a man in a modified scuba-diving suit topped by a fright mask, rubber fangs and Ping-Pong eyeballs, an impossibly cheap and unconvincing creature by any standards. Buchanan might be stating with this beast that man's dark side, his inner beast, is a pathetic buffoon. Certainly, the Creature does not merely "play" a bad monster in a bad monster movie, but exists as an expressionist sketch of how ugly and deranged Man is, a parody of Mankind as a hateful, killing clown. Significantly, though, this Creature, though supposedly representing man's "dark side," is in fact a *female*, being a manifestation of Doreena's primal self. Her attacks, primarily on men, are then symbolic as an expression of gender-based rage at the male of the species.

In *Creature,* as elsewhere, Buchanan uncannily captures the lethargic, somewhat ragged pace of spent postwar American culture. Buchanan's unique mixture of melancholic inertia and overwrought theatricality is vivid and arresting. At the Tanglewood, people sit around tables, getting drunk and politely smiling, bored out of their skulls; no one seems to be actually having fun. *Creature* chronicles well the dismal, desperate feel of leisure culture in America. Everyone looks tired, bored and washed-out as they labor to "play."

Creature of Destruction is inarguably one of the most unique made-for-television features of the 1960s. Although it is undeniably an excellent example of Buchanan-as-storyteller, with *Creature*, Buchanan also progressed greatly as a film artist. In *Creature,* as in *Mars Needs Women* (1967), Buchanan emancipates himself from the punitive financial and expositional constraints of low-budget feature film production, and allows himself the luxury of crafting something personal, something beyond the reach of cash or genre, something intimate and singular, something closely akin to an art film. Having attempted since the start of the Azalea telefilm series, with *Creature of Destruction* Buchanan finally succeeds in jumping genres from television film to narrative-based experimental feature, creating in the process a micro-budget masterpiece.

15

It's Alive!

It's Alive! (1969) is the final Azalea telefilm and is a singular entry in the low-budget narrative genre, a melodrama with traditional roots and an engaging, oftimes experimental structure. It completes a discussion of sexual politics started with Larry Buchanan's *Mars Needs Woman* and continued in *Creature of Destruction*, making the three films a trilogy commenting on the 1960s sexual revolution. In *It's Alive!* the entrenched patriarchy rears its ugly head one last time as it tries to drag civilization down, literally, to the bowels of the earth. Among its victims are a woman who finds herself fatally trapped by the machinations of male evil, and an arrogant, self-absorbed male who assumed the male domination of the planet would go on indefinitely. The heroes are a female who manages, like Doreena in *Creature of Destruction*, to break free from oppressive slavery to a boorish mate, and a New Age male who, with the aid of the woman, destroys the old order so that a new one may dawn. This dark fable of phallocentric order overthrown by an egalitarian sexual enclave has strong parallels to the astrological notion of the end of the Piscean Age, with its attendant emphasis on the male-dominated Judeo-Christian philosophy, and the dawning of the more balanced Aquarian age, an age promising to usher in enlightenment and equality between the sexes. With its celebratory title, *It's Alive!* seems to be Buchanan's wish for this dawning of a much-needed revision to the oppressive sociopolitical system which was, even in 1969, suffering severe upheaval. *It's Alive!* also alludes to the ongoing battle between the urban, progressive forces of the American middle class versus the traditional, regressive politics of rural America, a subject addressed in Buchanan films as diverse as *Common Law Wife* and *Free, White and 21*.

As well, Buchanan stretches his creative muscles in *It's Alive!* by tackling some unusual visual and structural techniques, making the film a unique and haunting experience. *It's Alive!* was filmed on location in the Ozarks, at locations as diverse as Beaver Dam, Spider Creek Camp, Onyx Cave, and Dinosaur Valley State Park near Glen Rose, Texas. The cavern scenes were filmed at Longhorn Cavern State Park near Burnet, Texas.[1] The film is loosely based, uncredited, on Richard Matheson's short story "The Being." The film begins with a narrated prologue, spoken by the director:

> The poets would have called the place pastoral, the day tranquil. For Lesland Sterns and her husband, Norman, it was another day in a country tour. But as they entered the Ozark plateau, an

ominous feeling invaded the privacy of the car, a feeling that intensified with each turn in the winding highway. There were reassurances from time to time, usually in the form of some familiar landmark, but soon, these were behind them. And then it began to rain. There is a legend in these hills, that when it rains and the sun shines at the same time, the devil is kissing his wife. And speaking of the devil, 'Look Norman!' An exclamation at something out of time, out of place. Then a simple request to explore another in the strange oddities that dock the roadside of a thousand highways, oddities that beckon the traveler to stop and see. But terror knows no time or place, and jeopardy can hide behind gentle rain or shine. And if Norman Sterns had known what danger lay, screened by an Ozark forest, he never would have left the highway....

In addition to setting up the general premise of the piece, with its emphasis on the urban middle class invading rural America, the prologue emphasizes that the tale involves "Lesland Sterns, and her husband, Norman." Like so many Buchanan films, *It's Alive!* is about the woman.

This narration is visualized via long, leisurely scenes of the Sternses driving along endless highways, the pair significantly silent. From the forlorn expressions of the unspeaking couple, it is clear that the two are in the midst of serious romantic discord, sharing that particular lack of communication so endemic to the generation as a whole. The sullen energy between the two also depicts the burden of the leisure class, that incessant and neurotic search for amusement and stimulation outside of one's self that virtually defines both a generation and an economic class. The dreary compulsion to "vacation" and "sightsee," the compulsion to check out each tacky diversion along any new highway, mirrors the existential and spiritual vacuum of the time, the deep and unfulfilled inner needs people hope will be met from superficial attractions without. Buchanan pinpoints and sketches this existential alienation and spiritual lack so endemic to the period with broad, revealing brushstrokes.

When the rain begins, it signals not only the end to the Sternses' adventure, but indeed the end to all civilization. Even the continual squeaking of the wipers sounds like weeping. The dreary rainfall not only dampens the travelers' hopes but also reduces their visibility of the future. The haunting p.o.v. ambience of this prologue, proceeding in deafening silence but for narration, underscore, the faint sounds of tires on wet pavement and the windshield wipers, well illustrates the barren, loveless soul of the American middle class. There is little love in these sad, perfunctory couplings. The Sternses' drive into nowhere seems to take place in real time, almost in slow motion, well depicting the genesis of a doomed spiritual journey in which time and space is radically twisted.

As the Sternses drive on, they spot an anachronism: a giant Brontosaurus squatting placidly by the roadside. A closer shot reveals the creature to be a sculpture for a tourist attraction, and, perhaps, under construction, alluding not only to the regression of the couple into a primitive environment, but the essential fragility of that environment. As the film also relates the mobile nature of the American middle class, as symbolized by the automobile, it is noteworthy foreshadowing to feature an emblem to that society's lifeblood, fossil fuel. As the narrator informs, if Norman Sterns knew what danger lay ahead of him, "he never would have left the highway," i.e., the safety and order of urban ritual for the unmapped adventure of unknown rural spaces, symbolic of the primal (and existential) unknown.

The main title—*It's Alive!*—appears surrounded by quotes and punctuated with an exclamation point, surely referring to something greater than a monster incarnate. After the credits, the voices of the couple are finally heard via a harsh, bickering dialogue full of accusation and anger, succinctly depicting the bourgeoisie in discord. Lost and stranded with no gas or directions available, Norman halts his oversized automobile near a jeep parked on the roadside, apparently abandoned. The Sternses share an uneasy glance. Norman hops out of the car, runs to the jeep, looks around to make sure nobody is watching, and steals a cup of water from the jeep's canteen. First, however, he washes out the cup, using precious water, suggesting that he feels the cup's owner is unclean and liable to contaminate him. Norman is thus painted as an elitist snob with notable social prejudices. In addition, he is a thief and exploiter of other's resources, and shockingly selfish. He doesn't even offer his wife a drink. Norman is the prototypical Capitalist: amoral, opportunistic and self-absorbed, obsessed solely with personal gain.

As portrayed by Corveth Ousterhouse, an actor who appears to have made no other films, at least under this name, Norman Sterns is an indelible archetype. He is angry, pouty and disgusted throughout the film. He has no patience for anyone, especially his lovely, long-suffering wife, who he clearly loathes. Norman attacks his wife continually, blaming her for all their travails. He is a tiny, bitter man, hateful of women specifically and mankind in general, a perfect emblem of the lower ranks of the patriarchy, a would-be ruler who is as frustrated by his own personal impotence as he is by the relative freedom and kindness practiced by those around him. Lesland, well played by Shirley Bonne, is a subservient, repressed and abused female. She sits, quietly simmering, as her husband berates her, criticizing the entire world around him and blaming it all on her. It is little wonder that Lesland virtually flies into the arms of the first male who will treat her with a modicum of respect.

The owner of the jeep approaches and introduces himself as Wayne Thomas, a paleontologist. As played by Tommy Kirk in a manner not dissimilar to his role as the Martian Dop in *Mars Needs Women*, Wayne immediately symbolizes the "new" male. Although he thus identifies himself with a study of, and thus reverence for, things old and traditional, Wayne comes across as immediately modern by his casual attire, charismatic smile and forgiving nature towards Norman, who has just trespassed on his property. Wayne thus sets himself up as an egalitarian person who may well represent a new age, free from the oppression of the patriarchal world represented so vividly by Norman. Even the fact that Wayne is a paleontologist, who takes the old world and reconciles it with the new, reinforces this notion. Wayne graciously tells Norman to continue drinking his water. As Norman inquires as to their whereabouts, Leland joins the men, uninvited. Norman greets her arrival by shouting at her: "Fine! We're lost! I hope you're satisfied!" Showing this anger and distaste in front of another man paints Norman as both a creep and a bully, and Lesland shrinks back, ashamed.

Wayne introduces himself to Lesland and offers her a drink, which the woman, thirsty for water and compassion, gratefully accepts. As she drinks, Norman gives the two a dirty look, angered that anyone would usurp his tyrannical role over his wife. Lesland hands the water cup back to Wayne in a pronounced gesture of gratitude, complete with meaningful eye contact. Norman grabs his wife by the hand and virtually drags this person he considers his possession back to the car, glancing back angrily at Wayne. The humorless, paranoid, territorial old-world male has met his nemesis, the sensitive male who treats a woman as an equal, and as a worthy partner. The oppressed female also sees the vast difference between the two males, and apparently likes what she sees in Wayne.

Norman Sterns (Corveth Ousterhouse, center) and Horace Greevy (Bill Thurman) take turns reproaching Lesland Sterns (Shirley Bonne) for the world's ills, in Larry Buchanan's dark fable on the collapse of patriarchal culture, *It's Alive!*

The setting changes to a wildlife sanctuary, where a stocky man wearing a cowboy hat feeds snakes and lizards which reside in makeshift wood-and-wire cages. He speaks to one creature thusly, "Clara, you're out of your cage again." This first glimpse of the villain of the piece (played to perfection by Buchanan stalwart Bill Thurman), paints him as apparently benign, and the viewer might surmise that this cowboy-like figure is kind, and actually *likes* living creatures.

Soon the Sternses pull up to a white, mansion-like house. Norman immediately blasts the horn, expecting immediate service, as if he were at a big-city filling station. The stocky man arrives, and Norman explains their situation, making sure to make his wife look like the guilty party yet again. The man introduces himself as Horace Greevy (Thurman), the owner of the estate. Greevy is an inspired name for the evil, psychotic villain, a mixture of "greedy," "seedy" and "creepy," with "grieving" thrown in for good measure. Greevy invites the couple inside, first asking them if they know anybody in the area. Answering in the negative, Greevy smiles sinisterly and says, "Don't worry, you'll like it here." Inside the house, a woman cowers at the window, her face a mask of dread. She sees the trio approaching, and flees with a look of terror on her face. The viewer senses that the frightened woman is a prisoner. The Sternses enter Greevy's living room, which he calls his "parlor." The viewer may then equate this with the old children's rhyme, "Come into my parlor, said the spider to the fly."

Greevy goes off, looking for his "housekeeper," called Bella, the woman just seen. Lesland looks curiously around Greevy's house, perturbed and mystified. Norman notices his wife's intrigue, and bleats, "What's the matter with you?" By this time, it is abundantly apparent that Norman absolutely hates his wife. Lesland describes her foreboding about the house and its owner. One charming and "arty" touch occurs as Lesland ruminates about their strange host: "Did you see his eyes? They were like a..." As she says this, Lesland looks off-screen and screams. The camera follows her glance and zooms in on a grotesquely grimacing stuffed lizard standing on the fireplace mantle, the lizard thus symbolizing both the hideous, cold-blooded personality of their host, and the potential fate of his victims.

The couple sit down on a loveseat, and Norman chastises his wife yet again, reminding her that he offered to take her to the Bahamas, where they would not have ended up in this predicament. Lesland reminds Norman that she has lived her whole life in New York City and had always wanted to see "the towns, the villages, the people who live there," i.e., the real America. The modern, urban curiosity towards older, rural America is portrayed here, as in other films and television programs of the era, such as *Green Acres*, as problematic and fraught with obstacle, if not outright danger. The modern curiosity seeker often finds in these treatments that the rules of conduct in the rural environment are shockingly different. Tourists often find themselves swallowed up by the insular, hardy, self-preserving logic of their backward backwoods brethren.

Greevy finds Bella cowering like a frightened mouse. The terrified woman (a powerful performance by Annabelle Weenick as "Annabelle MacAdams") begs Greevy not to make her aid in his apparently diabolical plans for the lost couple, but Greevy slaps her into frightful submission, the patriarchy lording over its slaves with brutal, abusive clarity. This first scene between Bella and Greevy is significant, quickly establishing that Greevy is a sadistic brute who has the woman in his complete power. Greevy's face of twisted rage as he shouts commands is disturbing.

Wayne approaches Greevy's house, looking for the Sternses. Greevy intercepts him outside. As the two attempt to repair the Sternses' car, Greevy knocks Wayne unconscious with a monkey wrench and drags him into the house. Greevy's brutal philosophy is thus revealed: kill or be killed. Bella brings some iced tea to the Sternses. Norman orders the "servant" to open the drapes, but seeing Greevy dragging an apparently lifeless body, she cannot bear to expose her master's evil deeds, even in her pained servitude. In morbidly dependent fashion, Bella is not merely a prisoner and victim but also a reluctant coconspirator in Greevy's machinations, a tragic element that makes her character entirely sympathetic. Bella queries the Sternses: "Why did you come here?" The compassionless Norman bleats his stock answer to all female inquiry: "What's the matter with you?"

Greevy returns to the Sternses, who are now sufficiently scared to declare they are going to depart, a statement to which Greevy, somewhat sarcastically, responds, "Where would you go?" The Sternses mention Wayne, and Greevy lies, saying that the young man was here but has gone off to fetch some gasoline. Greevy suggests that the Sternses bide their time by looking at his "collection," presumably of reptiles. Lesland is hesitant, but Norman goads her by stating, "You were the one who wanted to see some *wild life*," now clearly, albeit subconsciously colluding with the head patriarch in some sinister plan for the female(s). The scene changes to show various animals, including snakes, lizards, monkeys and bobcats, imprisoned in makeshift cages. Greevy suggests that the Sternses see the "prize" of his collection. Lesland has no interest in whatever this might be, but Norman literally pushes the woman down the entrance to "Onyx Cave," into some assuredly hellish fate in the bowels of the earth. Norman feebly placates his wife's concern by asking Greevy, "It won't take long?" Greevy replies, "It'll be over before you know it," followed by a zoom-in to some caged monkeys.

Unearthly animal cries dominate the soundtrack as the trio descend into some dank, ill-lit caverns, the literal bowels of the patriarchy, the dark heart of phallocentric culture, with allusions to the rings of Dante's Inferno. The trio is soon plunged into pitch darkness. When the lights come on, the Sternses are alone in a small cave replete with cots and washing supplies. Norman cracks, "What kind of place is this? It looks like someone *lives* here!" Lesland pleads with Norman to leave, but Norman dismisses her womanly intuition. At that moment, the two hear steel hitting rock and look around, horrified to find that Greevy has shut them into a jail-like cell. Norman yells at Greevy to let them out, but the deranged misanthrope just laughs and exits.

Only now realizing the grave danger they are in, Norman takes the opportunity to further blame the victim of his idiot rage, and vents pent-up frustrations to Lesland, chastising her for her desire to see the "real" world, as opposed to being sheltered by the rich lifestyle they are accustomed to. Lesland nervously states, "This room wasn't just intended for us. There have been others here." Indeed, the traps set up for the slaves of the patriarchy have had long and industrious use, as history will attest. Suddenly, Lesland looks behind her and screams, for Wayne is just now coming to consciousness behind some rocks.

In the house, Greevy and Bella share an uncomfortably silent supper. Greevy notices that Bella is not eating, and chastises her for being wasteful. Then he recites his philosophy of life:

The duplicitous Horace Greevy (Bill Thurman) is the face of kindness one moment, and a vision of pure evil as soon as his latest victim's back is turned, in the harrowing *It's Alive!*

> You are wasteful! That's a sin here in the mountains, you know that! Everything is used, again and again. Even when it rains, a drop of water falls from the sky, and a plant catches it. An insect eats the plant, and it falls prey to a lizard. A snake devours the lizard and his blood in turn quenches the thirst of a hawk, so you see, that little drop of water sustains life

in one animal after the other. The besieged animal is served by another, and each must serve his turn.

Bella counters, angrily, "A human being is not an *animal*!" to which Greevy retorts, "Who can tell?" Greevy's brutal "big fish/little fish" philosophy makes him purely emblematic of the old-world patriarchy, a monster ripe for overthrow by New Age revolution. Greevy may also be seen to represent the old, Piscean age of domination guilt and repentance, whereas Wayne and Lesland represent the new, Aquarian age of tolerance and forgiveness. One might also intuit a polymorphous "Aquarian" sexuality to Greevy's "hotel" for his prisoners, in which resides one cot for as many as three people, the cot being thus emblematic of group sex.

Back in the cave, Lesland tends to Wayne's wounds while Norman stews silently. Bella arrives with food for the trio. Norman demands to know what is going on, and where an escape route might be. He browbeats the terrified woman until Lesland intervenes. Bella professes she would like to help the group, but dares not, for Greevy would throw her to some horrible unseen beast she refers to as "The Thing!" Bella leaves, the trail of her escape route unclear, as well as why the trapped prisoners could not follow. The prison is obviously meant to be more metaphorical than literal.

The trio discuss the situation. Norman believes that Bella is merely acting to Greevy's script, part of a plot by some "country bumpkins" to fleece money from "city slickers." Norman is arrogant and self-absorbed, literally unto death. Wayne thinks there may indeed be some strange creature living down in the farthest depths of the cavern, and he decides to go take a look. After a small earth tremor, Norman declares that it would be foolish to venture further into the cave, for safety reasons, but he is clearly a coward. Lesland, in her first pivotal break from her boorish mate, decides to join Wayne on his exploratory trip. Defeated and humiliated, Norman sheepishly follows the others into the cave.

Deep in the caverns, the trio see what appears to be a bubbling hot springs. Wayne decides to venture further, to find out where the water leads. Lesland pleads with him, "Please be careful," to which Norman sarcastically adds, "By all means! We'd hate to lose *you*!" But before Wayne can descend, Greevy appears, pistol in hand, and warns the group not to venture into unknown territory. Greevy pontificates, "Perhaps you know of my creature — it's great and powerful!" Wayne and Norman try to convince Greevy to share his discovery with the world, but he knows they are only humoring him. Greevy offers for Lesland to join him, and says that he might spare her life. Submit to the patriarchy, he suggests, and your life might be spared. Lesland is repulsed by the idea, but Norman suggests she take the monster up on his offer of sexual slavery, for in this way *his* life might be spared. Norman thus reveals himself to be a purely loathsome creature.

Greevy shoots Wayne, and runs off, cackling like a madman. As Lesland attends to Wayne's wounds again, happy caretaker to a male who treats her with respect, Norman berates the two. Lesland, however, has found courage, and chastises her obnoxious partner: "I never realized before what my value to you was. I know you told me earlier today, but I didn't want to believe it. Well, now I know. I know how much I mean to you, *and it isn't enough!*"

Norman responds to his wife's honesty the only way he knows how, with a violent slap across the face, patriarchy knowing only abuse and control. Norman wonders off alone into the caverns, first giving his wife, and Wayne, one final dirty look. Norman descends towards the hot springs and retrieves the revolver, which Greevy let slip. He calls to Wayne to join him, apparently intending to shoot his new rival. However, just in time to thwart this conspiracy of the patriarchy to extinguish a revolutionary threat, a horrible, prehistoric creature arises out of the pool and kills Norman as Wayne and Lesland watch from above, horrified. The beast here is the same implausible creature first seen in *Creature of Destruction*: enhanced wet-suit body, glistening rubber mask, Ping-Pong eyes and goofy fangs, the perfect childlike vision of the beloved cultural notion of "cheap monster." What better emblem than a cartoon dinosaur from the murky deep to illustrate the brutal, yet ultimately pathetic patriarchy?

Wayne and Lesland run back to the relative safety of their prison cell, and, tellingly, discuss not the untimely death of Norman but the revelation of the bizarre beast from the pool. It seems as if the death of Norman was more of a godsend than a curse to both the wife and his rival, who now know that they may go forward and attempt to escape, and then dismantle, the evil old-world order which imprisons them. That the couple show no remorse over Norman's demise underlines the fact that he was of the old order, his death to be celebrated, not mourned. It is no accident that Norman is done in directly due to his rejection by the female. His refusal to accept the revised social contract renders him obsolete.

In the house, Bella passes her lonely day by playing hymns on an organ, an activity which alludes both to solace by faith to the downtrodden and to her almost religious devotion to this monster, who, after all, is the evil "god" figure in this little kingdom. Bella goes to see how the prisoners are and eavesdrops in the cave, listening in as Wayne explains to Lesland that the beast they just encountered was most likely a Mesosaurus, "a kind of aquatic lizard" very common to the area "about 75 million years ago." Bella returns to the house, clutching her stomach, visibly ill. She tries to sneak back into the house, but Greevy has been sitting in wait for her. He grabs her roughly by the wrist and makes her report on the disposition of his new prisoners. After Bella leaves, Greevy looks off in the distance, sad and weary, the care and maintenance of his empire clearly taking its toll.

Later, Bella decides to risk injury by eavesdropping on the prisoners again. As Wayne and Lesland share a cup of coffee, Greevy arrives. Wayne congratulates the

Somber paleontologist Wayne Thomas (Tommy Kirk) attempts to reason with his deranged captor in *It's Alive!* He soon realizes that only the violent overthrow of this obsolete political order will ensure his community's survival.

madman on his historic discovery. Greevy, flattered, agrees to tell the story of how he came here many years back, looking for gold. What gold he found was stolen from him, partially explaining his misanthropy. He dug further into the caves, and eventually stumbled onto the prehistoric creature. Greevy made the creature his friend, and fed it cattle, sheep, coyote, and eventually lost humans. Greevy makes another pass at Lesland, and informs her that if she agrees to become his new sexual slave Bella can be "taken care of." Bella listens, horrified at her master's cruel disloyalty. Wayne shouts to Greevy, "Do you realize the value of your discovery to mankind?" and the madman recites the misanthrope's credo: "Mankind? Whadda I care about mankind?"

Later, Bella arrives with bandages for Wayne. Having heard Greevy's plans for her, Bella decides that she will try to help the couple escape. Lesland asks Bella how she came to be in this sorry state, and Bella agrees to tell the young lovers her sad tale. The notable twenty-two minute flashback sequence which follows, shot silent and narrated, is the heart of *It's Alive!* This harrowing sequence distorts time and space effectively and ruthlessly illustrates the hopeless dementia of the patriarchy and the necessity of its immediate destruction. Bella reveals that two years ago she was on the last day of vacation as a schoolteacher, the vocation alluding to functions with which the patriarchy traditionally exploits women (reproduction, child-rearing, indoctrination of the young). Bella is thus revealed to be an underpaid servant of the phallocentric world, wiping its offsprings' bottoms for little pay and no glory. Her occupation might also peg Bella as a lonely, barren spinster, her fertility forsaken by serving others, her naive self trapped by sheer misfortune into being the "wife," sex slave and whipping girl of a mad brute. Yet what Bella ultimately suffers even more than Greevy's cruel exploitation is the dawning reality of her own complicity, a lifelong naiveté and vulnerability, neglecting herself in order to serve others. A long, dreary p.o.v. shot from the car shows a dark, lonely country road, at the end of which is a "road closed" sign, surely symbolic of the sad end to such a thankless, other-directed life.

Bella is next seen meeting Greevy at his house. Bella muses, "I know it's hard to believe, but he actually looked *kind* the first time I met him," acknowledging the charismatic allure of monsters. As Greevy leads Bella to a room to spend the night, the viewer sees his face turn from pleasant to distorted, the mask of civility removed. Greevy leads Bella to her fate just as a crafty dogcatcher lures a stray mutt to his doom. Greevy's guest room is barren and spooky, and looks not unlike a cage. Scenes follow which show the sad loneliness of Bella, sitting or pacing alone in her room, isolated from her peers. The viewer may wonder why Greevy does not entertain Bella. Surely the vast chasm between the sexes is illustrated by this heart-wrenching scene, in which the woman is isolated in a cage, far from the interests of the male.

Some time later, as Bella slowly undresses, Greevy sneaks back upstairs, ever closer yet ever so far away emotionally. In a moment of intuition, Bella thinks she hears Greevy lock the bedroom door, but she ignores the thought, assured in her lifelong conviction that nobody would be that cruel to a stranger. That night, Bella sleeps fitfully, fully aware of the evil energy pervading the house but unable to reconcile this with what she believes about mankind's basic goodness. Unable to rest, Bella finally rises from bed and heads to the door. Finding it locked as she secretly dreaded, her worst fears take over, and she panics. Bella runs to the window. It is barred like a prison cell. Her hope in man's basic goodness is shattered, her world is ended, a "prisoner to a man I would later learn was a madman!"

What follows are endless days of imprisoned solitude, as Greevy tortures Bella with a series of cruel tricks, the most significant being attempted starvation. Aside from the obvious physical deprivations, the psychological impact of forced solitude has a devastating impact on the psyche. These scenes of an innocent trapped in a tiny cell, waiting for nothing, is another of Buchanan's astute sketches of existential alienation. Certainly Bella's imprisonment, in which she is largely relegated to sleeping or rocking aimlessly, is metaphoric for man's pained and pointless existence. Bella's plight also mirrors in simplified, exaggerated form, the plight of the postwar wife in America, a person who was, in many ways, a servant to her male "master," and a functionary to the patriarchal empire en masse.

Bella is next seen sitting in a tattered easy chair, rocking herself into a stupor, and after three days without food or water, at the edge of madness. The desperate woman tries to reason with her new "master," but Greevy tells her only of his hatred of "the highway people" for circumventing his serpentorium. "The Highway People" certainly implies, in addition to the literal fact of progress circumventing Greevy's backwater kingdom, the hatred of the modern, urban world encroaching on and ignoring the largely psychotic mindset of rural America as exemplified by Greevy's nutty little empire. Finally promising Bella some sorely needed nourishment, Greevy instead offers her a dead rat, in a scene borrowed intact from *Whatever Happened to Baby Jane?* (1964, d: Robert Aldrich). This final act of wanton cruelty puts Bella over the edge, and via a hallucinatory montage it is implied that she loses her sanity.

Yet Bella is strong, finding the strength to throw hydrogen peroxide into Greevy's face the next time he assaults her. Bella escapes the house and runs into the woods. Slow-motion scenes of Bella running aimlessly through the woods evoke that eerie feeling common to many dreams, that of running endlessly but getting nowhere, "as on a treadmill," as Bella suggests, the notion that progress is merely an illusion. After what seems an eternity for both Bella and the audience, the woman is cornered by Greevy. Like any long-abused animal, Bella does not run further but stands stock still, paralyzed by fear and betrayed by exhaustion. She waits in silent obedience to her acknowledged master as he slowly removes his belt and whips the poor woman into fearful submission. This barbaric act punctuates the role of the patriarchy towards all its victims: complete and utter physical and mental domination. Tired of running and hypnotized into paralysis by their hunter, the victim participates in the ritual by letting their tormentor whip them into dog-like obedience. Yet Bella's experience, as painful as it is, allows her finally to see the truth of the dark side of man, and this will enable her to become proactive.

The scene reverts to the present, where Wayne and Lesland seem more concerned with their immediate survival than the horrible tale they have just heard. Perhaps it was too painful for them to address. The couple ask Bella to fetch Wayne's bag of explosives from his jeep. Perhaps it was the recounting of her travail to the new guests (along with overhearing Greevy's low opinion of her) which prompts Bella to rescind her former acceptance of cruel fate, and to challenge her oppressor, even at risk of her own peril. The "new" Bella has found the courage to help destroy the patriarch-monster. Now, perhaps for the first time, she is truly a woman, a person of strong, focused conviction, a creature with a noble purpose, and the will to battle oppression even at the possible cost of her life. Bella fetches the bag for the couple, but Greevy, spying on the woman all the while, questions her. Believing correctly that there is conspiracy afoot, Greevy poisons a pot of coffee destined for Wayne and Lesland. Bella brings Wayne's bag along with the deadly beverage. As Wayne prepares the dynamite, the two of them succumb to the drink. In an evil society, even trusting the food is ill-advised.

Wayne manages to toss the dynamite pack under the cot for safekeeping before he faints. Greevy enters to check on his prisoners, and, finding them comatose, carries Lesland off. Bella returns to the cell and awakens Wayne. The still-drugged man manages to grab the dynamite even as Greevy carries his prize downstairs to feed to his pet dinosaur. Bella leads Wayne to the cavern floor, where the monster awaits. Greevy asks Lesland one last time to become his sex slave. She refuses, so Greevy tries to shoot her. Wayne kicks the gun out of the madman's hand and rescues the girl.

In the grim *It's Alive!* Bella Pittman (Annabelle Weenick, as "Annabelle MacAdams") rocks listlessly in an easy chair, as the depth of her host's cruel depravity slowly dawns on her; she is being punished for the crime of being female, and will soon be both prisoner and slave in this evil microcosmic patriarchy.

Bella, now emboldened or resigned, is the one who throws the dynamite into the cavern, just as Greevy shoots her. Bella thus becomes Buchanan's token sacrifice, giving her life so that an evil regime may be destroyed.

The creature attacks Greevy, pawing him to death as the dynamite explodes. The cavern is destroyed, the patriarchal world and its fossil fuel philosophy of exploitation of resources ended. Wayne and Lesland make their way upstairs. When Lesland suggests telling others about this cataclysmic event, Wayne tearfully exclaims, "There's nothing left, do you hear me? Nothing! Maybe there never was *anything*!" In so doing, the New Age male not only destroys the evil patriarchy but also erases it from history, so that a new world can begin. Wayne and Lesland walk off, hand in hand, the Adam and Eve for a brave new world and possibly Buchanan's quintessential heterosexual savior-couple. For them, there can be no looking back, only the forgetting of past failure and the focusing on the future. The parting shot shows the bubbling lava pool, with the superimposed title, "THE END?" Buchanan, as well as anyone, knows that history, and political regimes, are cyclical, and although the patriarchal beast appears dead for now, there is no telling when it may successfully rise up from the bowels of Hell to claim another generation. As such, the movie may be seen as a rhetorical philosophical question, underscored by the uncertainty of the end title.

It's Alive! depicts an outdated political order destroyed via the sacrifice of one of its members, who suffers so that a new world might dawn. The evil beast of the thwarted patriarchy destroys its creator, as is proper and inevitable. The destruction of the caverns and the beast within is the destruction of the oppressive regime. It is no accident that, as in *Creature of Destruction*, the creature kills primarily only men. Also significant is the fact that New Age male Wayne uses his own tools to destroy Greevy's empire. It is certain that Greevy had explosive devices available, as witness the complex system of caves, but it is key that Wayne used his own dynamite, for this illustrates that powerful tools, heretofore seen as destructive and phallic (i.e., male), can also be used creatively. The destruction of evil a necessary precursor to growth, the use of traditionally destructive tools is valid. The main title now becomes clear, for "It's Alive!" is a celebratory exclamation of the anticipated ascendancy of the dawning new age, a shout of hope for the future of man. *It's Alive!* is also a rumination on the never-ending war between the sexes, a most enlightened perspective on the sexual revolution.

With *It's Alive!* Larry Buchanan concluded his wildly successful experiment in low-budget narrative film known as "The Azalea Pictures." He learned much, and mystified audiences worldwide with his ingenuity and virtuosity. He would lobby for, and receive, a budget ten times previous ones to fashion his first bonafide blockbuster, *A Bullet for Pretty Boy* (1970).

16

A Bullet for Pretty Boy

Faced with exhaustion and lack of tangible reward after delivering *It's Alive!* (1969) to American International, Larry Buchanan informed Sam Arkoff that he was through with producing tiny telefilms for preposterously low budgets. He was ready to forge a break with AIP, and in fact had returned to producing the same year, with the release of Falcon International's sexually emphatic documentary *Sex and the Animals* (1969). To Buchanan's surprise, Arkoff was willing to consider a big(ger)-budget theatrical feature, and Buchanan quickly submitted a proposal for a period action melodrama based on the life and times of real-life criminal Floyd Hamilton, dubbed by the popular press "Pretty Boy" Floyd. Buchanan's connection to Floyd was personal, as this was the very same bank robber who purportedly once shot at Buchanan's father, then a regional peace constable. Buchanan had since made peace with the legendary convict, and even featured the retired criminal as part of an earlier treatise on Depression-era outlaws, *The Other Side of Bonnie & Clyde* (1968).

In addition, Buchanan and Enrique Touceda had worked for the past year or so on a tentative screenplay for the film which would become *A Bullet for Pretty Boy* (1970). Inspired (some might say frustrated) by the huge success of Arthur Penn's *Bonnie & Clyde* (1967), Buchanan felt that he would be the perfect director for any film dealing with Depression-era politics in the rural South. It is clear he lobbied for *A Bullet for Pretty Boy* (henceforth referred to as *Bullet*) with this in mind, for the film is indeed his response to the romanticized violent excesses of Penn's film. Buchanan presented a package to AIP for a 35mm feature, budgeted at $900,000, to star an up-and-coming young actor named Jack Nicholson. Arkoff returned with an offer for a budget of $300,000, a paltry figure for a theatrical feature of the period. In addition, Arkoff insisted than the lead be played by Fabian Forte, a charismatic star of several AIP beach party movies.[1]

Buchanan humbly accepted these severe limitations, and shot his *Bullet* locally, making it a veritable valentine to the Lone Star State, as the credits proudly declare: "Filmed entirely on location in the state of Texas." Stylistically, *Bullet* shares much with other Depression-era gangster films of the time, including *Bonnie & Clyde*, *Killers Three* (1968, p: Dick Clark), and *Bloody Mama* (1970, d: Roger Corman). *Bullet* is faster-paced than earlier Buchanan films, and utilizes the quick editing and musical montages common to theatrical film of that period. Most notable is the use of brief, almost subliminal cutaways to previous scenes or characters in order to show a character's thought process, another often-used aesthetic quirk. Visually, *Bullet* is evocative, awash in lush landscapes and barren vistas. The country-flavored music is bouncy and pop-oriented, including an oft-repeated theme song, "I'm Gonna Love You (Till I Die)," by Harley Hatcher; *Bullet* begat a successful soundtrack album, released by AIP's offshoot, Tower Records.

Unfortunately, *Bullet* suffers dramatically from Buchanan's desire to underemphasize the viciousness of the outlaw mythos, and the violent trail it invariably leaves. While Charles Arthur Floyd,[2] as played by Fabian, is not a romantic character by any means, neither does his character convincingly show the metamorphosis from gentle farm boy to hard-boiled sociopath. The fault may be equally due to Buchanan's leisurely and simplistic script and Fabian's lackluster portrayal, the resultant gangster resembling nothing so much as a pouty adolescent with knee-jerk revenge on his mind. The apparent decision to make *Bullet* a PG, family-friendly picture also certainly hurt the film's potential impact, as the frequent shootout scenes are bloodless and quite tame by the standards of the time. Indeed, in the violence category, *Bullet* is far more timid than *Bonnie & Clyde* or *Bloody Mama*, two similarly themed pictures. Nor did Buchanan attempt to insert a dry gallows humor into the proceedings, a la *Butch Cassidy and the Sundance Kid* (1968). As a result, *Bullet* is a pleasant but unremarkable melodrama. In addition, it simplifies Floyd's real history for dramatic purposes to a point of almost comic-book absurdity; there is little psychological depth to any of the characters, and scenes have little or no allegorical meaning. *Bullet* is a simple story, simply told, and none the worse for that. One wonders, however, what Buchanan might have done without certain restrictions, both self-made and imposed by others.

Bullet opens as Charles Arthur Floyd (Fabian) and his new bride, Ruby (Astrid Warner), get married at a rural church in Southern Texas. A young preacher (Adam Rourke), also a friend, sends the congregation off to a wedding reception elsewhere. Under a big tent, everyone celebrates the newlyweds' joy. Soon, a sinister figure crashes the party. This is Jack (Hugh Feagin), a local thug and former lover of Ruby. Jack taunts Floyd with hints at his former sexual dalliance with his new bride, until Floyd explodes in anger and beats up the punk.

That evening, Floyd escorts his family home and helps his drunken father onto their front porch. A shot rings out, and the father falls dead. This pivotal death of the father, via a shooting obviously meant for Floyd, causes the young groom unbearable grief and guilt. Certainly this pivotal "death of the father" could have triggered much philosophic rumination and allegorical content in *Bullet*, but alas, such is not the case. The father's murder registers barely a mention in the subsequent scenario.

Flooded with rage and sorrow, Floyd soon visits Jack's farm in order to find the truth, and accidentally kills him while trying to defend himself against Jack's advances. Floyd is wrongfully convicted of the accidental death, and is sentenced to six years of hard labor on a chain gang. Ruby and "Preacher" bid Floyd a sad farewell, humbly aware of the casual, cruel serendipity of fate. On the backbreaking chain gang, it is revealed that four years have passed, and Floyd only has two years left of his sentence. Floyd is harassed by a sadistic guard. Another prisoner, Huddy (Bill Thurman), talks Floyd into attempting an escape. The two run. Huddy is wounded, and Floyd runs on.

Floyd soon ends up at a nearby whorehouse, run by a woman named Beryl (Anne MacAdams). Beryl takes pity on the young convict, and makes him a bouncer at her establishment. Beryl's brother Wallace (Jeff Alexander) is an abusive pimp. He takes an immediate dislike to Floyd when he comes to the rescue of Betty (Jocelyn Lane), one of the prostitutes, after Wallace tries to beat her. Betty befriends Floyd, and the two become lovers when Betty intrudes on Floyd as he takes a bath. This first of three water references in *Bullet* has much of the symbolic quality of the Christian baptism ritual, as Floyd is immersed in the healing fluids of kindly women, who nurture and protect him.

Wallace and his brother Lee scornfully dub the charismatic Floyd "Pretty Boy." Soon, Beryl fixes Floyd up with Bo (Ed Lo Russo) and Harvey (Desmond Bridge), two seasoned bank robbers who need a third hand for their next job. Another gangster, Ned Short (Michael Haynes), arrives, driven by a beautiful blonde (Morgan Fairchild). As Ned has a busted leg, it is agreed that Floyd will be the gun man. Floyd tries his hand at a machine gun, and practices by blasting a poster of President Hoover.

The robbers enter a small-town bank and stage their holdup; the sole teller, an old woman, is petrified, so Floyd grabs the money and manages a fast escape for all. Back at the whorehouse, everyone takes their cut of the successful theft. Floyd receives a letter from Ruby, saying that his mother has died. It may be this death of the other parent which sends Floyd over the edge, for soon after he states to his colleagues, speaking of the horrible economic deprivation which surrounds them, "Banks still got money." The depression of the 1930s, sketched only vaguely in *Bullet*, was certainly an example of the entrenched Patriarchy known as Capitalism leaving its children to die, penniless, in the streets. A trend towards a new, egalitarian economic system was forged by the criminals of the time, out of blood and hunger and fear, a revolt of the starving son over the greedy, murderous father. As Herbert Marcuse would say, the death of one Patriarchy soon summons another, which may or may not be an improvement.

Over a musical interlude, there is a montage of another bank robbery. At a Farmer's and Mechanics bank, law enforcement sets up an ambush, and in the bloody gunfight following, Floyd shows his talent with the machine gun. An exciting car chase ensues, culminating in a police car crashing into a filling station in a fiery explosion. The men are caught. Bo is slated for execution, Harvey gets life imprisonment, and Floyd gets fifteen years. A newspaperman visiting Beryl's hears Wallace's rude nickname for Floyd, and the headlines the next day dub the sad convict "Pretty Boy Floyd." On the train ride to prison, the cops mercilessly taunt Floyd with his new name. As the train moves on, Floyd suffers a heartrending montage of his accumulated memories. He manages to escape the train, and slowly make his way back home. He happens upon an old farmer friend, Seth (Ethan Allen), who offers him a ride and a place of shelter at his cotton storehouse. Soon Ruby joins Floyd, and the two have a long-awaited reunion. Ruby shares with Floyd photographs of his young son.

Preacher soon locates Floyd's hiding place. Preacher has become a hopeless alcoholic and begs Floyd to take him on as a partner, and to continue his crime spree. Ruby, thinking Floyd finally has a chance to go straight and be a good family man, insists that he stay in hiding, like an animal. Floyd, however, knows that he can never go back to innocence, since he has killed so many. Leaving a crestfallen Ruby, Floyd and Preacher return to Beryl's, where Floyd soon gets into a fight with Warren over Betty. Floyd wins and Betty agrees to join his gang.

Warren and Lee decide to kidnap Floyd for the reward money, but Floyd has been waiting for them, and machine-guns them to death when they enter his room. Beryl tells Floyd and his pals to leave her house. Floyd and Betty and Preacher and Helen (Camilia Carr),

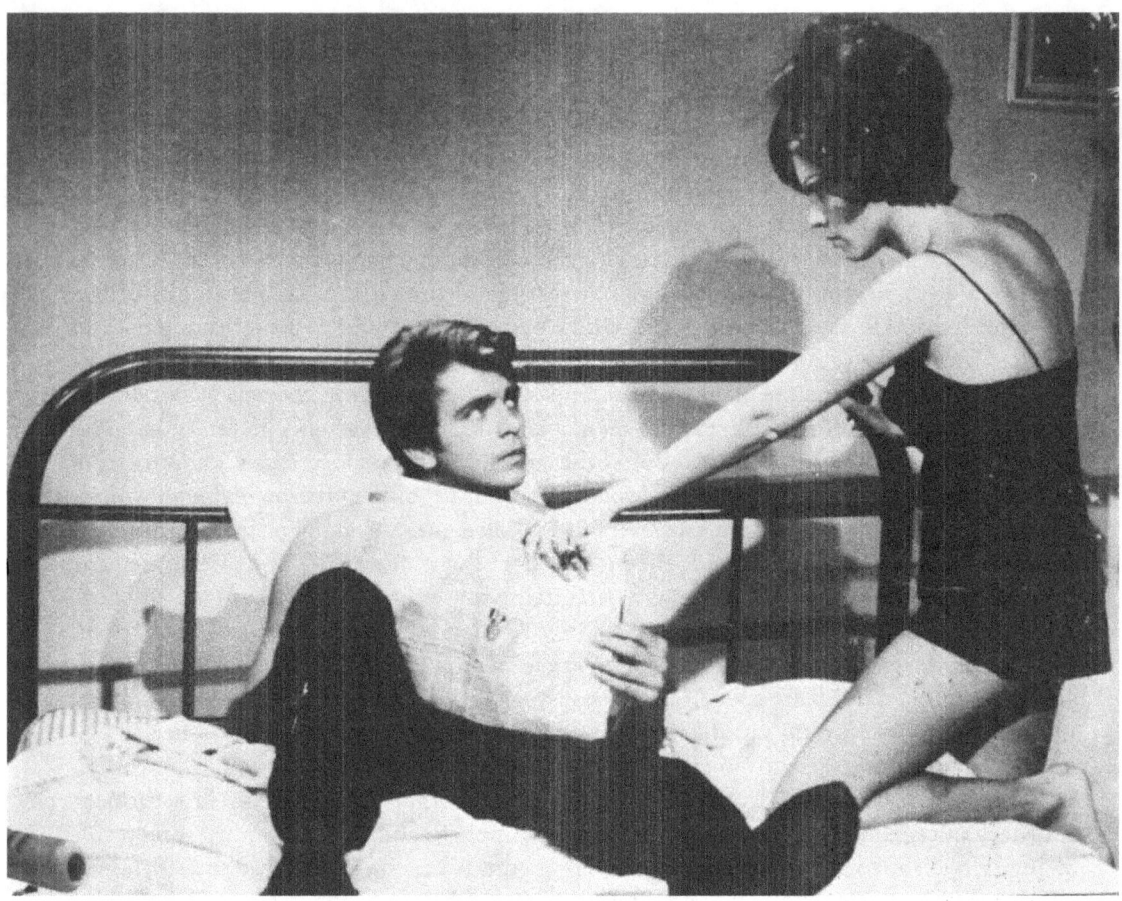

Amused by his new-found notoriety as a bank robber, Charles Arthur Floyd (Fabian Forte) reads the latest news about his fame as his road companion, the prostitute Betty (Jocelyn Lane), expresses her feelings in *A Bullet for Pretty Boy*.

another prostitute, all participate in their next, daring daylight bank robbery. As law enforcement officers have had no luck in capturing the criminals using a state-by-state approach, President Roosevelt signs into law the Federal Bank Robbery Act, making these robberies a federal crime. FBI prosecutor Hossler (Robert Glenn) arrives in Texas to coordinate efforts to capture Floyd's gang. An ambush is attempted at a local hotel, but the gang has moved on.

The gang's next stop is the Hayes City bank, where the sheriff happens upon the robbery in progress, and is summarily gunned down by Floyd. Local authorities soon tell Hossler that they have Floyd's gang surrounded in a tourist court. As the gang prepares to move out, the place is surrounded by cops. Over Floyd's objections, the gang decides to tackle one more robbery, at the bank at Groverton. As they leave their rooms, gunfire erupts, and Helen and Ned are killed. Floyd, Betty and Preacher drive on, and stop once again at Floyd's hometown. With a babbling brook dividing them, rivals Betty and Ruby discuss their mutual lover. Here the water suggests both the mutual power of the two women, who share some intimacies about their shared loved interest, while also illustrating the immense emotional and moral gulf which separates them.

Charles Arthur Floyd (Fabian Forte), escaped convict, attempts to defend his faltering marriage to Ruby (Astrid Warner) in *A Bullet for Pretty Boy.*

Realizing that she has lost Floyd to his new partner-in-crime, Ruby sadly acknowledges, "Everything's changing." The social mores of the time were indeed changing radically, with the sanctity of traditional marriage threatened and finally corrupted by the vicious economic upheaval of society, forcing new, ephemeral and dangerous liaisons. Back at the cotton house, Seth informs the gang that the law is coming down hard on the local community, whom they feel are harboring the criminals; the gang decides they cannot endanger their friends any longer. Early next morning, Floyd and Ruby share a teary farewell. Ruby senses it will be the last time she will ever see her true love. The gang's next bank robbery is met with indifferent stares from the townsfolk, who barely notice its occurrence. Crime has become a commonplace thing, and society has been significantly jaded. Soon, the gang's car suffers engine trouble, and they head north for needed repairs. O.J., an old friend, goes off to fetch a new water pump for them, but turns back when he spies a police roadblock nearby. O.J. warns Floyd of the impending trap. Floyd buys O.J.'s truck, and tells Betty to stay. Betty walks off, angry and dejected.

Floyd and Preacher drive towards home and certain death. Running through a police roadblock, they barely escape the law again. Afterward they rest. Hossler soon tracks the pair to Ralston, where the sheriff (Neil Fletcher) stumbles upon Preacher. The two shoot each other simultaneously. Floyd walks on alone, and happens upon a young man fixing his car. Floyd fixes the car and hitches a ride with the terrified youth. They soon encounter a roadblock and Floyd tries to run it. Floyd runs the car into a lake, and Floyd finishes his fight for life in the water, returning to the enveloping, baptismal redemption of the womb-like pool. He has finally achieved the death he most surely desired from the moment he begrudgingly killed his first man.

A Bullet for Pretty Boy did extremely well in its original theatrical release, and certainly gave Buchanan and AIP reason to be proud.[3] Yet in some ways, *Bullet* can be seen as a curious "reverse lesson" in Buchanan's beloved revisionist history theory. Rather than uprooting falsehoods and half-truths and replacing them with suppressed and obscured facts, here the filmmaker decided to modify and simplify, and thus stereotype Floyd's experience so that it might be both more easily filmed and accessible to a general audience. Floyd's tale in *Bullet* is a highly generic one, meant to be taken more as a period fable than a historical docudrama. Among many other historical errors in *Bullet*, Floyd's wedding to Ruby was a simple civil ceremony, and not church-bound.[4] There was no shooting of the father to trigger Floyd's life of crime. Floyd earned the nickname Pretty Boy from Beulah Baird, a lover and companion, and was not at all aggrieved at the affectionate moniker.[5] Finally, Floyd's death took place in a setting and manner far from its portrayal here.[6]

One cannot help but note the suppression of Buchanan's unique talents when faced with the larger canvas of this, his first mainstream 35mm feature. Much of the passion, philosophy and aesthetics of his more idiosyncratic, smaller works seem distilled here, and certainly the search for truth and justice seems largely absent in this generic, populist yarn. One might think that Buchanan's "Singing Cowboy" persona would have come to the fore in this, a film which showcased the characters, locales and culture Buchanan knew and loved, but this voice is absent in *Bullet*. Curiously, the sterile, emotionless quality of *Bullet* shares much with the existential weariness of Buchanan's Azalea Pictures, and one cannot help but wonder if *Bullet* might have worked better as a smaller, more intimate telefilm.

Still, one can enjoy *Bullet* for what it is. Certainly, no one could film rural Texas with as much love and affection as Buchanan, and the period ambience, although sketched broadly, is entirely convincing. As the filmmaker surely considered *Bullet* a reward of sorts for his backbreaking labors on the previous assignment pictures, one can also appreciate how much this opportunity meant to him. The end result, although not spectacular, is nothing to be ashamed of.

A curious coda to *Bullet*'s production history is the assertion that AIP was unhappy with the finished cut, and hired studio director Maury Dexter to reshoot some scenes.[7] Maury Dexter is a prolific director whose pedestrian melodramas (*Harbor Lights*, 1963; *Wild on the Beach*, 1965; *The Mini-Skirt Mob*, 1968) successfully mimicked bigger-budgeted films in various trendy genres of the day. Another version of the tale has Buchanan fired before shooting wrapped, and being replaced by Dexter.[8] Buchanan was mum on the subject, so this remains an unverified claim. However, if *Bullet* did indeed share two directors, and the resultant final cut reflects this divergent input, it may go some way to explain why *Bullet* seems to lack both commitment and soul, coming as it did from a director who lacked neither.

17

Strawberries Need Rain

After the financial success of *A Bullet for Pretty Boy*, Larry Buchanan decided to reward himself by tackling a more personal project. Buchanan had long been a fan of foreign cinema, stating that Marcel Carne's *Children of Paradise* (1945) was the greatest film ever made. However, a primary influence was Swedish director Ingmar Bergman, and two Bergman films particularly admired by Buchanan were *Wild Strawberries* (1957) and *The Seventh Seal* (1957). *The Seventh Seal* is an allegorical fantasy about Man's struggle against Death, centered on a chess game between a forlorn and cunning mortal and an omnipotent yet ultimately naïve grim reaper. *Wild Strawberries* features an elderly professor recounting the tragicomic events of his long and pointless life as he travels towards what he realizes is an encounter with his final destiny. Both films chronicle the psychological impact which the futility of life, haunted by the omnipresence of death, has on all mortals, via introspection, despair, and even madness.

Buchanan took several basic themes from the two films, and with Enrique Touceda III, fashioned *Strawberries Need Rain* (1970), an overt homage to the Bergman mythos. Buchanan based his screenplay on *In a Certain Village,* by Victor Bruns: "I had found a Scandinavian folk tale of a 16-year-old girl who is visited by the Grim Reaper. She is given 24 hours to live. She spends this precious time seeking out those who had expressed a love for her in hopes that before her departure, *she can know the sensual wonders of the fragile thing called desire.*"[1] Buchanan's florid euphemisms aside, the girl's quest is essentially to lose her virginity in the time she has left. Raising the meager production budget himself, Buchanan returned to Luckenbach, Texas, where he had filmed *The Naked Witch*; the Old World ambience of the tiny berg was ideal for this evocative project, as the environment mimics the look of a small European village from an earlier era, as well as consciously invoking a Bergmanesque setting. Leading the cast of *Strawberries Need Rain* (henceforth referred to as *Strawberries*) is Les Tremayne as the Grim Reaper, in a role not dissimilar to that he played as the diabolical Dr. Basso in *Creature of Destruction*. In both films, Tremayne plays a larger-than-life, hypnotic individual who holds the power of life and death over a mortal woman. Tremayne is effective as the Reaper, filling the role with required passion and pathos. His nemesis, played by newcomer Monica Gayle, would subsequently forge an

The Italian theatrical poster for *Strawberries Need Rain* featured evocative artwork emphasizing the sensual nature of the trial of poor Erica (Monica Gayle) against the ruthless onslaught of the Reaper (Les Tremayne).

impressive career in the adult entertainment industry. In *Strawberries*, Gayle portrays the fatalistic, virginal teenager Erica with efficacy and charm. When *Strawberries* was completed, Buchanan purportedly fashioned phony credits for the film and sneak-previewed it to the students of Southern Methodist University, where he "tested" many of his features. The audience readily accepted the film as the work of Ingmar Bergman.[2] Finding distribution for the arty film was another matter. According to Buchanan, one distributor wanted to retitle the film *Teenage Bait* (which, to be cynical, is not an altogether inaccurate title) and market it as sexploitation.[3] Compromises were made, and the film went out with Buchanan's title, but with lurid poster art and a suggestive advertising campaign, like early Ingmar Bergman films such as *Port of Call* (1948) and *The Magician* (1959), which were also retitled and marketed as exploitation product in their U.S. theatrical runs. Buchanan summarized *Strawberries'* box-office fate: "The arthouses loved it; the drive-ins and big hard-tops couldn't wait to cut short the engagement and ship the prints back to the exchange."[4]

As *Strawberries* opens, an elderly man (Les Tremayne) wearing a black suit and carrying a large sickle, walks down a country road: he is the Grim Reaper. Elsewhere, a teenage boy, Franz (Terry Mace), hides behind shrubbery, watching a beautiful young girl, Erica (Monica Gayle), swimming nude in a pond, Buchanan's idealized Woman and a voyeur lusting after the fetish-object. The boy falls to the ground, exhausted from watching, and perhaps gratifying himself. Franz walks back to his house, enters a dark tool shed, and pulls out a collection of girly magazines he has stored there. He kisses the images of smiling, naked women, still the voyeur whose sexual activity is entirely at the mercy of the purely visual. Franz spots his father (Bill Thurman) approaching with a herd of sheep, a quaint metaphor of Franz's existence under the harsh rule of a castrating father figure, and he hurriedly returns the contraband to their hiding place.

The Reaper walks on into the center of an unnamed small town, as a polka band plays in a gazebo. He walks ominously through the assembled townspeople, accompanied by somber music which threatens to drown out the carefree polka melodies. The Reaper walks on to a nearby farmhouse and encounters Erica; she sees the Reaper, flanked by what appear to be two tombstones, and runs. The Reaper corners Erica on the porch, and the girl, intuitively knowing that this dark figure somehow represents Death, begs him to spare her parents. However, the Reaper reveals that he is not here to collect her parents, but her. Erica is incredulous. The youth has barely even begun to live, and now Death wants her. It seems so arbitrary, so cruel and unfair. No one has, as yet, appreciated her as a person. Erica states, "I haven't even begun to love, and now I have to die?" She negotiates a deal with the reaper to allow her one more day of life, in that she was near death for the first twenty-four hours after her birth. The Reaper accepts this peculiar logic and agrees to return for her tomorrow at sunset.

That night, Erica lies in bed, contemplating her life, looking through the meager artifacts of her brief, sad and overworked life. Reading the Bible, Erica tries to understand the cruel realities of Fate, as the film's theme song plays. Erica goes to the mirror and puts her hair up, trying to see herself as someone worthy of love, worthy of Life, and desirable to the male. As with many women in Buchanan's films, there is a moment where the mirror-stage is acted out, in this case her entry into the Symbolic Order of culture and language. Indeed, after looking in the mirror, she composes a farewell letter to her parents, and, as she writes, Erica recalls a scene from her childhood, when a male teacher at school complimented her on her fine penmanship. For Lacan, language is the essence of the Symbolic Order, the order of signs and symbols the subject enters at the moment of the mirror-stage, and is tied to both the overriding presence of the father but also the death-drive. This moment of Erica's, looking in a mirror, expressing her apologies to her parents in a letter, and then recalling an early vote of confidence from a paternal male (father figure) can be seen as Erica's initial entry into the rules and regulations of the Symbolic Order and the Law organized by the "name-of-the father," a summation which richly echoes the film's conclusion.

Erica lies down on the cold, hard floor, and folds her arms over her chest in imitation of a corpse at a wake. She recalls the Reaper, and sits bolt upright. Erica returns to the mirror, and notices a hand-made Valentine card from her friend and neighbor, Franz, the voyeur seen earlier. Perhaps Franz can embrace Erica's need to access the full joys of life before it is too late, i.e., losing her virginity. Erica creeps out of her house, and makes her way over to Franz's house. Not surprisingly, Franz is in bed with the covers over his head, kissing pictures of naked ladies by flashlight in yet another display of self-gratification. Erica approaches, and the noise alerts Franz, shocked from his fantasy world by a real woman knocking on his window and asking to be let into his world. Taking Franz's flashlight, Erica shines it in his face, thus taking possession of the Phallus Franz needs to illuminate his fantasy life with women. Conversely, shining the "light of truth" in Franz's face forces him to admit he periodically spies on the young woman. Erica invites Franz to join him on his

Larry Buchanan (right) relaxes on location in Luckenbach, Texas, during the shooting of *Strawberries Need Rain*; with him are the Reaper (Les Tremayne) and Erica (Monica Gayle).

own bed. This dynamic of the woman as the sexual aggressor, indeed the virgin or the child-woman as sexual aggressor, is very modern in terms of traditional gender roles, and yet it also acts as a throwback of sorts to a typical male fantasy, the virgin-as-whore, and indicative of *Strawberries'* highly problematic sexual and gender politics as revealed throughout the film. Erica takes Franz's finger and puts it in her mouth, enigmatically stating, "It tastes better than Meyer's...." Franz is uncomfortably aroused by this act of symbolic fellatio, and pulls away from the seductress. Soon after, the flashlight goes dead, and Franz yells at Erica for wasting precious "energy," the failed flashlight used as an amusing metaphor for premature climax. Erica, who orchestrates much of the sexual energy between the two, lights a kerosene lamp (arguably a more "feminine" form) to illuminate the room, and the couple undress, attempting to consummate their relationship. Alas, Franz's worst fears are realized, and he cannot get an erection. Erica dismounts, disappointed that she has not achieved the sweet mystery of life. Franz, mortified by his own sexual failure, begs Erica to leave. As Erica climbs out the window, Franz pathetically bleats, "Will there be another time?" Sensing that the poor boy merely seeks a chance to save face, Erica lies and affirms a future meeting. Franz clutches his headboard, peering through the wrought-iron bars, his bedroom now a sexual prison of failure and remorse.

The scene changes to the next day, as another woman argues with a young man, Bruno (Paul Bertoya), who sits astride a motorcycle. Although filmed outside, the two seem to be speaking in an echo chamber, which lends an eerie, abstract quality to the scene. The woman reveals that she is pregnant, and Bruno asks sarcastically who the father is. The woman slaps him, insists that Bruno is the father, and suggests they get married. Bruno, however, is uninterested in adult responsibility. This scene stands in stark contrast to the previous scene: Franz is impotent, a man who fantasizes but can't act out his sexual needs. Alternately, Bruno is "cocksure" and an arrogant womanizer. Both are equally reprehensible in Buchanan's film world, and the problematic archetype of *Strawberries* is the masculine figure who will be ultimately elevated to the noble task of deflowering Erica.

Bruno rides into town and visits with a group of youths who sit outside a community center, talking about their luck in evading the army draft. Seen as the leader of the group, Bruno asks if there are any new girls in town whom he can stalk and violate. Suddenly, Erica approaches. As she walks by, Bruno notes cryptically, "She's changed." Erica enters the general store, and buys some sunglasses and a cheap bottle of perfume in a desperate attempt to become a woman by forcing society's "stink" onto her. She parades herself through town. If she began her day as the proverbial woman who came in thorough the bedroom window for voyeur Franz, she now becomes the stereotypical town slut and, of course, attracts the attention of whoremonger Bruno.

Offering her a ride on his motorcycle, Bruno and Erica go to a deserted mill. In a rather heavy-handed symbolic conversation, Erica runs to the brook and notes how, unlike life, "It goes on and on, forever," also a nod to water connected to female sexuality as in other Buchanan films, specifically *The Naked Witch*. Bruno reveals that he was born in the old mill house, and relates the sad tale of how the mill fell to ruin. Erica observes how sad it is that things die and become obsolete, but Bruno just puts it down to "progress," also represented by Bruno's motorcycle, one of the few modern devices in a film that exists primarily in an anachronistic, old-fashioned world. Bruno is now defined by the decaying family structure (the decrepit mill house business in ruins), Erica by the eternal flow of water (life and sex). Soon, Bruno takes Erica into the old mill to have sex with her, but when Erica attempts to become an active participant rather than a passive object of Bruno's macho seductions, he becomes enraged, and adopts a classic patriarchal stance by taking his belt to her and sadistically whipping her:

> You want to be taken, don't you? That's what all the baby girls say to Bruno: "Bruno made me do it!" So it doesn't bother your conscience?... You know why that turns you on? You pretend that it's your daddy that's spanking you, and you don't know why daddy can be mean to you, because when daddy's finished, he makes up! Daddy loves baby more than he loves momma!

In this sense, Bruno's sadism cannot be divorced from the holy family structure, as suggested by Giles Deleuze: "The paternal and patriarchal theme undoubtedly predominates in sadism.... In sadism the Oedipal image of woman is made, as it were, to explode: the mother becomes the victim *par excellence*, and *the daughter is elevated to the position of incestuous accomplice*"[5] (emphasis added). Bruno continues to whip Erica until she manages to escape and run down the highway, with Bruno in pursuit, until the Reaper intervenes and swings his sickle, killing the sadistic biker. The Reaper's action can be read as a patriarchal gesture of protection as well, and as will be discussed shortly, allows Erica to assume her role in a far more benign, romantic, but equally sadistic patriarchal order in which she indeed becomes the "incestuous accomplice."

Erica next walks through a meadow full of wildflowers, fully embracing nature, as a song is heard, "Yellow, Green and Blue." The montage is edited so the onscreen images correspond literally with song lyrics, in effect matching the visual with the word: image and sign. The camera pulls back to show a man (Gene Otis Shane) sitting on the rocks, *reading out loud from a book*. Erica comes upon the man, and, recognizing him, calls his name: "Mr. Seestrom!" Seestrom acknowledges Erica, who says, "I see you've discovered my private lake," certainly a *double-entendre*. Seestrom does not immediately recognize Erica, however, and when he does, he confesses, "You've changed a lot"—exactly the same remark Bruno made when first spotting Erica.

A flashback ensues, as a younger Erica runs to school. Taking her seat, she realizes the teacher is a younger Seestrom, the same teacher who complimented her on her penmanship during the flashback when she looked in the mirror. Returning to the present, Seestrom questions Erica about what she calls "her lake." Erica responds confidently, "Yes, it is a lake. Sometimes, it's an ocean," a clear reference to her burgeoning sexual appetite and arousal. Seestrom tells Erica she reminds him of Don Quixote, the main character in the book he is reading, a character of legend for whom erotic fantasy is paramount. Taking her by the hand, Seestrom leads Erica through the fields, and they pass by an untended strawberry patch, which leads to another flashback: a much younger Erica, and two other young girls, sneak up on a neighbor's strawberry patch, and begin to pluck and eat the berries. Seestrom, who lived next door at the time, runs out and chases the girls away. He scolds Erica. After shooing her away, Seestrom takes a half-eaten berry and finishes it himself, a none-too-subtle foreshadowing of a future sexual connection.

In this respect, Mr. Seestrom, the "good patriarch" teacher-figure, becomes the Symbolic father as the arbitrator of language, connected to the Symbolic Order of language (books, writing). As Lacan observed,

> The Primordial Law is therefore that which in imposing marriage ties superimposes the kingdom on that of a nature abandoned to a law of mating ... this law, then, is clearly revealed to be identical to an order of language ... it is *the name of the father* that we must recognize the support of the symbolic function which, from the dawn of history, has identified this person with the figure of the law.[6]

The Symbolic Order is constructed on the Oedipal complex, the incest taboo, and symbolic castration with the exchange of signifiers. The most troublesome aspect of *Strawberries* is how the sadistic order of patriarchal domination becomes a romantic incest fantasy with the Symbolic Father who transcends the Law becoming, if not God, certainly god-like as the center of metaphysical unity in the universe.

Back in the present, Erica questions Seestrom on finishing the strawberry she had stolen, but Seestrom explains, "I only ate the one you picked and had left to die." Erica understands, countering, "Nothing that's going to die should go to waste," another hint to Seestrom not to waste the sexual bounty she is poised to offer him. A downpour starts, (female) water pouring from the heavens, and the two find shelter in Seestrom's little log cabin (the antithesis to Bruno's decaying wood mill). Inside, Seestrom pretends to be Don Quixote, taking his umbrella as a prop lance. Holding out the object for Erica to anoint, she kisses the phallic symbol, and Seestrom-as-Quixote, thus empowered, rides out on his bicycle to fetch some food for his "lady fair." When he returns, they begin their romantic evening. Erica descends the stairs, wearing the simple white dress she had bought in town, looking to Seestrom like a virgin bride approaching the altar of wedding. The two share a glass of champagne, and Erica confesses she has never drunk before. She places the sacred liquid to her lips like a holy communion offering to God. Seestrom then dips strawberries into the champagne, and teasingly, erotically, inserts them into Erica's mouth, completing the faux-religious ceremony offering this innocent soul the blood and body of Christ (or simply shoving another Phallus into her mouth).

Inevitably, Seestrom is the man who deflowers Erica in what amounts to a soft-core pornographic sequence, replete with romantic clichés such as a roaring fire, and Erica's entreaties to Seestrom to be "gentle" for her first time. Afterwards, the two lovers run upstairs and have a pillow fight. Erica finally finds out her partner's first name, which is Gerte. The two make love again, and later Erica sneaks out while Gerte sleeps. Sunset arrives, and the Reaper returns to Erica. Erica stands, waiting, on the porch, resigned to her fate. However, he informs her that he cannot take her to Death now, for she is with child, and, "I came for only one soul. Now there are two." The Reaper hastens to add, "By the way, it'll be a boy," as if to affirm a triumph for the cosmic Patriarchy—her sexual-spiritual quest has resulted in a son, not a daughter. The Reaper departs, and Erica looks up towards the sun, ecstatic. The Virgin conquers Death by becoming the sexually active Woman. The Woman cheats Death by becoming a mother, and through her male progeny, the Woman becomes immortal.

In this respect, Buchanan's Jungian leanings feature prominently in *Strawberries*, which invoke Jung's archetypes of "the wise old man" and "the great mother." Erica is another of Buchanan's idealized women, in spirit and as a "great mother," while Gerte is emblematic of the wise old man archetype which Jung elucidated, and Buchanan referenced time and again. Yet, for all its progressive metaphysical concepts (which were frequently ascribed to Jung in the 1960s and 1970s), *Strawberries* is unquestionably Buchanan's most reactionary film, invested with a heterosexist, petit-bourgeois "couple logic" and sentimental romanticism. Ultimately, Buchanan declares that the traditional man-woman couple is the natural order of sexual relations, and the essential building blocks of the cosmos. Erica's journey of empowerment reveals her destiny is to be deflowered by an older man and become his wife and mother to his son, a tribute to patriarchy where the woman becomes "an incestuous accomplice." While *Strawberries* harkens back to *The Naked Witch* and the spiritual journey, the spiritual journey is being undertaken by a woman (Erica) in *Strawberries* and a man (the Student) in *The Naked Witch*. The difference is how the women protagonists function in each film. In *The Naked Witch*, the Widow is a supernatural avatar of revenge against the injustice of patriarchy; in *Strawberries*, Erica becomes patriarchy's metaphysical great mother by being impregnated not so much by Jung's wise old man archetype but by Lacan's Symbolic father incarnate: the Law made flesh. When Buchanan's stabs at feminism falter, it is then that they become haunted by the assumption that woman exists to provide man his missing sexual-spiritual self. The unification of male and female as a goal is a theme which regularly surfaces in Buchanan's film, and although this is indeed a prerequisite for sexual-spiritual happiness and growth in the filmmaker's eyes, it alludes to a more regressive heterosexual "couple logic" which tends to reinforce traditional sex roles and structures even as Buchanan challenges, often effectively, more untoward aspects of patriarchy. In this way, *Strawberries* ironically endorses the patriarchy Buchanan consciously, sincerely decries.

18

Goodbye, Norma Jean

Larry Buchanan's *Goodbye, Norma Jean* (1976) is more than lurid celebrity biography. It shatters many illusions about the movie business, and attempts to demystify the cultural creation known as Marilyn Monroe, questioning the cultural mythology which not only obscures but consumes the person (or its subjects, in both senses of the term). Her struggle shows the entertainment industry as a callous, dehumanizing system, a conglomerate of ruthless individuals prepared to exploit anyone in order to produce more products for an insatiable audience. Through straightforward narrative, *Goodbye, Norma Jean* (henceforth referred to as *Goodbye*) specifically seeks to lay bare the pleasant, preposterous banalities of how the public traditionally views a movie star's ascension to fame and fortune. In Norma Jean Baker's case, the road to success was not merely rocky, but criminally abusive and exploitative.

This may explain why *Goodbye* was enormously popular with audiences worldwide, yet was by and large reviled by critics. Filmed on a paltry budget ($180,000), it became Buchanan's biggest financial and artistic success. According to Buchanan, *Goodbye* played to favorable critical response at the Cannes Film Festival, and was almost distributed by studio giant Universal; a deal fell through when the two Australian producers (Mark Josem and Robert Ward) demanded more money than the film was realistically worth.[1] As Buchanan was quick to point out, if it were not for their mishandled negotiations, *Goodbye* might have ended up a smash hit along the lines of Frank Perry's *Mommie Dearest* (1978).

Certainly a degree of critical consternation was due to the sometimes-graphic exploitation-film content and the curious casting of Misty Rowe as Norma Jean Baker (and, it should be stressed, *not* Marilyn Monroe); Rowe was best known for her appearances in *Playboy* and as a regular on *Hee Haw* (and quite effective in the role of Baker). Perhaps most offensive to mainstream critics was the dim light *Goodbye* cast on the Hollywood movie industry's merciless methods, and the human wreckage that came with constructing what became one of the most iconic images in twentieth century American popular culture. Thus *Goodbye* is one of Buchanan's more interesting experiments in revisionist history, and as thoroughly political as *The Trial of Lee Harvey Oswald*; indeed, if Oswald became the patsy in a web of political conspiracies, Norma Jean Baker became the patsy of the Culture Industry.

One of the darker aspects of *Goodbye* deals with Norma Jean Baker not so much as a psychological character study but as a psychoanalytic study, the formation of a spilt personality through the fragmentation of the Self. The Baker/Monroe dichotomy is carried to a harrowing conclusion in Buchanan's sequel to *Goodbye*, which was *Goodnight, Sweet Marilyn* (1989), a dark treatise on conspiratorial intrigues intertwined with Monroe's mental deterioration. Yet Buchanan stated, "These are pictures that I used to try to look past the glamour and the scandal-ridden voyeurism to seek a truer insight, as I perceived it, mind you, *into a tragic and courageous life*."[2] This is not to say that Buchanan intended the film to be an "inspirational" story of empowerment, and it is perhaps a misnomer to self-describe the film's long studies of Baker's abuse, degradation, and eventual submission as a "courageous life." Nevertheless, it is an unflinching depiction of the person behind the image, the woman Buchanan knew as a casual acquaintance, starting from a time in the late 1940s when both aspiring performers were "meat" under punitive contracts to Fox Studios. Baker was an ideal subject for Buchanan, as she could be framed around his "parochial feminism": the innocent waif corrupted by the patriarchal, phallocentric, technocratic order.

In Hollywood, California, circa 1941, a beautiful teenaged orphan, Norma Jean Baker (Misty Rowe), lives with an abusive foster mother named Ruby, who takes every opportunity to remind Norma Jean that the reason she is an orphan is because her mother was "off her rocker," a taunt which constantly reinforces Norma Jean's own fears that she will one day succumb to a psychotic break. Ruby's boyfriend, George, simply prefers to surreptitiously ogle Norma Jean's body. Like many other disadvantaged and distressed teenagers during the Golden Age of Hollywood (Buchanan included), Norma Jean takes every opportunity to escape her world by indulging in culture's manufactured dream factory, "the Movies." After her guardians drive off for a date, the elated Norma Jean changes clothes, stripping for the camera in what certainly is some requisite gratuitous titillation. However, it also suggests Norma Jean's drive to escape her existing conditions by *becoming someone else*, even if the escape is as superficial as adopting fashion more appropriate for tramping through downtown Hollywood taking in all the glittery neon highlights of this debased wonderland. Norma Jean enters a movie theater and becomes absorbed in the newsreel, which suggests that movie stars are just real people after all, sharing casual parties and backyard barbecues like any poor working slob. In these carefully orchestrated, yet casual-appearing "home movies" of celebrity, a ubiquitous marketing tool of the entertainment industry, Hollywood baits and teases the obscure and unknown audience, suggesting, "you could be us," in what is surely a cruel misnomer. Norma Jean wholeheartedly absorbs this fanciful lie: for Norma Jean, who desperately wants her life to be Hollywood, the newsreel provides evidence that Hollywood is not only a dream-life of glamorous thrills, but theoretically attainable middle-class normalcy.

Instead, Norma Jean's life is one of continuous sexual exploitation. A young man sits down next to her, and tries to feel her up; she scares him off with a shower of popcorn. When she returns home later that same evening, another young man tries to molest her in the driveway, but she fights him off as well. Ruby and George return from their date, and stumble drunkenly into the house. George, a belligerent drunk, insists on sex from his companion: "I spent a buck-sixty on ya, and I want some action!" but Ruby falls on the bed, dead drunk. George spies Norma Jean undressing in the next room, and stumbles inside to molest her. Norma Jean wrestles with the old lecher, as Ruby awakens. Seeing her paramour and adopted daughter in an awkward embrace, Ruby becomes enraged, accuses Norma

Jean of leading George on, and orders her out of the house. Soon after, Norma Jean is pulled over by a motorcycle cop (Garth Pillsbury) for speeding. Seeing a sexual opportunity, he gives Norma Jean a warning with the implicit understanding that he may extract "payment" from her later. In short, Norm Jean's life is a constant battle for survival in a sexual jungle.

Norma Jean gains employment at Skylark Manufacturing, one of many industries making munitions for the U.S. military war effort under lucrative defense contracts. During a break, Ethel (Jean Sarah Frost), a coworker and friend, advises Norma Jean to give up her dreams of being a Hollywood starlet and just enjoy her proletarian lot: have fun and let guys pay her way through sexual favors. Relating her disappointing attempts to break into the "picture business," a story rife with exploitation and disappointment, Ethel underscores the brutal sexual reality of Hollywood as a symbol of patriarchal order by insisting that a dumb working girl has only one thing to offer the world: her ass. That night, as Norma Jean rests fitfully, the motorcycle cop returns to retrieve payment for his earlier "kindness" and rapes Norma Jean when she refuses "payment" for his benevolence — chilling evidence of Ethel's statement about a woman's sole value to men.

Her screams attract the attention of a neighbor, a young soldier named Ralph Johnson (Terrence Locke). He runs to the room as the cop escapes. Ralph covers the weeping Norma Jean and then, quite ironically, calls the police. Norma Jean hysterically ruminates to no one in particular over what she believes is an innate and accursed ability to drive men crazy, or the simple fact that she is an attractive woman in a man's world, and therefore fair game. Ultimately, Norma Jean will learn the rules of the game to not only survive but eventually become a star. Indeed, almost prophetically, she shouts, "I don't want anybody to touch me, with all their hands all over me. *Go fuck somebody else!*" (Emphasis added). The vulgarity of the line is also the succulent formula that occurs as "a star (Marilyn Monroe) is born"— Norma Jean can "get fucked" as the exploited or she can "fuck somebody else" as the exploiter. Norma Jean calls out to her long-absent mother, "They won't leave me alone! Make him keep his hands off me!" It is an allusion to memories of childhood sexual abuse. Later, after a doctor gives her a sedative, Norma Jean falls into a drugged stupor in which she pathetically murmurs, "I am not an orphan," while a montage of flashbacks reveals a life that has been one of only neglect and abuse: a man in a car drives away, leaving Norma Jean as a small child crying behind the gates of the Greenbriar Orphanage; a pedophile offers the skipping Norma Jean some candy in exchange for sexual favors; two women try to suffocate the small child with a pillow as she sleeps.

The next day at work, Ethel suggests Norma Jean enter an upcoming contest, in which the Armed Forces are going to choose the "Whammo Ammo Girl," a goodwill position which will serve the subcontractors for the military munitions industry (and a none-too-subtle comment on the sexually infused elements of the military-industrial complex that appears in many of Buchanan's films). As she contemplates this possible chance at low-level fame, a press photographer approaches her and asks, "Hey, little match girl, wanna be somebody?" Norma Jean offers her toothiest smile, and the photog snaps her picture. Later, at Myron's Ballroom, various contestants give speeches of acquiescence to impress the world. Finally, it is Norma Jean's turn; in answer to the question, "What would you say to all those soldiers out there," she pauses, and then whispers, "Hurry home." To riotous applause, the judges anoint Norma Jean Baker "Miss Whammo Ammo," and she walks offstage with a cheap tiara and a bouquet of roses. As she celebrates with her new beau Ralph, Norma Jean proclaims: "I am somebody, I really am somebody! I'm going to be a movie star!" In fact,

Norma Jean's first taste of public adulation is not that she has become somebody, but she has become *somebody else*. She is no longer Norma Jean to the world, but the public male fantasy of the coquettish "Whammo Ammo Girl." And as Norma Jean learns to become "somebody else" she can become to the world the object that can "go [to and] fuck somebody else."

Soon Ralph and Norma Jean are married in Tijuana, Mexico. During their honeymoon in a cheap hotel, Norma Jean muses, "I've never liked making love — except now, of course. I don't enjoy actual sex the way most girls do. It brings back bad memories...." She asks her husband to let her become the sexual aggressor, and, in effect, control the sexual encounter. This switching of roles is pivotal. Beyond the simple need to ensure her personal safety, the act underlines the vast difference between "making love" as an act of mutual respect and "being fucked" or "fucking somebody else" as acts of exploitation — the inherent relationship between sex and power that underscores Norma Jean's torturous transformation into Marilyn Monroe.

Soon Norma Jean takes her photography portfolio to a modeling agency. Beverly (Adele Claire), the tough dame who runs the place, sizes her up as a possible success. She suggests getting started at the lowest end of the entertainment industry: pulp magazines. These sexually saturated crime-and-punishment periodicals, which invariably featured cover art depicting a scantily clad girl about to be attacked and raped by a dark, faceless male figure, catered to the lowest titillation quotient in their predominately male audience, and brutally underlined the abusive, sadistic underpinning of patriarchal sexual roles in popular culture. Soon Norma Jean is posing in faked rape and torture scenes for the sleazy men's magazines. Inevitably, the lurid photography sessions not only trigger memories of sexual abuse, but Norma Jean is also forced to reenact them as a model, yet another aspect of sexual exploitation by a male-dominated culture.

This experience leads to what becomes the almost obligatory moment in a Buchanan film involving a woman and a mirror. In *Goodbye*, it is the first of *four* pivotal scenes involving Norma Jean looking into or reacting to a mirror: three scenes with mirrors proper and the fourth, the "silver screen," functioning as mirror in the conclusion. Each of the mirror scenes alternates with the exploitation Norma Jean endures to become a star. In this respect, Buchanan's early effort, *Naughty Dallas*, bears brief mention, where Toni's desire for stardom can be considered in terms of Lacan's paradox of the mirror-stage. As Toni watches her reflection as she practices her burlesque dance moves, the schism is established: the image-ideal of the Self that Toni sees and wants the world to see, versus the Other in the mirror that Toni sees as the world sees her: "the deflection from a specular *I* to a social *I*."[3] In Buchanan's films, the quest for stardom is precisely the desire of the subject to be seen as the image-ideal they want the world to see (the imaginary self-image), not the Other they see and who the world sees as a sign in the Symbolic Order (the reflection). Like Toni in *Naughty Dallas*, Norma Jean sees herself as the Other in the mirror, and seeks to replace her in the Symbolic Order with her narcissistic self-image — the image-ideal of Marilyn Monroe — a "somebody else" who is not her, and specifically a somebody else the world can "go fuck" as an object of abuse and exploitation.

In the first "mirror-stage" scene, as Norma Jean fixes her makeup between the tawdry photo sessions, she comforts herself by singing a childhood religious song, and then cryptically whispers, "Look, mamma, I'm getting there." Seeing herself in the mirror, she is "getting there" in both ways: getting famous and going mad, and both directly owing to sexual exploitation. Her next photo assignment is in a seedy hotel room, where the "photographer" is actually running a peepshow, with men paying to watch the action behind walls. Norma Jean is made to dress in a ripped sack dress, like a hillbilly slut. The creep handcuffs her to a bed, and covers her mouth with a tourniquet. As soon as Norma Jean is immobilized, the predatory male begins to molest and undress the terrified girl, as the men watch from secret peepholes. While *The Eye Creatures* suggested surveillance as a kind of organized voyeurism, in *Goodbye* voyeurism becomes a kind of organized surveillance where the voyeur (the man) can watch the assault without being seen, and the victim (woman) can be watched as an object of exploitation without knowing they are being watched. While the scene is undeniably designed to appeal to prurient interest as well, Norma Jean is reduced to the essence of what Laura Mulvey decried as the primary function of cinema: women as objects of sadistic punishment and fetishism.[4] Back at the rooming house, Norma Jean shares with Ralph her ongoing despair at exploitation by the male: "I can never get any sleep; there's always a bad taste in my mouth," which is also an obvious double entendre that foreshadows Norma Jean's road to stardom.

Soon Beverly introduces Norma Jean to Irving Olbach (Marty Zagon), a respected Hollywood talent agent. Briefly sizing her up, Olbach suggests that Norma Jean join him in a trip he is making to Palm Springs to attend a party held by famed movie producer Hal James (Preston Hanson), where he introduces her to several guests, including Randy Palmer (Sal Ponti), a famous movie star, and Ruth Latimer (Patch Mackenzie), a dismissive talent agent for the fictional Lion-Rampant Studios. Ruth openly mocks Norma Jean's naiveté yet agrees to arrange a screen test for the aspiring starlet if the girl will sleep with her. Buchanan's portrayal of Ruth as an "evil" lesbian is a punitive offshoot of the patriarchal system of sadistic power figures, taking everything that is wrong with the "masculine" realm of sexual role-playing and applying it, like her male counterparts, towards the exploitation and manipulation of the heterosexual female. Buchanan's usually restrained conflict with homosexual identity (manifest particularly with *Mars Needs Women*) becomes overt with this cartoon-like villain.

Meanwhile, Palmer tries to seduce Norma Jean by plying her with drink and promising her a bit part in his next picture, and the naive girl is too star-struck to object. Soon Palmer is forcing his way with Norma Jean in his Packard, when his wife shows up and becomes enraged. Norma Jean accuses him of rape, but no one believes her, and Palmer thinks the bickering over him by two females is all too funny: he is the perfect symbol of arrogant, ego-obsessed machismo, sheltered by a patriarchal culture and given license to do whatever he pleases, especially to women. Distraught, Norma Jean stumbles back into the house and literally falls into the arms of famed movie producer Hal James; a charismatic emblem of a tawdry business, he easily convinces the vulnerable starlet that he has her interests in mind. As James and Irving discuss the deterioration of the movie business, Norma Jean stands, silently obedient; a meeting is arranged at Lion-Rampant Studios where she meets an obese studio executive about a possible screen test. "I don't believe in preliminaries," he snarls and removes his trousers, signaling to the aspiring starlet to immediately fellate him. Norma Jean becomes angry, and mouths a poignant soliloquy which is the heart of *Goodbye*. Norma Jean speaks the lines in a tight close-up, directly at the camera, and at the movie audience:

> There was a time, not too long ago, that would have shocked me. Now, I am just disgusted! I gave up a modeling job to come here today! I spent my last two bucks on white gloves, for the "virgin"

look. That meant no lunch, but it didn't matter, because I came here with high hopes, thinking that this might be it, the break that gets me going to something I want so much that I am willing to let some "gentleman" like you completely destroy my self-respect by groveling at your feet, in the vain hope that you might consider me an actress! You win. I'll be your degraded whore, but not before I give you a message from every girl who ever had to kneel in front of a slimy bum like you for a chance to work: *how we hate you, because you make us hate ourselves*!

A somber Norma Jean Baker (Misty Rowe) contemplates the brutal Hollywood system on her road to becoming superstar Marilyn Monroe in Larry Buchanan's *Goodbye, Norma Jean*.

The angry and poignant speech articulates her rage at the patriarchal system, with its unlimited capacity to find ways to debase women and "how we hate you, because you make us hate ourselves!" Within the system of exploitation Norma Jean, who wanted to look the "virgin" part, agrees to play the role of the "whore," to become yet another *somebody else* they can go fuck, as she begins her entrance into the Hollywood order with her initiation on the casting couch.

That night, Norma Jean has a sleeping-pill induced hallucination in the mirror, the second mirror-stage sequence; Norma Jean sees her insane mother in a strait jacket, as she tells Norma Jean: "Take a good look at me, because this is how it will be for you before long, baby!... The Tomcats are after you, with their sweet words, and their hard cocks!" In the mirror, Norma Jean does not see herself, but a *new* "somebody else": the image of her equally abused and exploited mother, who explains it was not the poverty or the hard work that finally drove her insane but the betrayal of her husband, who cheated on her constantly and treated her, "like a toilet, just something to piss on...."

Later, Ralph and Norma Jean discuss their meager finances, and Norma Jean decides to do a "nudie film." Soon Norma Jean is prancing naked in a wooded mountain setting in a parody of the standard nudie-film convention, the "nature film." The same scene switches to grainy black and white, as the viewer sees the same actions as before, only this time projected on a movie screen. In this sense, what Norma Jean believes to be her first film role — the cinematic equivalent of Eve frolicking in the Garden of Eden—is revealed to be a cheap stag film being watched by a group of Hollywood celebrities sitting in a darkened room in Hal James' house, watching her innocent frolics projected via 16mm film, clearly both amused and aroused.

After the nudie reel ends, a man named Mortis (i.e., *"rigor mortis"?*) speaks to the group about his next offering, a new trend in the underworld of illicit cinema, something he calls a "snuff film." He describes the offering as a filmed record of two out-of-work actresses kidnapping a drunken hobo and killing him on camera. The debased and jaded audience are delighted about this new "kick," and agree to fork over $100 each as admission to see a heinous, immoral and obviously illegal act of voyeurism at its lowest. The evil film begins, and in murky underexposed black and white, two naked women paw at an unidentified figure as the camera shakes nervously. The scene ends with a quick, blurry close-up of the victim's face, wearing an expression of complete terror, indeed the face of civilized humanity at the moment of its utter annihilation.[5] Elsewhere, Hal James becomes nervous at the unearthly silence coming from the party. He peeks in to see what appears to be a man being killed on a movie screen. James shouts at the assembled to leave his house: this brave new world of debased ghouls disgusts the man and his traditional (read *obsolete*) Hollywood values.

Subsequently, James calls Irving, chastising him for letting Norma Jean appear in sleazy nudie films; he promises to get the young girl some legitimate work. James ruminates on his past behavior, which is revealed to be as implicitly exploitative as what is now occurring more overtly. In this regard, James becomes a symbol of two things; one, the romanticized myth of "Old Hollywood' and the studio system which, despite its excesses, made "great films" versus the "New Hollywood" of decadence and tawdry exploitation fare; second, the "good patriarch" (manifested previously and perversely in *Strawberries Need Rain*) whose benevolence is, at least in part, motivated by bad conscience and using Norma Jean for *his* moral redemption, an opportunity to be "a nice guy" while still fueling his reputation for "star-making."

Not surprisingly, Norma Jean's next encounter is with Ruth Latimer, who invites her to dinner that evening. Under the pretense of reading a scene from an upcoming movie, in which Ruth reads the man's part, the scene quickly turns into a seduction, which Norma Jean resists. Ruth becomes "ruthless," and slaps Norma Jean to the floor, telling her that if she wants to make it in the motion picture business, she must learn to obediently service any gatekeepers she meets along the way, in whatever sexual form that might take. Tearfully, Norma Jean walks into the bedroom, towards her newest humiliation. Later, Irving calls Norma Jean to say that Ruth has rejected her screen test, saying that she "needs to work on her diction," a reference by the lesbian toward soliciting further oral services in exchange for further career opportunities. An incensed Norma Jean soon barges her way into Ruth's office and demands to know why she was rejected; Ruth provides the caustic, official evaluation: "Just another cute ass and bosom, good for handing out samples at a sport convention." Unwilling to accept this assessment, Norma Jean barges into the studio head's office, and the bemused executive, Sam Dunn (Andre Philippe), dispassionately explains: "Your jaw is too firm. Your head is too large for your body. Your eyes would be difficult to make up. Your legs are too long. Your voice is absolutely void of color or timbre. No contract player ever shows her lower teeth the way you do." Not unlike *Mars Needs Women*, where women become female sexual-fantasy stereotypes and breeding stock, Dunn describes Norma Jean as a potential star-commodity as if he were grading an animal at a livestock auction.

Devastated by the rejection, Norma Jean considers herself an utter failure and undertakes the first of a string of suicide attempts, and a third "mirror-stage" moment occurs.

Ralph finds her on the ground, covered in blood, with the word "ugly" scrawled in blood on the mirror. "Ugly" is not only how she feels about herself but also how the world has deemed her. The Other in the mirror is no longer her reflection. The Norma Jean who sees herself as the world sees her in the Symbolic Order is literally reduced to a punitive word of her inadequacy to measure up to its standards.

Hal James invites Norma Jean to his home and takes her under his wing, giving make-up advice, and ordering a complete makeover, including nose job, hair color, and diction lessons. In true Pygmalion fashion — the old studio-system of star manufacturing — the "good patriarch" is revealed to be preoccupied with remaking the female body according to its own aesthetic construct. Soon the "new" Norma Jean is presented to a group of Hollywood celebrities at a party held in her honor. The difference is indeed stunning, but there is something missing from the "new" Norma Jean: the person who was dehumanized by the public image. James and Norma Jean become lovers as well, as James tries to find the right part for his "little girl." While indicative of the more sentimental, romantic (or romanticized) elements of Buchanan's work — the New Age couples and more specifically the perverse symbolic father-daughter couple in *Strawberries Need Rain*—the relationship between the good patriarch and his needy, innocent charge borders on incest fantasy. While in *Strawberries Need Rain* the union culminates in a metaphysical pregnancy, in *Goodbye* the incestuous overtones in the relationship between James and Norma Jean also results in progeny: "a star is born" as the persona of Marilyn Monroe. When the elderly James dies of a heart attack, Norma Jean again meets with Sam Dunn to not only demand a screen test but also a career of fame and fortune.

Embracing the Hollywood Walk of Fame, Norma Jean Baker (Misty Rowe), in platinum wig, smiles for her newfound audience in ***Goodbye, Norma Jean.***

The test is soon screened for the execs at Lion-Rampant. Norma Jean sneaks into the projection booth and watches herself with a mixture of fascination and fear — *narcissism and alienation.* The silver screen becomes the mirror and site of final fragmentation: Norma Jean and Marilyn Monroe, private individual and public persona, Self and Other, image and sign, "specular I to social I." The screen test ends, and the gathered executives share crude sexual remarks about Norma Jean, which she overhears in the projection booth. She defiantly shouts, "That's the last cock I'll ever have to suck!" The screen test is run again, and Ralph utters the film's title as he leaves the projection booth, knowing that he has lost Norma Jean forever: "Goodbye, Norma Jean." She doesn't hear him; she is completely entranced by the projected image (image-ideal) on the mirror-screen at the precise moment when Marilyn Monroe is born and Norma Jean Baker symbolically dies.

19

Hughes and Harlow: Angels in Hell

Larry Buchanan considered *Hughes and Harlow: Angels in Hell* (1977) his masterpiece, and, from an aesthetic viewpoint at least, one may be tempted to agree. By far his biggest production, Buchanan put all of his resources into this pseudo-historical melodrama. Produced immediately following his well-mounted but poorly distributed celebrity bio *Goodbye, Norma Jean*, Buchanan had high hopes that this new biopic, centering on the lives of two more Hollywood icons, would finally become the smash hit which had heretofore eluded him. Like *Goodbye, Norma Jean* and *A Bullet for Pretty Boy*, *Hughes and Harlow: Angels in Hell* (henceforth referred to as *H&H*) features yet another of Buchanan's uncanny re-creations of an earlier period, rich in artifact and nuance, utilizing resources usually allotted to the lowest tier of film production to create a high-gloss product comparing favorably to big-studio productions. Bringing more pop-culture heroes to life, *H&H* features lucid reincarnations of eccentric boy-millionaire Howard Hughes and sexy screen star Jean Harlow, sketched broadly yet vividly via stellar performances by Victor Holchak and Lindsay Bloom. The onscreen charisma of the pair is palpable, and it is easy to pretend that one is watching the real-life personages, not their fictional counterparts.

H&H captures an exciting moment in American history with unflagging passion and wit. The year is 1928, and the monolithic and insular entertainment industry known collectively as "Hollywood" is in the throes of painful growing pains due to the specter of talking pictures, an unprecedented technological advance which promises to both resurrect a depressed economy and brutally weed out obsolete performers and technologies. That this advance was both courted and loathed by all parties is part of the historical record. Giving the movies "a voice" has allegorical implications which are sadly unaddressed in *H&H*. In Hughes' case, his example to the world is that an obsolete system must be irrevocably and unemotionally torn down before a new system can be given its rightful trial. Even while it was embracing the new technology, the entertainment industry was clinging for dear life to the legacy of silent cinema, with its entrenched star system and fortuitous distribution design, and many observers accuse this dread of change of at least delaying, if not sabotaging, the emergence of "talking pictures" as a successful commercial venture.

As much as it centers on its title protagonists, *H&H* also depicts an unabashed love affair with the movies, and more specifically the making of movies. Chronicling the travails of Hughes as he struggles to bring his most recalcitrant cinematic "baby" to life, *H&H* obsesses lovingly on the minutiae of the filmmaking business, the shooting of film, the screening room with its omnipresent backroom banter, even the idiosyncratic technicalities of film laboratory processes. According to an interview Buchanan gave to Michael Price, *H&H* reflects Buchanan's "fascination with the inner workings of a big-league movie industry that I knew briefly from the inside, though never from a position of power."[1] This intimate knowledge of, and preoccupation with the movie industry is a source of much of the film's melodramatic integrity and historical authenticity.

As life eerily and unerringly imitates life, Buchanan would soon mount his own battle in bringing *H&H* to the screen, a battle he would ultimately lose. After garnering a meager $240,000 budget from a Los Angeles clothing manufacturer, and bringing in a remarkable melodrama complete with period setting, big cast, films-within-films and realistic World War I dogfight sequences, the duplicitous producer announced that *H&H* had been intended all along as a tax shelter and would not be released. Buchanan begged for the film to receive some distribution, to no avail. Buchanan maintained that *H&H* was never released theatrically, although two poster runs for the film do exist. To date, *H&H* has had one limited home video release and infrequent cable television screenings. The UCLA film archives purportedly owns a rare 35mm print of the film, available to film students, but for all intents and purposes, *H&H* is yet another Buchanan film unavailable to the general public.[2] The excruciating burdens of near fame had taken another ironic stab at Buchanan. Even after the success of *Goodbye, Norma Jean*, when the filmmaker had abundant offers for production money, he, like all artists, was still beholden to his sponsor for his work's eventual fate. The cynical Hollywood in-joke about the three rules of filmmaking ("Distribution, Distribution, Distribution") still rings frighteningly true for many a filmmaker, and Buchanan is certainly a most disheartening example. This makes the extant *H&H* all the more precious as a historical document of note.

H&H returns to one of Buchanan's most cherished themes, that of an outcast couple working against an antagonistic system and causing radical change in their community. Clarifying and fine tuning a similar theme from earlier films such as *The Naked Witch, The Eye Creatures, Mars Needs Women* and *It's Alive!*, Hughes and Harlow are perhaps Buchanan's most utopian couple, two good people who manifest apparent miracles in an effort to transform a corrupt and debased society. Perhaps Buchanan's ultimate heterosexual savior-couple, they could truly be called "Angels in Hell." Sociologists might be tempted to dub Howard Hughes and Jean Harlow an early example of the "New Age" couple which appeared later in the century, but, in fact, the two relied more on communal traditions of integrity, hard work and vision than current or trendy courses of action. Yet, like all visionaries, their actions did prophesy and to some degree usher in a new era of progress and growth for their communities. This makes Hughes and Harlow, at least in Buchanan's view, heroic and mythic characters.

H&H opens like a fable, via narration placed over effectively recreated scenes of a gala movie premiere: "Once upon a time, in a faraway land called Hollywood, there lived a people who manufactured dreams. They were so good at their work that it was hard to tell the real from the unreal. What you are about to see is the story of one such dream, and the two people who made it come true." Inside Grauman's Chinese Theater, the expectant crowd mingles in the lobby. A radio announcer introduces the stars of the evening, Howard Hughes, as "the tall young Texan" and his partner, Jean Harlow, as "the platinum blonde unknown." The announcer asks Hughes (Victor Holchak) what he thinks the critics will have to say about his new film, *Angels in Hell*. Hughes retorts, "I didn't make this movie for the critics," setting Hughes as having an antagonistic relationship with established power figures. To the same question, Harlow (Lindsay Bloom) chirps, "What's a critic?" This is perhaps a coy response, but one which suggests a sweet oblivion to the powers that be.

Hughes' assistant, Billy (David McLean), informs him that they are running behind at the film laboratory, even now processing the last reels of the film scheduled to run in mere minutes. Elsewhere, Harlow spouts an obscenity in front of a horrified Will Hayes (Royal Dano), all-powerful head of the motion picture censor board, nicely illustrating that while some people deliberately choose to run against established society, for others it is a destiny thrust upon them by circumstance. Hughes rushes off to the lab, where he encounters an apologetic lab technician. Hughes kindly responds, "It's my can, I'll carry it," clarifying with, "It's just an old Texas expression." Hughes spools up a freshly processed reel of film, showing himself to be, at heart, just a regular fellow. Buchanan seems intent here upon painting Hughes as a God-fearing Texas patriot.

The long-awaited *Angels in Hell* unreels, via some well-crafted black and white scenes. During the nightclub scene Harlow speaks, and the audience breaks into nervous titters. As soon as the war scenes begin, however, with impressive aerial dogfight footage, the audience turns to awed silence. In the balcony, Harlow leans over to Hughes and mutters, "Looks like you lose your bet, Sam."

The scene changes to a flashback, where Hughes is filming the dogfight scene just shown onscreen: Hughes tells the director to speed up production, and hops off the film truck. Inside the screening room, Hughes and his assistant watch the disappointing rushes. Billy leaves to get some fresh air, and stumbles onto a nearby set where a Hal Roach comedy, *Double Whoopee*, is being filmed. A sexy young blonde, Jean Harlow, stumbles out of a car and catches her dress in the car door. The crew is mesmerized by this sexy waif, who now wears only a slip. At the lunch wagon, Hughes buys a bowl of chili, but has no loose change with which to pay. Harlow pays for Hughes, thinking him a poor working slob like herself. Harlow soon joins the film crew in a dice game. Billy gives Harlow some of Hughes' money to gamble with. Hughes stands nearby, enchanted by this strange free spirit.

Later, Hughes visits a movie theater, enchanted by a gangster picture with actual sound effects. Hughes calls Billy and tells him they are going to remake *Angels in Hell*, with sound. At the studio, a director tells Hughes and the others why it would be foolhardy, and virtually impossible, to turn Hughes' war film into a "talkie" at this late stage, but Hughes refuses to listen and instead fires the director. The director tells off the arrogant millionaire, informing him that Hollywood considers him a joke, thus underlining Hughes' antithetical relationship with the establishment.

Soon Hughes and company are reviewing new rushes — of dogfights with authentic sound effects — and the result is encouraging to all. However, they still haven't found the perfect girl to accompany this revolution in entertainment. Hughes asks Billy about the sexy blonde at the lunch wagon, and Billy sadly informs him that the down-and-out actress is now working at a Hollywood brothel. Billy visits the brothel and discovers that Harlow

Boy-genius Howard Hughes (Victor Holchak) takes phallocentrism to a new, techno-fetishist level with his miniature flying machines in *Hughes and Harlow: Angels in Hell*.

is a dancer, not a whore. Billy convinces the suspicious young woman that the playboy millionaire, Howard Hughes, does indeed want to test her for a part in his upcoming movie.

Next morning Harlow arrives at the studio and recognizes the penniless man she lent money to arrive via motorcycle. Walking together into the soundstage, the film crew offers a hearty good morning to the man, who of course is Hughes. Harlow is incensed at Hughes' playful deception. Harlow gets dressed for her part as Hughes watches, and the two share some playful sexual banter. The screen test pits Harlow with Nick, an actor who appears to be homosexual. The screen chemistry is off, and Harlow performs badly. Harlow tries to get a rise out of her co-actor by putting ice on her breasts, thus enlarging the nipples. Returning to the set, Nick and Harlow achieve a slightly better rapport, ending their scene in a passionate kiss which floors the crew. That night, Hughes takes Harlow out for a date, driving to Caliente for some Mexican food. The two discuss their lives, as both are stuck in unhappy marriages.

The two stop at a speakeasy, where Hughes discovers that the men who are working as pilots for his film are also moonlighting for director Howard Hawks on a film he is shooting. Hughes fears that Hawks is stealing ideas from the pilots, so he decides to go visit the famed filmmaker. Although they arrive at Hawks' house uninvited at midnight, the gracious filmmaker (Adam Roarke) grants an audience to the cocky millionaire and his beautiful date. Hughes immediately goes in for the attack, accusing Hawks of stealing scenes. Hawks defends himself admirably, stating that ideas are essentially public domain and no film artist has a monopoly on how dramatic scenes are reenacted. This scene recreates in essence an actual meeting between an elderly Howard Hawks and Buchanan during the filming of *H&H*, in which Hawks purportedly told Buchanan of the pact made between Hughes and Harlow at the time, an important anecdote which figures prominently in *H&H*.[3]

Hughes and Harlow continue on to Mexico and soon arrive at a small shack in the country, where Hughes' good friends Emiliano and Inez live. Apparently Hughes made an emergency landing in the area last year and the kindly Latino helped Hughes fix the plane and put him up for the night. The four share a delicious dinner, complete with tequila. Harlow notices as Hughes passes some money to the poor farmer. This somewhat maudlin scene tries to portray Hughes as a down-to-earth man of the people, but he comes across as more patronizing than gracious.

The next morning Hughes and Harlow stop by a beachside on their way back to Los Angeles. Harlow clarifies for herself the two selves which battle within Hughes, the arrogant millionaire and the kindly patriarch nicknamed "Sam." Harlow makes a pass at Hughes, but Hughes declines. Hughes explains that he is determined to change Hollywood's opinion of him, and change Hollywood in the process: "I don't quit, and I don't fail!" Acknowledging his father as the source of his courage and determination, Hughes insists that *Angels in Hell* is going to be a significant success. He realizes that Harlow, as an untried screen goddess, is a major part of that challenge, and he pleads with her to work with him to make this project a legend. Hughes suggests that after *Angels in Hell* is successfully completed, the two of them may then "tie one on that'll make Louella Parsons crap in her pants!" This assertion on Hughes' part suggests that a creative couple must use their stored-up, unspent sexual energy towards the completion of creative acts. Instead of wasting this precious energy on frequent, orgasm-centered sexual activity, the fate of most sexually-oriented partnerships, by amassing and redirecting this bountiful fountain of energy one can manifest significant power towards the implementation and completion of mutual creative, social or political goals. This notion is very much in line with the philosophy of tantric sex in the Indian, Hindu and Buddhist esoteric traditions, which emphasize the sexual act as a powerful energizing force and spiritual ritual, one best left uncompleted, as orgasm tends to distill and deplete the sacred energy which is alternately enhanced and increased by the careful harnessing of sexual release.[4] Put another way, in order to manifest any sort of personal or societal change a partnership must forgo the lower, animal urges, and attempt to access the spiritual realm within each and as a unit. Therein lies creativity and genius, i.e., spiritual growth. Hughes and Harlow seal this fateful agreement with a passionate kiss, and the scene returns to the movie premiere, where the fruits of this energized sexual relationship are unfolding on the screen to an enrapt audience.

Harlow feels that the film is a failure, but Hughes remains confident. The scene returns to flashback, where Hughes and Harlow look over some rushes. Harlow ruminates over the obstacles encountered throughout this difficult project, and asks Hughes what's wrong with people who make movies. Hughes responds, "I guess we're just a nutty bunch. It sure as hell isn't the money," a statement which could easily have come from Buchanan. Continuing, Hughes states, "I don't see the pieces at all. I see the end of it, the finished product," surely the philosophy of any true artist.

An unnamed young woman shows up for a date with Hughes, leaving a rejected Harlow alone in the editing suite. Harlow returns home, distraught. She is having difficulty seeing the "finished product," and separating her emotional attachment to Hughes from her professional commitment. Disgusted with her lack of control, the actress undresses, hops into bed, tells God what a fool she is, and masturbates herself to sleep. This self-effacing, compulsive discharge of accumulated sexual tension is Harlow's offering to her vow to Hughes and the project, a sacrifice to the greater good.

The scene returns to the present, as *Angels in Hell* continues to unspool. Although the dogfight scenes are impressive, Hughes intuits that the audience is far more interested in Harlow's haunting sex appeal, and that it is her sultry screen presence which will make the film a hit. Harlow's unresolved sexual tension with Hughes may in fact be the energy which imbues *Angels in Hell* with its greatness, a good example of turning thwarted sexual energy into creative force. As another love scene unfolds, Harlow's sexual energy floods the screen. Even the stiff, pompous performance by her leading man cannot dampen her earthy erotic charms. Harlow whispers the immortal words, "I want to change into something more comfortable," and the silver screen's most passionate love scene to date unfolds. Movie censor Hayes looks on, disgusted.

The scene reverts to flashback, as Hughes drives his date home. Hughes accidentally hits a pedestrian and is arrested. Soon Harlow, Billy and a lawyer arrive at the police station to help out the jailed millionaire. The woman with Hughes also shows up, and this convinces Harlow that Hughes is indeed still playing around with whores and not keeping his end of their tantric bargain. An enraged Harlow leaves via taxi to return to the brothel, in the hopes of locating a "gang-bang" which could relieve both her pent-up sexual frustration and considerable self-loathing. Luckily the pedestrian is not fatally injured, and Hughes is released. Hearing of Harlow's angry departure, Hughes and Billy head for the brothel, where they battle several males-in-heat in order to rescue Harlow from her unwise reactionary decision.

Later Harlow yells at Hughes for his sexual double standards as he works on an airplane. Harlow harangues Hughes at length, while the cocky man remains silent. Harlow explains her sexual frustration in detail, and declares that their deal is off. Finally, a frustrated Harlow yells, "Will you say something, you sadistic bastard?" But Hughes still says nothing. He has clearly adapted a somewhat cruel, dominant role in this relationship, a chauvinistic trait unbecoming to the truly New Age individual but one which accurately reflects the real Hughes, who was considered by many to be an arrogant bully.

Hughes eventually stumbles onto what he feels is the missing factor in the existing aerial footage, a lack of voluptuous clouds which could somehow echo the erotic impact of the earth-bound love scenes. Searching for cloud formations in his airplane, Hughes dictates more conditions to Harlow about how she presents herself to the press. Hughes insists that during this devastating economic depression, moviegoers want to see "Cinderella stories" about poor girls making it big in the movies, and Harlow's actual past, which involved wealthy family members and finishing schools, will never do. Hughes then shows Harlow his new toy, a system by which an airplane can fly itself, which he coyly dubs "the automatic pilot."

Returning to the movie premiere, *Angels in Hell* concludes with an exciting aerial battle sequence. The film ends, and the audience sits in nervous silence. Suddenly, Will Hayes begins to applaud, and the sheeplike audience follows with riotous clapping.[5] Hughes and Harlow have turned their creative vigor into a political act. They have conquered Hollywood. Back in the lobby congratulations are passed all around. Hughes takes Harlow airborne, and they consummate their deal. Thanks to the boy genius's automatic pilot, Hughes

19. Hughes and Harlow: Angels in Hell

Jean Harlow (Lindsay Bloom, in white) taunts an offscreen Howard Hughes by flirting with a gigolo at a local whorehouse in *Hughes and Harlow: Angels in Hell*. (Other actors unknown). She is angered that the playboy billionaire is welching on their agreement to avoid sexual relations during the filming of *Angels in Hell*; Hughes is dating every Hollywood starlet in town, while Harlow is beholden to remain untouched.

and Harlow make love in the cockpit, while the airplane flies these "Angels in Hell" towards their desired Heaven. As in *The Eye Creatures* and *It's Alive!* the couple's immediate, symbolic reward for conquering the world is to finally indulge in mutually postponed sexual activity, an act which surely suggests the "birth" of a new era.

Although ultimately as disingenuous as its main protagonist, *H&H* is a highly entertaining and well-mounted production. The scenario by Buchanan and Lynn Shubert adopts the meandering, circuitous flashback structure Buchanan used in *Goodbye, Norma Jean*, and experimented with in the courtroom trilogy. This potentially confusing but dramatically rich structure assures the viewer that he will be taken down unexpected avenues of narrative adventure and character revelation, a shuffling of insular reality which owes much to the avant-garde literati of the era including the patchwork novels of William Burroughs. Although non-linear in appearance, the seemingly arbitrary structure of *H&H*, and *Goodbye, Norma Jean*, lends itself to a rapidly-accruing catalog of character development and raises the piece to an exciting dramatic crescendo.

What is unfortunate about *H&H* is that it takes the notion of revising history and turns it on its head. Rather than revealing unpleasant truths about its protagonists, it glosses them over, creating simplified, overly sympathetic characters which evoke the mythos of

Howard Hughes (Victor Holchak) puts the finishing touches on his experimental airborne guidance system, coyly dubbed "the automatic pilot," as Jean Harlow (Lindsay Bloom) ruminates on the glorious reception *Angels in Hell* was given by its premiere audience. The two will soon celebrate their victory by engaging in long-delayed sexual relations. From ***Hughes and Harlow: Angels in Hell.***

fairy tale characters more than real-life historical personages. Hughes, particularly, comes across in *H&H* as a tireless visionary and child-like genius, persecuted by his community and wrongfully accused of frivolity. Furthermore, *H&H* simplifies his sexual self into a mere cad. The real Howard Hughes was a much more complex and darker character, considered by many observers an "American Rasputin." In addition to possibly being a polygamist, he was an insatiable sex addict, courting dozens of casual girlfriends even while he maintained his marital façade. To muddy matters further, he was a bisexual and had clandestine affairs with young male models and aspiring actors. Finally, Hughes was a racist and anti-Semite, not at all an egalitarian "man of the people" as sketched here.[6]

As far as Hughes' relationship with Harlow is concerned, it appears that although the two of them may have had a brief fling during the production of *Hell's Angels* Hughes primarily saw Harlow as a commodity to be exploited and then discarded. Thus the frustrating scene in *H&H* where Harlow yells at a mute Hughes for his infidelities may ring closest to the truth of the matter, and yet in the overall framework of *H&H* it sticks out like a sore thumb, going against everything previously suggested about the man and his unerringly self-centered agenda. So, although Buchanan posits Hughes and Harlow in *H&H* as a real-life occurrence of his coveted savior-couple archetype who manage to assail and conquer a corrupted community, these characters are more of fable than of fact.[7]

Jean Harlow fares somewhat better in the film, although her character is simpler and sketched quite broadly. Bloom tends to portray Harlow as equal parts proletariat scrapper and ditzy flapper, whereas the real Harlow was an accomplished actress with astute timing who came from a well-to-do family. Bloom's version of Harlow, while somewhat fanciful, is not unsympathetic or patronizing.

This is not to say that *H&H* is without interest as a Hollywood fable of considerable charm. Indeed, the overarching message, that the determined and focused individual can overcome insurmountable odds to achieve success in their chosen field, especially if aided by a like-minded partner, is a universal and encouraging one, conveyed well. Also, the depiction of the motion picture industry is done well and may be of interest to any fan of the time period. Finally, the bringing to life of historical personages as identifiable, if not entirely accurate, genre archetypes is something Buchanan did exceedingly well, and his "Hughes and Harlow" may be his finest creations in this regard. His protagonists, for better or worse, do come across as mythic, larger than life, heroic in the best sense of the term. In the last analysis, *H&H* is best seen as allegorical fable and not biographical drama, a nostalgic period love story of an era conquered and a vision accomplished.

20

Mistress of the Apes

According to his autobiography, Larry Buchanan created *Mistress of the Apes* (1979) for distributor and friend John Rickert, who wanted a sexploitation film for the upcoming Cannes Film Festival. Buchanan produced an old treatment he had squirreled away, and proceeded to sell the film, on the spot, to Rickert.[1] While this may have been the economic motivation for *Mistress of the Apes* (henceforth referred to as *Mistress*), Buchanan certainly had other things in mind when he made this most unusual fantasy-thriller. After the huge disappointment of *Hughes and Harlow: Angels in Hell*, Buchanan likely felt the need to tackle something simpler and less personal.

Taking the time-honored template of white men going into the antagonistic jungle, battling internal strife and external threat, *Mistress* does deliver as a simple sexploitation yarn. However, *Mistress* also ends up as yet another treatise on the empowered female outsider escaping and overpowering an oppressive male-dominated society. In fact, *Mistress* brings Buchanan's disenchantment with patriarchal society — and his simultaneous fascination with the emancipated female — to new heights. Here the liberated woman rises to virtually godlike status, and lords over a new, male-populated society as their object of worship, educational mentor, and primary breeder.

Working with a meager budget of $100,000, Buchanan filmed *Mistress* in Malibu State Park in California, creating such an effective atmosphere that some reviewers insisted that the film was shot in Kenya! A good portion of the budget went to makeup for the tribal "Near-Men." The makeup designs were created by Greg Cannom, then an up-and-coming makeup artist who had just finished an assignment on the *Planet of the Apes* movie series. The excellent facial designs for the Near Men evoked the look of the Cro-Magnon Man, with a touch of "Hollywood Gorilla" thrown in. Cannom went on to become an esteemed makeup artist, winning Oscars for *Bram Stoker's Dracula* (1992; d: Francis Ford Coppola) and *Mrs. Doubtfire* (1993; d: Chris Columbus).

Mistress opens with a starkly misanthropic statement, conveyed via an onscreen title: "The skulls taken from Olduvai Gorge tell us we are the children of Cain — all of us." Credited to "African Genesis," this overt declaration that man is evil restates Buchanan's misanthropic philosophy in a fashion similar to the bold proclamation of Montaigne at the start of *Creature of Destruction*. The credits roll over nighttime scenes of New York City, ending with another editorial title: "A jungle somewhere on the eastern seaboard of the United States..." Buchanan thus gleefully offers two cynical references to Man and his civilization before the drama even commences, signaling that Buchanan-as-philosopher is in full force.

At a hospital, a woman, Susan Jamison (Jenny Neumann), is in the middle of giving birth when a drug-related robbery goes bad. In the ensuing chaos, Susan falls, and her baby is miscarried. Apparently, Susan was not meant to spawn men's children, but was destined for greater things. Soon Susan is recuperating, and a friend, David Thurston (Walt Robin), comes with flowers and news of Susan's explorer-husband, Earl, who has been lost in the Congo Basin for five weeks, and is presumed dead. Susan declares she is going to launch an expedition to search for Earl as soon as she gains her strength. Already, the character of Susan is sketched as a strong, focused and willful individual. The sleazy David, however, is next seen taking sexy photographs of his secretary (Suzy Mandel), and is a standard-issue exploiter of women. As the bimbo stands in front of an archery target, she bleats, "Am I the target for tonight?" and thus cleverly states her complicity in this ongoing dance of mutual abuse between men and women. The bimbo asks David why he is taking his wife, and not her, to Africa with him. David's reply fully reveals his opinion of the opposite sex: "Just shut up and function."

Susan arrives with a reporter, Paul Cory (Garth Pillsbury). David, a hobbyist-hunter, proudly shows Paul his new faux-penis, a mammoth Remington .308 hunting rifle. The pacific Paul is less than impressed, however, and the two bicker over the morality of big game hunting, and, in essence, the validity of the phallus as a weapon of conquest. Paul then presides over a slide show taken from pictures removed from Earl's recovered Leica camera. Much to their shock, the slides show images of prehistoric men similar to the "Australian Pleistocene Man," supposedly extinct for thousands of years and otherwise known as *Homo habilis*, the link between man and ape. The group decides to mount an immediate expedition to Nairobi in order to verify the existence of these remarkable ape-men. Susan, especially, seems intrigued by these unsullied primitives. As the group prepare to depart, Susan declares coyly, "I'm going to find my husband," and the viewer wonders if she thus intends to locate her old mate, or a new one.

Soon, Susan, Paul, David and his wife, Laura (Barbara Leigh), are navigating their Land Rover through darkest Africa and deep into the darkest heart of Man. They arrive at a trading outpost run by a scoundrel called Matthews (Mark Rhudy). Matthews summons David, and they argue over an apparent conspiracy between them to murder Earl's husband, a plan which may have gone awry. Paul maps the journey with his Bantu guide, but the guide warns against attempting the desired destination, due to a local superstition about "apes who walk like men." As the Bantu men will not take the perilous journey, it is suggested that young Bantu maidens be employed instead, as their lives are considered worthless until marriage. This leads Laura to comment, "Looks like women's lib hasn't penetrated equatorial Africa yet!" in one of Buchanan's more overt nods to feminist politics. Matthews runs off and locates his two henchmen, Brady (Stuart Lancaster) and Sikes (Marius Mazmanian). He yells at them for botching the murder of Earl Jamison, ordering the two to follow the new expedition in case they do actually discover the legendary "ape-men."

Soon the group has begun their expedition, with three comely Nubian women as porters. Unbeknownst to them, strange creatures watch from the bushes. That night the group pitches camp. Susan relaxes in her tent. David joins her, and brazenly makes a pass with his wife in the tent next door. Susan declines, as she has done several times in the past. The unrepentant macho man knows no boundaries, physical or ethical. David calls women, "Substitutes. Nothing but dumb broads that make up a twosome." Susan reminds him that although she has a healthy sexual appetite she is devoted to her husband, at least until she discovers his fate. David tries to assault the unwilling woman, but is rebuffed easily. The upset Susan takes a walk in the moonlight. Seeing two unidentified people making love on the ground, Susan becomes horny and enters Paul's tent with a bottle of liquor. Paul smiles. It is significant that Susan addresses her sexuality here, so that she cannot be written off as a prude, or neurotic. She, like any self-respecting empowered female, is comfortable with her sexual self and chooses partners based not on fear or emotional imbalance, but on natural desire and ethical considerations.

The next day, the expedition continues, with Brady and Sikes spying on the group from the distance. Sikes is shown becoming sexually aroused by the women in the group, all the more so as a "peeping tom." Finally they arrive at Earl's campsite, which lies barren and silent. After pitching camp, an unseen observer throws a spear at one of the tents. The group decides it must survey the area and discover who their enemies are. The men go off, leaving Laura with a revolver to use if necessary. Meanwhile, the Near-Men silently prowl the surrounding area, trying to uncover the nature of their adversaries. Paul and David soon see the extraordinary ape-men, and David's immediate reaction is to shoot randomly. Unfortunately, David shoots and kills the tribe's only female, certainly a symbolic act, even if not entirely deliberate.

The next day the group stumble upon a leopard hanging from a poacher's trap. The compassionate Susan runs into the clearing to cut down the creature, and she is shot at. Brady and Sikes enter the clearing, and they are about to rape Susan when David places a well-aimed shot from behind some trees. Paul gives the thugs a stern warning and sends them on their way. That night one of the Bantu maidens bathes nude in the brook. The young girl emerges from the safety of the water, and is beaten to death by one of the Near-Men in retribution for David's slaying of their female. That night Susan sleeps fitfully, suffering flashbacks to her traumatic miscarriage experience. She also relives the horrible shooting of the Near-Woman, a cruel fate for her sister-in-spirit.

The next morning Susan has made a decision. She packs her grip and prepares to go into the jungle in order to be with the Near-Men. Her stated goal is to study this most unusual anthropological find, but it is clear that she has far more personal reasons for desiring to be with this band of males, so unlike the sleaze she consorts with presently. Susan has been champing at the bit to escape this oppressive and duplicitous patriarchal community since the film's start, when its lower functionaries murdered her baby. As the African expedition progressed, Susan saw ever more of the evil deeds behind much of men's actions, and realized that this community was not merely unsupportive but antithetical to her interests. Seeing this new, virile, unsullied band of males has given her hope that perhaps a new society could exist, one without the corruption of Cain. Finally, the destruction of the lone female in the tribe signaled to Susan not only the homicidal agenda the patriarchy has for women but also the tribe's need for a new gender model.

David tries one last time to force himself on Susan, and when she defends herself admirably, David quips, "The Dove of Peace has claws after all!" Less cynically put, the so-called "weaker sex" has abundant strength and the courage of their convictions. Brady and Sikes enter the camp and introduce themselves to David, who greets them warmly. Realizing they are all sharing in the same conspiracy against cooperation, virtue and peace, i.e. the feminine principle, David then offers Laura to the thugs as a sexual reward for nefarious deeds done and impending. Surely this is the basest act a man can impose on his mate, and David clearly represents patriarchal values at their most mercenary. The two men viciously assault the woman as her debased husband looks on, sexually aroused, understandably a voyeur as well as an exploiter. Paul returns to camp, only to be ambushed by David and his gang. Soon Paul and Laura are staked to the ground, spread-eagle. Brady violates Laura sexually with his pocketknife, a lewd and brazen example of the inherent violence behind men's sexuality.

A primitive ape-man spies on human invaders in *Mistress of the Apes.*

Susan soon reaches the location of the Near-Men, and begins recording her observations on tape. She sees the Near-Men performing a burial ritual for one of their own, to Susan's eyes a clear sign that these "savages" are civilized. Susan enters the Near-Men's camp and lets herself be seen by the savages. Their reaction is one of cautious interest. Susan walks towards the sound of a baby crying, presumably the child of the slain woman. To the Near-Men's amazement, Susan bares herself and breast-feeds the hungry baby. This brazen act of self-exposure, although ostensibly an act of charity to the orphaned child, clearly shows Susan as a bold and fearless sexual aggressor, the type of woman most men either fear or detest. Effortlessly appropriating the traditionally male role of sexual conqueror, this act goes far in showing the Near-Men a new form of female creature to deal with, and eventually embrace. Susan could also be seen as an exhibitionist in this scene. As she lets the child suckle her, Susan smiles at the off-screen Near-Men, at the same time smiling at the audience. The audience, like the Near-Men, become "peeping toms" to this brash act by a fearless, imposing female.

Afterward Susan continues to observe the Near-Men in fascination, recording her thoughts on their language and rituals. She decides to befriend the savages by mimicking their behavior. Into her tape machine she declares, "I must become, in fact, Homo habilis myself." Susan knows she must become one with her primitive self if she is to shed her corrupt and tainted "civilized" self. Susan eats a banana as they eat theirs, and makes strange, affected physical gestures similar to theirs. This fascinating scene, showing a woman adopting behavior clearly archaic and primeval, is marred only by the insufferable rock song which accompanies it, replete with lyrics such as "She's an ape lady! She's the mistress of the apes!"

Paul and Laura make plans to disarm their captors. Laura convinces Sikes to untie her,

Bold, daring Susan Jamison (Jenny Neumann) takes an ape-man's hungry infant to her breast in *Mistress of the Apes,* also taking the opportunity to engage in some harmless exhibitionism.

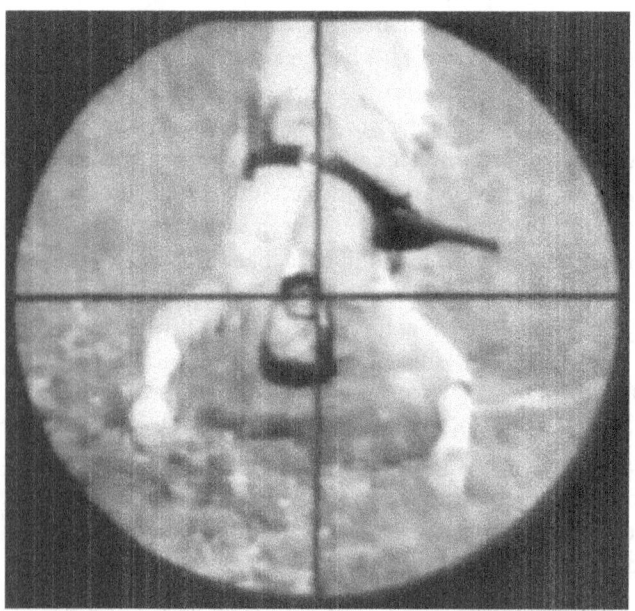

and she manages to steal his knife and stab him to death. Laura unties Paul. Brady buries his pal Sikes under a pile of rocks. Susan returns to camp to visit Paul and Laura, who fill her in on David's duplicity and Earl's murder. Susan tells of her adventures with the Near-Men. The two groups make their plans to outwit the evil ones.

Susan returns to the Near-Men community. When a gorilla attacks

David (Walt Robin), the designated predatory male on an ill-fated jungle expedition, ironically finds himself caught in one of his own cruel traps; even worse, he will soon be shot by his own gun in a moment of cosmic justice from *Mistress of the Apes.*

Larry Buchanan managed to interest popular erotic-fantasy illustrator Boris Vallejo in creating the gorgeous poster art for *Mistress of the Apes*.

her, the Near-Men attack and kill it, a sign of her acceptance into the group. That night, after supper, Susan lies down in the Near-Men's cave. A Near-Man joins her, fondling her breasts and finally mating with her. This is an extremely erotic scene, tinted as it is with hints of both interracial and inter-specie sexuality, and again paints Susan as a fearless sexual explorer. Afterwards, the sexually sated Near-Man is pummeled to death by the others, presumably for taking an outsider as his mate. This early sign of moral outrage on the part of the community, with its allusions to jealousy, competition and possessiveness of women by men, may signal that here is another destructive patriarchy, albeit in its "innocent" infancy.

A Near-Man becomes ensnared in a bear trap set by David, and as Susan, Paul and Laura look on, David shoots him. Soon the Near-Men work together with the others to trap and kill David and Brady. Afterwards, Paul and Laura prepare to head back to civilization, but Susan decides to stay with the Near-Men and continue her life with them. As it turns out, she has been impregnated. Perhaps this birth of a new, kinder infant will turn out better than Susan's tragic first attempt. Paul and Laura leave Susan standing on the rocks in front of her new kingdom, her arms outstretched to the sky, a new goddess lording over her strange new world.

Susan is perhaps Buchanan's ultimate heroine, as she not only follows in the footsteps of earlier heroines in Buchanan films but also, unlike many, does not suffer the fate of sacrificial martyr. Although she does indeed become "dead" to the patriarchal society she abandons, she retains her life, and indeed becomes a vital power figure in a new, egalitarian society much more to her liking. The emancipated and empowered female ironically becomes a New Age priestess to a modern manifestation of a most ancient societal archetype. Discovering a new and unsullied race living in isolation and safe from the corrupting influences of the civilized world could easily become a lifetime obsession to anyone with a passion for knowledge of primitive cultures, as well as anyone curious about occurrences of alternate societies, especially those which appear healthier and more supportive of the individual than current mainstream examples.

Mistress did well in limited theatrical runs, although producer Rickert made his primary promotional push for the film in the burgeoning videocassette market. Helpful in promoting the film was the beautiful artwork done by famed erotic-fantasy illustrator Boris Vallejo. The high-priced Vallejo was more than willing to do the poster art for *Mistress* because, according to Buchanan, "He had always wanted to do a movie poster, but no one had asked!"[2]

21

The Loch Ness Horror

At first glance, *The Loch Ness Horror* (1981) appears to be the anomaly in the Larry Buchanan filmography. It shares little with his other works, and precious little with other genre films of the early 1980s. It seems an anachronism, and this is part of its enigmatic charm. For all intents and purposes, *The Loch Ness Horror* (henceforth referred to as *Loch Ness*) is a throwback to a simple fantasy-genre template, that of the prehistoric monster on a rampage in the civilized world. Although the prototype for this type of film fantasy may well be the fabulous *King Kong* (1933; d: Meriam C. Cooper), the bulk of this film genre unspooled in the 1950s, with films like *The Beast from 20,000 Fathoms* (1953; d: Eugene Lourie) and *Godzilla, King of the Monsters* (1954; d: Inoshiro Honda) being two significant examples. The genre dwindled quickly as the didactic 1950s morphed into the turbulent 1960s, and examples of the somewhat simplistic "giant monster" movie were extremely rare in the 1970s. Thus, to find a charming, yet avowedly naïve monster movie in the early 1980s is somewhat of an enigma. The horror films of the later 1970s and early 1980s were by and large centered on human monsters such as serial killers, psychopaths and cannibalistic zombies.

As far as Buchanan was concerned, *Loch Ness* had many reasons to be made. And oddly enough, some of Buchanan's pet themes do manage to make appearances in *Loch Ness*, albeit in diluted form. Firstly, as the title creature, "Nessie," is considered a female by all parties concerned (and the creature confirms this assumption by the appearance of her egg), *Loch Ness* carries on Buchanan's obsession with the female as the driving creative spirit of mankind, a spirit abused and suppressed to be sure, but a spirit which nonetheless manifests powerful change in society, against formidable manmade barriers. As Nessie terrorizes the countryside, attacking men only, one is reminded of Doreena's monstrous alter ego in *Creature of Destruction* or the title heroine in *The Naked Witch*, both avenging female spirits wreaking havoc on corrupt patriarchal societies. As well, *Loch Ness* features a subplot involving a downed German warplane, and a British government attempt to retrieve the plane and cover up all evidence of its existence in order to hide earlier Allied misdeeds. This curious reference surely falls into the category of "government conspiracy," one of Buchanan's favorite meditations. Another cultural battle addressed briefly in *Loch Ness* is the ongoing strife between Religion, with its sacred reverence for tradition and taboo, and Science, with its insatiable thirst for knowledge and desire to extinguish outdated dogma.

Finally, continuing a theme first addressed clearly in *Goodbye, Norma Jean*, *Loch Ness* features a kindly elder patriarch who, as a father figure to the community, helps the female protagonist manifest positive change for herself and her community. This archetype, which will occur again in *Beyond the Doors*, may well represent an aspect of an older, kinder Buchanan, who sought to aid a younger generation in the ways of forging an egalitarian and livable society. This reference to generational differences is given much attention in *Loch Ness*, which features several older males attempting to pass on privileged information to an eager and intelligent younger generation.

As a filmmaker, Buchanan always sought to educate as well as entertain. This is clear from the dense informational texts in many of his films. Passing on interesting, historically significant information to an audience not only fueled the melodramas which carried this information but made available to the public alternate views of sociocultural phenomena which, in Buchanan's mind, had not yet been addressed sufficiently. In *Loch Ness*, Buchanan takes a playful turn with this concept by bringing to life not a suppressed historical truth but a beloved cultural myth, and treating it as bona fide reality.

From its inception, Buchanan considered *Loch Ness* a family project. Buchanan was a creative person who was blessed with a family of creative people, all of whom were proud and excited to have a successful filmmaker in their midst. According to Buchanan, all family members had expressed an interest in helping him on a future project, and sons Jeff and Randy had already begun to help their father in editing and other production duties in earlier films. The eldest son, Barry, wanted to become an actor, and *Loch Ness* enabled the handsome young man to showcase his considerable talents. Buchanan's wife, Jane, came on board as line producer, and daughter Dee acted both as script girl and an extra in the film.[1]

Loch Ness was filmed in and around Lake Tahoe, and manages to convey the look and feel of Scotland quite effectively. There are even several establishing shots of a local castle, which cleverly passes for an authentic Scottish fortress. One of the most visually impressive elements of *Loch Ness* is the title monster, "Nessie." It is certainly the biggest "monster" that Buchanan ever worked with, light years away from the threadbare rubber-suited beasts in the Azalea telefilms. Created by Tom Valentine and Peter Chesney, the hydraulically operated life-size prop features only the monster's head and neck, both of which are fully maneuverable in the fashion of the Walt Disney "animatronic" creations of the 1960s. Although the surface of Nessie has a plastic quality which belies the assumption of life, and the creature's perfect teeth sometimes create the undesired impression of a smile, the prop is filmed quite effectively and, especially in some nighttime scenes, comes across as surprisingly convincing.

The film opens as the credits roll over a melody played on bagpipe, setting the mood of the piece, albeit a bit heavy-handedly. A title announces a flashback: "Nineteen forty in the Scottish Highlands." A man, Jack Stuart (Doc Livingston), dressed in Scottish garb replete with kilt, hears something overhead and goes to his telescope. He sees a German warplane crash into the loch, as a giant sea monster simultaneously rises to the water's surface.

The scene changes to "Four decades later, in the year of the Scot." Two men in a rubber raft argue over their plans to search for and capture the legendary Loch Ness Monster. On cue, they spot the beast. Donning scuba gear, the men dive in to locate the beast.

Instead, they find the wreckage of the downed Nazi warplane, shown via a full-sized prop of some camouflage-painted wreckage. Nessie appears and attacks the men. Only one makes it back, carrying a strange package to his boss, an exiled professor named Pratt (Stuart Lancaster). Pratt examines the treasure, and is pleased to discover that it appears to be a dinosaur egg. He has stolen Nessie's offspring, and he immediately formulates plans to make money off this rare find, thus enunciating man's endemic exploitation of the female reproductive system.

Dyed-in-the-wool Scotsman Jack Stuart (Doc Livingston) snarls for his guests in *The Loch Ness Horror*.

Elsewhere, Professor George Sanderson (Sandy Kenyon) is doing his own research on Nessie. He soon meets a colleague, Spencer Dean (Barry Buchanan), from the University of Texas. Dean arrives in a huge white motorboat called the *Wet Bottom*, surely a symbol of American excess and decadence. Sanderson joins Dean on a trial run into the Loch to test Dean's sophisticated sonar equipment. Dean mentions that his scientific equipment is "courtesy of Bandera Oil," Buchanan taking care to add yet another reference to Texas's "Big Oil" industry. As they traverse the Loch, Sanderson tells Dean the legend of "The Mad Scotsman of Killy-Kranky Island," a former Scottish piper who is now a lunatic hermit and who acts out long-forgotten battles on his property.

Dean and Sanderson soon arrive back on land, and they visit Jack Stuart, the man seen in the World War II flashback. Stuart speaks in a ridiculous Scottish brogue which is overdrawn to the point of near parody. One wonders if this was merely the actor's choice, or if Buchanan was playfully mocking the role of "elder patriarch" in this family oriented film project. Alternately, Buchanan's son Barry, both dashing and confident, gives his lines a succinct, even candid reading as Dean. Sanderson introduces Dean and tells Stuart of the young American's exciting new research, but the old patriarch is incredulous. Stuart calls for his granddaughter, Kathleen (Miki Mackenzie), to join the group, and the winsome lass soon arrives. Immediately hostile to Dean, Kathleen asks, in a brogue almost as thick as that of her grandfather, "Is it true that Americans go to the picture show more than once a month, and spend a lot of time looking at magazines with naked women in them?" Dean answers, frankly, in the affirmative, which causes the embarrassed young woman to run upstairs. Aside from sheer sexual fear, Kathleen represents a very conservative, traditional order, perhaps as much as or more so than her grandfather.

As Stuart shares his collected Nessie findings with the two men, Nessie rises from the

Loch and walks ashore. The beast locates and kills the man who stole her egg, an avenging, gender-based killing not unlike similar events in *The Naked Witch* and *Creature of Destruction*. Pratt observes this killing, but does not interfere, as he now becomes sole possessor of the precious egg. Meanwhile, Sanderson and Dean take a late night excursion onto the Loch and spot the Nazi warplane with the help of Dean's sonar. Sanderson tells Dean what he knows about the plane, and asks if he can share these sonar scans with the War Office in London.

The next morning, a group of young students are enjoying a camping trip to the region. Their group leader, a Ms. Stowall (Pat Musick), informs the group that Sanderson will be giving a lecture this very evening on the existence of the Loch Ness Monster. Most of the students take the trip seriously, but one couple seems to be obsessed with having sex in their tent, until a classmate collapses their tent and dampens their ardor.

Elsewhere, Kathleen decides to visit the enigmatic American, Spencer Dean, who apparently has intrigued the young Scotswoman. Traveling via bicycle, Kathleen rides through the park where the students are simultaneously making a bike trip of their own. As the students ride en masse in one direction, like a school of fish, Kathleen rides through them in a perpendicular direction. This odd bit of choreography serves to punctuate the notion that Kathleen is an outsider, perhaps even a visionary, as she goes in an alternate direction to "the pack."

Arriving at the dock, the handsome young Dean easily convinces the curious, virginal child-woman to join him on a boating excursion. On board, Kathleen confesses to Dean, "I don't swim," another coded acknowledgement of her virginity. The churlish Dean soon scares Kathleen by announcing, "I think I just encountered Nessie," and then shoving his hand dripping with fish blood in her face. This bizarre sexual overture, disguised as a dumb adolescent prank, crudely alludes to the blood of a freshly broken hymen. Kathleen sighs to Dean, "We're worlds apart, you know. Worlds apart." Echoing the bicycle allegory from before, Kathleen sees clearly that, aside from the obvious chasm between the sexes, she represents the old world, with its traditional familial and religious values, forever intrigued by and yet contrary to this new world of Science, bold sexual aggressors, and the abandonment of old values. Dean asks Kathleen if she ever wears a dress, or shorts, and her curt and conservative answers reinforce that she is very sheltered and steeped in her ancestors' traditions. She is also overtly religious, ascribing the late daylight in the Loch to a "blessing from the gods," punctuating her assertion with, "Not so in America, with your pagan ways. Americans love the darkness more than the light, because their ways are wicked!" Dean responds to this curious bit of theologically fueled prejudice by reiterating Kathleen's earlier lament: "Worlds apart. Worlds apart."

Later that evening, Sanderson addresses the gathered students, showing rare slides of Nessie and revealing the accumulated evidence and some theories regarding the so-called monster. The oversexed boy from before sarcastically asks how Nessie "gets it on." Sanderson responds to the silly question with a sobering answer: "The courting cannot be called a quickie...." The scene returns to another "long courtship," that of Kathleen and Dean. Dean spots activity on the sonar equipment and curses. Kathleen replies in horror, "Never use profanity! It's bad luck on the Loch!" further revealing primitive and superstitious roots.

After Sanderson's lecture, the oversexed student couple take a boat out on the Loch, to try to reach the island where the "Mad Scotsman" supposedly resides. The couple soon land on the island. They hear creepy bagpipe music in the distance. As they sneak around in the dark, they soon encounter the dreaded madman, who comes at them with an ancient axe and shouts, "Remember Glencoe! The wanton slaughter!" The quick young man strikes the spectral elder over the head, apparently killing him. This enrages Nessie, who rises from the Loch, steaming mad. The couple rush back to their rubber boat, only to be attacked by Nessie for murdering her friend and protector. Nessie kills the boy, but the girl manages to swim to shore and soon reaches the others. Sanderson believes her bizarre story about a sea monster.

Kathleen leaves Dean, returning home late at night, but she is kidnapped by Pratt, who intends to hold her as a hostage until he escapes the area with Nessie's egg. Pratt tells Kathleen his plans for achieving fame and fortune with the dinosaur-child, elucidating Man's obsession with exploiting the female of the species for personal gain and self-aggrandizement.

Sanderson bikes to Stuart's residence to ask the whereabouts of Dean, whom he cannot locate. Stuart, however, is more worried about his missing granddaughter, and fears the worst regarding the young American's prurient motives. Sanderson calls the phone operator, and is informed that the military has taken over the area, including all communications, which introduces yet another in a long line of government conspiracies surfacing in the dark Buchanan universe.

The next morning Pratt prepares to leave the area with Nessie's egg and his virgin hostage in tow. Nessie, however, takes to land again, and follows Pratt to the highway, where the beast attacks and kills this unrepentant exploiter of the female, as Kathleen and armed sentries look on in horror. The scenes of Nessie traveling through the dark woods are impressive, but the attack on Pratt is thoroughly unconvincing. Pratt sticks his head into the mouth of the plastic dinosaur prop and pretends to be eaten, yelling and flailing his arms, while the music score offers a shameless appropriation of the "screaming strings" cue from the shower sequence in Alfred Hitchcock's *Psycho* (1960). The resultant scene is quite memorable, amusing in a likely unintended way.

After killing Pratt, Nessie peeks into the van, and, seeing her sister-in-spirit Kathleen protecting her egg, returns to the Loch, vindicated. Soon, the military arrives in the form of Colonel Laughton (Preston Hanson) and his subordinate, Derek (Garth Pillsbury). Laughton and Derrick discuss their dark plans to cover up an apparent crime by one of their own. They will enlist the aid of a local criminal, Alex, in order to fashion an explosion which will destroy the Nazi warplane and cover their collective sins. Laughton sends Derrick off to enlist the aid of Alex, while he visits his old friend, none other than Jack Stuart.

Kathleen drives home in Pratt's van and sneaks upstairs. She changes into a dress, presumably to impress Dean, who has joined the other men downstairs. Meanwhile, Derrick visits Alex (Don Myshrall). The two discuss the nefarious deeds to be done and strike a deal. This scene features a very brief appearance by Buchanan's daughter, Dee, as Alex's girlfriend. Dee and Don Myshrall were married in real life. What is odd about this cameo is that Buchanan films Dee always from the back, or in shadow, so that the viewer never sees her face. Buchanan appears to be thus attempting to protect his own daughter from the harsh world, just as the character Jack Stuart attempts to protect his beloved granddaughter from the harsh realities of the sinful world of evil men.

Kathleen joins the others and tries to convince her distraught grandfather that he had been drunk and thus unaware that she had been home all night. Laughton then explains

Like a cunning trapped animal, Kathleen (Miki MacKenzie) literally gnaws her way out of the lethal clutches of male domination in *The Loch Ness Horror*.

to the others that the Military desires to examine the Luftwaffe airplane because it was a propaganda plane, and may yet contain valuable information. Stuart interrupts, shouting at the Colonel, "You are lying! It was carrying high explosives! Harbor mines destined for the shipping lanes!" Stuart continues, sputtering, "Tr-r-r-r-ruth! Tr-r-r-r-reason! Your whole reason for being here is as a smokescreen to cover up the indiscretions of a fellow officer

Nessie, the female sea serpent, rushes to rescue her stolen egg from the virulent designs of greedy desperate men in *The Loch Ness Horror*.

Greedy entrepreneur Pratt (Stuart Lancaster) suffers the jaws of female rage in *The Loch Ness Horror*.

who cannot afford a blemish on his new knighthood!" In true Buchanan fashion, Stuart then tells the others "what really happened."

The war was going badly for the Allies. Hitler's savage U-boat attacks had driven the American convoys into the British North Channel. Göring conceived a grand plan, called "Operation Jugular," to mine the North Channel with explosives. The plan involved moving through the loch with the explosives plane and on to the North Channel. The loch had been used as a training center, and, at the time, there was an antiaircraft station manned by "Donald Gregory, now known as Sir Donald Gregory, member of parliament, knight of the realm!" The night when "Luftwaffe B-79" flew overhead, Gregory was away from his post, dallying with a prostitute in nearby Inverness. But, as Stuart notes, "the influence of the highly-placed is formidable." British Intelligence covered up the blunder and wired the Germans to tell them that Gregory had in fact blown the bomber out of the sky. Göring abandoned his plans, and Gregory became an undeserving hero. The reason for Laughton's apparent concern, Stuart concludes, is not to retrieve war booty, but to obscure the fact that the plane crashed due to engine failure, not engagement by British artillery as official propaganda stated. Were this to be revealed, the highly placed Sir Gregory's heroic act would be exposed as a fabrication. Stuart finishes his shocking lesson in revisionist history as the others stand in awkward silence. Kathleen runs upstairs and looks into the telescope. There she sees Alex preparing to dive into the loch to set off explosives. Kathleen takes Dean aside and enlists his support. The two go outside, and Kathleen shows Nessie's egg to a startled Dean.

Inside, Stuart ruminates on the different roads men take in their lives, and how their character is revealed by how they desire to treat Nessie, and by extension, all Womankind. The Scientist, while not evil or cruel, would be more than happy to kill and dissect Nessie to further his own knowledge. The military, of course, knows nothing but death and destruction, and merely wishes to annihilate her as it desires to destroy all creation. Stuart, the kindly elder patriarch, would be more than happy to "let her be, and not let her mystery be known for another 1400 years." Sanderson agrees, and quips, "Ah, Jack Stuart, you are an endangered species," as is any man who truly reveres women.

Alex reaches the wreckage of the warplane and places the explosives, but he is attacked by Nessie, who kills him. Dean and Kathleen make haste to the location of the impending disaster, but the explosives ignite, presumably destroying both the warplane and Nessie. Dean and Kathleen are devastated. They have arrived too late to save dear Nessie. Man's evil has won this round. Kathleen ruminates, "So, what is the sum of it all? Your fancy Lord Gregory will retire to his place in Kent. And your professors and your classrooms will have all the parts of Nessie they need for their microscopes." The two decide the least they can do is honor Nessie's memory by returning its offspring to the cradle of its mother's womb. Dean tosses the egg back into the water. It falls to the lake bottom, where its embryonic heartbeat echoes throughout the Loch.

Ostensibly a lightweight horror-fantasy entertainment, it is worth restating that *Loch Ness* does offer, in sketch form, a few themes from earlier, more "serious" Buchanan dramas. The overt generational emphasis in *Loch Ness* is a carryover from earlier films such as *The Eye Creatures* and *In the Year 2889*, in which an obsolete or spent patriarchy hands over the reins of power to the younger generation. It is thus both functional and playful on Buchanan's part that this project of "Clan Buchanan," as he dubbed the film's production company, also featured a gregarious patriarch giving over some of his creative duties to his offspring. The showcased young people in *Loch Ness*, Spencer Dean and Kathleen Stuart, although "worlds apart" in their sociopolitical underpinnings, are able to come together to manifest radical change in their troubled community. Although Dean is a cad by traditional standards, whining to see his partner in a dress, he does finally pull through to serve his community as dictated by duty and conscience. Likewise, Kathleen is able to overcome her sheltered, ultraconservative upbringing to grow significantly as a person, and thus help the community in crisis. The elders in the film fall into two distinct categories. The evil figures of Laughton and Pratt represent, respectively, falsehood and greed. The heroic figures are Sanderson and Stuart, of the old school certainly but devoted to truth and justice at all costs. Their ability to successfully pass on these worthy traits to the younger generation is the sole cause of whatever success is manifested.

As for the title creature, she is a sacrificial martyr, like so many females in the Buchanan universe, and her acts of aggression, although devastating, are dictated by an abiding sense of justice. Nessie kills three times, each act being highly symbolic. The killing of "Shorty" is in response to the barbarous theft of her offspring-in-egg form. The killing of the oversexed teenager is to avenge the murder of the Mad Scotsman, Nessie's guardian and advocate, and perhaps spiritually her mate. The killing of Pratt is essentially a protest against the exploitation of chaste virgin Kathleen. As mentioned earlier, these killings are gender-based and essentially political in nature. In the end, Nessie is sacrificed so that the community may endure. Nessie's fate clearly follows the "tragic heroine" template which Buchanan used so often, from *The Naked Witch* through *Goodnight, Sweet Marilyn*, making *Loch Ness* yet another Buchanan text which observes the simultaneous obsession with, and exploitation of, the feminine principle in modern patriarchal society. Finally, there is nary a Buchanan film of note which does not allude to conspiracy in high places.

The Loch Ness Horror did well in its relatively short run at drive-in theaters, managing to sneak onto the tail of the decade-long "speculative documentary" trend of the 1970s, which took historical events and cultural phenomena and attempted to scrutinize them from new perspectives. Pseudo-documentaries such as *Chariots of the Gods* (1974; d: Harald Reinl) and *In Search of Historic Jesus* (1980; d: Gary Conway) were often comprised more of conjecture than fact, but they did follow the spirit of Buchanan films such as *Free, White and 21* and *Goodbye, Norma Jean* in their stated quest to find new explanations for unsolved mysteries, and this spirit of unfettered contemplation was part of their enduring popularity. In this sense, this fad, of which *The Loch Ness Horror* was little more than a footnote, continued the tradition of positing the filmmaker as revisionist historian.

22

Beyond the Doors

In his autobiography, Larry Buchanan decried the label "conspiracy theorist," which had been pinned on him by both fans and detractors. Perhaps the filmmaker was being disingenuous, as so many of his films deal with the secret, backdoor machinations of sinister power figures, especially in the employ of the U.S. government.

What probably rankled him most about the label was its allusion to "crank" theory — unfounded and weird assertions about unsolved mysteries — and he insisted that his "theories" were well-researched and backed up with substantial if, by necessity, circumstantial evidence.

One of the most haunting collective tragedies of the 1960s was the death, within a year, of three of the most popular and influential rock musicians of the decade: Jim Morrison, Jimi Hendrix and Janis Joplin. Although all three were known for their reckless personal lives and histories of substance abuse, their demise nonetheless prompted waves of conspiracy theories, including that they had been assassinated by the government, and most famously that Morrison faked his death. Buchanan found the subject most compelling, not merely because he had a fondness for fellow Texan Joplin, but because it looked like the Nixon presidency, paranoid and out of control, could conceivably have been behind the deaths. As he had with Lyndon Baines Johnson, Buchanan had a healthy skepticism towards then-president Nixon, who was increasingly revealed to be both a crook and a madman.

Buchanan took this current obsession and fashioned *Down on Us*. It chronicles the last year or so of the three aforementioned "Pied Pipers of Rock," and offers a speculative subplot regarding the nefarious personages who orchestrated and actualized their demise. *Down on Us* premiered in 1984 at the University of Texas to enthusiastic response, but was not released at the time due to economic considerations.[1] The film was shortened by several minutes and released to videocassette in 1989 under the title *Beyond the Doors*, and that is the version which will be discussed here.

Beyond the Doors (henceforth referred to as *Beyond*) opens in "1984, near Cumberland, Maryland." Three men are hunting, and one, Alex Stanley (Sandy Kenyon), shoots at a tiny quail in the bush. Just as suddenly, one of the other hunters (Joe Camp) shoots Alex, who looks back at his colleague with a mixture of shock and understanding. As Alex lies dying, the shooter mumbles, "Rock and Roll is dead. Long live Rock and Roll!" The main credits introduce the three rock icons who are the subject of the film: Jimi Hendrix (Gregory Allen Chatman), Janis Joplin (Riba Meryl) and Jim Morrison (Bryan Wolf). Another title, *Assassination is the extreme form of censorship*, appears, attributed to George Bernard Shaw and succinctly expressing *Beyond*'s central theme. The scene changes to urban Maryland, where Alex's family are returning from his funeral services. Once at home, the victim's wife (Toni Sawyer) ruminates on how strange it was for her husband, who had been intimately familiar with guns for his entire life, to fall victim to a "hunting accident." Much more ominous was the morning after his death, when two men representing themselves as government agents confiscated Alex's files. The wife confesses to her son, Frank (Steven Tice), and his fiancée, Ellen (Jennifer Wilde), that she thought something was amiss, but there was nothing she could do at the time. Managing to save her husband's briefcase, which contained his most sensitive papers, she entrusts this sacred object to Frank. Suspecting something sinister, Frank peers into the briefcase. Inside is a letter addressed to him from his father, informing him that he was, indeed, the victim of conspiracy: "I, the hunter, become the hunted.... All my adult life, through four presidents, has been spent in the twilight world of covert intelligence for my country. Our assignment: neutralize the three 'Pied Pipers of Rock Music,' Jim Morrison, Janis Joplin and Jimi Hendrix." For all practical purposes representing an average, middle-class father figure and nondescript businessman, Alex Stanley is suddenly revealed to be a vile character, a duplicitous and murderous functionary of an evil government and its amoral intelligence arm, the dark side of the supposedly benign middle-class man and a secretive "alter ego" both enigmatic and fatal, with duties and passions completely at odds with his public image. To some extent, this frumpy, dog-faced assassin illustrates the utter banality of evil, a force which is nonetheless lethal for its off-putting appearance. The character Alex Stanley was loosely based on FBI agent William Sullivan, who is mentioned by name later in the film.[2]

The scene changes to 1968 in New York, and a raucous Jimi Hendrix concert where Joplin and Hendrix first meet. The scene shifts to Amsterdam, where a comatose Jim Morrison lies on a bed in his hotel room, while footage of B-52s bombing North Vietnam plays on the television. Morrison's band members enter and awaken the drugged-out rock star, who spouts antiwar poetry as they drag him off for a concert performance. While the hotel room is empty, the TV is still on and President Lyndon Baines Johnson assures his TV audience, "I don't want a man in here, going home, to think otherwise. We are going to win!" The statement, while likely referring to the war in Vietnam, also suggests the older generation's plans to suppress and exterminate their offspring. This grim foreshadowing is manifest later, when Morrison is entertaining a young woman, known only as "She" (Susanna Barnes). The woman, exasperated by his legendary silence, asks Morrison, "Why don't you, for once, say the things that would be left unsaid?" Morrison is unshakably pessimistic, his vision entirely apocalyptic: "In the capitals of the world men who can no longer get their peckers up have found a new way to getting turned on. They're the butchers of the world with their eighteen-pound sledge hammers. The bacon for tomorrow's breakfast will have the peculiar taste of ash."

Back in Washington, an unnamed bureaucrat holds a meeting with Alex. The bureaucrat adjusts a photograph of newly elected President Richard M. Nixon which hangs on the wall, and asks for Alex's comment. "A little crooked," he answers in a response applicable to both the photograph and its subject. Alex straightens Nixon's photograph himself, a futile gesture to "straighten out" the crooked bosses for whom he works. The bureaucrat informs Alex (whom he oddly refers to as "Harry,") that the president is entirely paranoid about the New Left, comprised of the hippies, the rock stars and the drug people. Nixon has become so obsessed with these young people and their hatred of him that he has set up clandestine, and surely illegal, suboperations within the intelligence community to battle this newly perceived generational threat.

The scene changes to March 1, 1969, in Miami, Florida, where Morrison addresses another rapt audience with ruminations about politicians, their cop and soldier functionaries, and their death-dealing ways, as he chastises his audience: "You don't want to change the world, you just want to make love. You don't want to hear about napalm, you just want to rock.... I'll flash my cock, if you'll burn your draft card." As Morrison strips for the stunned audience, baton-wielding peace officers drag him offstage.[3] Morrison is clearly disenchanted with the apathy of his peers, and correctly intuits that the generational paranoia of the Establishment is largely irrational, that the young people of the day indeed were more interested in free love and rock and roll than in mounting an effective collective assault on a corrupt and broken government.

This ascending clash of generations reaches its apex at the pivotal event of the counterculture era: August 15, 1969, and the Woodstock concert, where Hendrix finishes his avant garde, politically subversive performance of the "Star Spangled Banner." Hendrix's screeching electric guitar eerily mimics the sounds of bombs, explosions, and machine guns, as a television screen elsewhere offers grisly war footage of Thanatos in orgasmic sexual release. The political implications of Hendrix's music literally hits home with Alex Stanley a short time later. Holding a meeting at his house with two other covert operatives, Alex states: "From the moment Nixon took office, he has been preoccupied with reelection. The youth in this country, and their idols, are an incredible power bloc. Musicians, artists, campus radicals. These voices must be stilled. And we'll use anything. Internal Revenue, interrogation, wiretaps, streetwalkers, if you need. We're well-funded." The lines of war drawn, the elders plot to crush their own children. Suddenly, Hendrix's subversive music is heard, and Alex excuses himself. He runs to his son's room, grabs the 45 rpm record and breaks it, then yelling at the boy, "I told you, no nigger music while I have guests in this house!" For Alex Stanley, the generation gap is both a national and personal struggle; his sworn enemies are his son's idols, baring middle-class White America in its most polarized and troubled state.

The scene changes to Le George, a popular night spot in New York City, where the evening's festivities are in full swing. All three "Pied Pipers of Rock" are in attendance. Hendrix chats with "Stony," the club manager, who shows him his new toy, a full-screen movie projector which can throw images over an entire wall of the club. Hendrix asks if he can play with it, and Stony instructs him to switch the controls to "Cinéma Vérité," (i.e., "Cinema of Truth.")

The music changes to a strident, march-like drumbeat, and the wall is filled with pulsating lights. A conga line of patrons dances by the projected lightscape. The line stops, and a female impersonator tells the crowd that she is "Morrison, the poet who fills stadiums with fans, and cops, using his *cock!*" As a disgusted Morrison gets up to leave, the conga line continues, stopping at a man dressed vaguely like Joplin. He states that Joplin was voted "the ugliest *man* on campus," and trots offstage. Joplin is incensed at this cruel parody.

The conga line moves on, until it stops to highlight a drunken black woman, who tells the crowd how Hendrix has sold out his fellow African Americans in the service of the White Man's capitalism. A saddened Hendrix shakes his head, and sympathetically leads the distraught woman backstage. This pivotal scene, the heart of *Beyond*, illustrates something darkly significant about the younger generation of the time. Contrary to the simplistic paranoia of the elders, the younger generation was not a single-minded group, set in unity against their parents, but a quixotic, eclectic gathering of many social, cultural and political viewpoints. Thus they never entailed the universal threat which the "square" establishment so feared and tried so hard to annihilate. Indeed, it is sobering and distressing to see the three "Pied Pipers of Rock," these supposedly adored cultural icons, being mocked and derided not by their generational enemies, *but by their own peers.* It belies the popular notion of the time, that the solidarity of the younger generation was cohesive and unshakable, set to make great strides towards a more egalitarian society, via well-orchestrated revolution if necessary. This particular group of people suffered as much petty jealousy, infighting and difference of opinion as any previous generation. Simultaneously, Buchanan illuminates the highly contradictory sexual politics of the counterculture, which were ultimately as conservative as those of their parents. The counterculture was notorious for its sexism, male chauvinism, and homophobia. The fact that Morrison and Joplin, two supposed "revolutionaries," are so indignant over mild jokes about their sexuality betrays this contradiction. *Beyond* shines a harsh light on various sobering generational misconceptions in this most provocative moment in Buchanan's "Cinema of Truth."

Loving family man Alex Stanley (Sandy Kenyon) effortlessly transforms into a cold-blooded killer and conspirator towards youth in ***Beyond the Doors.***

Sometime later, Hendrix receives the infamous "Plaster Casters," two young women who attended rock concerts during the period for the sole purpose of making plaster casts of rock stars' phalluses. Hendrix gleefully accepts their offer to immortalize his genitals, as the women explain their overtly phallocentric philosophy: "There's nothing new about penis worship. It's a part of all cultures. Well, even church steeples, they're really phallic symbols, aren't they? But nobody'd ever thought of preserving the penises of famous persons for prosperity. I mean, as an art form!" Indeed, the counterculture is steeped in the same patriarchal order and phallus worship as the Establishment and "men who can no longer get their peckers up have found a new way to getting turned on." The Establishment's phallic missiles and rifles become the counterculture's kitsch mementos to their rock gods. At worst, the counterculture were mirror images of their parents but for their fashion and revolutionary rhetoric.

On September 3, 1970, in London, Alex and two other operatives plot to assassinate Hendrix. The female agent telephones Hendrix's hotel room, pretending to be "Pat Egmont, amusement editor of the London Times," who wishes to arrange an interview with the rock star. Hendrix's female companion answers the phone, and tells the phony reporter to leave the young musician alone, as he hasn't slept for three days. The young woman leaves the room to fetch a pack of cigarettes, which gives one of the operatives time to enter the room and plant drugs next to the comatose Hendrix. Hendrix's companion returns and, seeing the drugs scattered out next to the unconscious man, panics and calls for medical assistance. The phone call is diverted to the FBI operatives' lair, and a phony medical team is sent. Hendrix is strapped to a stretcher, and a phony doctor gives the hysterical young woman a strong sedative. Hendrix is taken away in an ambulance, where he begins to come to. He starts to vomit from his intoxication, and one of the operatives covers his mouth, so that Hendrix suffocates on his own vomit, as history will dutifully report.[4]

The scene changes to September 19, 1970, in Washington, DC. FBI head Hoover watches closed-circuit television footage of the recently held Woodstock concert, at which the youth movement seems in full swing as a cultural and political force. An agent enters, and tells Hoover of a communication regarding a covert assignment neither man has heard of. Hoover queries the man as to the nature of this apparent security breach, and the man mentions the name William Sullivan. The man continues, suggesting the dark possibility that "a very elite, very illegal and well-funded command of special agents are operating as deep cover in this country, and around the world, and they are operating with full termination powers." Hoover sighs, "I love Washington, especially *this* time of year." This meeting foreshadows events in Hollywood, on October 3, 1970, where Joplin is similarly assassinated in a display of espionage worthy of a James Bond film: her oranges are injected with poison. When she succumbs to their effect, Alex enters the apartment and injects her with pure heroin, which will be seen as the official cause of death. As Alex works, the phone rings. Alex picks up the receiver, and drops it to the floor next to the dying woman, leaving it as a further prop for his theatrical recreation of the death of a rock star.[5]

In Paris on July 8, 1971, "She" makes a frantic call to a friend, to announce that Jim Morrison is dead! A closed coffin, covered with flowers, sits in the room. "She" then informs Morrison, who is sitting in bed in the next room, that she has dutifully informed all their friends of Morrison's untimely "death." Morrison coughs, obviously ill, and quips, "Aside from bad lungs, liver, tired blood, respiratory problems, I'm in great shape." "She" pleads with Morrison to reconsider this premature drop-out from society, but Morrison is adamant: "It won't be the first time a poet's dropped out. Death has a hell of a plus: privacy." Morrison goes on to explain that he intends to join a monastery in Spain where he can be anonymous and translate ancient Gregorian chants all day. To the exhausted idol, this sounds like paradise. Morrison bids farewell to his girl, saying, "Don't worry, in a couple of years, they'll be saying, 'Jim who?'"

Beyond now returns to the present day, as Frank continues his father's letter. Alex states that he did not believe that Jim Morrison was dead, and that he may still be alive, in exile, somewhere in Europe. He asks Frank to follow this lead, if he dares, and discover the truth, finally confessing that he is writing a book about his misadventures in the FBI, which will be "bigger than Watergate." Frank reads his father's final words: "Tomorrow I'm going quail hunting with some old Georgetown friends. Next week I'll fly to Paris to finish this book...."

Now realizing the dark truth about his father's death, Frank decides to investigate, locating the Spanish monastery where Alex traced Morrison after his faked death. As Gregorian chants are heard, a monk leads Frank to a graveyard and points to one of many gravesites, marked only by a generic wooden cross. The monk recalls the ailing rock star: "And he played such sweet music. Not melancholy, but happy! I think he found here something he'd been searching for a long, long time. In the beginning, we thought he was getting better, but the winters were too severe, and in 1974, February, he died." The monk recalls Morrison smiling at the moment of death, something he rarely did in his public life. Frank notes, "But there are no names. The graves are unmarked." The monk replies, "How else would he be free?" Only after he left the world, and became nameless and faceless–"Jim who?"—could Jim Morrison escape the destiny the U.S. government plotted for him, and actualized with Hendrix and Joplin. To escape assassination, the most extreme form of censorship, Morrison had to censor and assassinate himself. With the Gregorian chants still playing, *Beyond* ends with a cryptic quote from Nixon, attributed to a 1977 British television interview:

> TV Host: Did you give your approval to an intelligence program that contemplated clearly illegal acts?
> Nixon: When the president does it, that means it is not illegal.
> TV Host: Would not that rationale also permit a president to order murder?
> Nixon: There are degrees — nuances — which are difficult to explain.... the deciding line would be the president's judgment.

This chilling assertion of supra-legal powers assumed by the president, with its delusional inferences, rings true to current events, and it is somewhat shocking to see that Buchanan saw fit to insert it into this film, made over twenty years ago. It restates well Alexander Pope's old adage, "Power corrupts, and absolute power corrupts absolutely."

Beyond ends up being one of Buchanan's brightest and most uncompromising works, clarifying the ongoing battle between conservative and liberal, old and young, Thanatos and Eros, with clarity and passion. *Beyond* is first and foremost a most interesting take on youth empowerment by someone from the elder generation. Painting the youth movement of the 1960s, and its musician-heroes, in a largely favorable light, *Beyond* pits these young innocents against a sinister army at first surprising: their collective parents. Although Buchanan may have been more or less targeting an intended market for his film by focusing on the younger segment of the movie-going demographic, he certainly did his own generation no favors in the way he represented them, as a duplicitous, paranoid, amoral and genocidal bunch who seem obsessed with squashing anyone half their age.

This battle between young and old, commonly dubbed "the generation gap," is portrayed vividly and ruthlessly in *Beyond*, and the lines of demarcation could not be clearer. The younger generation certainly represents Eros, the forces of love and creativity and growth. The elders are, without exception, agents of Thanatos, purveyors of death and despair and destruction. To some extent, *Beyond* is an allegorical battle between Eros and Thanatos, as the stifling forces of Death become obsessed with squashing their rivals, the Love children. The death-dealing "adults" live in a sterile, deeply repressed world, a world which nonetheless hides many dark and murderous tendencies. The life-loving "youngsters" threaten this repressed world, and the adults rise up to defend their sick and insular world

Laid to rest in an anonymous grave in a Spanish monastery, rock legend Jim Morrison finally achieves peace in death, concluding *Beyond the Doors*.

from encroachment from the outside. Not surprisingly, the world in which the death-obsessed adults live is claustrophobic, artificial and lifeless, whereas the world of the young is exciting, expansive, vital and real. This glaring juxtaposition of the drab existence of the elders, trapped in their dreary clothing, lackluster hotel rooms and flavorless offices, against the unabashedly colorful and carefree existence of the younger generation, suggests that the elders are, indeed, jealous of the youngers' devil-may-care attitude towards life.

Beyond also ruminates on the dichotomy between public and private space, and how the two are often merged or compromised. By and large, the private spaces are dominated by the elders, who hide in their concrete caves to plan exterminations. The young rock artists play in arenas with masses of their peers, unafraid of the potential of open spaces. Even the sanctity of the recording studio is often breached by unwanted intruders. Perhaps the only thing these adversarial groups have in common is the omnipresent television set, which invades both camps' spaces, providing information, curiously enough, on each others' enemies. The old killers watch footage of hippie communes, rock concerts and antiwar protests, while the young artists watch speeches of crooked politicians and footage of war atrocities. Indeed, *Beyond* illustrates not just a political and cultural but also a generational turf war. And as seen throughout *Beyond*, the younger generation were not at all united in their perspectives and causes, and in fact were at times as antithetical to their peers as any threat from the older, "square" establishment.

Beyond has the somewhat drab and stillborn spirit of a stage-bound made-for-television feature, which admittedly would have made it difficult to compete theatrically with the glitzy blockbusters of the day, including Oliver Stone's phantasmagoric *The Doors* (1991), which was likely inspired by Buchanan's film. But for the exciting concert footage, *Beyond* takes place primarily in dreary hotel rooms and fake forests.

Curiously, the lackluster, generic hotel room, so iconic in Buchanan's mise-en-scène, is shared and suffered by both parties in *Beyond*, the homicidal elders and the sacrificial young ones. It is perhaps Buchanan's trademark setting, symbolizing the faceless, sterile and claustrophobic atmosphere of middle-class America, a space completely lacking in character, personality, or soul. Buchanan's ubiquitous hotel room is the perfect emblematic space for anonymous, interchangeable individuals in a mass society. Indeed, the unrelentingly dreary world in which these people lived and died and, most importantly, tried to escape through art and drugs, makes their demise all the more tragic, and their journey through the political and cultural minefields of evil, stultifying America all the more mythic.

As in many other Buchanan films, the clash of cultures which exemplified the 1960s is seen filtered through its effects on a middle-class family. The killer, Alex, is just another nice father figure to his family, who mourn his untimely death as if he were the nicest guy in the world. That he was a vicious and heartless killer of innocents doesn't seem to enter the equation at all. His death still impacts the family profoundly. *Beyond* also revels in one of Buchanan's most consistent and darker obsessions, that of a government conspiracy against unpopular political targets. From *The Trial of Lee Harvey Oswald* to *Mars Needs Women* and on through *Goodnight, Sweet Marilyn*, Buchanan returned often to examine the sinister duplicity of the U.S. government, and its military and intelligence branches, with *Beyond* perhaps the most illustrious example. The government overtly and consistently targets the younger generation, and its appointed heroes, as enemies of the state and extinguishes marked members with ruthless efficiency.

23

Goodnight, Sweet Marilyn

Larry Buchanan's final film, *Goodnight, Sweet Marilyn* (1989, henceforth referred to as *Goodnight*), adroitly combines three themes consistent to his works: historical revision, conspiracy, and the function of women in society. The scenario depicted in *Goodnight*, a chronicle of the last day of Marilyn Monroe's life, is straightforward, although certain events are surmised rather than dramatized. In many ways, it is a direct sequel to *Goodbye, Norma Jean* (1976, henceforth referred to as *Goodbye*). Indeed, what is notable is that *Goodbye* ends with the birth of Marilyn Monroe, while *Goodnight* ruminates on the last day of her life. Buchanan is in essence making two film biographies of Marilyn Monroe which barely addressed her career, instead focusing on the initial construction and the final destruction of the pop-culture icon known as "Marilyn Monroe."

Goodnight begins burdened with the accumulated stresses of Monroe's whirlwind career and the cruel machinations of studio heads, culminating in the filming of the ill-fated, aptly titled *Something's Got to Give* (circa 1962). Confined to her bed, the physically and mentally exhausted actress succumbs to a long-feared psychotic break (foreshadowed in *Goodbye*) as she hallucinates seeing her insane mother in the bureau mirror. Bound in a straitjacket, the mother beckons: "I have come for you." Monroe, realizing the mirror image portents her own dissent into terminal madness, frantically calls her close friend and bodyguard "Mesquite" (a pseudonym given by Buchanan) to fulfill a promise he had made years before. After sharing some parting words of eternal devotion, Mesquite anally inserts a strychnine-laced suppository and covers her with the bedsheets. Within minutes after Mesquite departs and Monroe lapses into a coma, two assistants of Attorney General Robert Kennedy, alerted of Monroe's imminent demise by means of a telephone wiretap, rearrange the room and key props including pill containers, liquor bottles and the telephone in order to create the enduring popular fiction that Monroe's death was self-inflicted. In a final act of historical manipulation, Monroe was stripped naked and laid out on her bed like an exhausted prostitute, so that the world would view her, even in death, as a dumb, drunken whore, a laughable and bizarre sex object both tragic and feeble.

Put simply, Monroe's death was not a suicide but a carefully planned mercy killing fabricated into a pathetic suicide by forces with their own agenda. This is the unflinching thesis mounted by Buchanan in *Goodnight*. According to Buchanan, it was imperative for the world to see Monroe as a bad person, evil and weak, perhaps redeemable and forgivable but terminally flawed, as opposed to a cruelly exploited victim of manipulation by male-owned corporate interests. The truth about her death would reflect harsh and revealing light on her life, pointing an accusing finger toward the entire entertainment industry and its endemic, two-pronged crusade against woman (perpetuation of the collective psychosexual fantasy where woman is sex slave to man, and its exploitation and annihilation of innumerable females to feed and serve this insatiable slave/fantasy machine). The notoriously fickle and compromised Los Angeles medical examiner, Thomas Noguchi, was easily persuaded to buy into the fiction created by Kennedy and company, and likely augmented by publicists at Fox Studios, to announce "incontrovertible evidence" that Monroe killed herself with a toxic combination of barbiturates and alcohol. An accurately performed and reported autopsy would have certainly found ample evidence of the poison's presence in the actress, as well as its entry point, so the published autopsy report can be dismissed as a scripted public relations artifact of a very dark kind. Curiously, Noguchi went public twenty years later to announce that the only conceivable cause of death for Marilyn Monroe was an anally inserted suppository, but at that moment in time no one in the press or public cared a whit about this shocking revelation, and the assertion remains obscure to this day.

Buchanan devotes several pages in his autobiography to relating his conversations with Mesquite, a good friend from the time of their first meeting as contract players for Twentieth Century Fox in the early 1950s until the enigmatic man's death from AIDS in the mid-1980s.[1] *Goodnight* is as much a homage to Buchanan's colleague as it is to Monroe. As the film opens, the character nicknamed Mesquite (portrayed by Jeremy Slate) addresses the audience directly, a frequent film strategy employed by Buchanan to break the "fourth wall" between the audience and the performance and immediately situate the audience not merely as spectators watching a film but as critical participants in a political debate (as with his early courtroom films): "You've all heard the lies about my sweet Marilyn.... The trouble with half-truths and innuendo are you are left with no image at all, or worse, cruel distortion. The mind boggles at the ocean of lies about her." The scene dissolves to a montage of famous Marilyn "moments," reenacted by Paula Lane, who plays Marilyn in the film, as Mesquite continues: "Had she lived, the most powerful political dynasty in the history of America would have toppled." The narrator states that he earned the nickname Mesquite after the small town in Texas where he grew up, and he takes care to briefly mention his bisexuality, perhaps a deliberate reference on Buchanan's part to the ever-shifting duality of the modern self, seen through a sexual filter. Mesquite ends his dark edict with the following confession: "There's no mystery here — I took her life." As the main credits roll, the audience is given two important factors to consider: there was a conspiracy, and her death was not suicide. Buchanan, for the final time, uses film as a means of revisionist history to present an alternative to the official story.

In *Goodnight*, Paula Lane is billed as playing "Marilyn Monroe," while Misty Rowe is billed as playing "Norma Jean Baker." This billing is primarily due to the unfolding scenario, in which Lane plays Marilyn on her deathbed, while her earlier life is recounted in flashbacks through recycled scenes from *Goodbye*. Yet this surreal pairing of two different actresses to play two different aspects of the same person magnifies and explodes the "split personality" between the private and troubled life of Norma Jean Baker and the iconic public persona of Marilyn Monroe. As Laurence Olivier caustically observed in his memoirs to

The Prince and the Showgirl (1957), "There were two entirely unrelated sides to Marilyn. You would not be far out if you described her as a schizoid; the two people that she was could hardly have been more different."[2] This fragmentation of the subject as the Self and the Other, the two selves which comprised Baker/Monroe, is suggested throughout *Goodbye*: the need to become the "somebody else" the world can "go fuck" on the road to stardom; seeing the image of her insane, abused mother as her own reflection after her first "casting couch" audition; scrawling the word "ugly" on the mirror during her first suicide attempt, the verbal signifier replacing her reflection to define her status in the Symbolic Order; the final fragmentation of the mirror Self and the Other with the "symbolic" death of Norma Jean the moment she sees herself "born again" on the silver screen. Norma Jean's doomed quest for adulation via her movie star persona, Marilyn, illustrates Lacan's misrecognition of the self, born in the "mirror-stage" of a child's development and triggering the lifelong process of identifying the imaginary Self in terms of the symbolic Other. With *Goodnight*, the Self and the Other literally become two separate entities: Norma Jean (Misty Rowe) and Marilyn Monroe (Paula Lane).

The scene now shifts to Marilyn's bedroom, a sacred, empty space, dark and still, like a funeral sepulchre. The camera searches the darkness in vain for some sign of life. Finally, a dark figure emerges out of the blackness, walks up to Marilyn's empty bed, and looks at the array of discarded pill bottles which adorn the night table. Another figure joins the first, and the two are soon outside, now inexplicably pulling Marilyn's naked, bloated body from the pool (a moment of narrative confusion that is addressed later on in the film). Inside the bedroom, the unnamed woman (Joyce Lower) forces the barely conscious actress to look at her reflection in the mirror, reminding her how important it is to obsess on *how she appears to her public*; Marilyn was being a "two-faced" puppet of the entertainment industry. The unnamed man (Kenneth Hicks) begins to interrogate the disoriented, dying Marilyn, offering neither her nor the audience anything about himself, but demanding answers from the disorientated figure on the bed. The moment alludes to the opening sequence in Kafka's *The Trial*, in which the protagonist is assaulted, interrogated with unanswerable questions, and finally arrested by nameless functionaries of a malevolent authority. The Kafkaesque implications of *Oswald* and *Goodbye* reach their final conclusion here. A political conspiracy needed a patsy in Lee Harvey Oswald, as the Culture Industry needed a patsy in Norma Jean Baker. As the web tightens between Washington, DC, and Hollywood, between the conspiratorial agendas of politics and culture, Marilyn Monroe becomes the ideal (or *"image-ideal"*) patsy.

Moreover, the characters of the woman and the man, billed as "Psychiatrist" and "Medical Doctor" in the credits but never addressed as such in the film, are ominous archetypes, working as functionaries to an unseen, omniscient organization whose prime directive is to contort reality to its own agenda by any means necessary. The woman "Psychiatrist" indeed assumes the role of psychotherapist to Monroe, the dying patient, as the film itself becomes a fragmented psychoanalytic account of Monroe's career. In this way, the erratic structure of *Goodnight* is determinedly confusing, with its eclectic shuffling of real-time events, fourth-wall asides by an onscreen narrator, recent flashbacks to times earlier the same evening, patchwork remembrances of long-past events, and, of course, the recycling of footage from *Goodbye*. *Goodnight* becomes an effective psychological chronology of the fragmented subject — Marilyn Monroe — who only existed as a public icon, a construct of others' fantasies and motivations.

The Medical Doctor injects Marilyn with sodium pentathol in order to extract further information from her. The Psychiatrist insists, "I can't help you until I get some information." The woman intones, "We are going to go back to when you were an orphan." Against brief flashback footage from *Goodbye* Marilyn insists, "I am *not* an orphan!"—the same line which underlined her life of exploitation in *Goodbye*. The Psychiatrist whispers to the Doctor, "Throw away all the liquor bottles, anything that looks like a party." The man replies, "You know, when we're through here, drowning might be an option." These chilling plans are uttered in front of the victim, who receives no acknowledgement. The Psychiatrist turns back to the subject: "We're not talking about Marilyn. We're talking about Norma Jean Baker. Aren't we? And it becomes even more complex when we remember that you are a Gemini. You are *two* people." Turning to her colleague, the woman reiterates: "She's *two!*" Again, Buchanan, intentional or otherwise, recalls Lacan: the Norma Jean/Marilyn fragmented subject—Marilyn as Norma Jean's image-ideal, who has replaced Norma Jean as a public persona, a "moving image" on the silver screen, a sign in the Symbolic Order.

The telephone rings, and an answering machine retrieves the message as a helpless Marilyn and her interrogators listen in: the unidentified male caller warns Marilyn that there are wiretaps on her telephone, and that she might want to reconsider her upcoming press conference, where she has threatened to tell "all she knows" (presumably about the Kennedy dynasty and other corrupt power institutions of the day). The Psychiatrist, amused by this bit of fortuitous espionage, quips to Marilyn, "You have always trusted in the kindness of men of power." The scene changes to another flashback from *Goodbye, Norma Jean* in which an insulted Norma Jean barges into the offices of Lion-Rampant Studios after the results of her screen test, only to be further humiliated, a defeat which spurs her first suicide attempt.

Returning to the present, the Psychiatrist coldly states, "After they bedded you, and spent their power inside you, it took you further and further from Norma Jean Baker," a cruel but accurate assessment of the evolution of Norma Jean's fragmentation. Much of *Goodnight* is a chronicle of Norma Jean's alienation from the Self, as Marilyn became the object of public adoration and, as noted, a fittingly fragmented film alternating between a nonlinear narrative of her final day, key scenes recycled from *Goodbye*, and allusions to her involvement with JFK and RFK. Yet it is the Psychiatrist who ironically becomes the main character in *Goodnight*, who simultaneously narrates, comments, and psychoanalyzes the dying Monroe:

> Could the adoring public, your fans, have it all wrong? The frightened one is "Marilyn." The tough one is "Norma Jean." Marilyn is the commodity, the product.... You went through that basket of pictures, and brought back "Norma Jean." Psychiatry has a word for this shifting of personalities: the Orphan Syndrome.... After all, "Marilyn Monroe" had the world by the tail, but rejection was a steady diet for Norma Jean.

After a lengthy flashback of truncated events seen in *Goodbye*, focusing on the more traumatic moments in Norma Jean's life as they formed "Marilyn Monroe," the Psychiatrist notes:

> So, it was "Goodbye, Norma Jean," and "Hello, Marilyn." You had fame, adoration, but it wasn't enough, was it? The "little match girl" found that her appetites were insatiable, so the demons from her private hell came back for a visit. You wouldn't be satisfied until you could seduce any man alive, no matter how powerful! You love your country, don't you? So do we....

The scene shifts to a reenactment of Marilyn's infamous "Happy Birthday, Mr. President" performance, recreated effectively by Lane. After being introduced by Peter Lawford (Gerry Hopkins) with the sinister, prophetic words, "And now, the late, the very late, Marilyn Monroe," the movie star scuttles onstage and sings the birthday song, but she appears nervous, disoriented, and intoxicated as much as intoxicating. Back at the bedroom, the Psychiatrist asks Marilyn bluntly, "Were you intimate with the president that evening, after the party? And the attorney general, that same evening?" After Marilyn nods affirmative to both questions, the woman continues: "It was a ritual. You had become an embarrassment to the president." The reasons behind the conspiracy are now revealed: Marilyn was going to "tell everything" at a press conference about the Kennedys, the Mafia, the CIA, and her affairs with the president and attorney general. Monroe, as the potential voice of America's moral and political conscience, had to be silenced. Much like the Widow in *The Naked Witch*, Monroe had now become a "naked witch," whose powers of seduction were only matched by her potential powers of destruction to the status quo.

However, the Psychiatrist ascertains Monroe has not told anyone of her potentially incendiary plans. The damage assessed and deemed confinable, the interrogators continue their gruesome work. The woman prods Marilyn: "Someone tried to drown you tonight. Who was it?" Unable to answer, Marilyn sinks into an ever-deeper slumber. The Psychiatrist consults Marilyn's address book, and plays back another telephone message, from a masseuse who came earlier that evening to service Marilyn. The scene reverts to a few hours earlier, as a drunken Marilyn enjoys a rubdown from a disgusted male masseuse. As she enjoys her paid companionship, Marilyn ruminates ironically, "In all her movies, you never see Marilyn Monroe, the world's greatest sex symbol, actually making love onscreen." She refers to herself here in the third-person — as "somebody else." Soon Marilyn and the young masseuse are having sex, with Marilyn on top. Marilyn seems to be on the verge of achieving orgasm, when the two stop abruptly. Marilyn curses and the young man apologizes. Apparently he has lost his erection. He pleads, "I'm sorry, I can't help it. It's who you are." This telling remark reveals that, indeed, the bigger-than-life commodity known as "Marilyn Monroe" is something to adore and revere, too big an icon to "fuck." The "real" Marilyn, however, is incensed: "Just for once, can't somebody love me?" Yet even Marilyn is not a "me," but a "somebody else," a public perception and persona that fucked while "getting fucked." Jumping naked into the pool, a bitter, drunken Marilyn insults the masseuse's manhood, and the masseuse then tries to drown the actress. Back in the present, the Psychiatrist asks the Doctor, "The phony masseuse. One of ours?" The man answers with scorn, "We'll never know. Probably an amateur. A persistent fan. They could have been from the Hoffa camp. They do tacky work. Let's not make the same mistake." It is a moment of dark comedy that the conspiracy has become so vast and convoluted that even the participants cannot sort out the events. The Psychiatrist and Doctor leave the room and Marilyn briefly regains consciousness to see the image of her insane mother. The mirror-image calls, "Norma Jean! Come to me, baby!" and Marilyn fittingly retorts, "I'm not Norma Jean! I'm Marilyn!"

Mesquite enters the room, as the mirror-mother announces gleefully, "Mesquite's here!" He sits on Marilyn's bed, strokes her hair, and tells her what she already knows: "They tease you about all the time you spend in front of the mirror, your tardiness, but we know, don't we? It's not vanity. You're looking for the first signs of madness." To again utilize Lacan, Norma-Jean-as-Marilyn has all her life been locked in the perpetual trauma of the mirror-stage, the imaginary realm versus the symbolic Order, the dialectic of the specular I and

Sinister shadow-figures (Kenneth Hicks and Joyce Lower) violate Marilyn Monroe's bedroom sanctuary in Larry Buchanan's harrowing political thriller, ***Goodnight, Sweet Marilyn.*** These agents of deceit will not be satisfied until her death has been completely rescripted, for public consumption, as the suicide of a neurotic whore.

the social I, that merges fitfully into the state Lacan called the "body-in-pieces." Marilyn is considerably calmer in Mesquite's presence, and they share some frivolous gallows humor concerning her imminent demise. Mesquite goes to the bathroom to prepare a suppository. As Mesquite inserts the suppository, Marilyn coos, "Do they have cameras in heaven?" Mesquite replies, "They will now." The two share an awkward embrace. Marilyn whispers, "Good night, sweet prince," a line suggesting past lives as well as referencing the death of Shakespeare's Hamlet. Mesquite responds with the film's title, "Goodnight, Sweet Marilyn," and kisses the sex goddess on the cheek. As he leaves, Mesquite removes his picture from the dresser, thus erasing all evidence, and memory, of his tortured yet devoted relationship with her. He then provides an epilogue:

> And that's how I left her, in the fetal position, common to anyone who has gone over to the Elysian fields with the help of drugs. I wish it could have ended that way, but again, in the end it had to be someone else's scenario. She was just a prime cut for other appetites, with their dark motives. I know now that I had hardly left the house when they came. It doesn't matter a damn who they were. Whether their actions were Bostonian, English or Swahili.

He describes a clandestine trip to St. John's hospital with Marilyn's dying body, a trip carried out in inexplicable radio silence. Marilyn died en route, and it was decided by those in charge to return her to the house and reset the scene as a morbid melodrama for mass consumption. In addition to being laid out bare on her bed like a common whore, Mari-

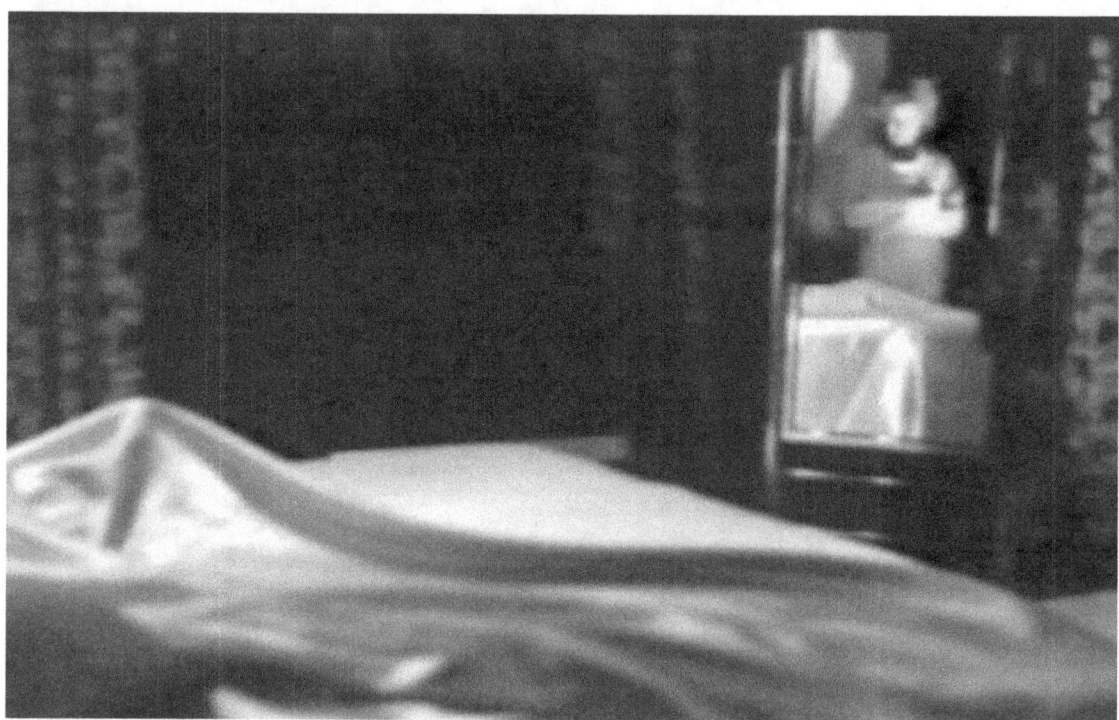

When Marilyn Monroe (Paula Lane) sees the specter of her insane mother, Gladys Baker (Phyllis Coates), in the mirror, she knows it is time to finally say "Goodnight, Sweet Marilyn."

lyn's hand was symbolically posed clutching the telephone, her lifeline to society, and, some might say, sanity. Mesquite continues:

> There was a new set of rules. "Situation ethics," they call it. "Plausible denial." "National security." Then they retreated to a corner of the room to map strategy, as casually as they would discuss the time of day. There was much to do. Alibies to rehearse, money to change hands, so the well-oiled machine slipped into gear and purred into the black morning hours.

Mesquite finishes his tale back onscreen, saying that "finally, at 3:30 a.m., the West Los Angeles Police Department received the official call, that my sweet Marilyn was dead."

Goodnight ends on this disturbing note, with inferences to a massive conspiracy against Marilyn Monroe. *Goodnight* joins other Buchanan films such as *The Trial of Lee Harvey Oswald* and *Beyond the Doors* in suggesting an alternative and even highly unorthodox interpretation of a significant historical event. Second, *Goodnight* continues what is arguably Buchanan's most consistent theme, from *The Naked Witch* to *Mars Needs Women*, by depicting the subjection of women in a patriarchal order. Third, *Goodnight* elaborates on the psychoanalytic component of Buchanan's texts and, whether intended or not, Lacan's "mirror-stage," explored most specifically in *Naughty Dallas* and *Goodbye, Norma Jean*. Indeed, *Goodnight*, arguably Buchanan's most avant garde film, well expresses his passion as historical revisionist, parochial feminist, and psychoanalytic filmmaker.

24

The Ghost of Larry B

As someone once stated, "all art is political." Any artist worth his salt will entertain and provoke, comfort and challenge, reinforce and contradict his audience. This is his strength and his allure. Drawing equally from generational experience — surrounding culture and personal, creative well — the artist contains within an essentially political creation, a messenger who underlines current notions while imagining new trends, conveying the resulting theses in a pleasing aesthetic and structural form. Applying this formula, Larry Buchanan is a film artist of note. Buchanan is not an auteur in the classical sense and his films have less a dramatic or aesthetic signature than a political or philosophical one, but they are no less memorable or engaging for that. Indeed, Buchanan's strength as a storyteller is the power and courage of his prevailing theses, with no punches pulled and few speculative stones left unturned.

Buchanan was one of the last independents to inject both a personal philosophy and a sense of regional culture into his films. Buchanan juggles both storyteller and political provocateur in his screenplays, and in the end becomes primarily a philosopher. The twin themes of revising cultural history and redrafting period setting, both within modest financial resources, are two poles of Buchanan's work which consistently charge his melodramas with their uncanny hyper-reality, creating a curiously familiar, neorealistic universe which is simultaneously fantastic. Buchanan crafts fabulous melodramatic sketches, something akin yet superior to a first draft. All low-budget filmmakers must paint with broad strokes; they cannot afford subtlety. As their budget and resources are minimal, it is the screenplay, with its infinite flexibility, spliced with the filmmaker's visual ingenuity (i.e. aesthetic vision), which holds the key to the successful low-budget film. Buchanan was a master at painting the wildest, most vivid and alluring works on these smallest of filmic canvases.

A person's fantasies always outrun his dreams, just as his dreams always outreach his works. All are valid, permissible, even essential to the other. Yet the one who not only embraces his dreams but also some part of his fantasies and applies it to his "works" is the true artist. Buchanan did this time and time again, fashioning provocative, fantastic and often confrontational melodramas that challenged the audience even while charming them. Buchanan's films all have very good "hearts," progressive sociological themes and a great sympathy for, though by no means uncritical of, the human condition. Although almost invariably done in a traditional melodramatic style, Buchanan's films are in many ways shockingly modern, even avant garde. His lashing of current trends to the traditional B-movie structure make for bigger-than-life pieces, set in familiar small-town America and featuring a cast of players that look like the people next door. Buchanan's films, with their highly theatrical flavor, often play like filmed theater.

One can see the genesis of Buchanan's disenfranchisement with entrenched cultural and political institutions from his early dust-bowl roots. A sensitive and creative orphan, wrested from his beloved mother and family and tossed into a church-run orphanage, arguably one of the more diabolical and corrupt organizations man has ever devised, Buchanan's films reflect the deep moral degradation of white, middle-class America, as his orphanage experience presented it to him in microcosmic form.

The Ghost of Larry B: Buchanan's impact on the independent film scene is inestimable, and with the release of his magnum opus, *The Copper Scroll of Mary Magdalene*, will surely grow even further. The ghost of Texas's own Singing Cowboy can still be heard, echoing throughout a world of suppressed and altered history.

In youth, Buchanan himself became the rebel outsider he later fashioned in many of his films. This protagonist rebels against a repressive cultural environment, and is persecuted for his beliefs or his attempts to enlighten or infiltrate same, as Buchanan did as a tortured adolescent. The orphanage became, in Buchanan's art, the cold, calculating establishment of postwar America (the justice system, the military-industrial complex, the government or the entertainment industry) which conspires to thwart, suppress and destroy the protagonist at every opportunity.

Most important in the task of exposing and revising corrupt institutions are the discovery and revelation of the actual truths behind the institution being examined, to counter the self-serving half-truths, distortions and outright fabrications which often pass for history. The mercurial, subjective nature of history, which compromised parties can successfully distort, is one of Buchanan's most frequent warnings, and uncovering and disseminating alternative views of accepted history are among Buchanan's most cherished causes. Buchanan knows that "the truth" is never what it appears to be, and the truth seeker must endlessly battle the sinister forces which work behind the scenes to craft "reality" to their own ends.

In his search for truth, the Buchanan protagonist often seeks a spiritual guide, an omniscient authority figure. Being naïve or flawed, the hero has the tendency to ascribe untoward qualities to questionable imposters. In Buchanan's surely knowing opinion, the search for a God figure must be undertaken with as much intellectual honesty as the search for righteous world leaders.

Buchanan assuredly saw Woman not only as a potential savior for Mankind but also as an avenging force against evil patriarchal institutions. Understandably, Buchanan's dearly missed mother figures most prominently in his art. She returns time and time again as a pivotal and powerful central archetype in the films, a stoic figure of virtually supernatural powers, yet one who is often martyred for her attempts at personal empowerment or for saving the diseased community from which she springs. The prominence of the female in Buchanan's films seems almost an effort to resurrect the ghost of the dead mother as a religious figure, an all-powerful, sacrificial saint, one who manifests great societal change before her untimely martyr's death.

Being a devoted family man himself, it is not surprising that the bulk of Buchanan's films, no matter how far afield they venture, always comment on the middle-class experience. Even such fantastic fables as *Zontar, the Thing from Venus* and *Beyond the Doors* focus heavily on the impact of cultural upheaval on a typical middle-class family. This impact is invariably destructive, and often fatal. Buchanan consistently declares that unwise decisions made at the pinnacles of power will negatively resonate all the way down to the common man in his little domicile, so the common man must be ever vigilant to what his leaders are up to. The macrocosm is the microcosm.

Ultimately, Buchanan's philosophical verdict is an understated but undeniable misanthropy, a mistrust of the collective human experience, a rejection of religious solutions to flaws within that experience, and a belief in the healing power of humanism. Most importantly, Buchanan senses that entrenched, male-dominated organizational systems are the most prone to error and corruption, and its members, although perhaps noble in spirit, can easily slip and descend into mere "creatures of destruction." The outsider male, usually in tandem with an empowered female, are to Buchanan the only hope for the reparation of such corrupt institutional constructs, although the road to societal salvation may be strewn with travail and even death. This avowedly heterosexist perspective, which may alienate some even while it endears others, is the genesis for Buchanan's recurring savior couple, a heterosexual unit whose devotion to each other and the spirit of truth leads them to tirelessly battle corrupt societies and institutions, often unto death. This familial warrior duo is surely the ghost of the mother and father Buchanan missed so dearly throughout his traumatic childhood and tortured adolescence; that they appear so frequently and so sympathetically (one might even say romantically) in the vast majority of Buchanan's films suggests not only that they are enduring, useful societal archetypes, but that Buchanan, like all good artists, was trying to understand and exorcise his unique psychological past by filtering experience through creative effort. That this savior couple resonate so well with a large portion of Buchanan's audience reveals that they indeed represent a beloved and desired modern mythology for the postwar generation, in effect, the baby

Cheap Monster: The Gill Monster in the 1967 film *Creature of Destruction*. Buchanan considered the beast in his Azalea telefilms to be a conscious parody of the traditional B-movie creature, a reckless pun on the beloved cultural icon known as the "cheap movie monster."

boomers' subconscious wish for all-knowing, omniscient "super-parents" who might protect them from all evil.

    The strength of Buchanan as storyteller is essentially the spirit of the oral folk tale as personified by the modern-day singing cowboy, a prolific folk artist telling sad and lurid tales of a fallen culture and the people who strive valiantly to restore it. The films become mythical in nature due to this unique narrative perspective. They are, in some ways, modern American fairy tales. Bearing the distinct imprint of Southern culture, they convey a very identifiable and treasured cultural universe. Thanks to fantastic screenplays filtered through a neorealist mise-en-scène, what is created is a very topical yet timeless filmed theater which nonetheless acknowledges traditional narrative structure. This is why Buchanan's films are both idiosyncratic and universal, generic yet wholly unique. The ghost of "Larry B" surely lives, in the unforgettable films he made, in the hearts of those who have enjoyed them, in the myriad unresolved psychological, philosophical and historical issues raised in his work, in the creative efforts of the many artists influenced by this most talented and visionary filmmaker.

Filmography

(This filmography does not contain films Larry Buchanan produced while at the U.S. Army Signal Corps circa 1945, as these titles are largely unknown.)

The Cowboy (1951)

Director: Larry Buchanan *Screenplay:* Larry Buchanan *Producer:* Larry Buchanan *Cinematography:* Larry Buchanan, Hal Hunt *Film Editing:* Larry Buchanan *Produced by:* First Departure Films, 20 minutes, black and white, 35mm.

Cast: Larry Buchanan (the Cowboy), Bill Free (Narrator)

Grubstake (1952)

Director: Larry Buchanan *Screenplay:* Larry Buchanan, Lynn Shubert *Producer:* Larry Buchanan *Cinematography:* Carl Sturgess *Sound:* Kort Falkenberg, Sol Fol *Assistant Camera:* Gil Margolis *Wardrobe:* Toby Wyman *Produced by:* Tejano Productions, a.k.a. *Apache Gold*, 60 minutes, black and white, 35mm.

Cast: Stephen Wyman, Jack Klugman, Neile Adams, Lynn Shubert, Kort Falkenberg

Venus in Furs (circa 1957)

Director: Larry Buchanan *Screenplay:* Larry Buchanan (from works by Marquis de Sade) *Cinematography:* Ralph K. Johnson, format unknown.

The Naked Witch (1961)

Director: Claude Alexander, Larry Buchanan *Screenplay:* Claude Alexander, Larry Buchanan *Producer:* Claude Alexander *Original Music:* Ray Plagens *Film Editing:* Claude Alexander, Larry Buchanan *Production Manager:* John F. Rickert *Sound:* S.F. Brownrigg *Camera Operator:* Ralph Johnson *Color Consultant:* Adrian Mosser Alexander Enterprises, 59 minutes, color, shot in 16mm, released in 35mm. *VHS:* Sinister Cinema, Something Weird Video; *DVD:* Something Weird Video.

Cast: Libby Hall (the Witch), Robert Short (the Student), Jo Maryman (Kirska), Denis Adams, Charles West, Howard Ware, Jack Herman, Marilyn Pope (schoolteacher), Der Saengerbund Children's Choir, Rae Forbes (uncredited), Gary Owens (narrator of prologue, uncredited), Beth Porter (uncredited)

Common Law Wife (1963)

Director: Eric Sayers, Larry Buchanan (uncredited) *Screenplay:* Grace Nolan *Editing:* Frank Forestieri *Producer:* Fred A. Kadane, M.A. Ripps (uncredited) Cinema Distributors of America / Texas Film Producers, a.k.a. *Swamp Rose*, 76 minutes, black and white, shot in

16mm and 35mm, released in 35mm. *DVD:* Something Weird Video.

Cast: Annabelle Weenick (as "Anne MacAdams") (Linda Farnum/Mrs. Rainey), George Edgley (Shugfoot Rainey), Lacey Kelly ("Baby Doll"/Jonelle #1), Max Anderson (Jake, the Sheriff), Bert Masters (Bull, a moonshiner), Libby Booth (Brenda, Jakes' wife), Norman Smith (Lewis, an attorney), Dale Berry (Jess, owner of the White Rock Terrace)

Free, White and 21 (1963)

Director: Larry Buchanan *Screenplay:* Larry Buchanan, Harold Hoffman (as "Harold Dwain"), Cliff Pope *Producer:* Larry Buchanan, *Original Music* "The Hobo Twist" by Joey Johnson *Cinematography:* Ralph K. Johnson *Film Editing:* Larry Buchanan *Art Direction:* Dennis Adams *Sound:* Robert Redd *Assistant Camera:* Laney Duck *Design Consultant:* Dick Danne *Crew Chief:* Jim Finley *Production Assistant:* Betty Sooter *Produced by:* Falcon International Pictures *Distributed by:* American International Pictures, filmed at P.S.I. Studios, Dallas, Texas, a.k.a. *A Question of Consent*, 104 minutes, black and white, 35mm. *VHS:* All-Seasons Entertainment.

Cast: Frederick O'Neal (Ernie Jones), Annalena Lund (Greta Mae Hansen), George Edgley (judge), Johnny Hicks (Prosecuting Attorney Atkins), George Russell (Defense Attorney Tyler), Hugh Crenshaw (Assistant Prosecuting Attorney), Miles Middough (witness), James Altgens (witness), Jonathan Ledford (witness), Bill McGee (witness), Ted Mitchell (witness), Jack Dunlop (witness)

Under Age (1964)

Director: Larry Buchanan *Screenplay:* Larry Buchanan, Harold Hoffman *Producer:* Harold Hoffman, Title Song ("Under Age") by Harold Hoffman and Larry Buchanan, "Boil Them Cabbage Down" by The Alpine Trio, "Turtledove Song" by the Lost River Trio *Cinematography:* Henry A. Kokojan *Film Editing:* Larry Buchanan, filmed at Southwest Film Center, Dallas, Texas *Produced by:* Falcon International Pictures *Distributed by:* American International Pictures, 90 minutes, black and white, 35mm. *VHS:* Simitar Entertainment.

Cast: Annabelle Weenick (as "Anne MacAdams") (Ruby Jenkins), Judy Adler (Linda Jenkins), Roland Royter (George Gomez), George Russell (D.A. Tyler), John Hicks (Prosecutor Adkins), George Edgley (the Judge), Tommie Russell (Mrs. Sybel Riley), Regina Cassidy (Dr. Vivian Scott), Joseph Cranshaw (W.J. Earnhardt), Raymond Bradford (Wilbur Neal), Jonathan Ledford (Barney Jenkins), Howard Ware (bailiff), Joreta C. Cherry (court reporter), Robert B. Alcott (Assistant District Attorney), William Peck (news photographer), Barnett Shaw (news reporter)

Naughty Dallas (1964)

Director: Larry Buchanan *Screenplay:* Larry Buchanan *Producer:* Larry Buchanan *Associate Producers:* Marilyn Pope, Jimmy Rhodes *Executive Producer:* John F. Rickert *Musical Consultant:* William F. Pecchi *Musical direction and score:* Wallace V. Pettit *Band:* The Bill Peck Quintet *Special Music:* Joe Garcia *Bongo Solo:* Pat Woods *Cinematography:* Ralph K. Johnson (as "P.K. Johnson") *Editing:* Jerry Caraway, sequences filmed at Jimmie and Don Youras' Club Montmart, and Abe's Colony Club, Dallas *Production Facilities:* Producer Services Inc., Dallas, Texas, a Double Bob Production *Produced by:* Diamond International Pictures *Distributed by:* Paul Mart Productions, a.k.a. *Life in the Raw; A Stripper Is Born; Mondo Exotico; Naughty Cuties*; 72 minutes, color, shot in 16mm, released in 35mm. *VHS:* Something Weird Video.

Cast: Marilyn Pope (as "Toni Shannon") (Toni), Jada (stripper), Kim Athas (stripper), Peggy Steele (stripper), Breck Wall (comedian, emcee), Bill Fanning (comedian), Bill Demar (comedian, emcee), Buddy Raymon (old drunk), White Boyd, Dale Berry, Bill Peck (himself, bandleader), Jack Cole (himself), Abe Weinstein (himself), Suzanna Long (herself), Larry Buchanan (narrator, uncredited), "and the Amatuers!"

The Trial of Lee Harvey Oswald (1964)

Director: Larry Buchanan *Screenplay:* Larry Buchanan, Harold Hoffman *Producer:* Harold

Hoffman *Cinematography:* James R. Davidson *Film Editing:* Larry Buchanan *Set Decoration:* Bill Mitchell *Sound:* Bruce Howard, Sheilds Mitchell *Gaffer:* Roy E. Adams *Key Grip:* J.H. Beall *Assistant Camera:* Olin W. Dalton *Production Assistant:* Ralph Johnson *Camera Operator:* Henry Kokojan *Script Supervisor:* Betty Sooter *Assistant Camera:* Jack Specht, filmed at Southwest Film Center *Produced by:* Falcon International Pictures *Distributed by:* Capital Film Enterprises, 94/98 minutes, black and white, shot in 16mm and 35mm, released in 35mm. *VHS:* Burbank Video; *DVD:* Something Weird Video.

Cast: George Russell (Defense Attorney Tyler), George Edgley (the judge), Arthur Nations (Prosecuting Attorney Atkins), Charles Mazyrack (Lee Harvey Oswald), Joreta C. Cherry (court reporter), Howard Ware (bailiff), Don Gillespie (attorney), Dan Terrell (attorney), Bill Peck (attorney), Jenna Jordan (witness), Raymond Bradford (witness), Theodore Mitchell (witness), Edwin Cherry (witness), Bill Bell (witness), William McGhee (witness), Jonathan Ledford (witness), Bill Thurman (witness), Charles McLine (witness), Tommie Russell (witness), Annabelle Weenick (as "Anne MacAdams") (witness), Dale Howard (witness), Bob French (witness), Jack Dunlop (witness), Bill Carter (witness), Nathan Wyle (witness), Bob Dracup (witness), Max Anderson (witness), Shirley McLine (witness), Jim Altgens (witness), Barnett Shaw (witness), Wallace Edwards (witness), Armand Jones (witness), Charles W. Tessmer (himself), Desmond Dhooge (uncredited)

The Eye Creatures (1965)

Director: Larry Buchanan *Story:* Paul W. Fairman (from his short story "The Cosmic Frame," uncredited) *Screenplay:* Larry Buchanan (uncredited), based on an original screenplay by Robert J. Gurney Jr. and Al Martin *Producer:* Larry Buchanan *Associate Producer:* Edwin Tobolowsky *Original Music:* Les Baxter, Ronald Stein (uncredited) *Cinematography:* Ralph K. Johnson *Film Editing:* S.F. Brownrigg *Production Manager:* James A. Sullivan, Second Unit Director: Hillman Taylor *Sound:* Bruce Shearin, Assistant to Director: Joreta Cherry *Key Grip:* Melvin Clark *Camera Operator:* Ted Liles II, Dialogue *Director:* Annabelle Weenick *Produced by:* Azalea Pictures, Academy Pictures Corp. *Distributed by:* American International Television, a.k.a. *Attack of the Eye Creatures*, 80 minutes, color, 16mm. *VHS:* Sinister Cinema, Something Weird Video; *DVD:* Retromedia.

Cast: John Ashley (Stan Kenyon), Cynthia Hull (Susan Rogers), Warren Hammack (Lt. Robertson), Chet Davis (Mike Lawrence), Bill Peck (Carl Fenton), Ethan Allen, Charles McLine, Nathan Wyle, Bob Cowan, Enrique Touceda III (as "Tony Huston") (Culver), Jonathan Ledford, Shirley McLine, Bob Brown, Donna Lindberg, Larry Tanner, Gordon Bulow, Jody Daniel, Travis Wayne, George Edgley (Medical Examiner), Bill Thurman (Air Force Sergeant), Hillman Taylor, Edwin Cherry, Jody Daniels (Unnamed), Peter Graves (Narrator of USAF Briefing Film (uncredited), Larry Buchanan (soldier, uncredited)

High Yellow (1965)

Director: Larry Buchanan *Screenplay:* Larry Buchanan *Producer:* Clyde Knudsen *Stunts:* Stuart Spates (uncredited) *Production Assistant:* Stuart Spates, Dinero Productions, Thunder Pictures Inc., 83 minutes, black and white, 35mm.

Cast: Cynthia Hull (Cynthia "Cindy" Wood), Warren Hammack (George), Kay Taylor (Judy), Bill McGhee (Joseph), Annabelle Weenick (Mrs. Langley), Bob Brown (Mr. Langley), Bill Thurman (Major Bates), Jonathan Ledford (Reverend Hatfield), Max W. Anderson (officer), Jody Daniels, Stuart Spates (cowboy in saloon, uncredited)

Zontar, the Thing from Venus (1966)

Director: Larry Buchanan *Screenplay:* Larry Buchanan, Hillman Taylor *Associate Producer:* Edwin Tobolowsky, Larry Buchanan (uncredited) *Original Music:* Ronald Stein (uncredited) *Cinematography:* Robert B. Alcott *Art Direction:* Robert Dracup *Sound:* S.F. Brownrigg, Bruce Shearin *Production Coordinator:* Joreta C. Cherry *Camera Operator:* Ralph K. Johnson *Best Boy:* Ted Liles II *Assistant Camera:* James A. Sullivan Dialogue *Direc-*

tor: Annabelle Weenick *Produced by:* Azalea Pictures *Distributed by:* American International Television, a.k.a. *Zontar, Invader From Space,* 80 minutes, color, 16mm. *VHS:* Sinister Cinema, Something Weird Video; *DVD:* Retromedia.

Cast: John Agar (Dr. Curt Taylor), Susan Bjurman (Martha Ritchie), Enrique Touceda III (as "Anthony Houston") (Keith Ritchie), Pat Delaney (as "Pat De Laney") (Anne Taylor), Neil Fletcher (General Young), Warren Hammack (Rocket Scientist at Zone 6), Colleen Carr, Jeff Alexander (Rocket Scientist at Zone 6), Bill Thurman (Sheriff Brad Crenshaw), Andrew Traister, Jonathan Ledford, George Edgley (Mr. Ledford, Newspaper Editor), Carol Gilley (Alice), Bertha Holmes

Curse of the Swamp Creature (1966)

Director: Larry Buchanan *Screenplay:* Enrique Touceda III (as "Tony Houston") *Producer:* Larry Buchanan *Associate Producer:* Edwin Tobolowsky *Original Music:* Ronald Stein (uncredited) *Cinematography:* Ralph K. Johnson *Art Direction:* Robert Dracup *Production Management:* James A. Sullivan *Sound:* Ted Liles II, Bruce Shearin *Special Effects:* Jack Bennett *Key Grip:* Jack Carney *Production Coordinator:* Joreta Cherry *Continuity:* Annabelle Weenick *Produced by:* Azalea Pictures *Distributed by:* American International Television, 80 minutes, color, 16mm. *VHS:* Sinister Cinema, Something Weird Video; *DVD:* Elite Entertainment, Family Value Collection.

Cast: John Agar (Barry Rogers), Francine York (Pat Trent), Jeff Alexander (Dr. Simon Trent), Shirley McLine (Brenda Simmons), Cal Duggan (Ritchie), Charles McLine, Bill McGhee (as Bill McGee), Ted Mitchell, Roger Ready (Frenchie), Bill Thurman (Driscoll West/The Swamp Creature), Enrique Touceda III (as "Tony Houston") (Tom), Gayle Johnson, Michael Tolden, Annabelle Weenick (Hotel Clerk), Patrick Cranshaw (as Pat Crenshaw), J.V. Lee, Naomi Bruton

Sam (1967)

Director: Larry Buchanan *Screenplay:* Larry Buchanan *Producer:* Larry Buchanan *Cinematography:* James R. Davidson *Film Editing:* Larry Buchanan *Production Coordinator:* Joreta Cherry *Camera Operator:* Henry Kokojan, a.k.a. *The Hottest Fourth of July in the History of Brewster County,* color, 35mm.

Cast: Jody McCrea, Pat Delaney, Enrique Touceda III (as "Tony Huston"), Caruth C. Byrd, Bill Thurman, Jack Carney, Ethan Allen, Neil Fletcher, Bud Breen, Bob Harris, Ross Thompson

Creature of Destruction (1967)

Director: Larry Buchanan *Screenplay:* Enrique Touceda III (as "Enrique Touceda") *Producer:* Larry Buchanan *Associate Producer:* Edwin Tobolowsky *Original Music:* Ronald Stein (uncredited) *Cinematography:* Robert C. Jessup *Sound:* Rex Cromwell, Don Ross *Special Effects:* Jack Bennett *Assistant Camera:* R.L. Buchanan *Production Coordinator:* Joreta C. Cherry *Gaffer:* Robert Dracup *Key Grip:* James Finley *Dialogue Director:* Annabelle Weenick *Produced by:* Azalea Pictures *Distributed by:* American International Television, 80 minutes, color, 16mm. *VHS:* Sinister Cinema, Something Weird Video.

Cast: Les Tremayne (Dr. John Basso), Pat Delaney (Doreena), Aron Kincaid (Captain Theodore Dell), Neil Fletcher (Sam Crane), Annabelle Weenick (as "Anne McAdams") (Mrs. Crane), Roger Ready (Lt. Blake), Ron Scott, Suzanne Roy (Lynn Crane), Byron Lord (investigating psychiatrist/the creature), Barnett Shaw (investigating psychiatrist), Scotty McKay (himself)

Mars Needs Women (1967)

Director: Larry Buchanan *Screenplay:* Larry Buchanan *Producer:* Larry Buchanan *Associate Producer:* Edwin Tobolowsky *Original Music:* Ronald Stein (uncredited) *Cinematography:* Robert C. Jessup *Film Editing:* Larry Buchanan *Makeup Artist:* Annabelle Weenick *Sound:* Rex Cromwell, Don Ross *Assistant Camera:* Robert L. Buchanan *Production Coordinator:* Joreta C. Cherry *Gaffer:* Robert Dracup *Key Grip:* Jim Finley *Produced by:* Azalea Pictures *Distributed by:* American International Television, 83 minutes, color, 16mm. *VHS:* Sinister Cinema, Something Weird Video, MGM Home Entertainment; *DVD:* MGM Home Entertainment.

Cast: Tommy Kirk (Dop), Yvonne Craig (Dr. Marjorie Bolen), Warren Hammack (Martian Doctor/Fellow #2), Enrique Touceda III (as "Tony Huston") (Martian Fellow #3), Larry Tanner (Martian Fellow #4), Cal Duggan (Martian Fellow #5), Pat Delaney (artist abducted by Martians), Sherry Roberts (Brenda Knowlan, abductee), Donna Lindberg (stewardess abducted by Martians), "Bubbles" Cash (stripper abducted by Martians), Byron Lord (Col. Bob Page, U.S.D.S.), Roger Ready (Stimmons, a reporter), Barnett Shaw (man at military conference), Neil Fletcher (Secretary of Defense), Chet Davis (Mr. Fast, of the *Seattle Sun*), Ron Scott, George Edgley (planetarium director), Dick Simpson, Don Campbell, Bob Hazlett (James, gas station attendant), Ann Palmer (U.S.D.S. Tech), Gordon Bulow, Bill Thurman (drunk on pier), Patrick Cranshaw, Claude Earls, Sally Casey, Bob Lorenz, Sylvia Rundell, David England (planetarium manager), Terry Davis, Larry Buchanan (narrator of planetarium film, uncredited)

In the Year 2889 (1967)

Director: Larry Buchanan *Screenplay:* Harold Hoffman, from an original story by Lou Rusoff *Producer:* Larry Buchanan Associate *Producer:* Edwin Tobolowsky *Cinematography:* Robert C. Jessup *Film Editing:* Larry Buchanan (uncredited) *Original Music:* Ronald Stein (uncredited) *Sound:* Rex Cromwell, Don Ross *Special Effects:* Jack Bennett *Assistant Camera:* R.L. Buchanan *Production Coordinator:* Joreta Cherry *Gaffer:* Robert Dracup *Key Grip:* James Finley *Dialogue Director:* Annabelle Weenick *Produced by:* Azalea Pictures *Distributed by:* American International Television, 80 minutes, color, 16mm. *VHS:* Sinister Cinema, Something Weird Video; *DVD:* Retromedia, American Home Treasures.

Cast: Paul Petersen (Steve), Quinn O'Hara (Jada), Charla Doherty (Joanna Ramsey), Neil Fletcher (Captain John Ramsey), Hugh Feagin (Mickey Brown), Max W. Anderson (Granger), Bill Thurman (Tim Henderson), Byron Lord (Mutant)

Hell Raiders (1968)

Director: Larry Buchanan *Producer:* Larry Buchanan, Edwin Tobolowsky *Cinematography:* Robert C. Jessup *Film Editing:* James Ferguson *Sound:* Danny Brown, Gary Ferguson *Special Effects:* Jack Bennett, Byron Lord *Production Coordinator:* Joreta C. Cherry *Gaffer:* Jim Finley *Assistant Camera:* Charles Smith *Produced by:* Azalea Pictures *Distributed by:* American International Television, 80 minutes, color, 16mm.

Cast: John Agar (Maj. Ronald Paxton), Richard Webb, Joan Huntington (Laura Grant), Bill Thurman (Tex), Annabelle Weenick, Jeff Alexander, Laura Clepack, Eddie Edwards, John Finley, Ross Interrante, Gary McLain, Tom Mularky, Ron Paxton, Tom Paxton, Tony Purcell, Synthia Rodgers, Ron Scott, Bob Strauss

Comanche Crossing (1968)

Director: Larry Buchanan *Screenplay:* Larry Buchanan, Enrique Touceda III (as "Anthony Houston") *Producer:* Larry Buchanan, Caruth C. Byrd *Cinematography:* Ralph K. Johnson *Film Editing:* Larry Buchanan *Stunts:* Bob Harris *Production Coordinator:* Joreta Cherry, color, format unknown.

Cast: Cynthia Hull, Enrique Touceda III (as "Tony Huston"), Caruth C. Byrd

The Other Side of Bonnie and Clyde (1968)

Director: Larry Buchanan *Screenplay:* Larry Buchanan, based on the book *"I'm Frank Hamer"* by Frank Hamer *Producer:* Larry Buchanan Associate *Producer:* Joreta Cherry *Original Music:* "Clyde & Bonnie Theme" by Don Zimmers; "Frank Hamer's Theme" by Jack Carney *Cinematography:* Charles Smith *Film Editing:* J.C. Ferguson *Sound:* Skip Frazee *Second Unit:* David Beckman *Special Effects:* Jack Bennett *Gaffer:* Byron Lord *Assistant Camera:* Curtis Poe *Producer:* Larry Buchanan Productions *Distributed by:* Dal-Art Films, a.k.a. *Bonnie & Clyde: Myth or Madness?*, 61/75 minutes, color, shot in 16mm & 35mm, released in 35mm. *DVD:* Something Weird Video.

Cast: Burl Ives (narrator), Jo Enterentree (Bonnie Parker), Frank Hamer, Jr. (himself), Mrs. Frank Hamer (herself), Sofia Cook (herself), Floyd Hamilton (himself), John Jenkins (himself), Lucky Mosley (Clyde Barrow), George Edgley (man killed at service station, uncredited), Harold Hoffman (himself, uncredited), Bill Thurman (policeman, uncredited)

It's Alive! (1969)

Director: Larry Buchanan, from an original short story by Richard Matheson ("Being," uncredited) *Screenplay:* Larry Buchanan (uncredited) *Producer:* Larry Buchanan Associate *Producer:* Edwin Tobolowsky *Cinematography:* Robert B. Alcott *Film Editing:* Larry Buchanan *Sound:* Conrad Lee Reed Special *Effects:* Jack Bennett *Production Coordinator:* Joreta C. Cherry *Paleontology:* Skip Frazee *Produced by:* Azalea Pictures *Distributed by:* American International Television, 80 minutes, color, 16mm. *VHS:* Sinister Cinema, Something Weird Video; *DVD:* Retromedia.

Cast: Tommy Kirk (Wayne Thomas), Shirley Bonne (Lesland Sterns), Bill Thurman (Greevy), Annabelle Weenick (as "Annabelle Macadams") (Bella Pittman), Corveth Ousterhouse (Norman Sterns), Larry Buchanan (narrator)

Sex and the Animals (1969)

Director: Harold Hoffman (as "Hal Dwain") *Producer:* Larry Buchanan (uncredited), George Costello *Editing:* Larry Buchanan, Harold Hoffman (as "Hal Dwain"), David Korn, Roger Carter *Story by:* Dr. Lorus J. Milne, Dr. Margery Milne (based on their book, "The Mating Instinct") *Screenplay:* Harold Hoffman (as "Hal Dwain"), Dr. Lorus J. Milne, Dr. Margery Milne *Music:* Ravi Shankar (uncredited) Music *Editor:* Andre Brummer *Narrated by:* Dr. Lorus J. Milne, Dr. Margery Milne *Produced by:* Falcon International Pictures *Distributed by:* Dal-Art Films, a.k.a. *Love and the Animals*, color/widescreen, 85 minutes, shot in 16mm, released in 35mm. *VHS:* Prism Entertainment, Video City Productions.

A Bullet for Pretty Boy (1970)

Director: Larry Buchanan, Maury Dexter (uncredited) *Story by:* Enrique Touceda III (as "Enrique Touceda"), Larry Buchanan *Screenplay:* Henry Rosenbaum *Producer:* Larry Buchanan *Original Music:* Harley Hatcher *Cinematography:* James R. Davidson *Film Editing:* Miguel Levin *Makeup Artist:* Lynne Brooks *Sound:* Lawrence Gianneschi, Sr. *Stunts:* Lucky Mosley (uncredited) *Script Supervisor:* Joretta Cherry *Wardrobe:* Ron Scott *Musical Supervisor:* Al Simms First *Assistant Camera:* Larry Gianneschi III (uncredited), American International Pictures, original soundtrack, published by American International Records, songs performed by The Source, 84/89 minutes, color, 35mm. *VHS:* Orion Home Entertainment, Virgin Video, Guild Video.

Cast: Fabian (as "Fabian Forte") (Charles Arthur "Pretty Boy" Floyd), Jocelyn Lane (Betty), Astrid Warner (Ruby), Adam Roarke ("Preacher"), Michael Haynes (Ned Short), Robert Glenn (Hossler), Annabelle Weenick (as "Anne MacAdams") (Beryl), Camilia Carr (Helen), Jeff Alexander (Wallace), Desmond Bridge (Harvey), Bill Thurman (Huddy), Hugh Feagin (Jack Dowler), Jessie Lee Fulton (Mrs. Floyd), James N. Harrell (as James Harrell) (Mr. Sam Floyd), Gene Ross (William), Eddie Lo Russo (as Ed Lo Russo) (Bo), Charlie Dell (Charlie), Frank De Benedetto (as Frank DeBenedett) (Lester Floyd), Eddie Thomas (Ben Dowler), Ethan Allen (Seth), Troy Hoskins (as Troy K. Hoskins) (Sheriff Taylor), Lucky Mosley (Deputy), Ron Scott (Deputy), Charles Redding (Deputy), David Beuret (Deputy), Walt Becklund (Deputy), Sheriff of Ralston (Neil Fletcher, uncredited), Morgan Fairchild (Gangster Moll, uncredited)

Strawberries Need Rain (1970)

Director: Larry Buchanan *Screenplay:* Enrique Touceda III (as "Anthony Houston"),

Larry Buchanan *Story:* Victor Brun ("In a Certain Village") *Producer:* Larry Buchanan *Executive Producer:* Leslie Lagoni *Original Music:* Ray Martin *Cinematography:* Robert C. Jessup *Film Editing:* Larry Buchanan, Jeff Buchanan *Art Direction:* Byron Lord *Key Grip:* Bill Thurman *Production Coordinator:* Joretta Cherry *Produced by:* Larry Buchanan Productions & Dinero Productions *Distributed by:* American International Pictures, Futurama International, 86 minutes, color, 35mm.

Cast: Monica Gayle (Erica), Gene Otis Shayne (Gerte Seestrom), Les Tremayne (The Reaper), Paul Bertoya (Bruno Miller), Terry Mace (Franz).

Goodbye, Norma Jean (1976)

Director: Larry Buchanan *Screenplay:* Larry Buchanan, Lynn Shubert *Producer:* Larry Buchanan, Mark Josem, Robert Ward *Executive Producer:* Amadeo Curcio *Original Music:* Joe Beck *Theme Song:* Johnny Cunningham *Performed by:* "The Sundown Company" *Cinematography:* Robert A. Sherry *Film Editing:* John Buchanan, John S. Curran *Sound:* Jim Bryan *Gaffer:* Tommy Estridge *Script Supervisor:* Debra Hill, Austamerican Productions, 97 minutes, Australia / USA, color, 35mm. *VHS:* Thorn-EMI Video; *DVD:* Madacy Entertainment Group.

Cast: Misty Rowe (Norma Jean Baker), Terence Locke (Ralph Johnson), Patch Mackenzie (Ruth Latimer), Preston Hanson (Hal James), Marty Zagon (Irving Oblach), Andre Philippe (Sam Dunn), Adele Claire (Beverly), Sal Ponti (Randy Palmer), Paula Mitchell (Cynthia Palmer), Jean Sarah Frost (Ethel), Lilyan McBride (House Mother), Burr Middleton (Sleazy Photographer), Stuart Lancaster (George), Ivy Bethune (Ruby Kirshner), Robert Gribbon (Terry), Garth Pillsbury (Police Officer), Steve Brown (M.C.), Anthony Giger (Sid), Darla Leroy (receptionist), J.R. Clarke (Morris), Frank Curcio (Mel), Duncan McLeod (doctor), Charles Edwards (Stuart), Laurel Barnett (Margaret), Steve Sikes (Masher), Charles Aidikoff (director), Don Brodie (projectionist), Bill J. Stevens (Birdwell), Debbie Daniels (Snuff Girl), Sherry Kay Campbell (Snuff Girl), Harry Woolman (Wino), Sheila Sisco (aspiring actress), Edward Ansara (doctor)

Hughes and Harlow: Angels in Hell (1977)

Director: Larry Buchanan *Screenplay:* Lynn Shubert, Larry Buchanan *Associate Producer:* Frank V. Bianchini, Malcolm Cobrink, Eugene Maday *Producer:* Larry Buchanan, William B. Silberkleit *Original Music:* Jimmie Haskell *Songs:* Estelle Silberkleit *Sung by:* Terri Pierce *Cinematography:* Nickolas Josef von Sternberg *Film Editing:* Robert A. Fitzgerald *Art Direction:* George Costello *Costume Design:* Lennie Barin *Makeup Artist:* Ray Sebastian *Special Makeup Artist for Ms. Bloom:* Tina Bushelman *Production Management:* Joe Price *Assistant Director:* John Curran *Boom Operator:* Mark Buckalew *Score Recordist:* Ron Malo *Sound Mixer:* Alfredo Ramirez *Stunts:* Peter Horak, Gary Taramaschi *Costume Supervisor:* Lenny Baron *First Grip:* Alan Caso *Still Photographer:* Tommy Estridge *Wardrobe Assistant:* Holgie Forrester *Key Grip:* Robert C. George *Key Grip:* Jimmie Haskell *Vintage Cars Cie Owner:* Robert Jenson *Production Assistant:* Thomas Keir *First Assistant Camera:* Lowell Peterson *Gaffer Best Boy:* Ernie Roebuck *Assistant Editor:* Linda Sande *Script Supervisor:* Jackie Saunders *Second Assistant Camera:* David Schmier *Technical Advisor:* Dr. S. Shearing *Production Assistant:* Tommy Silberkleit *Best Boy Grip:* Ray Spadero *Produced by:* H & H Films *Distributed by:* PRO International Pictures, 95 minutes, color, 35mm. *VHS:* Monterey Home Video.

Cast: Victor Holchak (Howard Hughes), Lindsay Bloom (Jean Harlow), David McLean ("Billy"), Charles Aidikoff (projectionist), James S. Appleby (pilot), Wally K. Berns (announcer), James E. Brodhead (lawyer), Don Brodie (director), Barry Buchanan (Pilot), Adele Claire (Mother), David Clover (George), Rita Conde (Inez), Tony Cortez (Emiliano), Brian Cummings (assistant director), John S. Curran (chase cop), Peter Dane (director), Royal Dano (Will Hayes), Richard Dano (theater manager), Charlie Dell (chili wagon man), Dane Denick (bartender), Bud Ekins (chase cop), Michael J. Finn (drunk), Clement St. George (Reggie), Haji (as "Hadji") (Laura), Jim

Hensley (police sergeant), Stephen Hartman (pilot), Erik Holland (Nick), Daniel Knapp (Cabbie), Stuart Lancaster (Charlie), Marius Mazmanian (French waiter), Duncan McLeod (lawyer), Linda Ann Napolitano (hat check girl), Nelson Olmsted (judge), Sage Parker (flapper), Terri Pierce (chanteuse), Garth Pillsbury (Paul), Adam Roarke (Howard Hawks), Walt Robin (Maitre d'), Toni Sawyer (Paul's Wife), Estelle Silberkleit (Candy Francis), Tommy Silberkleit (lab man), Paula Sills (Madeleine), Dave Silverman (pilot), Anthony Sirico (Frankie Rio), Sheila Sisco (other woman), Joel Stedman (Bruno), Harry Woolman (very drunk), Marty Zagon (Sid Grauman), Peter Horak (stuntman), Gary Taramaschi (stuntman)

Mistress of the Apes (1979)

Director: Larry Buchanan *Screenplay:* Larry Buchanan *Associate Producers:* John S. Curran, Joe Price *Producer:* John F. Rickert *Cinematography:* Nicholas Josef von Sternberg *Music and Lyrics ("Mistress of the Apes"):* J.R.F. Peel, W. Malone *Music and Lyrics ("Ape Lady"):* Doug James, Tray Christopher *Sung by:* Billy Hocher *Makeup Artists:* Rob Bottin, Greg Cannom *Special Lighting:* Ron Batzdorff *Distributed by:* Cineworld, 84 minutes, color, 35mm. *VHS:* Monterey Home Video.

Cast: Jenny Neumann (Susan Jamison), Barbara Leigh (Laura), Garth Pillsbury (Paul Cory), Walt Robin (David), Stuart Lancaster (Brady), Mark Rhudy (Matthews), Marius Mazmanian (Sikes), Maida Belove (Near-Woman), Barry Buchanan (first cop), Angela De Joseph (Bantu Maiden), Blayne Dennis (second cop), Ric Drasina (Near-Man), Dennis Gable (Near-Man), Dale Kalberg (nurse), Sandra Kaye (Bantu Maiden), Suzy Mandel (secretary), Frank Martone (Near-Man), Burr Middleton (doctor), Dale Park (Gorilla Savage), Joseph Leo Sexton (Near-Man), Paula Sills (Bantu Maiden), Vince Torrente (Near-Man), George Travis (Bantu Chief), Raymond Vellucci (junkie), Satir González (druggie, uncredited)

The Loch Ness Horror (1981)

Director: Larry Buchanan *Screenplay:* Larry Buchanan, Lynn Shubert *Associate Producer:* Irvin Berwick *Executive Producer:* Jane Buchanan *Producer:* Larry Buchanan, John F. Rickert *Original Music:* Richard H. Theiss *Cinematography:* Robert Ebinger *Assistant Cameraman:* Steve Mann *Film Editing:* Larry Buchanan, Jeff D. Buchanan, Randy Buchanan *Production Manager:* John S. Curran *Assistant Director:* John S. Curran *Second Assistant Director:* Hans Beimler *Sound:* Wayne Berwick, Randy Buchanan *Gaffer:* Ernie Roebuck *Boom Operator:* Randy Buchanan *Script Supervisor:* Dee Buchanan *Best Boy:* Jeff D. Buchanan *Key Grip:* Adam Jones *Special Effects:* Tom Valentine, Peter Chesney, Image Engineering, The Film Business Inc. *Wardrobe:* Theresa Nicholls *Producer:* Clan Buchanan *Distributed by:* Omni-Leisure and Cineworld International, 89 minutes, color, 35mm.

Cast: Sandy Kenyon (Professor George Sanderson), Miki McKenzie (Kathleen Stuart), Barry Buchanan (Spencer Dean), Eric Scott (Brad), Karey-Louis Scott (Fran), Doc Livingston (Jack Stuart), Stuart Lancaster (Professor Pratt), Preston Hanson (Colonel Laughton), Garth Pillsbury (Sergeant Derek), David Clover (Red), Pat Musick (Ms. Stowall), Ronald Cohen (Shorty), Don Myshrall (Alex Nicholson), Dee Buchanan (Alex's Girl)

Down on Us (1984)

Director: Larry Buchanan *Screenplay:* Larry Buchanan *Executive Producer:* Murray K. Kaplan *Producer:* Larry Buchanan *Cinematography:* Nicholas Joseph von Sternberg *Music Supervision:* Jeffrey Dann, David Shorey *Casting:* Susan Margarette-Havins *Art Direction:* Shay Austin *Makeup Artist:* Blake Shepard *Production Manager:* John Curran *First Assistant Director:* John Curran *Second Assistant Director:* Joseph John Kontra *Assistant Art Director:* Debra Combs *Sound:* Alfredo Ramirez *Boom Operator:* José Sedano *Distributed by:* Omni-Leisure Entertainment, a.k.a. *Beyond the Doors*, 134/118 minutes, color, 35mm. *VHS:* Unicorn Video.

Cast: Gregory Allen Chatman (Jimi Hendrix), Riba Meryl (Janis Joplin), Bryan Wolf (Jim Morrison), Sandy Kenyon (Alex Stanley), Joe Camp (Hunter), Toni Sawyer (Mrs. Stanley), Steven Tice (Frank Stanley),

Jennifer Wilde (Ellen), David DeShay (Al Long), Mark Madison (stage manager), Ernie Roebuck (road manager), Pete M. Robinson (musician), Peter M. Robinson (musician), John J. Casino (musician), Dan Priest (limo driver), Phyllis Durant (Christine), Les Hatfield (McElroy), Harold Wayne Jones (Sullivan), Susanne Barnes (she), Granville D. Wolfe (promoter), Michael D. Green (Miami cop), Richard Kennedy (J. Edgar Hoover), Sallee Young (newswoman), Ray Laska (mole), Russ Dumas (talent manager), Mike Gluskin (mole), Diane Wise (prostitute), Darryl Milton (pimp, "Rainbow" Brown), Chris Woods (photographer), Joe Tornatore (Disco owner, "Smokey"), Logan Carter (transvestite), Mark Niclas (impersonator), Derek Barton (technician), Peter Whittle (road manager), Karen Mayo-Chandler (Sue Rigg), Stuart Lancaster (New York cabbie), Marius Mazmanian (French cop), Roger Rochon (mace cop), Loren Cedar (New Orleans girl), Randy Polk (Joplin's engineer), Jodi Harrison (Disco groupie), Nick Ullett (London mole), Lisa Wills (London mole), John Lykes (bodyguard), George N. Marco (Monk), James Maness (Monk), Gordon Hueston (FBI Agent), Helene Bodner (concert groupie), Danièlle Arnaud (London blonde).

Goodnight, Sweet Marilyn (1989)

Director: Larry Buchanan *Screenplay:* Larry Buchanan *Producer:* Larry Buchanan *Associate Producers:* Marlene O'Connell, Scott Pastore *Cinematography:* Miles Anderson *Film Editing:* Jeff Buchanan, Larry Buchanan *Art Direction:* C. Cracko *Makeup Artist:* Constance Gamiere *Production Supervisor:* Jeff Buchanan *Boom Operator:* Skip Clarke *Sound Recordist:* Peter Wolff *First Assistant Camera:* Dave Drysdale *Script Supervisor:* Kate Hoogner *Gaffer:* Jack Wiley *Distributed by:* Arkoff International Pictures, 93/95/104 minutes, color, 35mm. *VHS:* Off-Hollywood Video.

Cast: Paula Lane (Marilyn), Misty Rowe (Norma Jean Baker), Jeremy Slate ("Mesquite"), Joyce Lower (psychiatrist), Kenneth Hicks (medical doctor), Phyllis Coates (Gladys Baker), George Niles Berry (Masseur), Gerry Hopkins (Peter Lawford), Terence Locke (Ralph Johnson), Patch Mackenzie (Ruth Latimer), Preston Hanson (Hal James), Marty Zagon (Irving), Andre Philippe (Sam Dunn), Adele Claire (Beverly), Sal Ponti (Randy Palmer), Paula Mitchell (Cynthia), Jean Frost (Ethel), Lillian McBride (House Mother), Stuart Lancaster (George), Ivy Bethune (Ruby Kirshner), Robert Gribbon (Terry), Garth Pillsbury (police officer), Steve Brown (Dance M.C.), Darla Leroy (receptionist), J.R. Clarke (Morris), Frank Curcio (Mel), Laurel Barnett (Margaret), Charles Edwards (Stuart), Don Brodie (projectionist), Sheila Sisco (aspiring actress).

The Copper Scroll of Mary Magdalene (circa 2006)

Director: Larry Buchanan *Producer:* Larry Buchanan *Associate Producers:* George Costello, Stuart Lancaster *Assistant Directors:* Hammida Ben-Amar, Abdellatif Ben-Ammar *Executive Producer:* Kenneth Kreisel *Original Music:* Alex North *Cinematography:* Robert C. Jessup *Production Manager:* Steve Williams *Unit Coordinator:* Joreta C. Cherry, Michael B. Druxman (publicist, uncredited), a.k.a. *The Rebel Jesus, Live From the Dead Sea,* color, 35mm.

Cast: Gene Shane (Jesus), Garth Pillsbury (Quintar), Gilleigh McLain (Mary Magdalene), Jean Fadal (John the Baptist), Warren Hammack (Judas), Roberta Haynes (Mary the Mother), Rosalind Saunders (The Madam), Howard Rubin (Shammai).

Additional Credits

Armstrong Circle Theatre (1950), *The Men* (1950), *The Gunfighter* (1950) (performer)

The Gabby Hayes Show (1950) (performer, writer, musical director)

The Marrying Kind (1952) (assistant director)

Chapter Notes

Chapter 1

1. Larry Buchanan. *It Came from Hunger: Confessions of a Cinema Schlockmeister* (Jefferson, NC: McFarland, 1996), 12.
2. Ibid.
3. Ibid., 14.
4. Laura Mulvey. "Visual Pleasure and Narrative Cinema," in *Feminism and Film Theory*, ed. Constance Penley (New York: Routledge, 1988), 57.

Chapter 2

1. Larry Buchanan. *It Came from Hunger: Tales of a Cinema Schlockmeister* (Jefferson, NC: McFarland, 1996), 30.
2. Duncan Emrich. *Folklore on the American Land* (New York: Little, Brown, 1972), 23.
3. Buchanan, 132–133.
4. Buchanan, in personal correspondence with author.
5. Larry Buchanan. *The Trial of Lee Harvey Oswald/The Other Side of Bonnie & Clyde* (audio commentary, DVD special edition, Something Weird Video, 2003).

Chapter 3

1. Larry Buchanan. *Common Law Wife* (audio commentary, DVD special edition. Something Weird Video, 2003).
2. Ibid.
3. Ibid.
4. Larry Buchanan. *It Came from Hunger: Tales of a Cinema Schlockmeister* (Jefferson, NC: McFarland, 1996), 59.
5. Ibid., 60.
6. Hilariously, some of the newspaper advertisements for the film changed the source material to the fictitious "Erskine William's 'Diary of a Negro Maid'"!
7. Michael Price. "Larry Buchanan: The Life and Times of a Hungry Visionary," *Psychotronic Video Magazine* 24 (1997), 53.
8. Ibid., 53–54.
9. Buchanan. *It Came from Hunger*, 85–86.
10. Larry Buchanan. *The Other Side of Bonnie & Clyde* (audio commentary, DVD special edition, Something Weird Video, 2003).
11. Frank Hamer. *"I'm Frank Hamer"* (Pemberton, 1968), 122.
12. Although Jo Entreetee and Lucky Mosely are billed as the title characters, other press material bills Sonny Wayne and Bonnie Shefield as the outlaw pair. This contradiction likely reflects a casting change during production.
13. Buchanan. *The Other Side of Bonnie & Clyde*, audio commentary.
14. Ibid.
15. Buchanan. *It Came from Hunger*, 115
16. Buchanan. *The Other Side of Bonnie & Clyde*, audio commentary.
17. *Sex and the Animals* (1969) pressbook.
18. Ibid.
19. Price, 56.

Chapter 4

1. Betty Friedan. *The Feminine Mystique*, twentieth anniversary edition (New York: W.W. Norton, 1983), 380.
2. Larry Buchanan. *It Came from Hunger: Tales of a Cinema Schlockmeister* (Jefferson, NC: McFarland, 1996), 48.
3. Ibid.
4. Kate Millet. *Sexual Politics* (Berkeley, CA: Granada, 1969), 3.
5. Edwin Mullins. *The Painted Witch: How Western Artists Have Viewed the Sexuality of Women* (New York: Carroll & Graf, 1985), 60, 39.
6. Kenneth Turan and Stephen F. Zito. *Sinema: American Pornographic Films and the People Who Make Them* (New York: Praeger, 1974), 25.
7. The recent color DVD release of *The Naked Witch* by Something Weird Video features extended, full-nude bathing scenes, not seen in the slightly truncated black and white versions previously released to home video.
8. Friedan, 384–385.
9. Luckenbach, Texas, is currently a popular tourist

destination, owned and operated by singer Willie Nelson and featuring well-attended, yearly country and western concerts, a curious descendent of the "Saengerfests" of old.

Chapter 5

1. Doyle Greene. *Lips, Hips, Tits, Power: The Films of Russ Meyer* (London: Creation Books, 2004), 40.
2. Larry Buchanan. *It Came from Hunger: Tales of a Cinema Schlockmeister* (Jefferson, NC: McFarland & Company, 1996), 55.
3. Ibid.
4. Ibid., 58.
5. Ibid., 57.
6. Ibid., 58.
7. Felicia Feaster and Bret Wood. *Forbidden Fruit: The Golden Age of the Exploitation Film* (Baltimore: Midnight Marquee, 1999), 185.
8. Roland Barthes. "Striptease," in *Mythologies,* trans. Annette Lavers (New York: Hill and Wang, 1991), 84–87.
9. Bill Demar (sometimes billed Bill DeMar) is an intriguing figure in the Dallas entertainment netherworld. Demar (nee William D. Crowe, Jr.) began his show business career as a stage hypnotist, a talent he learned during a stint in the U.S. army. He apparently included the hypnotism as part of his stage act up until the time of the JFK assassination. In addition, Demar included a "memory act" as part of his performance, wherein he would recall objects and information invoked by club patrons. Demar later evolved into a popular ventriloquist and continues this aspect of his artistry to this day, offering books, seminars and video tapes on the art of ventriloquism. Demar was involved in the aftermath of the JFK assassination and also gave testimony to the Warren Commission which shines an inquisitive light on the production history of *Naughty Dallas*. At the time of the assassination, Demar claimed to reporters that he had seen Lee Harvey Oswald in the audience of Ruby's nightclub at one of his performances during the week of November 22, 1963, and claimed that Oswald was one of the participants in his "memory act" of the night in question. When Demar testified to the Warren Commission, he carefully avoided any reference to the hypnotism aspect of his performances and, as mentioned, dropped this part of his act shortly thereafter. As to why Demar is seen in *Naughty Dallas* doing only a tame musical-comedy routine, not his usual hypnotism act, is open to conjecture.
10. Breck Wall (nee Billy Wilson Ray) and Bill Fanning were entertainers who began as a team in the early 1960s, soon coming up with a musical-comedy act called "Bottoms Up," which premiered at the Adolphus Hotel in Dallas. By 1964, Wall and Fanning had migrated to Las Vegas, and "Bottoms Up" became a staple for years at the Castaway Hotel, running well into the 1970s. Due to his involvement with Jack Ruby and presence in the Dallas entertainment scene, Wall was among many entertainers subpoenaed for testimony by the Warren Commission investigating the assassination of John F. Kennedy. Wall's testimony regarding Ruby centered around the club owner's ongoing disputes with performer's unions, as well as personal grudges against rival club owners, including *Naughty Dallas*'s own Abe Weinstein. (See Elizabeth Foyt, "Stars Fill the Audience at 'Bottoms Up' Show,' *Las Vegas Sun,* September 06, 2000, archived at http://www.lasvegassun.com/sunbin/stories/text/2000/sep/06/510728233.html. Accessed on March 21, 2006.)

11. Anonymous. "Texas Tornado!," *Man's Adventure,* November 1957, 12.
12. The bikini, first introduced in France in the late 1940s, was seen as a sinister influence by "decadent" European interests on the morals of America's youth upon its introduction to the States circa 1960.
13. MR. HUBERT: Do you know who I mean when I say Jada, do you know who that person is?
   MR. CROWE: I met her once but I have never worked with her.
   MR. HUBERT: Where did you meet her?
   MR. CROWE: In Dallas.
   MR. HUBERT: Was she then working for Ruby?
   MR. CROWE: No.
   MR. HUBERT: Do you recall when you met her?
   MR. CROWE: Around November 30, maybe.
   MR. HUBERT: Of what year?
   MR. CROWE: At the same time I was there.
   MR. HUBERT: 1963?
   MR. CROWE: 1963.
   MR. HUBERT: You met her after the death of the president and after the death of Oswald?
   MR. CROWE: Yes.
   MR. HUBERT: Where did you meet her?
   MR. CROWE: I don't remember the name of the club. It begins with an *M,* upstairs private club, about 3 blocks from the Carousel.
   MR. HUBERT: She was playing there?
   MR. CROWE: No, she was shooting a film there.
   MR. HUBERT: What sort of a film was that?
   MR. CROWE: A film that Diamond Pictures was making.
   MR. HUBERT: Do you know what the subject of it was?
   MR. CROWE: A stripper in Dallas, I think.
   MR. HUBERT: Were you part of that film?
   MR. CROWE: I did a relief, a comedy relief segment.
   MR. HUBERT: That was about the thirtieth of November, you say?
   MR. CROWE: Approximately, I don't know for sure.
   MR. HUBERT: It lasted only a few days, I take it?
   MR. CROWE: A couple of days I know of.
   MR. HUBERT: You had not met her before?
   MR. CROWE: No.

(See "Warren Commission Hearings, Transcripts," archived at http://www.jfk-assassination.com/warren/wch/v01115/page101.php. Accessed on March 21, 2006.)
14. *The Official Warren Commission Report on the Assassination of President John F. Kennedy* (Garden City: Doubleday, 1964), 350.
15. Gary Cartwright. "Who Was Jack Ruby? How a Small-time Strip Joint Operator Ushered in America's Age of Violence," *Texas Monthly* (November 1975), archived at: http://www.texasmonthly.com/mag/issues/1975-11-01/feature.php. Accessed on October 5, 2006.
16. Ibid.
17. *Warren Commission Report,* 796.
18. Buchanan, *It Came from Hunger,* 59.

Chapter 6

1. Larry Buchanan. *It Came from Hunger: Confessions of a Cinema Schlockmeister* (Jefferson, NC: McFarland, 1996), 63
2. Ibid.
3. Mark Donald. "Good Time Charlie," *The Dallas Observer,* Thursday, December 23, 1999, archived at

http://www.dallasobserver.com/issues/1999-12-23/news/feature_5.html. Accessed on October 2, 2005.)
    4. Buchanan, 63.
    5. Larry Buchanan. *Common Law Wife* (audio commentary, DVD special edition, Something Weird Video, 2003).
    6. Ibid., 69.

Chapter 7

1. Barr McClellan. *Blood, Money & Power: How L.B.J. Killed J.F.K.* (Boston: Hanover House, 2003), xi.
2. Larry Buchanan. *The Trial of Lee Harvey Oswald* (audio commentary, Something Weird Video, 2003).
3. Ibid.
4. Larry Buchanan. *It Came from Hunger: Tales of a Cinema Schlockmeister* (Jefferson, NC: McFarland, 1996), 77.
5. Buchanan. *The Trial of Lee Harvey Oswald*, audio commentary.
6. George Edgley had been a real judge in England before coming to the States to work as an actor, and like Buchanan was an avid student of conspiracy theories.
7. Buchanan. *The Trial of Lee Harvey Oswald*, audio commentary.
8. Ibid.
9. Ibid.
10. Ibid.
11. Ibid.
12. McClellan, xiv.
13. Buchanan. *The Trial of Lee Harvey Oswald*, audio commentary.

Chapter 8

1. Kevin Heffernan. *Ghouls, Gimmicks, and Gold: Horror Films and the American Movie Business, 1953–1968* (Durham, NC: Duke University Press, 2004), 155.
2. Larry Buchanan. *The Trial of Lee Harvey Oswald* (audio commentary, special edition DVD, Something Weird Video, 2003).
3. Larry Buchanan. "Of Zontar and Azalea Street," *Horror-Wood Online Magazine* interview by Rob Craig, March 23, 2003, archived at: http://www.horror-wood.com.zontar.html. Accessed March 23, 2003.
4. Larry Buchanan. *It Came from Hunger: Tales of a Cinema Schlockmeister* (Jefferson, NC: McFarland, 1996), 89, 121.
5. This average is based on a sample survey of production budgets taken from various sources, such as the Internet Movie Database (http://www.imdb.com), and including the following films: *The Flesh Eaters* (1964), $170,000; *The Navy vs. the Night Monsters* (1966), $178,000; *The Pit and the Pendulum* (1962), $200,000; *The Time Travelers* (1964), $250,000; *Beach Party* (1963), $350,000; *The Wild Angels* (1967), $360,000; *Bikini Beach* (1964), $600,000; *Wild in the Streets* (1968) $1,000,000.
6. Buchanan. *It Came from Hunger*, 89.
7. Although some have noted marked similarities between *Curse of the Swamp Creature* and Edward L. Cahn's *Voodoo Woman* (1957), the differences in scenario outweigh the parallels, and it cannot be considered a remake. If anything, Buchanan took the rudimentary framework of *Voodoo Woman* and fashioned a new screenplay around it.
8. Buchanan. *The Trial of Lee Harvey Oswald*, audio commentary.

9. Ronald Stein, an accomplished film score composer, and studying for a time under classical giant Paul Hindemith, is intimately familiar with the classical tradition in film music. His movie scores, primarily for B-movies of the 1950s and 1960s, are consistently haunting, thrilling and evocative, and he surely deserves a place among the composer giants of the day such as Ferde Grofe and Bernard Herrmann. In *Zontar*, Buchanan was apparently given free rein to mix and match "stock" cues from earlier Stein scores including *The She-Creature* (1956), *Invasion of the Saucer Men* (1957), and even *Zontar's* prototype, *It Conquered the World*. The resultant musical collage is extremely evocative and, as mentioned before, the overriding theme is of a curious enervation, a sense of passive despair and melancholy. Stein's compilation-score gives *Zontar* much of its emotional strength. It would appear that the music from the Azalea telefilms, although primarily scored by Ronald Stein from existing library tracks, was to some extent "lifted," that is, used without proper permission. Cue sheets on the Azalea telefilms name cues which were not in the finished films, as well as cues erroneously credited to other people such as Al Simms, a music producer for Bell Records. Additionally, Stein became aware in the early 1970s of AIP's use of his library cues without his permission. It may thus be nearly impossible to identify all of the source music used in the Azalea telefilms. (See John Takis, "Invasion of the Score Man!" *Film Score Monthly* 6, no. 9 (October/November 2001): 18–21.)

Chapter 9

1. The props in the surveillance sequence primarily consist of film processing equipment, so it is likely this scene was filmed at the Jamieson Film Laboratory in Dallas, a business with which Buchanan had a long history.
2. Larry Buchanan. *It Came from Hunger: Tales of a Cinema Schlockmeister* (Jefferson, NC: McFarland, 1996), 80.
3. Carl Sagan. "The Saucerian Cult: An Astronomer's Interpretation," *Scientific Review* (August 6, 1966): 50–52.

Chapter 10

1. It may well be pondered why Buchanan, penultimate Texan, didn't retain the original line from *It Conquered the World*: "You look like a man who's just inherited Texas!"

Chapter 12

1. Larry Buchanan. *It Came from Hunger: Tales of a Cinema Schlockmeister* (Jefferson, NC: McFarland & Company, 1996), 100.
2. Ibid., 99.
3. Ibid., 100.
4. Ibid., 101.
5. Sigmund Freud. *Civilization and Its Discontents*, trans. James Strachey (New York: W.W. Norton, 1961), 66.
6. Christopher J. Jarmick. "Larry Buchanan: Fast, Cheap & Under Control," *Brutarian*, Fall 2005, 44.
7. Buchanan, *It Came from Hunger*, 102.
8. Larry Buchanan with Rob Craig. "Of Zontar and Azalea Street," *Horror-Wood* online magazine, archived at: http://www.horror-wood.com/zontar.html. Accessed March 1, 2006.

Chapter 13

1. Filmed in murky black and white and boasting significant atmosphere, *Day the World Ended* stands as one of the best thrillers of the Cold-War era. *Day* opens where most films of this type end, with the literal end of the world. The superpowers have unleashed the atom bomb on the world, and human civilization, for all intents and purposes, is ended. Seven survivors of this man-made holocaust manage to find their way to a lone house in a remote unnamed valley, where the deadly atomic mist has not yet penetrated. The survivors, led by a retired military man (Paul Birch), attempt to remain rational while battling threats internal and external, the most significant being a gruesome mutant who stalks the tiny human fortress. Among many outstanding features in *Day* is the atomic mutant, a magnificent creation by f/x whiz Paul Blaisdell. With its grimacing sneer and triad of bulging eyes, Blaisdell fashioned one of the first of his indelible, fanciful monsters which embodied in their facial sculpting the evocation of *hate* and *rage*, making the creatures as much *character* as *object*, highly symbolic of Mankind's monstrous collective ego, thus more frightening and memorable than many other "horror creatures" of the era. Also outstanding is *Day*'s haunting, melancholy score by Ronald Stein, one of his best early compositions and one of his only uses of the then-popular theramin instrument. In *Day* Corman introduces subjects which he would virtually fetishize in subsequent work, most significantly the strange, symbiotic relationship between female intuition and telepathy, and the troubled reality of mind control versus the psychological "fiction" of paranoia. *Day* is an intense, dark and grim melodrama which did extremely well at the box office and helped the fledgling American International Pictures (temporarily called "American Releasing Corporation" for legal reasons) get off to an auspicious start.

2. The actual photograph shows a young Buchanan in a striped blazer. This in-joke is more than mere self-aggrandizement, for in *2889*'s prototype, *Day the World Ended*, Lori Nelson's boyfriend is depicted by director Roger Corman in a similar photograph.

3. It is significant that Buchanan named the stripper in *2889* "Jada," after real-life exotic dancer Jada, nee Janet Conforti, who performed in Dallas at the time and figured prominently in Buchanan's exploitation opus, *Naughty Dallas* (1964).

4. Jonathan M. Weisgall. *Operation Crossroads: The Atomic Tests at Bikini Atoll* (Annapolis: Naval Institute Press, 1994), 120.

5. Ibid., 158.

6. Larry Buchanan. *It Came from Hunger: Tales of a Cinema Schlockmeister* (Jefferson, NC: McFarland, 1996), 106

7. An interesting side-note to the history of *2889* is its synchronistic relation to a pop music hit. In 1969, RCA Records released a dystopian pop ballad called "In the Year 2525," created by a folk-rock duo from Nebraska called "Zager & Evans." At first blush it would appear that the title for the song was borrowed from Buchanan's 1967 film, which had received wide play on national television by the time the pop song hit the national airwaves in June 1969. Yet other sources claim that Danny Zager and Rick Evans originally wrote their tune in 1964, predating Buchanan's film by several years. Adding confusion to the issue is the fact that Zager & Evans were performing the song in and around the Texas/Nebraska area during the mid–1960s. The repetitive, dirge-like song details how life will deteriorate and become more automated and impersonal as the years, decades and centuries progress. Although no particular plot points from *2889* are used in "In the Year 2525," the general despairing air of the song, with its vapid depiction of a mechanized, totalitarian future, was perhaps inspired by the grim postwar setting of Buchanan's film. Although the possibility exists that the two cultural documents are in fact coincidental in title, the allusion to synchronicity is fascinating, and a definitive statement on any influences between the two works would be welcome. (See Joel Whitburn, *The Billboard Book of Top 40 Hits,* 6th ed. [New York: Billboard Books. 1996], 669.)

Chapter 14

1. *The She-Creature* is based on the notorious "Bridey Murphy" case of the 1950s. In 1952 hypnotist Morey Bernstein claimed that he was able to "regress" his subject, one Virginia Tighe, to reveal an alleged past life, in which she was "Bridey Murphy," a young Irish woman who lived in the nineteenth century. According to Bernstein, Tighe-as-Murphy was able to recall significant historical details of the period. Bernstein published his accounting of this unusual experiment in 1956 in a book entitled *The Search for Bridey Murphy,* which became an instant bestseller and started a controversial, if short-lived obsession with hypnotic regression. (See Paul Edwards, *Reincarnation: A Critical Examination* (Amherst, NY: Prometheus Books, 1996), 72–74.) *The She-Creature* is a strong melodrama with very dark overtones. It illustrates, quite brutally, the darker side of the postwar domestic couple. The "She-Creature" itself is a magnificent man-in-suit creation by an unsung genius of 1950s film-creature design, Paul Blaisdell. Here, Blaisdell fashioned what may have been his masterpiece, a huge, hulking beast with allusions to both the amphibious sea-creature and the prehistoric reptile. One noteworthy touch is a gaping mouth-like orifice in the creature's mid-section, lined on both sides with monstrous teeth, an expressionist depiction of Woman's "all-devouring vagina" as seen by fearful Man. The Blaisdell touch is also seen in the "She-Creature's" face, grimacing and full of rage, and so emblematic of the violence and anger which the creature's existence represents.

2. Michel de Montaigne. *Selected Essays,* trans. Donald M. Frame (New York. Walter J. Blake 1943), xxix.

Chapter 15

1. Michael Price. "Larry Buchanan: The Life and Times of a Hungry Visionary," *Psychotronic Video Magazine* 24 (1997), 58.

Chapter 16

1. Larry Buchanan. *It Came from Hunger: Tales of a Cinema Schlockmeister* (Jefferson, NC: McFarland, 1996), 121.

2. Buchanan renamed his title character "Charles Arthur Floyd," possibly to avoid potential legal troubles.

3. Buchanan, 123.

4. Michael Wallis. *Pretty Boy: The Life and Times of Charles Arthur Floyd* (New York: St. Martin's. 1992), 135.
5. Ibid., 186.
6. Ibid., 338.
7. Michael Price. "Larry Buchanan: The Life and Times of a Hungry Visionary," *Psychotronic Video Magazine* 24 (1997), 56.
8. Christopher J. Jarmick. "Larry Buchanan: Fast, Cheap & Under Control," *Brutarian*, Fall 2005, 59.

Chapter 17

1. Larry Buchanan. *It Came from Hunger: Tales of a Cinema Schlockmeister* Jefferson, NC: McFarland, 1996, 127.
2. Christopher J. Jarmick. "Larry Buchanan: Fast, Cheap & Under Control," *Brutarian*, Fall 2005, 59.
3. Buchanan, *It Came from Hunger*, 128.
4. Ibid., 127.
5. Gilles Deleuze. *Coldness and Cruelty* (New York: Zone Books, 1989), 59–60.
6. Jacques Lacan. *Ecrits: A Selection,* trans. Alan Sheridan (New York: W.W. Norton, 1977), 66–67.

Chapter 18

1. Larry Buchanan. *It Came from Hunger: Tales of a Cinema Schlockmeister* (Jefferson, NC: McFarland, 1996), 143.
2. Michael Price. "Larry Buchanan: The Life and Times of a Hungry Visionary," *Psychotronic Video Magazine* 24 (1997), 56.
3. Jacque Lacan. *Ecrits: A Selection*, trans. Alan Sheridan (New York: W.W. Norton, 1977), 5.
4. Laura Mulvey. "Visual Pleasure and Narrative Cinema," in *Feminism and Film Theory*, ed. Constance Penley (New York: Routledge, 1988), 58.
5. This disturbing scene, cut from the theatrical release of *Goodbye* and appearing only on the DVD, is another example of Buchanan addressing dark historical subjects which mainstream cinema rarely addresses. The history of the "snuff film" has been admittedly controversial. Much effort has been spent recently in conveying the wishful notion that the phenomenon of the "snuff film" is primarily an urban legend, and few if any such films were produced. Others, including many in the entertainment industry, have long maintained that this most diabolical exploitation subgenre does exist, and there is a thriving underground industry in filmed slaughter. Buchanan, for one, seems to know whereof he speaks. In a 1995 interview, he states: "I have a script which is the result of my having seen a snuff film in Rio in which they killed children. The children were bought from their parents and killed and — as an Aquarius — it just boils my blood." (See Kris Gilpin. "The Larry Buchanan Innerview," *Bijouflix*, 1995, archived at http://www.bijouflix.com/innerviews/buchanan_innerview4.htm. Accessed on May 6, 2006.)

Chapter 19

1. Michael Price. "Larry Buchanan: The Life and Times of a Hungry Visionary," *Psychotronic Video Magazine* 24 (1997), 56, 58.
2. Larry Buchanan. *It Came from Hunger: Tales of a Cinema Schlockmeister* (Jefferson, NC: McFarland, 1996), 158.
3. Ibid., 159–160.
4. Allen Edwardes and R.E.L. Masters. *The Cradle of Erotica* (New York: Lancer, 1962), 84.
5. In actuality, the premiere audience responded enthusiastically, without any goading from Hollywood censors. (See Charles Higham. *"Howard Hughes: The Secret Life"* [New York: G.P. Putnam's, 1993], 48.)
6. Higham, 48.
7. The same obscuring of history regarding Howard Hughes is still with us, as witness Martin Scorcese's preposterous *The Aviator* (2005), in which Hughes once again is portrayed as a guileless, charismatic man-child with a gleam in his eye and a heart full of gold. Thanks to the absurd casting of Leonardo DeCaprio as the mad millionaire, the illusion of authenticity was even further shattered, making Scorcese's character of Hughes a comic caricature of a sullen teenage idol. Even Scorcese's bloated f/x budget couldn't hide the fact that *The Aviator* was a story hung on the slimmest of historical and narrative threads.

Chapter 20

1. Larry Buchanan. *It Came from Hunger: Tales of a Cinema Schlockmeister* (Jefferson, NC: McFarland, 1996), 161.
2. Ibid., 163.

Chapter 21

1. Larry Buchanan. *It Came from Hunger: Tales of a Cinema Schlockmeister* (Jefferson, NC: McFarland, 1996), 166.

Chapter 22

1. Larry Buchanan. *It Came from Hunger: Tales of a Cinema Schlockmeister* (Jefferson, NC: McFarland, 1996), 171.
2. William Sullivan worked for many years at "The Bureau," and for a time was its third-ranking official, under J. Edgar Hoover. He was put in charge of the agency's Division Five, a covert operation designed to harass the New Left. After Hoover's Death, Sullivan worked directly for Nixon, in increasingly illegal surveillance operations. Sullivan was shot dead in 1977 while hunting. An inquest concluded that he had been shot accidentally by another hunter. At the time of his death Sullivan was scheduled to appear before the House Select Committee on Assassinations, and many feel his death was murder, more damage control on the part of a beleaguered FBI. Sullivan had been writing a book dealing with his experiences in the Bureau, a book which was published after his death. Called *The Bureau: My Thirty Years with the FBI* (New York: Pinnacle Books, 1982), the book was critical of many aspects of the bureau, including Hoover. (See "William S. Sullivan," archived at http://www.spartacus.schoolnet.co.uk/JFKSullivan.html. Accessed May 25, 2006.)
3. According to some sources, this event may have been apocryphal. Morrison may have only threatened to expose himself, and this in itself was enough to incite the ire of law enforcement officials.

4. Some twenty years later, Dr. John Bannister, the doctor who treated Jimi Hendrix at the St. Mary Abbot's Hospital, claimed that the rock star died from drowning in red wine, an assertion clearly suggesting murder. Although his alcohol blood level was low, Hendrix' lungs were filled with liquid.

5. Joplin was indeed found to have been killed by a lethal dose of heroin. According to the official report, she did not accidentally overdose, but injected a lethal batch of heroin which also killed others the same weekend. "According to Sunshine, the dope killed eight other people in L.A. that weekend." (See Alice Echols, *Scars of Sweet Paradise: The Life and Times of Janis Joplin* [New York: Metropolitan, 1999], 300.)

Chapter 23

1. Larry Buchanan. *It Came from Hunger: Tales of a Cinema Schlockmeister* (Jefferson, NC: McFarland, 1996), 173.

2. Sir Laurence Olivier. "The Prince and the Showgirl," in *All the Available Light: A Marilyn Monroe Reader*, ed. Yona Zeldis McDonough (New York: Touchstone, 2002), 150.

Bibliography

Barthes, Roland. "Striptease." In *Mythologies*. Translated by Annette Lavers. New York: Hill and Wang, 1991.
Buchanan, Larry. *It Came from Hunger: Tales of a Cinema Schlockmeister*. Jefferson, NC: McFarland, 1996.
Caro, Robert. *The Years of Lyndon Johnson: The Path to Power*. New York: Alfred A. Knopf, 1983.
Cartwright, Gary. "Who Was Jack Ruby?" *Texas Monthly*, November 1975. http://www.texasmonthly.com/mag/issues/1975-11-01/feature.php (accessed October 5, 2006).
Colgan, Mark K. "When a Mysterious Death Is No Longer Mysterious." *Kennedy Assassination Chronicles* 6, no. 1 (Spring 2000).
Craig, Rob. "The Cheap Chillers of Larry Buchanan." *Horror-Wood Online Magazine*, September 1, 2001. http://www.horror-wood.com/buchanan.html.
____. "Of Zontar and Azalea Street." Interview with Larry Buchanan. *Horror-Wood Online Magazine*, March 23, 2003. http://www.horror-wood.com/zontar.html.
Deleuze, Gilles. *Coldness and Cruelty*. New York: Zone Books, 1989.
Dye, David. *Child and Youth Actors: Filmographies of Their Entire Careers, 1914–1985*. Jefferson, NC: McFarland, 1988.
Echols, Alice. *Scars of Sweet Paradise: The Life and Times of Janis Joplin*. New York: Metropolitan, 1999.
Edwardes, Allen, and R.E.L. Masters. *The Cradle of Erotica*. New York: Lancer, 1962.
Edwards, Paul. *Reincarnation: A Critical Examination*. Amherst, NY: Prometheus, 1996.
Emrich, Duncan. *Folklore on the American Land*. New York: Little, Brown, 1972.
Feaster, Felicia, and Bret Wood. *Forbidden Fruit: The Golden Age of the Exploitation Film*. Baltimore: Midnight Marquee, 1999.
Foyt, Elizabeth. "Stars Fill the Audience at 'Bottoms Up' Show." *Las Vegas Sun*, September 6, 2000. http://www.lasvegassun.com/sunbin/stories/text/2000/sep/06/510728233.html (accessed March 21, 2006).
Freud, Sigmund. *Civilization and Its Discontents*. Translated by James Strachey. New York: W.W. Norton, 1961.
Friedan, Betty. *The Feminine Mystique*. 20th anniversary edition. New York: W.W. Norton, 1983.
Gilpin, Kris. "The Larry Buchanan Innerview." *Bijouflix* (1995). http://www.bijouflix.com/innerviews/buchanan_innerview1.htm (accessed May 6, 2006).
Greene, Doyle. *Lips, Hips, Tits and Power: The Films of Russ Meyer*. London: Creation Books, 2004.
Hamer, Frank. *"I'm Frank Hamer."* London: Pemberton Publishing, 1968.
Heffernan, Kevin. *Ghouls, Gimmicks, and Gold: Horror Films and the American Movie Business, 1953–1968*. Durham, NC: Duke University Press, 2004.
Higham, Charles. *Howard Hughes: The Secret Life*. New York: Putnam, 1993.
Hunter, Diana, and Alice Anderson. *Jack Ruby's Girls*. Atlanta: Hallux, 1970.
Jarmick, Christopher J. "Larry Buchanan: Fast, Cheap and Under Control." *Brutarian*, Fall 2005.
Lacan, Jacques. *Ecrits: A Selection*. Translated by Alan Sheridan. New York: W.W. Norton, 1977.
Marcuse, Herbert. *Eros and Civilization*. New York: Vintage, 1955.
____. *One Dimensional Man*. Boston: Beacon, 1964.
McClellan, Barr. *Blood, Money and Power: How L.B.J. Killed J.F.K*. New York: Hanover House, 2003.

Millet, Kate. *Sexual Politics*. Berkeley, CA: Granada, 1969.

Montaigne, Michel. *Selected Essays*. Translated by Donald M. Frame. New York: Walter J. Blake, 1943.Mullins, Edwin. *The Painted Witch: How Western Artists Have Viewed the Sexuality of Women*. New York: Carroll & Graf, 1985.

Mulvey, Laura. "Visual Pleasure and Narrative Cinema." In *Feminism and Film Theory*. Edited by Constance Penley. New York: Routledge, 1988.

Official Warren Commission Report on the Assassination of President John. F. Kennedy. Garden City, NY: Doubleday, 1964.

Olivier, Laurence. "The Prince and the Showgirl." In *All the Available Light: A Marilyn Monroe Reader*. Edited by Yona Zeldis McDonough. New York: Touchstone, 2002.

Penley, Constance. "The Lady Doesn't Vanish: Feminism and Film Theory." In *Feminism and Film Theory*. Edited by Constance Penley. New York: Routledge, 1988.

Price, Michael. "Larry Buchanan: The Life and Times of a Hungry Visionary." *Psychotronic Video Magazine* 24, 1997.

Sagan, Carl. "The Saucerian Cult: An Astronomer's Interpretation." *Scientific Review*, August 6, 1966.

Sarris, Andrew. "Notes on the Auteur Theory in 1962." In *Film Theory and Criticism: Introductory Reading*. 2d ed. Edited by Gerald Mast and Marshall Cohen. New York: Oxford, 1979.

Steele, Phillip W., and Marie Barrow Scoma. *The Family Story of Bonnie & Clyde*. Gretna, LA: Pelican, 2000.

Sullivan, William. *The Bureau: My Thirty Years in Hoover's FBI*. New York: Pinnacle, 1982.

Takis, John. "Invasion of the Score Man!" *Film Score Monthly* 6, no. 9 (October/November, 2001).

Turan, Kenneth, and Stephen F. Zito. *Sinema: American Pornographic Films and the People Who Make Them*. New York: Praeger, 1974.

Tyler, Parker. *Magic and Myth of the Movies*. New York: Simon & Schuster, 1970.

Wallis, Michael. *Pretty Boy: The Life and Times of Charles Arthur Floyd*. New York: St. Martin's, 1992.

"Warren Commission Hearings, Transcripts." http://www.jfk-assassination.com/warren/wch/v01115/page101.php (accessed March 21, 2006).

Weaver, Tom. *Return of the B Science Fiction and Horror Heroes*. Jefferson, NC: McFarland, 2000.

Weisgall, Jonathan M. *Operation Crossroads: The Atomic Tests at Bikini Atoll*. Annapolis: Naval Institute Press, 1994.

Whitburn, Joel. *The Billboard Book of Top 40 Hits*. 6th ed. New York: Billboard Books, 1996.

"William S. Sullivan." http://www.spartacus.schoolnet.co.uk/JFKSullivan.html (accessed May 25, 2006).

Zirbel, Craig I. *The Texas Connection: The Assassination of John F. Kennedy*. Scottsdale, AZ: The Texas Connection Company, 1991.

Index

Numbers in ***bold italics*** represent pages with photographs.

A-bomb tests 136
ABC Television network 77, 78, 147
Adler, Judy ***65***
Adolphus Hotel 248ch5n10
Adorno, Theodor 144, 157
advertising industry 59
Agar, John 17, 77, 79, 111, ***118***, 120
AIDS 227
alcoholism, in Buchanan films 137, 139, 142, 143, 173
Aldrich, Robert 168
Alexander, Claude 33, 41
Alexander, Jeff 110, ***112***, ***118***, 172
Alexander, William 42
Allen, Dede 25
Allen, Ethan 173
American International Pictures 16, 23, 28, 64, 65, 67, 84, 96, 171, 144, 250ch13n1
American International Television 17, 84, 96, 76, 77, 79, 122, 146
American Releasing Corporation 250ch13n1
Anderson, Max 21
anima & animus (Jung) 40, 41
animals, exploitation of 145
"Animatronics" 210
Antonioni, Michelangelo 3, 54, 55, 129
Apache Gold see *Grubstake*
Archer, Eugene 64
Arkoff, Samuel Z. 23, 28, 64, 171
artistic appropriation 83
Asher, William 8

Ashley, John 79, 84, 87, ***94***
Athas, Kim 43, 49–50
atheism 107
Athens Strip Club 126
Attack of the Crab Monsters 84
Australian Pleistocene Man 203
auteur theory 8
"automatic pilot" 198, 200
L'Aventurra 54
The Aviator 251ch19n7
Avnet, Jon 132
The Azalea Pictures 16, 17, 23, 76–83, 89, 100, 120, 132, 133, 137, 141, 142, 144, 151, 158, 159, 170, 176, 210, 249ch8n9

B-52 Superfortress (aircraft) 124, 219
B-Western genre 6, 15, 142
babyboomers 80
Baghdad After Midnight 42
Baird, Beulah 176
Baker, Norma Jean 44, 47, 184–192, 227–229
Baldwin, Sidney 42
Bannister, Dr. John 252ch22n4
Barnes, Susanna 219
Barr, Candy 43
Barrow, Clyde 23, 25
Barthes, Roland 47
Batman (TV series) 147
Beach Party 249ch8n5
The Beast from 20,000 Fathoms 209
Beatty, Warren 25, 26

Bennett, Jack 85, 89, 108, 121, 137
Bergman, Ingmar 3, 8, 177
Bernstein, Morey 250ch14n1
Bertoya, Paul 181
Bewitched (TV series) 39
Beyond the Doors 36, 58, 74, 135, 210, 218–225, ***221***, ***224***, 232, 235
bikini 248ch5n12
Bikini Atoll 135
Bikini Beach 249ch8n5
Birch, Paul 250ch13n1
Birds Do It, Bees Do It 29
black empowerment 110, 119, 120
Black Like Me 23
Blasidell, Paul 84, 96, 250ch13n1, 250ch14n1
Blood, Money & Power: How LBJ Killed JFK (McClellan) 67
Bloody Mama 171, 172
Bloom, Lindsay 193, 195, ***199***, ***200***, 201
Bogdanovich, Peter 76
Bonne, Shirley 161, ***162***
Bonnie & Clyde 5, 28
Bonnie & Clyde (1967) 25, 28, 171, 172
The Bonnie Parker Story 28
Booth, Libby 21, 35, ***36***
Born Free 29
Borzage, Frank 3, 5
Bosch, Heironymus 33
"Bottoms Up" (Las Vegas Revue) 248ch5n10

255

Brahms, Johannes 83
Bram Stoker's Dracula 202
Brecht, Bertolt 69
"Bridey Murphy" 250ch14n1
Bridge, Desmond 173
Brown & Root 82
Bruns, Victor 177
"Bubba Justice" 73, 75
Buchanan, Barry 210, 211
Buchanan, Dee 210, 213
Buchanan, Jane 210
Buchanan, Jeff 210
Buchanan, Larry 4–8, 11, 13, 20, 44, 233–234, **234**, 249ch9n1; autobiography 143, 202, 207, 208; and Azalea Pictures 77, 78, 84, 249ch8n9; *Beyond the Doors* 218, 223; *A Bullet for Pretty Boy* 171, 172; childhood 5, **6**, 9, 11; father 5, 8, 28, 171, 172; *Free, White & 21* 53, 63–66; *Goodbye, Norma Jean* 184, 187; *Goodnight, Sweet Marilyn* 226, 227, 232; *Hughes & Harlow: Angels in Hell* 193, 194, 196; *In the Year 2889* 250ch13n2, 250ch13n3; labeled conspiracy theorist 218; *The Loch Ness Horror* 209, 210, 213, 216; as male model 6; *Mars Needs Women* 132; mother 8, 9, 234, 235; *The Naked Witch* 41, 43; as narrator 33, 34, 129; *Naughty Dallas* 48, 51; *The Other Side of Bonnie & Clyde* 28; as performer 3, **4**, 89; *Sex and the Animals* 31; *Strawberries Need Rain* 177, **180**; as television's first singing cowboy 6, 11, 12; *The Trial of Lee Harvey Oswald* 67, 68, 73
Buchanan, Randy 210
Buckner Orphans Home 5, 6, 234
A Bullet for Pretty Boy 27, 28, 36, 77, 170, 171–176, **174, 175**, 177
The Bureau: My Thirty Years with the FBI (Sullivan) 251ch22n2
burlesque, in film 42, 46, 47, 50, 51
Burlesque in Harlem 42
Burner, Texas 159
Burroughs, William 199
Butch Cassidy and the Sundance Kid 172

Caddo Lakes 20, 112
Cahn, Edward L. 77, 110, 249ch8n7
Caldwell, Erskine 21

Camp, Joe 18
Cannes Film Festival 184, 202
Cannom, Greg 202
capitalism 149, 150, 173, 161
Carne, Marcel 7, 177
The Carousel Club 43, 45, 51, 52, 248ch5n13
Carr, Camilla 173
Cartwright, Gary 51
Castaway Hotel 248ch5n10
Castle, William 62
Central Intelligence Agency (CIA) 4, 230
Chariots of the Gods 217
"Charles Arthur Floyd" 172
Chatman, Gregory Allen 219
Chesney, Peter 210
childbirth footage 30
Children of Paradise 7, 177
Chisos Hills, Texas 14
Christianity 106; angel of death 97, 108; baptism ritual 173
cinéma vérité 220
Civil Rights era 55, 123
Claire, Adele 87
"Clan Buchanan" 10, 216
Clark, Dick 171
Clark, Edward 75
Club Montmarte 43, 48, 51
Coates, Phyllis 232
Cocteau, Jean 3, 7
Cole, Jack 47, 50
Colony Club 43, 47
Columbia Pictures 29
Columbus, Chris 202
Comanche Crossing 16–17
Comanche Indians 17
Common Law Wife 20–21, **22**, 112, 159
Conforti, Janet *see* Jada
Conway, Gary 217
Cook, Sofia 26
Cooper, Meriam C. 209
The Copper Scroll of Mary Magdalene see The Rebel Jesus
Coppola, Francis Ford 76, 202
CORE (Congress of Racial Equality) 55
Corman, Roger 3, 7, 23, 76, 77, 96, 133, 171, 250ch13n1
counterculture movement 123, 221, 222
couple logic, in Buchanan films 81, 107, 183
The Cowboy 7, 13–14, 16
Craig, Yvonne 122, **132**
Cranshaw, Pat 125
The Creature from the Black Lagoon 81
Creature of Destruction 58, 77, 81, 121, 144–158, **145, 149, 151**,

159, 166, 170, 177, 203, 209, 212
Crowe, William D. *see* DeMar, Bill
culture industry 184, 228
Curse of the Swamp Creature 77, 81, 110–121, **112, 114, 118, 120**, 249ch8n7

Dallas (TV series) 23
Dallas, Texas 5, 13, 16, 17, 41, 248ch5n13, 249ch9n1, 250ch13n3; in *Free White and 21* 53, 55, 56; in *Naughty Dallas* 42–46, 48, 51, 52; in *The Trial of Lee Harvey Oswald* 67–70, 73, 75
Dano, Royal 195
Dante's Inferno 164
Davis, Chet 87, **128**
Davis, Tony 53, 54, 63
The Day the Earth Stood Still 96
Day the World Ended 77, 133, 135, 136, 138, 140, 141, 142, 143, 250ch13n1, 250ch13n2
Dead Sea Scrolls 17
"dead space," in Buchanan films 54, 70, 111, 129
Death of a Salesman (1951) 14
DeCaprio, Leonardo 251ch19n7
Delaney, Pat **145**, 146, **149**, 157, 79, **99, 101**, 108, 130
Deleuze, Giles 181
DeMar, Bill 48, 51, 52, 248ch5n9, 248ch5n13
De Montaigne, Michel 102, 146, 156
Denning, Richard 143
de Sade, Marquis 16
Il Deserto Rosso 54
Dexter, Maury 176
Diamond Pictures 51, 248ch5n13
Diary of a Chambermaid (Mirbeau) 23
Diary of a Negro Maid 247ch3n6
Dies Irae 82
Dinero Productions 23
Director's line of sight 107
Disney, Walt 210
Dr. Strangelove 124
Doherty, Charla 134, **141**
Don Quixote (Cervantes) 182
The Donna Reed Show (TV series) 143
The Doors (1990) 74, 225
Double Whoopee 195
Douglas Aircraft 6
Down on Us 218; see also *Beyond the Doors*
Dracula (1932) 82
drive-in theatres 20

Duckworth, Wanda 65
Duggan, Cal 126
Dunaway, Faye 25, 26
Dwain, Hal *see* Hoffman, Harold
Dwain, Harold *see* Hoffman, Harold

Eden, Barbara 32
Edgley George 21, 55, 68, **74**, 79, 128, 249ch7n6
Eisenstein, Sergei 57
Elm Street, Dallas 68, **70**
Emrich, Duncan 14
Les Enfants du Paradis see Children of Paradise
entertainment industry, in Buchanan films 9, 184, 187, 193, 194, 201, 227, 228, 234
Entreetee, Jo 247ch3n12
Eros & Thanatos (Freud) 123, 131, 223
"Erskine Williams" 247ch3n6
Evans, Rick 250ch13n7
evolution 115, 116
exhibitionism 205, 206
existential alienation, in Buchanan films 47, 80, 129 160, 168, 191
exploitation film genre 10, 20, 28, 30, 32, 42, 46, 47, 51, 57, 59, 78
The Eye Creatures 41, 58, 77, 81, 84–95, **86, 88, 90**, 110, 131, 135, 188, 194, 199, 216

F-16 (aircraft) 124
factory farms 145
"Fair Play for Cuba" 71
Fairchild, Morgan 173
Falcon International Pictures 31, 171
Fanning, Bill 248ch5n10
Faulkner, William 21
FBI (Federal Bureau of Investigation) 219, 221, 222, 251ch22n2
Feagin, Hugh 134, 172
Fear and Desire 7
The Feminine Mystique (Freidan) 32, 115
feminism, in Buchanan films 33, 36, 39, 40, 41, 82, 98, 105, 115, 122, 157, 183, 203, 205, 217
feminist movement 51
fetishism 38
film noir 42
The Flesh Eaters 249ch8n5
Fletcher, Neil 104, **106**, 124, 147, 134, **135**, 142
Fly-n-Fish hotel 111, 120

Ford, John 120
Forte, Fabian 171, 172, **174, 175**
The Fortune Cookie 126
fourth-wall moments, in Buchanan films 69, 74, 150, 227, 228
fragmentation of the self 185, 228
Frankenstein (1932) 82
Free, White & 21 16, 21, 23, 31, 53–65, **56, 57, 60**, 72, 110, 155, 159, 217
Freidan, Betty 32, 36, 40, 115
Freudian symbology 40, 123
Fried Green Tomatoes 132
Fright Night 131
Frisco Mansion 23
Frisco, Texas 23
Frost, Sarah Jean 186
Fuller, Sam 3, 7

The Gabby Hayes Show (TV series) 6, 13
The Garden of Earthly Delights (Bosch) 33
Gayle, Monica 177, 178, **180**
Gemini (astrological sign) 229
gender and sex roles 33, 39, 40
General Dynamics 82
Generation gap 135, 210, 216, 223
Gibbons, Louisiana 25, 26
Gibson, Mel 17
Glass House 7
Glenn, Robert 174
Godzilla, King of the Monsters 209
Goodbye, Norma Jean 36, 44, 47, 50, 56, 184–192, **189, 191**, 193, 194, 199, 210, 217, 226, 228, 229, 251ch18n5
Goodnight, Sweet Marilyn 36, 44, 47, 185, 217, 225, 226–232
gore in film 84
government conspiracy in Buchanan films 85, 94, 95, 111, 112, 185, 209, 213, 217, 218, 225, 226, 232
grassy knoll (Dallas) 68, 69, 75
Grauman's Chinese Theatre 195
Great Depression of the 1930s 25, 173, 193
Green Acres (TV series) 163
Greene, Doyle 42
Greenwich Village 26
grindhouses 20
Il Grito 54
Grofe, Ferde 249ch8n9
Grubstake 14–16, **15**

Halliburton 82
Halperin brothers 110
Hamer, Frank 25, 26

Hamilton, "Pretty Boy" Floyd 5, 27, **27**, 28, 171–176
Hamilton, Roy 27
Hammack, Warren 23, 85, 126
Hansen, Greta Mae 54
Hanson, Preston 188, 213
Harbor Lights 176
Harlow, Jean 193–197, 200, 201
Harrington, Curtis 76
Hass, Hugo 8
Hatcher, Harley 172
Hawks, Howard 196, 197
The Hay Wagon (Bosch) 33
Haydn, Franz 83
Hayes, Will 195, 198
Haynes, Michael 173
Hee Haw (TV series) 184
Heffernan, Kevin 76
Hefti, Neal 147
Hegelian dialectic 10, 82, 106
Hell (Bosch) 33
Hell Raiders 17, 77
Hendrix, Jimi 218, 219, 220, 221, 252ch22n4
Herrmann, Bernard 249ch8n9
heterosexuality, in Buchanan films 11; couples and 40, 92, 119, 122, 136, 142, 144, 169, 191, 194, 235; and exploitation 47, 185, 187; and impotence 113, 149; and sex roles 102
Hicks, Edward 83
Hicks, Johnny 55, 68
Hicks, Kenneth 228
High Noon 13
High Yellow 21, 23, **24**, 110
Hindemith, Paul 249ch8n9
Hiroshima, Japan, bombing of 133
historical revisionism: in the Azalea Pictures 83; in Buchanan films 11, 14, 28, 233, 251ch18n5; in *A Bullet for Pretty Boy* 176; in *Creature of Destruction* 155; in *Free, White and 21* 59; in *Goodbye, Norma Jean* 184; in *Goodnight, Sweet Marilyn* 226, 227, 232; in *Hughes & Harlow: Angels in Hell* 199; in *The Loch Ness Horror* 217; in *The Naked Witch* 36; in *Zontar, the Thing from Venus* 104
History Is Made at Night 3, 5
Hitchcock, Alfred 8, 213
Hitler, Adolf 215
Hoffman, Harold 21, 27, 28, 30, 31, 53, 64, 65, 66, 68, 77
Holchak, Victor 193, 195, **196, 200**
Hollywood 3, 4, 5, 6, 19, 43, 64,

185, 186, 193, 194, 201; walk of fame 191
home movie footage 69, 71
home videocassette market 207
Homer Goes Hygienic 4
Homo habilis 203
homoeroticism 126, 131
homophobia 131, 221
homosexuality 87, 89, 122, 124, 127, 188
Honda, Inoshiro 209
Hoover, Herbert 173
Hoover, J. Edgar 251ch22n2
Hopkins, Gerry 230
House Select Committee on Assassinations 251ch22n2
Houston, Anthony *see* Touceda, Enrique, III
Houston, Texas 124
Hughes, Howard 193–197, 199, 200, 251ch19n7
Hughes & Harlow: Angels in Hell 123, 142, 193–201, **196, 199, 200**, 202
Hull, Cynthia 17, 23, 24, 87, **94**
humanism 106
"hyperspace hypnotism" 100

I Crossed the Color Line 23
I Dream of Jeannie (1966, TV series) 32
The Immoral Mr. Teas 42
In a Certain Village (Bruns) 177
In Search of Historic Jesus 217
In the Year 2525 250ch13n7
In the Year 2889 77, 81, 133–143, **134, 135, 137, 141**, 216, 250ch13n2, 250ch13n3, 250ch13n7
Incest taboo 182
"Injecta-Pods" 102
The Intruder 23
Invaders from Mars (1953) 87
invasion of privacy, in Buchanan films 81, 85, 91, 94, 95, 111, 137
Invasion of the Saucer Men 77, 84, 87, 88, 91, 92, 93, 95, 249ch8n9
It Conquered the World 77, 83, 95, 96, 97, 98, 99, 102, 249ch8n9, 249ch10n1
It's Alive! 77, 81, 120, 121, 131, 159–170, **162, 164, 166, 169**, 171, 194, 199
Ives, Burl 26

Jackson, Mississippi 55
"Jacob's Ladder" 106
Jada 43, 45, 48, 51, 52, 250ch13n3
Jamieson Film Laboratories 14, 16, 249ch9n1
Janus (Roman god) 103
Jarmick, Christopher 131
Jessup, Robert 133
Jesus Christ 5, 17
JFK (1990) 73
Johnson, Lyndon Baines 52, 67, 75, 218, 219
Johnson, Ralph 69
Johnson, Robert 95
Joplin, Janis 218–220, 222, 252ch22n5
Josem, Mark 184
justice system 9, 234

Kael, Pauline 26
Kafka, Franz 70, 228
Kellogg, Brown & Root 82
Kelly, Lacey 20, 21
Kennedy, John Fitzgerald 51, 52, 67, 68, 69, 70, 73, 75, 80, 229, 80, 248ch5n9, 248ch5n10; assassination 51, 52, 70 80, 248ch5n9, 248ch5n10; *see also* Johnson, Lyndon Baines
Kennedy, Robert 226, 227, 229, 230
Kent, Willis 3
Kenyon, Sandy 211, 218, **221**
Kerner, Jordan 132
Kerouac, Jack 95
Kiddie Matinees 29
The Killers 7
Killer's Kiss 7
Killers Three 171
Kincaid, Aron 147, **149**
King Kong (1933) 209
Kirk, Tommy 79, 122, **128, 132**, 161, **166**
Klaw, Irving 42
Klugman, Jack 14, **15**
Kubrick, Stanley 7, 124
Kurosawa, Akira 59

Lacan, Jacques: and the alienated other 47; in Buchanan films 40; and the fragmented self 229; and image-ideal 47, 192; and mirror-stage 47, 179, 187, 189, 190, 228, 230, 232; and symbolic order 47, 182, 187, 191, 179, 182, 228, 230
Lake Dallas 16
Lake Tahoe 210
Lake Texoma 146
Lancaster, Stuart 203, 211, **215**
Lane, Jocelyn 173
Lane, Paula 227, 228
The Last Temptation of Christ 17
Law enforcement 89, 92, 94, 95
Lawford, Peter 230
Leigh, Barbara 203
Lemmon, Jack 126
Lerner, Carl 23
lesbianism 39, 188, 190
Lewis, Herschel Gordon 42, 48
Ley, Willy 85
Life in the Raw see *Naughty Dallas*
Life magazine 6, 136
Lindberg, Donna 127, **130**
Lindberg Corporation 85
Livingston, Doc 210, **211**
Lo Russo, Ed 173
The Loch Ness Horror 209–217, **211, 214, 215**
Loch Ness Monster 209, 210
Locke, Terrence 186
Lone Star Baptist Evangelical Circuit 6
Longhorn Cavern State Park 159
Lord, Byron 79, 123, 157
Lorna 42
Louisiana 20, 22, 110, 111, 112
Lourie, Eugene 209
Lower, Joyce 228
Luckenbach, Texas 33, 35, 39, 177, 180, 247ch4n9
Lund, Annalena 54, 56, **57, 60, 61**

MacAdams, Anne *see* Weenick, Annabelle
Mace, Terry 178
Mackenzie, Miki 211, **214**
Mackenzie, Patch 188
The Magician (1959) 178
Mahon, Barry 3
male chauvinism 221
Malibu State Park 202
Mandel, Suzy 203
Marcus, Stanley 53
Marcuse, Herbert 173
Mars, greek god 124
Mars Needs Cigars 131
Mars Needs Women 3, 40, 56, 58, 68, 77, 81, 95, 122–132, **125, 128, 130, 132**, 141, 144, 158, 159, 161, 188, 190, 194, 225, 232
Mars Needs Women Too! 132; see also *Mars Needs Women*
Mars Still Needs Women 132; see also *Mars Needs Women*
Mars Wants Flesh! 131
Martin Dreadnought Guitar 6
Maryman, Jo 33
master-slave dialectic (Adorno) 113, 144, 157
Masters, Bert 21
Matheson, Richard 159

The Mating Instinct (Milne) 29
Matthau, Walter 126
Mazmanian, Marius 203
Mazyrack, Charles **74**
McClellan, Barr 67
McCrea, Jody 16
McGhee, William 23, 79
McKay, Scotty 147, 151
McLean, David 195
McLine, Shirley 111
megalomania 108, 113
Menzies, William Cameron 87
Meryl, Riba 219
Mesosaurus 166
Meyer, Russ 42, 48
Micheaux, Oscar 3
middle-class America, in Buchanan films 9, 80, 98, 120, 141, 144, 147, 152, 159, 160, 220, 225, 234, 235
Mikels, Ted V. 23
military-industrial complex, in Buchanan films 4, 9, 82, 84, 85, 87, 92, 94, 95, 102, 105, 106, 131, 186, 234
Miller, Arthur 14
Millett, Kate 37
Milne, Dr. Lorus 28, **29**, 30
Milne, Dr. Margery 28, **29**, 30
Minelli, Vincent 100
The Mini-Skirt Mob 176
Mirbeau, Octave 23
misanthropy, in Buchanan films 11, 28, 80, 81, 146–148, 153, 156, 157, 167, 202, 235
misogyny 148, 152, 153
Mr. Sardonicus 62
Mistress of the Apes 3, 202–208, **205, 206, 207**
Mommie Dearest 184
Monroe, Marilyn 44, 47, 184–192, 226–230
Montgomery, Elizabeth 32
Moorehead, Agnes 32
Morrison, Jim 218–220, 222–224, 251ch22n3
Mosely, Lucky 247ch3n12
"Movie of the Week" 78
movie remakes 97
Movielab 64
Moyers, Bill 75
Mrs. Doubtfire 202
Mullins, Edward 38
Mulvey, Laura 10, 58, 188
Museum of Modern Art 7
Musick, Pat 212
Myshrall, Don 213

NAACP (National Association for the Advancement of Colored Persons) 55

The Naked Witch 3, 16, 17, 21, 23 32–41, **34, 36**, 43, 55, 131, 177, 181, 183, 194, 209, 212, 217, 230, 232, 247ch4n7
narcissism 47, 191
NASA space launches 99
Nations, Arthur 68
Naughty Dallas 16, 42–52, **45**, 55, 56, 126, 187, 248ch5n9, 248ch5n10, 250ch13n3
Naughty New Orleans 42
The Navy vs. the Night Monsters 249ch8n5
Neiman-Marcus 53
Nelson, Lori 250ch13n2
Nelson, Willie 248ch4n9
Neumann, Jenny 203, **206**
"New Left" 220, 251ch22n2
New York City 6, 203
New York Times 64
newsreel footage 69, 185
Nicholson, Jack 171
Nicholson, James H. 64
Nixon, Richard Milhaus 74, 218, 219, 223, 251ch22n2
Noguchi, Thomas 227
North, Alex 19
Nothing Sacred 16
"nudie-cuties" 42, 51
nudist films 189, 190

occult rituals 110, 114, 116, 120
Oedipal complex 182
O'Hara, Quinn 134, 143
"Old Europe," in Buchanan films 17, 35, 55, 61
Olivier, Laurence 227
On the Waterfront 6
O'Neal, Frederick 54, **56, 60**
Onyx Cave 164
"Operation Crossroads" 135
Oswald, Lee Harvey 52, 67–75, 228, 248ch5n9, 248ch5n13
The Other Side of Bonnie & Clyde 3, 23–28, **25, 27**, 171
Ousterhouse, Carveth 161, **162**

Page, Betty 42
The Painted Witch (Mullins) 38
paranoia, in Buchanan films 61, 85, 86, 89, 90, 92, 95, 137, 220, 250ch13n1
paraphrasing, as artistic method 82, 83
Parker, Bonnie 23, 25
parochial feminism, in Buchanan films 185, 232
Parsons, Louella 197
The Passion of the Christ 17
patriarchal order: in *Beyond the Doors* 221; in Buchanan films

10, 32, 39, 40, 47, 57, 235; in *A Bullet for Pretty Boy* 173; in *Creature of Destruction* 145, 148, 152, 153, 156, 157; in *Curse of the Swamp Creature* 110, 111, 113–117, 119; in *The Eye Creatures* 90, 91, 94; in *Goodbye, Norma Jean* 185, 187–189, 191; in *Goodnight, Sweet Marilyn* 232; in *In the Year 2889* 138, 139, 141–143; in *It's Alive!* 159, 162–169; in *The Loch Ness Horror* 216, 217; in *Mars Needs Women* 131; in *Mistress of the Apes* 202, 204, 205, 208; in *The Naked Witch* 35, 37; in *Strawberries Need Rain* 181–183; in *Zontar, the Thing from Venus* 98, 105
The Peaceable Kingdom (Hicks) 83
Peck, Bill 49, 87
peep show 59, 124, 154, 188
Penn, Arthur 25, 26, 28, 171
Penn, Irving 6
Perry, Frank 184
Perry Mason (TV series) 54
Petersen, Paul 79, **134**, 143
phallic symbols 38, 39, 41
phallocentrism 115, 116, 129, 196
Phillipe, Andre 190
"Pig 311" 136
Pillsbury, Garth 186, 203, 213
pin-up photography 39, 42
The Pit and the Pendulum 249ch8n5
Planet of the Apes (1968) 202
Playboy (magazine) 42, 50, 184
Ponti, Sal 188
Poor White Trash Part 2 20
Pope, Alexander 223
Pope, Marilyn *see* Shannon, Toni
pornography 145, 151
Port of Call 178
Presley, Elvis 92
Price, Michael 194
The Prince and the Showgirl 228, 230
procreation, in Buchanan films 110, 113, 115, 119, 121
provincialism 40
Psycho (1960) 213
pulp magazines 44, 187

A Question of Consent see Free, White and 21

racial integration 53
racial politics 11, 23, 53, 55, 110
racism 36, 63, 111

radiation poisoning 136
Rashomon 59
Ray, Billy Wilson *see* Wall, Breck
Ray, Nicholas 91
Raymon, Buddy 48
Ready, Roger 111, 123, 134, 148
The Rebel Jesus 17–19, **18**, 234
Rebel Without a Cause 91
Reinl, Harold 217
religion, in Buchanan films 101, 102, 106, 113, 133, 150, 183, 212, 235
remake, as cultural phenomenon 82, 155
Remington .308 hunting rifle 203
rhythmic montage (Eisenstein) 57
Rickert, John 202, 207
Ripps, Mike (aka M.A. Ripps) 20
ritual sacrifice 148
Roach, Hal 195
Roarke, Adam 196
Roberts, Sherry 129
Robin, Walt 203, **206**
Rothman, Stephanie 76
"roughies" 42, 51
Rourke, Adam 172
Rowe, Misty 184, 185, **189**, **191**, 227, 228
Roy, Suzanne 147
Royter, Roland **65**
Ruby, Jack 43, 45, 48, 51, 52, 68, 69, 73, 248ch5n9, 248ch5n10, 248ch5n13
rural America 111, 160, 163, 168, 171
Rusoff, Lou 96, 97, 133, 144
Russell, George 55, 68

sadism 10, 181
Saengerfests 33, 248ch4n9
Sagan, Carl 95
Sam (or The Hottest Fourth of July in the History of Brewster County) 16
San Antonio, Texas 51
Sawyer, Toni 219
Sayers, Eric 20
science 110, 119, 212
Scorcese, Martin 17, 251ch19n7
Screen Building (New York City) 7
Scum of the Earth 42
Seale, Larry Marcus 5, **6**; *see also* Buchanan, Larry
The Search for Bridey Murphy (Bernstein) 250ch14n1
Self-Portrait in Red (Oswald) 72
self-reflexivity 99
The Seventh Seal 177

Sex and the Animals 28–31, **29**, **30**, 171
sexism 63, 92, 221
sexual exploitation in film 47, 185, 187, 202
sexual impotence 113, 149
sexual politics 34, 37, 81, 102, 144, 221
"The Sexual Revolution," in Buchanan films 29, 30, 51, 122, 128, 129, 131, 145, 157, 159, 170
Shakespeare, William 33
Shane, Gene Otis 18, 182
Shankar, Ravi 29
Shannon, Toni 43, 44
Shaw, George Bernard 219
The She-Creature 77, 95, 144, 147, 249ch8n9, 250ch14n1
She Wore a Yellow Ribbon 120
Shefield, Bonnie 247ch3n12
Short, Robert 33
Shubert, Lynn **15**, 199
Signal Corps Photographic Center 6
silent cinema 193
Simms, Al 249ch8n9
Singer, Alex 7
16mm film 20, 84, 85, 189
slapstick comedy 42, 51
Slate, Jeremy 227
Slusher, Juanita *see* Barr, Candy
snuff films 189, 251 ch18n5
Socratic dialogue 10, 97, 98, 106, 147
Something Weird Video 52, 247ch4n7
Something's Got to Give 226
Southern Methodist University 67, 178
"Southfork" (*Dallas* TV series) 23
speculative documentary 217
split personality 185, 227
A Star Is Born 16, 43, 44
"Star Probe Space Station" 85
"The Star Spangled Banner," Jimi Hendrix's rendition 220
Steele, Peggy 43, 47
Steiger, Rod 6
Stein, Ronald 80, 84, 95, 108, 249ch8n9, 250ch13n1
stock footage 15, 133
Stone, Oliver 73, 74, 225
Strategic Air Command 124
Strawberries Need Rain 3, 8, 41, 131, 177–183, **178**, **180**, 190, 191
Strip Tease (Barthes) 47
Striporama 42
A Stripper in Dallas 248ch5n13; see also *Naughty Dallas*

A Stripper Is Born 43; see also *Naughty Dallas*
striptease 42, 47, 126, 139
suburbia, in Buchanan films 4, 9, 79, 80, 97–106, 108, 115, 141, 142, 144, 152
Sullivan, William 219, 222, 251ch22n2
superstition 35
Swamp Rose 20, 22, 112
Symphonie Fantastique (Berlioz) 82

talking pictures 194, 195
Tanglewood Lodge 146, 148, 154, 157
Tanner, Larry 126
tantric sex 197
Taurog, Norman 8
Taylor, Kay 23
Technicolor 17
Techniscope 17
Teenage Bait 178; see also *Strawberries Need Rain*
telepathy 100, 118, 135, 137, 138, 140, 250ch13n1
television 15, 16, 32, 99, 100, 107, 163, 219, 224; syndication 76, 77
Tessmer, Charles 53, 54, 68, 73
Texas, and Buchanan 4, 5, 16, 20, 35, 43, 79, 82, 111, 112, 171, 176, 195, 218, 221, 227
Texas Justice 73, 75
Texas Rangers 25, 26
Texas Schoolbook Depository 69, **70**, 71
Thurman, Bill 23, 24, 79, 85, 111, 120, **121**, 125, 134, 142, **162**, **164**, 172, 179
Tice, Steven 219
Tighe, Virginia 250ch14n1
Tijuana After Midnight 42
Time (magazine) 26
The Time Travelers 249ch8n5
Totalitarianism 119
Totentanz (Liszt) 83
Touceda, Enrique, III 17, 79, 85, 112, **101**, 108, 126, 144, 157, 171
Tower Records 172
Track of the Vampire 76
Tremayne, Les 79, 146, 151, 177, 178, **180**
The Trial (Kafka) 70, 228
The Trial of Lee Harvey Oswald 36, 52, 54, 58, 67–75, **70**, **71**, **74**, 184, 225, 228, 232
Tucker, Phil 42
Tunisia 18
20th Century–Fox Studios 5, 227

U-boats 215
UCLA film archives 194
UFOs 85, 87, 88, 95
Ulmer, Edgar G. 3, 7
Under Age 54, 65–66, **63, 64, 65**, 72
underground cinema 78
United Artists 7, 14
U.S. government 4, 9, 234
universal order 40
Universal Studios 81, 184
University of Texas 211, 218

Valentine, Tom 210
Vallejo, Boris 207, 208
Van Gogh, Vincent 83
vaudeville, in film 47, 48
Venus in Furs 16
Vietnam War 100, 219
Visual Pleasure and Narrative Cinema (Mulvey) 10, 58
Voodoo Woman 110, 249ch8n7
Voyage to the Planet of Prehistoric Women 76
Voyage to the Prehistoric Planet 76
voyeurism, in Buchanan film 46, 57, 59, 81, 85–87, 93, 188, 190

Wall, Breck 49, 51, 248ch5n10
Wallace, George 53
Walley, Deborah 87
Ward, Robert 184
Warner, Astrid 172, **175**
Warren Commission on the Assassination of President John F. Kennedy 51, 52, 71, 248ch5n9, 248ch5n10
Watts, race riots 117
Wayne, Sonny 247ch3n12
Webb, Richard 77
Weenick, Annabelle 21, 23, **64**, 79, 111, 147, 163, **169**, 172
Weinstein, Abe 43, 47, 50, 248ch5n10
Weisgall, Jonathan 136
Welles, Orson 7
Wellman, William 16
Whatever Happened to Baby Jane? (1964) 168
White Rock Terrace 87
White Zombie 110
The Wild Angels 249ch8n5
Wild in the Streets 249ch8n5
Wild on the Beach 176
Wild Strawberries 177
Wilde, Jennifer 219
Williams, Tennessee 21
Wise, Robert 96
witch, as archetype 32, 39
witchcraft 32, 35, 36, 38, 40
Witney, William 28
The Wizard of Oz 100
Wolf, Bryan 219
Wolper, David L. 29
woman's suffrage 32

women: in Buchanan films 91, 98, 105, 179, 226, 235; and emancipation 37, 110, 113, 119; and empowerment 146, 202, 207; and exploitation 145, 155, 157, 203, 232; and idealization 131; and objectification 57; and preeminence 82; and rage against patriarchy 38, 144, 145, 156, 157; and roles in patriarchal society 32, 168; and the Women's Liberation movement 203; in the workplace 32; in World War II 32
Wood, Edward D., Jr. 3
Woodstock 220, 222
World War I 194, 195, 198
World War II 13, 17, 211

X—The Unknown 84
xenophobia 63

Yin and Yang 106
York, Francine 113, **114, 118**
Youras, Jimmie & Don 43

Zager, Danny 250ch13n7
Zager & Evans 250ch13n7
Zagon, Marty 188
Zontar, the Thing from Venus 3, 77, 81, 83, 96–109, **99, 101, 106, 108**, 110, 120, 147, 156, 235, 249ch8n9

www.ingramcontent.com/pod-product-compliance
Lightning Source LLC
Chambersburg PA
CBHW060258240426
43661CB00060B/2829